THE GENDERED WORLDS

OF LATIN AMERICAN

WOMEN WORKERS

DUKE UNIVERSITY PRESS   *Durham and London, 1997*

A book in the series COMPARATIVE AND
INTERNATIONAL WORKING-CLASS HISTORY
General Editors: ANDREW GORDON/Harvard University
DANIEL JAMES/Duke University
ALEXANDER KEYSSAR/Duke University

The

Gendered Worlds

of Latin American

Women Workers

From Household and Factory to

the Union Hall and Ballot Box

JOHN D. FRENCH AND

DANIEL JAMES, EDITORS

© 1997 Duke University Press
All rights reserved
Printed in the United States
of America on acid-free paper ∞
Typeset in Monotype Garamond
by Tseng Information Systems, Inc.
Library of Congress Cataloging-in-
Publication Data appear on the last
printed page of this book.
The publisher thanks the Center for
International Studies at Duke University
for support of the publication of this book.

Contents

Preface

This book has its origin in the Latin American Labor History Conference held annually since 1984, first at Yale, occasionally at Princeton and Stony Brook, and for the last four years at Duke University. Most of the essays were first presented at this conference. The editors of the volume founded the conference and have helped organize it ever since. Part formal conference, part informal workshop, part *grupo de afinidad,* the annual gathering has provided a vital intellectual space where the issues of labor history in Latin America can be debated. The editors, and, we are sure, the other contributors to this volume, are indebted to one another and to all the participants who over the years have made this such a fertile intellectual environment.

A larger intellectual debt looms for many of us. Emília Viotti da Costa was a decisive presence for many of the contributors—as a colleague, as a dissertation adviser, and as an incisive participant in many of the conferences. The breadth of her intellectual concerns, her dedication to advancing the work of her students and colleagues, and the passion of her commitment to reconstructing the history of the oppressed of Latin America have provided a model for all of us involved in this collection. A long time ago, she explained to a young assistant professor anxious to make his mark on the field that, while ambition is laudable, the most lasting intellectual contributions in history have come not from attacking parodied versions of the work of earlier generations of scholars but from critical and respectful engagement with that work. Each generation of scholars sees clearer and farther if it can stand on the shoulders of its predecessors. Those of us who have worked with Emília Viotti have indeed been privileged to stand on the shoulders of a giant. While she may not agree with all of the conclusions reached, and while she may question some of the theoretical paths followed, her spirit pervades this volume.

Other thanks are in order. Long-time participants in the conference, such as Jeff Gould and Mike Jiménez, did much to help sustain the creative ambience. Institutional support from the Center for International Studies at Duke University and the Duke University Council for Latin American Studies has been invaluable for both the success of the conference and the appearance of this book. Particular thanks are due to Debbie Jakubs, Natalie Hartman, Adriana Brodsky, and Silvia González. Nancy Hewitt, who has been such a forceful spokesperson for women's studies, has been a generous supporter of the conference and an astute commentator on several of its papers. In finalizing this volume we benefited from the comments of Aldo Lauria-Santiago and the anonymous readers of the manuscript. Asunción Lavrin generously gave us insightful comments on the introduction, as did Jody Pavilack on the introduction and conclusion in addition to producing the index. A 1995–96 National Humanities Center fellowship enjoyed by John D. French provided ideal conditions for writing the volume's introduction and conclusion. The usual caveats concerning the final judgments that appear in the volume apply. Finally, Valerie Millholland has been a patient and supportive editor, and for that many thanks are due from the editors and contributors.

Squaring the Circle

Women's Factory Labor, Gender
Ideology, and Necessity

JOHN D. FRENCH AND DANIEL JAMES

The aims and ambitions of this volume can best be understood by looking back to an early attempt, twenty years ago, to define the scope and direction of labor history. At the Fifth Conference of Mexican and North American Historians in Pátzcuaro in October 1977, John Womack Jr. was given the task of reviewing presentations on workers and labor in Mexico in the national period. This was a formidable undertaking, given its inclusion in a massive 1979 volume, whose bulk and scope reflected the depth and richness of historical studies of labor in Mexico compared with labor studies elsewhere in Latin America, where the field was largely in its infancy.[1] Womack's essay also came during a decade in which, in Latin America as a whole, workers and the urban labor movement had been proven central to contemporary politics and were increasingly attracting the attention of scholars both within and outside of the region.

Under these circumstances, Womack's 1979 essay offers a privileged point of departure as we examine the trajectory of the new labor history in Latin America over the intervening two decades. As befitted a historiographical essay, Womack noted how much was "missing from the papers . . . [and] the frequent failure . . . to ask certain kinds of questions about the facts that do appear."[2] Having cited Harry Braverman's then new book *Labor and Monopoly Capital* as the inspiration for a new "critical intellectual tradition" on labor, Womack argued that the time had come to address "altogether new kinds of historical problems." A list of nine topics followed, beginning with productive structures and technology and ending with studies of "working-class consciousness" and the "economic, social, political, and cultural histories of other classes," since "the history of the working class is not the history of workers only, but the history of their relations with other classes."[3]

Looking back on Womack's ambitious agenda for future research, one is struck by the vehemence of his emphasis on production and work. Yet, in this regard, his prescriptions failed to capture the collective imagination of those who were creating the field of Latin American labor history in the 1970s and 1980s. Unlike Womack, this emerging cohort was most attracted to the political issues that were marginalized in his work-centered program of research, especially those regarding populist and leftist politics.

Yet despite their divergences, most of the new Latin American labor historians shared certain underlying assumptions with Womack that are sharply revealed in his Pátzcuaro text. The most striking is the absence of any mention of women in Womack's historiographical review.[4] This lacuna is all the more striking because of Womack's quite apt criticism of those contributors who "wrote as if one worker was practically the same as another" while ignoring occupational differences among the apparently all-male laboring classes.[5]

Not only are women workers absent, but the presence of any women is touched on only once in Womack's list of research priorities, in an item that calls for "studies in the history of family structures among workers, to understand the psychology of their class."[6] Womack's only other indirect reference to women comes in a comment about how roles in "a particular process of production . . . determined the organization of their subjects' daily lives, geographic mobility, education, *the phase in life for marriage, the schedule for having children,* the readiness to truckle or to rebel, and so on" (emphasis added).[7] The unilateral model of social causation and identity formation underlying Womack's comment is worthy of note: a single determining factor is given exclusive sway over the lesser realms of social reproduction and human subjectivity and consciousness.[8]

Womack's gesture of subsuming women into the family and then accounting for the family via its male head was typical of a collective blindness among historians of Latin American labor.[9] In spite of the breakthroughs in the study of women workers in the North Atlantic world at that time, it is clear that the emerging field of Latin American labor history was largely impervious to the new interest in women workers as such. In part, this reflected the conditions under which this new academic specialization was created, within and about a late-developing peripheral region with a weak academic infrastructure, where the political importance of wage-earning laborers, a twentieth-century phenomenon, was widely recognized if little studied.

Although labor is central to both political and academic discourse in Latin America (the distinction between the two is not as clearly drawn in the region as elsewhere), the actual study of labor is a very recent phenomenon undertaken largely by scholars in sociology, the region's premier integrative intellectual enterprise. Looked at from the point of view of labor history, much of this literature has been politically driven in the narrow sense and marked by a type of sociological reductionism with a bias toward structural determinism.[10]

This intellectual context helps to explain, in large part, why so many young labor historians of Latin America were drawn to the politically charged question of workers and populism, the focus of the first Latin American Labor History Conference held at Yale University in 1984.[11] Revisionist in thrust, the founders of the conference rejected deterministic approaches, insisted on a rigorous empiricism in research, and abhorred a priori deductive approaches to working-class consciousness. Aware of the by then burgeoning field of women's labor history, the conference eventually chose women and labor as the subject of its fourth meeting in 1987.[12]

The new generation of historians of labor came to the subject of women workers in Latin America after a group of pioneering sociologists and anthropologists had already undertaken much pathbreaking research.[13] Writing with passionate partisanship on behalf of women and workers, scholars such as June Nash, Helen Safa, and María Patricia Fernández-Kelly combined feminist and Marxist analysis to produce an exciting body of empirical research that explores the relationship between capitalism and patriarchy.[14] Indeed, June Nash's broad-ranging 1979 ethnography *We Eat the Mines and the Mines Eat Us* pays close attention to male-female relations and anticipates, in its scope and ambition, the objectives set forth in this volume by today's cohort of gender-conscious Latin American labor historians.[15] In joining this ongoing women's-labor-studies dialogue, our collection seeks to demonstrate that historical research makes its own special contribution, especially since the "snapshot" nature of most anthropological and sociological fieldwork sometimes obscures patterns of development over time.

Overall, much of this pioneering work could be characterized, in Joan Scott's terms, as "herstory," an attempt to overcome the neglect of women workers by reaffirming the existence of women within the traditional categories.[16] As with the North Atlantic "herstory," but somewhat delayed, this effort in Latin America sought to document the importance of women workers while establishing women's roles as active and autonomous agents in labor's history.[17] This was combined with the exposure and denunciation of sexism, discrimination in employment, male violence and domination in the household, and the neglect or suppression of working women's interests by male labor leaders.[18]

This important bridging maneuver, although somewhat defensive in nature, was typical of the study of women and labor in many world regions, as studies of women's "lost" or "hidden" histories proliferated throughout the 1980s. Although women emerged from this literature as active agents, the approach was premised on placing women into the traditional narratives of a male-defined labor history (women as workers, as union members, and as political and union activists). It did not, however, challenge the conceptual framework and categories that have traditionally constituted labor history as a field. The result was that the study of women workers, in the words of U.S. historian Ava Baron, remained "ghettoized and segregated from men's labor history." [19]

The key conceptual breakthrough, reflected in this volume, could only be found through engagement with the theoretical category of gender. [20] In the words of Baron, a gendered analysis of labor requires "going beyond the study of women workers and women's work." [21] The challenge facing labor historians is to explore the articulation of gender and class in the lives of working-class subjects, both male and female. [22] In this nonessentialist approach, gender is understood as a relationship rather than a thing; it is viewed as a verb rather than a noun. [23] It must be seen as a social process of construction in which meaning is ascribed to sexual difference, which is reproduced by and within institutions (such as the family, factory, or polity) that generate and sustain gender hierarchies and patriarchal ideologies. The formation of male and female identities and subjectivities should not, however, be taken as transhistorical processes. Far from being givens, they are socially and discursively constructed and simultaneously contested in specific historical contexts.

The title of this book reflects these ambitions. We speak not of the "World of Latin American Women Workers" but rather of their *worlds* because we reject the dualistic implication of such dichotomous categories as male/female, public/private, or capitalism/patriarchy. In the words of two Latin American sociologists, Lourdes Benería and Martha Roldán, "The specificity of real life does not present itself in a dualistic manner but as an integrated *whole,* where multiple relations of domination/subordination—based on race, age, ethnicity, nationality, sexual preference—interact dialectically with class and gender relations." [24]

We speak of *gendered* worlds because women's identities are not constituted apart from those of men. Rather, gender is constituted by and implicated in a whole array of sites in which historical agency and individual and collective consciousness are formed. Nor can the identity of individuals or groups be derived, in a deterministic fashion, from any single dimension of their lives.

As June Nash suggests, questions of identity are fundamentally empirical and not deductive in nature.

The worlds of our title refer not only to men's and women's different experiences but also to the different spheres that make up the lives of working-class women, be they within the home, the community, or the workplace. Thus these essays deal with many different levels of analysis: the individual, the family, the experience of work, community and electoral life, and the discourse about women workers produced by employers and other elites. The challenge is to discover innovative ways to combine the analysis of structural conditioning features with the study of gendered agents. The objective is to achieve a fullness of representation and understanding that is adequate to the multidimensional, integrated nature of how people actually experience their lives.

Let us examine, for example, the case of a hypothetical woman worker and her life as drawn from the chapters in this volume. She enters a factory as an individual and, once at work, becomes part of a process of material production subject to the domination of employers, appearing as part of a statistical aggregate in employment or census records. This woman has feelings about the social position she now occupies, both at an individual level in terms of the work she now performs (given her skill level or the male/female balance within her department) and in terms of her past history, whether as a domestic servant or as the daughter of a factory worker. At work, she has entered a power matrix of sexual and gender relations between male and female, both workers and nonworkers—relations of affect as well as effect, attraction and repulsion, anxiety and self-confidence.

She also experiences her new role in terms of how, as a woman worker, she is now viewed by those outside the factory, be they members of her family, the community, or the non-working-class elite worried about "losing" women to the sexualized ambience of the factory. Her understanding of life is also shaped by the nature of her spiritual beliefs and the depth of her religious convictions.

This composite woman worker is also, however, living at a particular moment in her own and her family's life cycle, since her entry into paid labor occurs with certain regularities. In this process, she is by no means always a victim, forced to work against her own will, since work may in fact function as an integral part of marriage, childbearing, and consumption strategies. In this regard, she has been raised with certain expectations about respectability and about appropriate roles for women workers as well as for wives and mothers (both gender ideals and compromises imposed by material restraints). It is within this context that predatory male sexuality and violence are understood and contested, both within and outside the family.

Trained in the "domestic arts" by her mother, she enters into marriage or consensual unions with a man (whom she may have met in the factory), who is himself shaped by another web of both shared and gender-specific understandings of the male role. Together, the new family unit is part of a community with its own mores, contested identities, and community narratives. Yet this family is also influenced by the discourses about class, gender, and citizenship available to them within their respective nations and the regions within those nations.

The lives of this woman, her husband, her children, and her neighbors are also decisively shaped, in even their most private spheres, by initiatives from the public spheres of nation, state, and citizenship. Class identity in Latin America, after all, is constituted as much in the plaza as in the factory and is also shaped by structural economic trends (surpluses or scarcity in the labor market, shifts in wage levels, or the intensity of inflation).[25] Within this world, there also occur various forms of what would be more narrowly considered the only politically relevant practices of workers, such as trade unionism and electoral participation. Such participation in the "public sphere" was the exclusive focus of an earlier labor history, which tended to neglect nonclass forms of identity and mobilization found among workers (be they based on gender, race or ethnicity, religion, or community).

The interconnected and multidimensional nature of working-class women's lives, as suggested by this composite, challenges the many falsely dichotomized categories with which we have traditionally understood working-class life (home/work, public/private, family/community, labor/leisure, workers/nonworkers). Working-class women and men do not simply reproduce within their class the dominant gender ideologies of the society. Nor do they create their own distinct gender identities as a class. Rather there is a dynamic interaction between the two.[26] Just as there are male and female ways of being a worker, there is a working-class way of being a man or woman.

Yet the greatest challenge still lies ahead of us: to produce fully gendered accounts of class formation and working-class subjectivity. The goal must be to rethink the categories within which male labor history is written so as to broaden our understanding of working-class identities for both men and women. This book is a step on the road toward this objective, a work in progress, a call for a future volume to deal with "the gendered worlds of Latin American *workers*," male and female.

The potential for a truly gendered labor history can be glimpsed in recent research on work and the production process itself, subjects that might appear at first to be less-than-promising terrain for the application of a gendered analysis. Yet "gender is created not simply outside production but within it," as Ava Baron observes. "It is not a set of ideas developed separately from the economic structure but a part of it, built into the organization and social relations of work."[27] Sociologist John Humphrey's rich study of the labor process in contemporary Brazil convincingly demonstrates that gender permeates "all aspects of factory life, going much deeper than merely the allocation of workers to certain types of jobs. . . . [A] gender perspective," he concludes, is essential "for the analysis of male workers as well as female."[28]

This promising line of inquiry is represented in this volume by Thomas Klubock's chapter, which establishes the centrality of gender to the process of class formation, even in the case of an all-male mining workforce. After the strikes of the post–World War I era, the Kennecott Copper Company came to associate single men with high turnover, disorder, and labor militancy. They adopted a new policy designed to reshape the workforce and community life by giving preference to married men in "stable" family units. Klubock shows that gender was central to company policy and that this reconfiguration of family arrangements changed the terrain on which class conflict occurred in subsequent decades.

The essays in this book all explore the material conditions under which women operate, live their lives, and construct their histories. Yet this emphasis on material or structural constraints does not take analytical priority over the investigation of the specific forms of subjectivity and consciousness through which women negotiate their material and affective relations. Indeed, this integration of what has sometimes been called the "objective" and the "subjective" is linked to a redefinition of the subject of labor history, the concept of agency, and the role of language and discourse.

The ongoing theoretical debate, initiated by the work of Joan Scott, has led to much discussion in women's history and feminist studies in the North Atlantic world. Yet her work has left an ambivalent legacy. On the one hand, she has helped to popularize the concept of gender, with its capacity to remake traditional categories of historical analysis.[29] In addition, she and others have made a strong case for the need to historicize our understanding of the construction of identity. Yet Scott's poststructuralist espousal of the primacy of language and discursive structures has had the effect of minimizing the relevance of agency.[30] In addition, her attacks on the pretension of his-

torians to reconstruct or reconstitute "women's experience" have threatened
to undermine much of the foundational ethic of feminist and labor scholarship.[31]

Latin American labor history as a whole has been relatively "immune" to
the poststructuralist vogue.[32] Yet theoretical innocence can come at a price,
and there is much to be gained, as this volume demonstrates, from a greater
engagement with the theoretical and historiographical questions raised by
this debate. Whether implicitly or explicitly, most of the chapters in this volume pay close attention to the role of language and discourse in the making
of working-class women's identities. At the same time, they do not embrace
the bifurcated image of the Latin American woman either as entirely dominated by and accepting of patriarchal discourses and practices or as wholly
"autonomous" agents resisting such pressures.

Women and Work

The women whose experiences are examined in this volume were engaged
primarily in industrial labor, lived for the most part in urban settings, and
came from a wide variety of backgrounds, some as immigrants and others as
rural migrants. They were employed as textile workers in Colombia, Brazil,
and Guatemala, as meatpacking workers in Argentina, and as fruit-packing
workers in Chile. Thomas Klubock deals with the only case, Chilean copper
mining, where women were totally excluded from the main source of paid
employment, while Theresa Veccia explores, among other issues, women's
oft-neglected and unpaid work within the family and home. Overwhelmingly, the essays deal with working-class women from the 1930s to the 1950s,
dramatic decades which altered the face of modern Latin America through
the new forms of mass political participation and union activism associated
with the rise of populism and the Left.

Despite the different industrial, community, and national contexts dealt
with in this volume, there is a remarkable similarity in workers' adherence to
the ideal that the woman's place is in the home and that her "natural" vocation
is motherhood. In this familiar construct, the family is the woman's "natural" sphere, the man is the breadwinner, and women's work outside the home
is an anomaly to be discouraged. At midcentury, adherence to these traditional views about the gender division of labor was characteristic not only of
working-class men and women but also of industrialists, other elite groups,
the state, and would-be social reformers.[33]

Yet the reality was that women *did* work outside the home and were present and visible in the expanding and still-alien world of the factory. Moreover, women's factory labor was quite unlike domestic service, women's most common paid occupation, because it involved work outside of a family, even if not her own. The experience of women factory workers thus serves as the crux of this volume precisely because it posed, in the clearest fashion, the contradiction between gender prescriptions and workers' lived experiences in a world of need and scarcity. Unable or unwilling to give up deeply ingrained beliefs, those who engaged in, profited by, or contemplated women's industrial labor were left with the impossible task of squaring the circle.

The woman who went to work in the factory not only violated the socially accepted definitions of male and female roles, but her work outside the home—and the factory itself—was viewed as a potential threat to honor.[34] In the early twentieth century, the factory was more than just an economic reality that served as a source of wages, profits, or goods; it had quickly acquired a potent social imagery in Latin America that was cast in moral and sexual terms. For the various contending voices in the ensuing debate, the factory was perceived as a hostile sexualized space that threatened not only women's virtue but the survival of the family and, with it, the very future of the nation.[35]

These anxieties placed the emerging industrialists on the defensive vis-à-vis other established elites. Criticized by the medical community, social reformers, politicians, and the Catholic Church, industrialists were seen as fostering the violation of women's natural social role and biological vocation. In the striking case of the textile industry in Medellín, Colombia, discussed by Ann Farnsworth-Alvear, such concerns led to the institution of factory inspections and various legal restrictions on women's labor after World War I. In response, local employers developed a defensive counterdiscourse of highly gendered Catholic paternalism over the following decades. This discourse was combined with an ambitious reorganization of the labor force, aimed at diminishing women's employment, and the adoption of a system of discipline designed to control male sexuality while policing women's honor and virtue. The resulting decline in female employment was accompanied by the employers' pretension to total control that provides the context for Farnsworth-Alvear's subtle discussion of workers' sociability in the factory.

Barbara Weinstein's treatment of industrialists' associations in São Paulo, Brazil, provides an interesting contrast to the Colombian case. The generation of industrialist leaders who founded job training and social service agencies at the end of World War II faced a formidable challenge because a very high percentage of female and child labor had long been employed in industry, especially in textiles, as shown by Theresa Veccia. Facing an avalanche of interventionist social and labor legislation under the regime of Getúlio Vargas (1930–1945) and a postwar strike wave, they sought and received government approval in 1946 to establish the industrialist-controlled Industrial Social Service (Serviço Social de Indústria). Employing large numbers of middle-class women in the new occupation of social worker, the latter agency did not focus on the workplace as such but sought instead to foster modern forms of motherhood and a home-centered female domesticity among workers through extensive educational programs. Blunting elite criticism, the industrialists of the state finessed the question of female factory labor while offering a set of gender prescriptions that reinforced societal norms.

In their own lives, working-class men and women also faced the challenge of squaring the circle given their simultaneous adherence to prescribed gender roles and acceptance of women's paid work outside the home under some circumstances. For male breadwinners and their daughters and spouses, this challenge was met by continuing to affirm the ideal while accepting its violation due to the pressure of necessity. Moreover, women's factory labor was always presented as a matter of "helping" the family under exceptional circumstances.

This self-representation defined women's paid labor outside the home as complementary and atypical, and thus not a threat to male status or women's own self-conceptions. As Theresa Veccia notes, the retired women textile workers she interviewed "defined their paid work in a helping capacity . . . [which in turn] gave a tacit nod to the (ideal) masculine breadwinning role, although it was one that in actuality found scant expression in their everyday lives." Indeed, the discursive construct of "help" is a common trope used by the women in this volume when they discuss their lives: they "help" the family in James, Veccia, French and Cluff, and Lobato and they "help out" in the factory in Farnsworth-Alvear.

Yet as Mirta Lobato demonstrates, this attempt to square the circle does not provide a stable solution to the tension occasioned by women's de facto violation of the norms to which they formally declare their loyalty. Unlike middle-class women in the early twentieth century who increasingly worked outside the home by choice, working-class women were "driven" into the factories and meatpacking plants by necessity. Given the economic realities of urban working-class families, the labor of wives, daughters, and sons was often essential to the household economy, as is discussed by Veccia and French and Cluff.

In Lobato's analysis of women's oral histories, we find a rich understanding of the hidden maneuver present behind their invocation of "necessity." Necessity, she suggests, was not a purely functional or empirical statement about survival in a narrowly economic sense. Rather the word "necessity" contained a built-in flexibility that allowed it to expand or contract depending upon the family's objectives.[36] More important, she shows that women workers used "necessity" as a defense against disapproval and as a means, however imperfect, of claiming legitimacy for their decisions. This was vital in a world where women's factory labor was regarded as "jeopardizing women's morals" because it placed them "with the male sex in public where the protection of the family was absent."[37]

The linkages between factory employment, family life, and female honor, which generated debates among elites, also made female employment a flash point for conflict between male workers and employers. Despite differences in location and time frame, French and Cluff, Farnsworth-Alvear, and Levenson-Estrada all point to strike actions that originated in male anger at the sexual harassment of working-class women. In choosing this type of abuse as the focus of resistance against employers, male workers fulfilled an aspect of their masculine role: they acted to protect the weaker members of their class by defending "their women" against attack by men of "another class." Such action also represented an effort to neutralize the threat posed by the factory as a sexually "promiscuous" space in which fathers and husbands lost control of their daughters and wives.

The vision of the factory as a male-dominated terrain that threatened women's honor varied but was especially powerful for the meatpacking industry. "I think that all the women who ended up working in the frigorífico felt the same," recalled former Berisso worker Doña María Roldán, "because it is a place, well it's like a monster when you go in there, in that darkness, that dampness, in that situation of lines of men with knives in their hands, I don't think that was very nice, you felt bad, but necessity made you get used to it." Yet once alternative employment in textiles became available in Berisso, Lobato reports, working-class families found it more acceptable than meatpacking precisely because that type of employment was viewed as less threatening to female honor.

This preoccupation with the factory as a place that posed "certain risks, to one's reputation and to one's person," in the words of Farnsworth-Alvear, is to be found throughout this volume. In an interesting parallel to Lobato's observation, Veccia finds that working-class families in São Paulo also viewed women's job options in terms of female honor, but in this case judged textile labor to be less threatening than domestic service. The continued power of notions of "proper male and female being" is suggested in Deborah Levenson-Estrada's study of workers in contemporary Guatemala City who also confront the challenge of squaring the circle. "The gap between the real and ideal male and female has been wide," she says, and although "the gender rules are neither overturned nor strictly adhered to. . . . working-class people have lived in a gray area of gender 'imperfection.'" Underlying it all is a barely hidden "'secret' that women and children are breadwinners, and that fathers often abandon the family." Given the ubiquity of male abandonment and/or female-headed households, she observes that "although perhaps few men have been 'feminine,' many women have been 'masculine.'" In her exploration of the nature of single motherhood under such conditions, Levenson-Estrada notes that these women "stay with their children and they work hard inside and outside of the house, and they are revered for this by their children. . . . In their children's eyes, mothers working outside the home are not suspect."

For women workers with children, the decision to enter the paid workforce could best be legitimized by resorting to this powerful image of the long-suffering mother willing to do anything necessary to care for her children. Blue-collar women did not feel that they could defend their paid work on the basis of an openly avowed discourse about their own needs, whether for independence, self-affirmation, or autonomy. Although many women valued and derived satisfaction from their work outside the home, whether in terms of skills learned or enjoyment of workplace sociability, they could not offer these as valid reasons for working. In a similar way, as French and Cluff suggest, women workers' declared aversion to work outside the home could also be a protest against the types of jobs that were actually open to them, as well as an attempt to avoid the double shift from the factory to the kitchen that still characterized the lives of married working women. Most of all, however, they could not admit publicly that they valued paid employment because of the greater independence it afforded them in relation to their male partners; in the saying cited by French and Cluff, the married woman who works is "more the master of her own nose."

However women's work was handled discursively, the fact that women worked outside the home was bound to have an impact on the dynamics of power within the patriarchal structure of the family. To the extent that wage earning by women lessened economic dependency, even if only slightly (given discrimination in wages and job opportunities), it did provide women with somewhat greater leverage vis-à-vis their male partners. This is well illustrated in Heidi Tinsman's study of the changing reasons for wife-beating among rural workers in Aconcagua, Chile. She shows how a significant shift in the balance of power in the household occurred after the 1973 military coup. There was an increase in the economic vulnerability of rural men while women increasingly found jobs in the booming fruit-export industry. "If women's packing-plant work meant that husbands ceased to determine a wife's comings and goings, men also ceased to unilaterally decide household budgets and expenditures. Most women insisted on retaining control over their own wages and on their right to make basic purchases for themselves and the family." [38]

The case of Aconcagua also sheds light on the balance between material interest and gender ideology that underlies marriage among working people. After the Pinochet regime liquidated the agrarian reform of the Christian Democratic and Popular Unity eras, the resulting immiseration and proletarianization undermined the gender reciprocity that was claimed as the basis for the male/female household. [39] If the men were unable to fulfill their prescribed role as breadwinners, there was far less reason for women to put up with the inequalities of the patriarchal pact within the family. Despite the military regime's abundant rhetoric glorifying traditional family roles, the result was, as Tinsman shows, a startling increase in female-headed households: from three percent of all households in Aconcagua in 1970 to one-third in 1986. "While in the majority of cases it was men who left women, women's access to waged employment made survival without a male partner a more viable, if still extremely economically difficult, option than it had been twenty years earlier."

The material and sexual roots of male/female inequality within the family are forcefully highlighted by Tinsman and Klubock, who place the issue of male violence against women on the agenda of Latin American labor history. [40] Wife-beating, Tinsman argues, is not a timeless unfolding of an ahistorical logic of patriarchy. Conjugal violence can only fully be understood when inserted into the cultural, socioeconomic, and political dynamics of the broader society; in a word, by historicizing it. [41] Although men's ability to control women, or their aspiration to do so, were characteristic of both the pre- and post-1973 periods, Tinsman suggests that rural men beat their wives for qualitatively different reasons in the two periods. Before 1973, men beat their wives in "defense" of their right to sexual control and over issues of male household authority and male sexual freedom. After 1973, spouses fought about men's inadequacy as providers and about women's new access to paid employment through factory work and the expansion of social freedom that implied. As had been true in the earlier period, wife-beating continued to involve conflict over sexuality, but it now stemmed from a presumed or real increase in women's sexual opportunities due to their work in the packing plant.

Tinsman deals with flirting in the packing plants as a rhetorical construction or male fantasy whose empirical truth in any individual case is difficult to document. Her account echoes a larger theme raised by most of the essays in this book. When dealing with women workers, the image of the factory has been construed in negative sexualized terms by both men and women. And this construction both draws sustenance from and reinforces an existing discourse concerning women's honor, sexuality, and factory work. Using company disciplinary records and oral histories, Ann Farnsworth-Alvear approaches this problematic from a radically different point of view, that of women as desiring and desired subjects. Her discussion of flirting between male and female textile workers is all the more striking because she is dealing with Medellín, where a Catholic paternalist project to control sexuality was carried to its logical extreme, both inside and outside the factory. Indeed, Farnsworth-Alvear suggests that on-the-job sociability, including flirting, was a key if unstudied strategy by workers to humanize the factory as a system of human domination.[42] She also offers thoughtful observations about the distinction between "mutual flirtation and sexual intimidation."

Farnsworth-Alvear is well aware of the ambiguities of flirting within the context of gender inequality. She shows, however, that flirting is not reducible to sexual harassment.[43] This possibility is also hinted at in one of the interviews cited by Tinsman. Yet the comments offered by this woman, whose sister was beaten by her husband, suggest that honor still weighs heavily in women's views about interactions with men outside the family. Such female concerns about honor undoubtedly vary by generation and between groups. Doña María Roldán is outspoken in her conviction that "the woman who knows her place never lacks for respect, nothing strange ever happened to me," she says, "but then it never did because I never went around being cute, joking around with the men in the patio" of the *conventillo* where she lived.

As we further explore the issues of sexuality raised by Farnsworth-Alvear, Tinsman, and Klubock, we must also be careful to avoid anachronism when dealing at midcentury with a precontraceptive world where the risk of pregnancy was high. In the bitter words about marriage by one of Veccia's informants, the problem with men is that they drink their *pinga* (an alcoholic beverage), and women pay the price. In a world of male jealousy often exacerbated by alcohol, Klubock and Tinsman show that there is much to be learned from studying the history of domestic violence and government efforts to punish or prevent it. Women's recourse to the courts in response to male violence suggests women's right to be free from an "unacceptable" level of violence from men. As Klubock suggests, these "private" family questions became increasingly the object of state action by the late 1930s in Chile and elsewhere.[44]

Given its neglect by an earlier historiography, it is exciting to see how recent research has demonstrated that gender was central to the national projects associated with populism and the Left in midcentury Latin America. As part of what some scholars have called the modernization of patriarchy, efforts were aimed, in particular, at controlling male sexuality and reconfiguring the working-class domestic sphere.[45] The result was a paradoxical one. In the case of post–World War II Argentina, for example, the discourse of the Peronist regime fervently embraced traditional patriarchal categories for women, while giving roles such as motherhood and guardian of the household a new public dimension and validation. Yet, the regime's conservatism was combined with a new discourse of rights for women—not only the right to vote or to participate politically through the Partido Peronista Feminino, but also the right to entitlements based on women's contributions to the nation as mothers.[46] What is needed now, more than ever, is a full exploration of the impact of government social and labor legislation on working-class women and their families.

Politics in twentieth-century Latin America has been fundamental to the daily lives, outlooks, and struggles of women as well as men.[47] In a century of revolution and profound social transformations, women have never been limited, in reality as opposed to myth, to the "private" sphere of the family. The Bolivian National Revolution of 1952, as Lesley Gill has shown, had an important impact—direct and indirect—on the lives and outlooks of the women who worked as servants in the homes of others. And even something as private as cooking can and has been touched by politics, as shown by Dawn Keremitsis, who documented the gender conflicts that accompanied the introduction of the machine for making tortilla dough into Cardenista Mexico.[48]

Toward a Gendered Labor History: New Research Terrain

The essays in this book suggest that a gendered history of Latin American workers is within reach. While demonstrating the progress that has been made, they also leave us with many unanswered questions and suggest productive avenues for future research. Perhaps the greatest gap stems from our inability to adequately historicize and particularize our understanding of the gender ideologies and practices of the popular classes in Latin America. For analytical purposes, it has proven convenient to naturalize the category of patriarchy by treating it as a given, when in fact there may be not one but many patriarchies. French and Cluff, for example, refer in passing to "gender traditionalism," but this construct, although perhaps unavoidable at this stage, tells us little about the specific historical content of such a category.

To meet this challenge, we need a richer understanding of the variation in patriarchal norms, ideologies, and practices, in all their nuances, among both men and women in the region. The cultural specificity of patriarchy and its codes of female honor is eloquently suggested by one of Theresa Veccia's informants. This young woman recalled with anger how her immigrant mother enforced "one of those strict customs of the Portuguese," by refusing to allow her to cut her hair because such a woman "was a tramp [*mulher vagabunda*] . . . [with] no morals, no shame." As this example suggests, we must pay special attention to differences derived from the still too-often neglected influences of ethnicity, race, region, and generation.

A call to historicize gender also raises the fundamental issue of the rural-to-urban transition in twentieth-century Latin America. The overwhelmingly rural origin of the working-class populations discussed in this book calls attention to the incomplete nature of our understanding of the worlds of women workers. Without an adequate gendered history of patriarchy in the areas of origin, it is difficult to know to what extent we are dealing with a "carryover" in attitudes or practices, as opposed to documenting the impact of the new social and economic relations of urban and/or industrial life.[49] In June Nash's ethnography of Bolivian tin miners, for example, we are able to see how gender dynamics in the mining camps were structured, in part at least, by the difference between male and female roles in the rural villages from which the miners came.[50]

As the effort to gender labor history advances, Latin Americanists must remain alert to the dangers that stem from the unexamined transposition of concepts from the center to the periphery.[51] It would be misleading if the gender norms and ideals documented in this volume were taken simply as a Latin American version of what has come to be known as the ideology of separate spheres and the cult of domesticity in the North Atlantic literature. In the case of the cult of domesticity, one can rightly ask whether a concept designed to capture certain themes in the ideology of middle-class Victorian life can be meaningfully applied to working-class life, much less to the popular classes in other national and cultural contexts in other time periods.[52] Moreover, the ideal of domesticity need not have the same content or function for industrial working-class women as it has for those employed in white-collar occupations in twentieth-century Latin America.

The historiography of the study of labor in Latin America provides ample evidence of the dangers that stem from the utilization of "universal" categories in an ahistorical fashion.[53] In the past, the unexamined use of the European/North Atlantic category *class,* derived as it is from a nineteenth-century context, brought with it a set of assumptions about social boundaries, class institutions, modes of political action, and "appropriate" consciousness. Having moved away from such essentialist notions in the study of labor, it would be unfortunate if the gendering of labor history were to inadvertently reproduce earlier postures in which the consciousness and practice of the subaltern were measured against an abstract model derived from the North Atlantic world.

Even for midcentury Latin America, we do not yet have an adequate understanding of the cultural connotations of the fundamental category of class,[54] much less the complex interrelationship between class and gender, or between men and women. At this point, we do not yet fully grasp what being a "worker" meant to a *male* industrial wage earner in Brazil in 1950, much less how that experience and self-representation differs from what is found in Medellín or El Teniente. Nor have we reached an adequate understanding of how a female textile worker differs from a male one, even in a single locale, despite the positive steps taken by the essays in this volume.[55]

Nor do we fully grasp the different meanings that women attached to the various occupations and types of work in which they engaged, whether urban or rural, skilled or unskilled. Was women's contribution to the household economy handled differently, in discursive and experiential terms, among the rural and urban poor, or between blue-collar and white-collar urban populations? And, for working women as a whole, we need to know how they viewed the desirability of different forms of work, especially as non-manual occupations became an increasingly important employment option for women in Latin America.[56]

Latin America's relatively weak archival infrastructure and its historically modest levels of popular literacy (often lower for women) can easily tempt scholars of gender to opt for textual analysis of the discourses generated by dominant groups. To avoid reproducing the older paradigm in which the subaltern are "spoken of" more than they actually "speak," it is important not to overestimate the dearth of sources for a gendered labor history—at least for the twentieth century. After all, ten years ago one might have been surprised to encounter so much creative historical research on women drawn from legal and governmental sources, from mutual aid society documents, or from company employment and disciplinary records. And much will be revealed in the future, from initiatives such as the "Berisso Obrero" project, directed by Daniel James and Mirta Lobato, which draws on all these forms of evidence in addition to having gathered 250 male and female testimonies.[57]

Even when a sufficiently rich array of sources cannot be located, it is essential that scholars be aware of the problems and limitations inherent in research undertaken in this textualizing mode. This is especially important as scholarly attention increasingly focuses on the public debates regarding women's roles at midcentury in Latin America. We must be cautious about the extent to which these debates about women's labor, centered on the state and expressed through the print media, reflect, respond to, or shape popular attitudes, as opposed to being part of an elite dialogue with "modernity" in the North Atlantic world.[58] A similar caution must be exercised in interpreting the cultural products disseminated through the modern mass media, such as records, radio, film, and television. Ultimately, we must insist that propositions about popular attitudes derived from such sources be subjected to careful empirical validation.

Given such strictures, the ambitious goal of gendering labor history is most likely to proceed productively, at this point, through intensive local studies of particular social and cultural universes in relatively restricted time periods. Without falling into the self-limiting ethnographic conceit that the study of yet one more village must precede any generalization, there can be little doubt that a firm foundation for a gendered labor history requires many more local and regional microhistories.[59] Only in this way can we tackle the formidable challenges resulting from other major gaps in our knowledge.

Although women's labor outside the home was common among rural and urban populations, the industrial forms of women's labor studied in this book were, for the most part, new in early-twentieth-century Latin America. Even today, the factory labor situation is still the experience of a minority of working women, while the majority work in the poorly documented service and informal sectors.[60] And even the men employed in these areas of the economy continue to be neglected by the historians of labor in much of Latin America.[61] A labor history of the informal and tertiary sectors, where women's participation is central, will also be necessary if we are to construct a fully gender-conscious labor history. After all, the boundaries between formal and informal subsistence activities are often blurred for women, even those who are employed in the industrial sector of the economy. Facing the need to generate cash, working-class women choose from a menu that differs from that of men: washing clothes, cleaning homes, sewing, petty commerce, industrial homework, domestic service, the taking in of tenants, or factory labor. And women factory workers have often engaged in such "informal" subsistence activities during, as well as before and after, their waged employment in industry.

Asunción Lavrin has rightly suggested that we also know far too little about "what happens when women *stop* working," particularly how or if women acquire access to state pension systems. "There is little sensitivity towards the topic of aging or older women," she observes. "So much of the population in Latin America is young, that the graying of a certain sector seems to be no issue at all. It should be."[62] Moreover, the impact of aging on gender dynamics is eloquently illustrated in June Nash's oral history of a Bolivian tin miner's family. As Petrona Rojas and her husband Juan age, Petrona's role grows in importance with the decline of her husband's income that accompanies his sickness and retirement, especially given the high or even hyperinflation that characterized the era.[63]

Petrona Rojas's story illustrates the impact of the life cycle on the experience of class and gender. The Rojas family is also characterized by a multi-generational household structure, which has important implications for gender dynamics and the possibility of passing on a type of class or community memory.[64] The family or household is also a key site for both gender socialization and generational conflict over differing ideas of work, sexuality, and marriage. Discourses about gender roles themselves, after all, are constructed and negotiated within the family or household, perhaps even more crucially than in the workplace or public square.

Within the family, gender discourses can be reinforced or undermined by daily practice in a process in which ideals of femininity and masculinity are articulated, inculcated, and contested. Given the unexamined masculinist bias of much of labor history, it is ironic that the history of masculinity is one of the least researched aspects of gender relations in the region. To the extent to which it is addressed, scholars have been content, for the most part, with an unexamined "common sense" image of Latin American working-class males as *machos*. Some recent anthropological work on Mexico has suggested, however, that there is far more to popular masculinity than merely the macho stereotype. Even male gender identities, anthropologist Matthew Gutmann underlines, are "products and manifestations of cultures in motion . . . [and] do not emanate from some primordial essence."[65]

Working-class masculinity will have to be historicized if we are to arrive at a fully gendered understanding of Latin American working-class life. As in all societies characterized by gender inequality, there are indeed cultural constructs and practices of male-supremacist and misogynist masculinity that approximate the stereotypical image of the macho or, in the case of rural Chile, the *huaso*. And recent studies have shown how these practices, which idealize male "independence" and a predatory male sexuality, explain, at least in part, the attraction of Pentecostal religious sects for poor and working-class women.[66]

It is unwise to assume, however, that the macho is the only ideal of masculinity available to Latin American men; we must begin to study, as Gutmann observes for Mexico, the "variety, as opposed to the homogeneity, of masculinities among working class" men.[67] After all, there exists another influential model of patriarchal masculinity, one that is configured in terms of male obligation and duty to the family.[68] This is not to say that such working-class men were or are necessarily sensitive and egalitarian, but their behavior is subject to an accepted community understanding of what constitutes respectable and honorable behavior.[69] The minimum expectation was well illustrated by Veccia's informant who, despite criticizing her abusive deceased husband, nonetheless praised him for going to work every day, no matter how hungover, and for bringing his wage home to support the family.

How is *machismo* constructed discursively in the social and culturally specific contexts of the Latin American working class over time? What does "being a man" mean for male workers, and what are the tensions, conflicts, and ambiguities bound up in this identity? Working-class men *may* identify with a predatory macho ideal, in part or in whole, especially when young. They may also participate in its perpetuation, even if only vicariously, through verbal interaction with men in bars and workplaces.[70] Yet how does this dimension coexist with their adherence, in their daily lives, to a practice of paternal masculinity linked to the larger cultural construct of working-class respectability? In other words, although being the stereotypical macho may be the ideal, not all men achieve it, some probably do not accept it, and many do not practice it.[71]

Without substantial further research on masculinity, such abstractions will continue to be treated as if they were real, thus causing us to lose sight of the men and women, living in particular and concrete circumstances and relations, who should always be the object of our study. The warning of Emília Viotti da Costa is apropos:

We have become so habituated to seeing history as a product of reified historical categories, to talking about "variables" and "factors," to dealing with abstractions . . . [such as class, gender, masculinity] and the like, that we often forget that history is made by men and women, even though they make it under conditions they themselves have not chosen. In the last instance, what matters is the way people interact, the way they think about the world and act upon it, and how in this process they transform the world and themselves.[72]

Analytical categories and abstractions only make sense if they are developed from and understood through a dialogue with the everyday lives of working people. As June Nash has observed, their personal stories remind us "that the structural parameters derived from aggregate data [or discourses] must be interpreted in terms of the decisions made by human beings who have the illusion, if not the reality, of autonomous control over their lives. Structuralist premises are good for postmortems."[73] And as Emília Viotti further observes, "History is not the result of some mysterious and transcendental 'human agency,' but neither are men and women the puppets of historical 'forces.' Their actions constitute the point at which the constant tension between freedom and necessity is momentarily resolved."[74]

Notes

1   John Womack Jr., "The Historiography of Mexican Labor," in *Labor and Laborers through Mexican History,* ed. Elsa Frost, Michael Meyer, Josefina Zoraida Vázquez, and Lilia Díaz (Mexico City: Colegio de México, 1979), pp. 739–56. Work on labor from the pre-Conquest through the colonial period is particularly rich, with a number of papers on Indian, black, and mulatto laborers in the colonial period.

2   Ibid., p. 753.

3   Ibid., pp. 755–56. For labor historians, the importance of studying the industrialists is well demonstrated by Peter Winn, *Weavers of Revolution: The Yarur Workers and Chile's Road to Socialism* (Oxford: Oxford University Press, 1986), pp. 13–52. Industrialists have also begun to attract attention from historians in their own right (Barbara Weinstein, *For Social Peace in Brazil: Industrialists and the Remaking of the Working Class in São Paulo, 1920–1964* [Chapel Hill: University of North Carolina Press, 1996]). James P. Brennan's excellent recent monograph is the most ambitious labor history investigation to place technology and labor process at the center of its concerns (*The Labor Wars of Córdoba, 1955–1976: Ideology, Work, and Labor Politics in an Argentine Industrial City* [Cambridge: Harvard University Press, 1994]).

4   This invisibility is demonstrated by the fact that only one of the twenty-six
     papers in the published volume deals with women's labor. The title of this chap-
     ter by Beatriz Ruiz Gaytán is itself suggestive, "Un grupo trabajador importante
     no incluido en la historia laboral mexicana (trabajadoras domésticas)," in Frost
     et al., *Labor and Laborers,* pp. 419–55.

5   Womack, "Historiography," p. 754.

6   Ibid., p. 755.

7   Ibid., p. 753.

8   Womack did not entirely exclude the subjective world of feeling and emotion
     from scholarly consideration, but judged it of importance largely in relation to
     the productive process itself (ibid., p. 755).

9   Womack's comment on Ruiz Gaytán's essay about domestic servants is illustra-
     tive in this regard: "The problem with her topic is that the domestic servant has
     only recently emerged into the labor market, so that only recently could histori-
     ans have identified her as worth studying in herself, separate from the household
     in which she labors" (ibid., p. 746).

10   Some of the themes that characterized this sociological literature on labor in the
     region were the aristocracy of labor, rural migration, social mobility, margin-
     ality, new versus old working classes, and heteronomy in class formation. See
     Daniel James, "Dependency and Organized Labor in Latin America," *Radical
     History Review* No. 18 (1978), pp. 155–60, for a critical review of Spalding's pioneer-
     ing 1977 volume. In almost all cases, working-class consciousness was assumed
     to be a known quantity, defined by what was believed to be a European model.

11   For a review of the historiography on labor and populism in Brazil see John D.
     French, *The Brazilian Workers' ABC: Class Conflicts and Alliances in Modern São Paulo*
     (Chapel Hill: University of North Carolina Press, 1992), pp. 1–16. See also Steve
     Stein, *Populism in Peru* (Madison: University of Wisconsin Press, 1980); Winn,
     Weavers of Revolution; Daniel James, *Resistance and Integration: Peronism and the Argen-
     tine Working Class, 1946–1976* (Cambridge: Cambridge University Press, 1988); and
     Jeffrey Gould, *To Lead as Equals: Rural Protest and Political Consciousness in Chinan-
     dega, Nicaragua, 1912–1979* (Chapel Hill: University of North Carolina Press, 1990).
     All have been participants in the annual Latin American Labor History Confer-
     ences.

         Initiated with the strong support and continuing inspiration of Brazilian his-
     torian Emília Viotti da Costa, the Latin American Labor History Conference
     has met annually since 1984 at Yale, Princeton, the State University of New York
     at Stony Brook, and Duke University. On the early conferences, see the brief re-
     ports in *International Labor and Working Class History* 41 (1992), pp. 76–79; 35 (1989),
     pp. 84–87; 33 (1988), pp. 87–89; 32 (1987), pp. 80–82; and 28 (1985), pp. 94–95.

12   All of the contributions to this volume originated in presentations to the annual
     Latin American Labor History Conference. The essays by Levenson-Estrada and
     French and Cluff were originally presented at the 1987 conference, which focused

on women and labor as major lacunae in the field of Latin American labor history (a paper presented there by Michael Jiménez was published as "Class, Gender, and Peasant Resistance in Central Colombia, 1900–1930," in *Everyday Forms of Peasant Resistance,* ed. Forrest Colburn [Armonk, N.Y.: M. E. Sharpe, 1989], pp. 122–50). In 1986, the conference highlighted the question of class and culture, a subject which had received little attention in the Latin American versus North Atlantic new labor history.

13 Among Latin Americanists, women's history and studies and labor history and studies have tended to be two separate fields, barely overlapping and not in any consistent dialogue with each other. Judging from a recent review essay by Richard Oestreicher, this state of affairs does not appear to be unique to Latin America ("Separate Tribes? Working-Class and Women's History," *Reviews in American History* 19 [1992]: pp. 228–31).

14 See the two collections edited by June Nash and Helen I. Safa: *Sex and Class in Latin America* (South Hadley, Mass.: Bergin, 1980); and *Women and Change in Latin America* (South Hadley, Mass.: Bergin and Garvey, 1986). Another fundamental work is María Patricia Fernández-Kelly's study of women workers in the *maquiladoras: For We Are Sold, I and My People: Women and Industry in Mexico's Frontier* (Albany: State University of New York Press, 1993). Much of this pioneering work adopted what might be called a dual systems approach that emphasized the parallel dynamics of patriarchy and capitalism, although its analytical categories, viewed retrospectively, can easily seem too rigid and its models of causation mechanistic.

15 June Nash, *We Eat the Mines and the Mines Eat Us: Dependency and Exploitation in Bolivian Tin Mines* (New York: Columbia University Press, 1979). In 1992, she published a compilation of oral histories over several decades with family members of one of her key informants: *I Spent My Life in the Mines: The Story of Juan Rojas, Bolivian Tin Miner* (New York: Columbia University Press, 1992). This fascinating volume did not, however, offer any detailed analysis of the oral testimony itself. See also Nash's interview with female former miner Basília in June Nash and Manuel María Rocca, *Dos mujeres indígenas: Basília, Facundina* (Mexico City: Instituto Indigenista Interamericano, 1976).

16 Joan Wallach Scott, "Women's History," in *Gender and the Politics of History* (New York: Columbia University Press, 1988), pp. 15–28.

17 The breakthrough text in this regard was Domitila Barrios de Chungara, *Let Me Speak! Testimony of Domitila, A Woman of the Bolivian Mines* (New York: Monthly Review Press, 1978). See also Domitila Barrios de Chungara, *Aquí también Domitila* (La Paz: n.p., 1984).

18 For an early contribution by a historian see Maryssa Navarro, "Hidden, Silent, and Anonymous: Women Workers in the Argentine Trade Union Movement," in *The World of Women's Trade Unionism: Comparative Historical Essays,* ed. Norbert C. Soldon (Westport, Conn.: Greenwood, 1985).

19   Ava Baron, "Gender and Labor History: Learning from the Past, Looking to the Future," in *Work Engendered: Towards a New History of American Labor,* ed. Ava Baron (Ithaca: Cornell University Press, 1991), pp. 16–17.

20   Joan Wallach Scott, "Gender as a Useful Category for Historical Analysis," in *Gender and the Politics of History,* pp. 28–53.

21   Baron, "Gender and Labor History," p. 36.

22   A similar formulation is offered to sociologists by Lourdes Benería and Martha Roldán, who call for "the study of how class and gender are articulated in a concrete working and living situation" as part of an effort "to develop an integrated analysis in which class and gender formation, struggle, and recomposition are looked at simultaneously as necessary steps . . . [in order to] capture the wholeness of the reality we want to describe" (*The Crossroads of Class and Gender: Industrial Homework, Subcontracting, and Household Dynamics in Mexico City* [Chicago: University of Chicago Press, 1987], pp. 1–2).

23   Baron, "Gender and Labor History," p. 36.

24   Benería and Roldán, "Crossroads," p. 10.

25   This formula regarding the originality of class formation in Latin America was first advanced by Silvia Sigal and Juan Carlos Torre ("Una reflexión en torno de los movimientos laborales en América Latina," in *Fuerza de trabajo y movimientos laborales en América Latina,* ed. José Luis Reyna and Rubén Katzman [Mexico City: Colegio de México, 1979], p. 145).

26   This point is also made by sociologist John Humphrey, who observes that "clearly the identities of male and female workers are related to the constructs of masculinity [and femininity] in the wider society, but they are by no means reducible to them" (*Gender and Work in the Third World: Sexual Divisions in Brazilian Industry* [London: Routledge, 1989], p. 6).

27   Baron, "Gender and Labor History," p. 37.

28   Humphrey, "Gender and Work," pp. 2, 6.

29   See Eleni Varikas, "Gender, Experience, and Subjectivity: The Tilly-Scott Disagreement," *New Left Review* 211 (1995): pp. 89–101.

30   "Language or discourse position subjects and produce their experiences," Scott writes in "The Evidence of Experience," *Critical Inquiry* 17, no. 3 (summer 1991).

31   See the exchange between Scott and Linda Gordon in *Signs* 15, no. 4 (1990), pp. 852–59. An analogous point is made in Leon Fink, "The New Labor History and the Powers of Historical Pessimism: Consensus, Hegemony, and the Case of the Knights of Labor," in *In Search of the Working Class* (Urbana: University of Illinois Press, 1994), pp. 135–36.

32   Social historian Geoff Eley has recently advanced the metaphor of a train journey to best capture the attitude of historians toward the "linguistic turn" of the mid-1980s. Some take the train to the end of the line, "to the land of discourse and deconstruction"; a much larger group is aware of what is happening but is uninterested in the theory and "essentially wishing it would go away"; a third

group, in which he includes himself, is "partly there for the ride, partly curious to see where it goes and not at all sure they'll stay very long at the final destination" ("Is All the World a Text? From Social History to the History of Society Two Decades Later," in *The Historic Turn in the Human Sciences,* ed. Terrence J. McDonald [Ann Arbor: University of Michigan Press, 1994]). It seems that most Latin American labor historians fit within the second group while tempted by some of the scenic attractions of the journey.

33   In her impressive new book *Women, Feminism, and Social Change,* Asunción Lavrin offers an encyclopedic survey of the women's mobilization in the Southern Cone from 1890 to 1940 and the accompanying debates about their role. She pays special attention to the emerging controversy about working-class women's paid employment that "became the target of the gender-oriented legislation that created special rewards for working women, reinforced the cult of motherhood in society, and linked women and children to public health issues." Topics regarding women workers "were debated for four decades and at the end of the 1930s, when the process of female incorporation into the labor market was irreversible, the debate had come to a standoff in which no ideological position could claim a victory." A fuller exploration of these debates, she suggests, remains to be done "since labor history is beyond the scope" of her book (*Women, Feminism, and Social Change in Argentina, Chile, and Uruguay, 1890–1940* [Lincoln: University of Nebraska Press, 1995], pp. 54, 85).

34   A similar view of factory employment as threatening women's honor was reported in Brazil for a Pernambuco textile factory, in the 1930s and 1940s (Maria Rosilene Barbosa Alvim, "Trabalho infantil e reprodução social: O trabalho das crianças numa fábrica com vila operária," in *Condições de vida das camadas populares,* ed. Luiz Antônio Machado da Silva [Rio de Janeiro: Zahar, 1984], pp. 73–74). Concerns about female honor were also reported by Lloyd Reynolds and Peter Gregory in their 1953–1956 survey of 1,045 industrial workers in three cities in Puerto Rico. Gregory reported that "at the earliest stages of the [industrial] expansion, and particularly in the smaller and less cosmopolitan towns, the new employment opportunities were regarded with some suspicion by the conservative elders and husbands. . . . Once women had taken such jobs, it was a familiar sight to see an unmarried daughter escorted to and from the factory by another family member, in order to protect her reputation and honor" (Peter Gregory, "The Labor Market in Puerto Rico," in *Labor Commitment and Social Change in Developing Areas,* ed. Wilbert Moore and Arnold Feldman [New York: Social Science Research Council, 1960], p. 151).

35   "By 1920," Asunción Lavrin notes, "female labor had become an economic and political issue transcending the boundaries of the home but still heavily charged with the emotions surrounding family issues." Public debate focused, in particular, on women's "blue-collar work because it was the most socially and politically controversial . . . [since] men who reached adulthood in the first decade

of the twentieth century, under nineteenth century mores, perceived women as mothers, sisters, or daughters in the safe environment of the home. The erosion of that image created an emotional climate that made female industrial labor a political issue" (*Women*, p. 54). A recent study by Yamandú González Sierra shows that some of these major themes were also present in the 1870s and 1880s in the Uruguayan public debate about women's labor (*Del Hogar a la Fábrica: ¿Deshonra o Virtud?* [Montevideo: Editorial Nordan-Communidad, 1994]).

36   This finding is echoed by French and Cluff who, after noting that "women's work outside the home is viewed as an exception," suggest that it can stem either "from economic difficulties or the family's desire for upward social mobility."

37   Lavrin, *Women*, pp. 89–90.

38   Male/female power dynamics within the family can also be explored through the study of the various strategies adopted for handling money within working-class households. Largely neglected by historians, the question has been central to anthropological and sociological studies of urban working-class households. In particular, see chapters 4 and 10 in the superb comparative study of textile workers' families in Brazil and Argentina carried out by Liliana Acero in collaboration with Claudia Minoliti, Alejandra Rotania, and Irma Nora Perez Vichich, *Textile Workers in Brazil and Argentina: A Study of the Interrelationships between Work and Households* (Tokyo: United Nations University Press, 1991).

39   This is a theme in Helen Safa's new book on women workers in Puerto Rico, the Dominican Republic, and Cuba: *The Myth of the Male Breadwinner: Women and Industrialization in the Caribbean* (Boulder, Colo.: Westview Press, 1995).

40   Anthropologist Verena Stolcke wrote a pioneering 1988 study on the impact of proletarianization on gender dynamics within the rural family (*Coffee Planters, Workers, and Wives: Class Conflict and Gender Relations on São Paulo Plantations, 1850–1980* [New York: St. Martin's Press, 1988], pp 208–46). She also examines the pattern of domestic violence among the rural laborers she studied.

41   See Ana María Alonso's treatment of wife-beating in a rural northern Mexican community in a chapter titled "Caciques at Home," in *Thread of Blood: Colonialism, Revolution, and Gender on Mexico's Northern Frontier* (Tucson: University of Arizona Press, 1995).

42   This theme is more fully developed in the everyday-life (*Alltagsgeschichte*) movement in German labor history in the 1980s. (Alf Lüdtke, ed., *The History of Everyday Life: Reconstructing Historical Experiences and Ways of Life* [Princeton: Princeton University Press, 1995]). For an introduction see Geoff Eley, "Labor History, Social History, *Alltagsgeschichte*: Experience, Culture, and the Politics of Everyday—A New Direction for German Social History," *Journal of Modern History* 61 (1989): pp. 297–343. For an example by one of its primary exponents see Alf Lüdtke, "Cash, Coffee-Breaks, Horseplay: *Eigensinn* and Politics among Factory Workers in Germany circa 1900," in *Confrontation, Class Consciousness, and the Labor*

Process: Studies in Proletarian Class Formation, ed. Michael Hanagan and Charles Stephenson (Westport, Conn.: Greenwood Press, 1986), pp. 65–95.

43   This issue is raised for the U.S. case in Christine Stansell, *City of Women: Sex and Class in New York, 1789–1860* (New York: Knopf, 1986). Anthropologist Kevin A. Yelvington offers interesting observations based on his ethnography of a small factory in Trinidad in "Flirting in the Factory," *Journal of the Royal Anthropological Institute* 2, no. 2 (1996): pp. 313–33.

44   See Lavrin, *Women;* Karen Rosemblatt, "Por un hogar bien constituido: El estado y su política familiar en los frentes populares," in *Disciplina y desacato: Construcción de identidad en Chile, siglos 19 y 20,* ed. Lorena Godoy et al. (Santiago: Sur/Cedem, 1995), pp. 181–222.

45   See Karen Rosemblatt, "Por un Hogar," and Susan K. Besse, *Restructuring Patriarchy: The Modernization of Gender Inequality in Brazil, 1914–1940* (Chapel Hill: University of North Carolina Press, 1996).

46   Although Lavrin's book ends in 1940, the Peronist regime's gender policies and discourse clearly built upon the politics of social motherhood developed by the earlier reformers and feminists she discusses (Lavrin, *Women,* pp. 353–62).

47   The historian, as Emília Viotti da Costa suggests, must never "forget that in modern societies, even more than in the past, politics is at the center of human life. This centrality of politics is a result of both the incorporation of increasing numbers of people into the market economy and the overwhelming presence of the modern state in the lives of people. As a consequence of these two processes, which are intimately related, political decisions have come to affect economic and social life in ways never seen before. The life of a peasant in some lost village in the backland, the labor conditions of a worker in a factory, a woman's status in a society, the opportunities denied or opened to a black person, all depend not only on their own struggle or on the cold logic of the market, but also on decisions taken by those in power" (*The Brazilian Empire: Myths and Histories* [Chicago: University of Chicago Press, 1985], p. xvii).

48   Lesley Gill, *Precarious Dependencies: Gender, Class, and Domestic Service in Bolivia* (New York: Columbia University Press, 1994), pp. 37, 145; Dawn Keremitsis, "Del metate al molino: La mujer mexicana de 1910 a 1940," *Historia Mexicana* 33, no. 2 (1983): pp. 285–302.

49   In her discussion of masculinity in a rural community in Chihuahua, Alonso finds that waged labor was conceptualized as servile and thus dishonoring to men. In this particular case, a "frontier ideology of gender-honor conflicted with the servile image of the docile worker. . . . Waged labor implied a form of subjectivity-subjection that did not permit *serrano* men to embody their ideals of masculine identity. The dependency wage labor entailed made a man like a child, like a woman, and like a 'tame' Indian." Such particularized local gender constructs would be of obvious relevance to a labor historian if men from

such a community were an important source of factory labor through migration (Alonso, *Thread*, pp. 192, 194).

50   Nash, *We Eat the Mines*, pp. 72–73. The interpenetration of the rural and the urban in early European industrialization is explored in Douglas R. Holmes, *Cultural Disenchantments: Worker Peasantries in Northeastern Italy* (Princeton: Princeton University Press, 1989). Raymond Buve's 1972 study of Tlaxcala textile workers showed that the mobilization of these *obrero-campesinos* [worker-peasants] could not be understood apart from their rural communities of origin ("Protestas de obreros y campesinos durante el porfiriato: Unas consideraciones sobre su desarollo e interelaciones en el este de México Central," *Boletín de Estudios Latinoamericanos* 13 [1972]: pp. 1–25).

51   Ana María Alonso criticizes attempts to link women's subjection to men in terms of a "universal homology between the structural contrasts nature-culture and female-male" (*Thread*, p. 79).

52   Even at the moment when the cult of domesticity was being constructed in England, Catherine Hall suggests, "working men and women developed their own notions of manliness and femininity which, while affected by [such] dominant conceptions, nevertheless had inflections of their own" ("The Tale of Samuel and Jemima: Gender and Working-Class Culture in Nineteenth-Century England," in *E. P. Thompson: Critical Perspectives*, ed. Harvey J. Kaye and Keith McClelland [Philadelphia: Temple University Press, 1990], p. 97).

53   The fundamental reference remains the compelling 1975 article by Sidney W. Mintz ("The Rural Proletariat and the Problem of Rural Proletarian Consciousness," in *Ideology and Social Change in Latin America*, ed. June Nash and Juan Corradi [New York: n.p., 1975], vol. 2, pp. 34–77) that explores such difficulties without falling into nominalism.

54   We still lack an exacting survey of the language of class along the lines of William H. Sewell, *Work and Revolution in France: The Language of Labor from the Old Regime to 1848* (Cambridge: Cambridge University Press, 1980). Nor do we have a detailed discussion of the subjective experience of work, much less class; for suggestive examples see Patrick Joyce, ed., *The Historical Meanings of Work* (New York: Cambridge University Press, 1987).

55   Concern with identifying differences between male and female workers should not, however, lead us to overlook similarities in outlook that cross the boundaries of gender. In a 1962 survey of 1,096 industrial workers in Lima and Callao, for example, Guillermo Briones found almost identical responses from men and women as to sources of job satisfaction ("Training and Adaptation of the Labor Force in the Early Stages of Industrialization," *International Social Science Journal* 15 [1963], p. 579).

56   Letter to authors by Asunción Lavrin, October 1996.

57   Funded by a two-year NEH Collaborative grant, the first fruits of the "Berisso Obrero" project can be seen in the various published works of Lobato and in the

forthcoming book by Daniel James, *Doña María's Story* (Durham, N.C.: Duke University Press).

58 Asunción Lavrin, *Women,* rightly avoids this error.

59 The labor historian of Brazil is in a unique situation when dealing with contemporary industrial workers in São Paulo. In the last twenty-five years, intense interest has been generated among an exceptionally talented group of social scientists by the rise of the New Unionism identified with Luis Inácio "Lula" da Silva and the subsequent success of the Partido dos Trabalhadores (PT); the result has been an amazingly rich and varied array of studies of contemporary workers in greater São Paulo (see John D. French's forthcoming book *The Metalworkers of ABC, 1950–1980*). Even for a generally less well-studied topic like sexuality, for example, one can find many interesting pieces on male and female workers in the region. See Rose Marie Muraro, *Sexualidade da mulher brasileira: Corpo e classe social no Brasil,* 2d ed. (Petrópolis: Vozes, 1983); Carmen Barroso and Cristina Bruschini, "Building Politics from Personal Lives: Discussions of Sexuality among Poor Women in Brazil," in *Third World Women and the Politics of Feminism,* ed. Chandra Mohanty, Ann Russo, and Lourdes Torres (Bloomington: Indiana University Press, 1991), pp. 153–72; and Donna M. Goldstein, "AIDS and Women in Brazil: The Emerging Problem," *Social Science Medicine* 39, no. 7 (1994): pp. 919–29.

60 Zulma Recchini de Lattes and Catalina H. Wainerman, *El trabajo feminino en el banquillo de los acusados: La medición censal en América Latina* (Mexico City: Terra Nova, 1981). For a short English discussion see "Unreliable Account of Women's Work: Evidence from Latin American Census Statistics," *Signs* 11, no. 4 (1986): pp. 740–50.

61 Labor historians of Latin America have lagged behind other social scientists in this regard. See, for example, Florence E. Babb, *Between Field and Cooking Pot: The Political Economy of Marketwomen in Peru* (Austin: University of Texas Press, 1989); and Ximena Bunster and Elsa M. Chaney, *Sellers and Servants: Working Women in Lima, Peru* (New York: Praeger, 1985).

62 Letter to authors by Asunción Lavrin, October 1996.

63 Nash, *I Spent My Life.* Women have been central to this epic if largely hidden daily struggle for survival in Latin America, which has been marked by historically high and often sustained levels of inflation. It is remarkable that we still lack studies of how urban working-class families have responded, over time, to the high cost of living. Beyond its impact on consumption patterns or trade union dynamics, inflation and currency instability must have also had a profound cultural influence on popular views of the nature of money and the economy.

64 On aging and memory see Ecléa Bosi, *Memória e sociedade: Lembranças de velhos,* 2d. ed. (1973; reprint, São Paulo: T. A. Queiroz, 1983); and Barbara Meyerhoff, *Remembered Lives: The Work of Ritual, Storytelling, and Growing Older* (Ann Arbor: University of Michigan Press, 1992).

65   Matthew C. Gutmann, *The Meanings of Macho: Being a Man in Mexico City* (Berkeley: University of California Press, 1996), p. 14.

66   See Gill, *Precarious Dependencies;* John Burdick, *Looking for God in Brazil: The Progressive Catholic Church in Urban Brazil's Religious Arena* (Berkeley: University of California Press, 1993); and Elizabeth Ellen Brusco, *The Reformation of Machismo: Evangelical Conversion and Gender in Colombia* (Austin: University of Texas Press, 1995). If we aspire to understand the many spheres of working-class women's lives, we cannot continue to ignore the spiritual dimension of their inner lives as well as its external manifestations through ritual and public participation (baptism, marriage, church attendance, prayer, references in speech). It is reductionist to view religion as primarily a form of social control or merely as an instrument to accomplish individual goals. As an aspect of interiority, spirituality is tied to the larger challenge of developing an anthropology of emotion, a history of sensibilities.

67   Gutmann, *Meanings,* p. 16. The existence of a range of masculinities is also suggested for rural northern Mexico in Alonso, *Thread,* pp. 79–80.

68   This is closely tied up with what Carole Pateman calls the sexual contract between men and women (*The Sexual Contract* [Stanford: Stanford University Press, 1988]).

69   See the oral history testimonies in Laura Miller, "La mujer obrera en Lima, 1900–1930," in *Lima obrera 1900–1930,* ed. Steve Stein (Lima: Ediciones El Virrey, 1987), pp. 11–152.

70   We still lack a rich literature on working-class sociability in Latin America, male or female. For an exception see the study by Luiz Antônio Machado da Silva, "O significado do botequim," *América Latina [Rio de Janeiro],* no. 3 (1969): pp. 160–82. It contains wonderful ethnographic material on the behavior, social mores, and views of the men who frequented the working-class *botequim* studied.

71   Gutmann, *Meanings,* pp. 14–15. The little-studied issue of nonheterosexual or same-sex relations among men would have obvious relevance here. See Joseph Carrier, *De Los Otros: Intimacy and Homosexuality among Mexican Men* (New York: Columbia University Press, 1995).

72   Emília Viotti da Costa, *Crowns of Glory, Tears of Blood: The Demerara Slave Rebellion of 1823* (New York: Oxford University Press, 1994), pp. xviii–xix. Bracketed material was added.

73   June Nash, "A Decade of Research on Women in Latin America," in *Women and Change in Latin America,* p. 13. Bracketed material was added.

74   Viotti da Costa, *Crowns,* p. xviii.

"Tales Told Out on the Borderlands"

Doña María's Story, Oral History,
and Issues of Gender

DANIEL JAMES

The processes of working class autobiography, of people's history and of the working class novel cannot show a proper and valid culture existing in its own right, underneath the official forms, waiting for revelation. Accounts of working class life are told by tension and ambiguity, out on the borderlands. —Carolyn Steedman, *Landscape for a Good Woman*

BERISSO: *Berisso is a city of 70,000 people (as of 1980) located some sixty miles south of the federal capital along the coast of the Rio de la Plata and seven miles from La Plata, the capital of the province of Buenos Aires. Armour and Swift meatpacking plants were established in Berisso in the first years of the century. These were large-scale plants using the most modern Chicago-based technology. They reached the height of production during the Second World War when they employed some 20,000 workers. The labor force initially was drawn largely from transatlantic migration. Lithuanians, Poles, Ukrainians, Albanians, Greeks, Syrians, Turks, Czechs, Slovaks, Bulgarians, Spaniards, and Italians were all drawn to the plants. By the 1940s a community of some 50,000 had established itself. Union organization was almost nonexistent until the 1940s. Under the leadership of Cipriano Reyes, Berisso workers established the Sindicato Autónomo de Obreros de la Indústria de la Carne in 1944. This was one of the first unions to be courted by Juan Perón when he was Secretary of Labor in the military government established in 1943. The meatpacking workers of Berisso played a crucial part in the mobilization of October 17, 1945, that obliged the military government to release Perón from prison and that launched him on his rise to the presidency. Berisso provided one of the main sources of inspiration for the foundation of the Partido Laborista in the last months of 1945. This party would be the chief vehicle for mobilizing working-class support for Perón in the elections of February 1946. Meatpacking workers in Berisso and elsewhere were rewarded for supporting Perón. Conditions of work and salaries improved in the plants in the 1946–1955 period. Much of this improvement was underwritten by state subsidies which offset company cutbacks in production. The period following the overthrow*

Doña María Roldán speaking at a rally of the Partido Laborista
in 1946. Courtesy of María Roldán.

of Perón in 1955 marked the decline of the large-scale meatpacking plants in Argentina: changing markets, changing consumer demands, new regulations, and aging plants combined to reduce the attractiveness of such concerns to the large multinational food combines who owned them. The 1960s were a period of slow agony in Berisso as the plants rapidly reduced their workforce. This process culminated in 1969 when Armour closed its doors; Swift struggled on into the 1970s with a much reduced capacity but closed in the late 1970s. Berisso now has some of the appearance of a ghost town, dominated by the empty shell of the old Swift plant, which still takes up an area of many city blocks. Berisso has remained staunchly Peronist. Despite its economic decline it has maintained its population and they remain politically active; in the Peronist internal elections in 1988 some 12,000 citizens of Berisso voted. The community voted overwhelmingly for Carlos Menem in 1989 and again in 1995.

DOÑA MARÍA ROLDÁN: *Doña María Roldán was born in 1915 in a suburb of Buenos Aires, San Martín. Her father was an Italian immigrant. Newly married, she moved to Berisso in 1931. She gave birth to three children in the 1930s. Her husband had been born in the province of Buenos Aires in a town close to Berisso and had had some experience as a butcher. While her husband worked in the Armour plant, Doña María herself did not enter the plants until 1944 when she got work in the* picada *section in Swift. Her job was to separate nerve and fat from meat that was to be used in preparation of soups, pâtés, and*

Doña María Roldán with candidate Carlos Menem in 1988 in
Berisso. Note the poster of Evita Perón in back left corner.
Courtesy of María Roldán.

other items. She was elected shop steward for her section shortly after her arrival and partici-
pated in the unionization drive which led to the establishment of the Sindicato Autónomo.
The union's presence in the plants was cemented during a ninety-six-day strike between
March and June 1945. Doña María became involved in the emerging political movement to
support Perón. An exceptional outdoor orator, she spoke in the Plaza de Mayo on the night
of October 17, 1945. She traveled the country as part of the laborista *campaign to support*
Perón during the elections of 1946. As part of her activism, she met both Juan and Evita
Perón several times. Doña María stayed in the meatpacking plants until 1958.

Her husband died in 1954 largely as a result of the undermining of his health by the
work he performed. Doña María remained active in local Peronist politics throughout the
following years and campaigned actively for Menem in the 1989 presidential election cam-
paign. She died in July 1989.

I first met Doña María Roldán in August 1985, in the house of Cipriano Reyes.
I was beginning to study the origins of Peronist unionism in Berisso and had
made Reyes's acquaintance. He had introduced me to several of his old union
and laborista colleagues, and one day he announced we would be meeting
the "first female shop steward" in the Swift plant, someone who had played
an important part in the emergence of the union in Berisso. The meeting in

Reyes's front room was a little formal. Doña María evidently had been told about the English professor who was researching the old days of Berisso's golden past; the emergence of the meatpacking union; the mobilization of October 17, 1945; the formation of the Partido Laborista; and, of course, the role of Cipriano Reyes. While I don't think that there had been any formal prior arrangement of an appropriate script, it was clear that during our meeting Reyes, as he was to be in other similar meetings, was very much the master of ceremonies, and Doña María willingly, and convincingly, played her role. The meeting lasted perhaps forty minutes, and I filed it away as an interesting encounter. I filed Doña María away, too, as a potential future source of information about Berisso's social and labor history.

I next met her eighteen months later when I returned to do a more prolonged stretch of research and began to seek out informants who could provide me with oral testimonies about Berisso's past, in particular its labor history and the history of work in the meatpacking plants. Although she had clearly kept to Reyes's script in our previous meeting, I had been impressed with her articulateness and her apparently well-tuned memory. That she had been among the first group of shop-floor representatives in Swift, an active participant in the struggles of the 1940s, and the fact that she had not been among the leadership group of the union or the Partido Laborista, drew me to her. I first went to her house in Berisso in January 1987, with the aim principally of obtaining from Doña María empirical information that I was missing in my attempt to reconstruct the unionization drive within the plants. There was also a hope on my part that I would emerge with that difficult-to-define, but always sought-after, commodity—a "feeling" for the period by way of some appropriate anecdotes that Doña María might be able to recall for me. I assumed that our conversation, which I intended to record, would last a few hours. As it turned out, I ended up recording some thirty hours of interviews over a nine-month period, visiting her house on average once a week to tape conversations, though I was frequently there more often.[1]

One reason for the change in my intentions was clearly that I found Doña María's testimony of great interest. Yet, this was not primarily for the reasons that I had initially chosen to interview her. Her testimony, which came to over six hundred pages of typed script, is a rich, multilayered, often puzzling narrative. It does contain passages that add considerably to an understanding of many basic issues that I wished to document and better understand. Doña María's account, for example, of the difficulties encountered by the activists during the unionization drive of 1944–1945, or her recounting of her experiences, and those of other women in her section, of the Taylorist system of

work organization, the "standard," adds considerably to our objective knowledge both of these issues and of how they were experienced and handled by
the historical actors.[2]

Nevertheless, it became clear to me that however rich a potential source of
empirical information, Doña María's narrative was both limited in this sense
and also involved something else besides. The limits had, of course, partly
to do with the problem of memory, its limits, its failing, and its distortions.
These would warrant an analysis of their own. What interests me in this essay,
however, has to do with the "something else" involved in Doña María's narrative. One of the reasons for the problems, the limits confronted in using
this narrative primarily as a source of empirical knowledge, is that it involves
a largely passive role for Doña María, as simply a repository of more or less
coherent, more or less available, historical data. Yet, it was clear to me before long that even in response to my most "factual," "information-seeking"
questions, Doña María was narrating, telling me a story about her life, reconstructing her past in a selective way that would both legitimize it to me and
make sense of it to herself.

If this is, therefore, indeed a story, the question arises as to how it is to
be read. The shift in focus from oral history as part of a verification process
for historical research to life history implies, among other things, coming to
terms with this question.[3] Contemporary oral history now rarely invokes a
claim to having privileged access to hitherto ignored historical facts and experience based on the practice of a sort of "naive realism."[4] Influenced by
trends in literary criticism that emphasize the importance of narrative and
the construction of texts—and that have tended by extension to see historical reality as another text—oral historians are increasingly aware of the limits
of oral testimony as a source for simply expanding our stock of historical
facts about the recent past. The form of oral narrative is now often taken
to be as significant as the content. This changing awareness has been much
influenced, too, by postmodernist anthropology, with its emphasis on the
authorial shaping of ethnographic narratives and the attendant textual and
rhetorical devices used to construct an apparently objective and authoritative
account of another's life and society.[5]

Increasingly, oral historians such as Luisa Passerini and Ronald Grele have
begun to challenge us to treat the subjective, textual quality of oral testimony as a unique opportunity rather than the obstacle to historical objectivity
and empirical rigor it had seemed to an earlier generation of practitioners.[6]
As a recent manifesto celebrating the subjective dimension of oral testimony
states: "At the same time the individuality of each life story ceases to be an

awkward impediment to generalization, and becomes instead a vital document of the construction of consciousness."[7] Following this invocation we can indeed begin to do justice to one of oral history's original claims: to give a voice to the voiceless, to those who would not normally enter the historical record. In particular oral testimony enables us to approach the issues of agency and subjective intervention in history.

Yet, once more, we must beware of falling back on the assumptions of a naive realism, of presupposing a mimetic quality in oral narratives as they express consciousness and feeling. The issue of using oral narratives to gain access to the domain of consciousness, of "lived experience," is one of the issues complicated by an attention to oral testimony as narrative. If oral testimony is indeed a window onto the subjective in history, the cultural, social, and ideological universe of historical actors, then it must be said that the view it affords is not a transparent one that simply reflects thoughts and feelings as they really were/are. At the very least the image is refracted, the glass of the window unclear.

Thus the relationship between personal narratives and history—as indeed between autobiography in general and history—is complex and problematic. Life stories are culturally determined constructs drawing on a public discourse structured by class, cultural conventions, and gender, and making use of a wide spectrum of possible roles, self-representations, repertoires, and available narratives. We have to learn to read these stories, and the symbols and logic embedded in them, as such if we are to attend to their deeper meaning and do justice to the complexity found in the lives and historical experiences of those who recount them.

In this essay I want to try to suggest what a "symptomatic" reading of a personal narrative might involve by looking at the theme of gender in Doña María's narrative. At first glance this is scarcely a promising theme to isolate from the narrative, particularly if one is interested in reclaiming through such personal testimony an authentic, repressed woman's voice, something approaching a counterdiscourse.

The central events and experiences of Doña María's life are recounted principally in class terms. The dominant events are clustered around her role in the formation of the union in the meatpacking plants, her actions as a shop steward, the October 17 demonstration in favor of Perón, her role in the election of 1946 campaigning with the Partido Laborista, and her later activism within the local Justicialist Party in Berisso. While she is clearly aware of the exploitation of women in the plants, this is placed within the overall context of the crucial and basic changes made in the quality of workers' lives—male and female—by the emergence of the union and Perón.

Doña María also emphasizes the respect and equality of treatment she received from male union leaders in the plants:

> On the contrary, I was accepted to such an extent that shop stewards came to ask me questions to clear up problems. For example: "María, what do you think, there is a worker who did such and such, what should I do, shall I take action, because he arrived late and every time he comes he gets mad"; "now leave it alone, at work you don't argue, later outside tell him to come to the union and we'll all talk about it for a while." . . . No I got on fine, they liked me a lot, I have no complaints.

In a similar vein, Doña María paints a picture of an ideal marriage, based on mutual respect and understanding between husband and wife. At different times throughout the narrative she emphasizes both her acceptance of the role of the good wife, as traditionally defined in Argentine society, and her husband's support of her activities outside the home. Describing her early life in a tenement house before she went to work, she stresses that she never had problems with lack of respect from the men who lived in the tenement, despite the forced intimacy of the situation:

> I always say that the woman who knows her place never lacks for respect, nothing strange ever happened to me, but then it never happened because I never went around being cute, joking around with the men in the patio, I waited for my husband, gave him his food, cleaned, stayed with my children.

Her account of the initiation of her activism in the union is framed in a similar tone:

> Reyes came to see me in my section, the picada, "I come on behalf of your husband, he is already in agreement, and if you want to be the delegate for this section, because you have the qualities, your husband says it is fine. . . ." I said to him, "If you have spoken to my husband and he has said yes, then I'll also say yes."

Once she is launched on a career beyond the home, she is careful to emphasize that she was able to do it with his support: "He supported me in everything I did, if I hadn't had him as a husband I wouldn't have done what I did."

If one of the forms of self-representation used by Doña María to construct her narrative is that of the "good wife," that of the "good mother" also figures prominently. This is often expressed in terms of the importance of providing good welfare and love for children as a basic social priority, and is the ultimate rationale for political and union struggles — "to give a piece of bread to our children"; "I often had to listen to my children go to bed crying because they were hungry." In Doña María's narrative we also find this generalized into a guiding principle which should be used to define the role of women in society. At one stage of her testimony she took out an old newspaper clipping of a speech she had made that was directed specifically at rallying women to the Partido Laborista. The speech started with an affirmation of a basic principle:

> The home is the place where the great national principles are nourished. . . . the home is the very image of the nation, the stronghold of the fatherland, where mothers sing to their children of the hope of a better world, in the home the invincible force is the woman, it is the woman who with her silent sacrifice entrusts the blood of her blood, her children, for the defense of national sovereignty. She is the people confronted with any state that persecutes, terrorizes, and kills.

In line with this general affirmation of the role of mothering and nurturance, Doña María also expresses opposition to both divorce and abortion within her narrative.

This all seems relatively unproblematic, and in some ways the "prototypical" Peronist woman's life-script, conforming to the dominant representation of women found in Peronist discourse and formally articulated in Peronist ideology. Yet we should be cautious about accepting this at face value. The very logic of the narrative argues against it; other elements and themes Doña María uses to create her story speak of a more complex, ambivalent process of self-identification and story construction. The typical elements of a working-class woman's biography are juxtaposed and overlain with other images, roles, and themes which give Doña María's story a different twist.

In Doña María's life story we have clear indications early on that her story will contain unconventional elements. Speaking of her childhood she says:

> I gave my family a little bit of concern because I had the rebelliousness that my father had, for me to be shut up inside with a needle sewing and hemming and that sort of thing was a waste of time, I thought that you had to go beyond that, do other things.
>
> I was very predisposed to curiosity as a kid, to know what was happening here, what was happening there, where there was a political meeting, for example, that's where I'd be, listening.

Once some friends and I stopped in a button factory and we said to the girls who worked there, Why are you working for free? Why don't you rebel one day and not come in? Or why don't you have a sit down strike inside? . . . We poked our noses in because we felt the pain, the pain of exploitation that was imposed on other girls. Because my father protected me, gave me clothes and food and a roof over my head, but these others no, they had to go out to get food for an invalid mother, a widowed mother or a father who had lost his wife.

The image of herself as irreverent, as disposed to rebel, forms a crucial part of the emerging plot in Doña María's narrative. Her refusal to turn a blind eye to suffering and injustice and her rebellious temperament lead her into a series of actions and situations after 1944 that form the core of the plot of her story. Yet these crucial elements of her story are made possible by events beyond her control. The emergence of Peronism, the consequent mobilization of the organized working class, with its greater access to the public sphere, all provide the context for her divergence from the accepted story line of a working-class woman. The emergence of Perón will provide the stage on which this individual woman will make her decision to break with her traditional domestic role. In her telling of this story two things are made clear. First, the prior establishment of her image of adolescent curiosity and rebellion enables her in a sense to stress the continuity and rationale of her decision in the mid-1940s, after more than ten years of apparently quiescent domestic bliss, to enter the workforce and adopt a role of union and political militancy. Second, she phrases her explanation of her crucial decision to start work in solidly material terms. She, like many other women in Berisso, went into the meatpacking plants for basic economic reasons. In her case, the medical bills that she faced after her second son caught polio could not be paid from her husband's salary alone. While she had no illusions about the nature of work in the plants, she thought it better than entering domestic service and cleaning up the "mess of others."

Her activism in the public sphere beyond the family, in both the union and in politics, in the course of the following decade forms the central theme in her life story. While the events cover a span of only a decade in a long life, they have a disproportionate weight in her narrative. While the issue of her role beyond the confines of the family is encountered in many forms in her testimony, it is most crucially expressed in a series of anecdotes that recall incidents of confrontation with authorities. These anecdotes become fundamental episodes imbued with symbolic significance in her life story, which gives them an almost mythical status. This impression is increased by the fact that they are frequently repeated throughout the narrative. They are frequently told in the same form, with almost identical wording. They are clearly stories that have been repeated, performed, and honed in family, social, and political settings.

Once I stopped in front of a foreman, this was when we had already come to believe in unions and we could defend ourselves better, this foreman said to a woman, "Señora, you're useless," when I saw that the woman didn't say anything I said to him, "This woman has a husband and she is a wife and mother of a family, what right do you have to call her useless?" "Well, she doesn't know how to work," he said to me. "Have the decency, señor *jefe,* to call her aside and explain to her what is happening, not insult her in front of everyone, remember that you were born of a woman, not from a plant, or weren't you born of a woman?" I said to him, the impulsive one they called me, yes, *la impulsiva,* because I shouted in their faces. Where does he get off telling her in front of all her *compañeras* that she is useless? The woman stayed there, like someone who had killed another person, like a condemned woman. I said to her, "Lift your head up, *querida,* you're not useless, you just arrived and haven't adapted yet, you'll soon work like us." This was when we already had the right to speak [*ya teníamos la palabra*], we had the union to defend us, when we knew that we weren't going to go into the streets for answering back, because they would have grabbed me by the hair and thrown me out twenty times a day otherwise, because as a steward I assumed the responsibility of defending my compañeras.

The order arrived from the union one day to call my section out . . . but I got to thinking, what about the women in the turkey section, who don't have a steward, so I took off from my section and went to the turkey section. No sooner had I got there than I met up with the foreman and he told me I was an intruder. I said to him, all right, I accept it but let's all get out girls, let's go outside, the *frigorífico* is on strike, no sooner had I said it than they were all outside, "He doesn't even let us go to the toilet, this son of a bitch, we can hardly work anymore for wanting to go to the bathroom."

Once they came to take me to the *sub-prefectura de marina,* I had to get out of my work clothes, the two guards who came for me wanted to come in while I took off my overall, so I said: "No, señor, you stay outside, let the forewoman watch me in here, I am not going to escape since I know that I am in the hands of the oligarchy, the shameless ones who have so many dollars, so that I will surrender, but you can't come in here." The subchief of the maritime police said to me, "Sit down, señora." So I said, "Good afternoon, señor," because he hadn't even had the courtesy to greet me. He asked me, "What are you?" "An Argentine," I said. "No," he said to me, "What party do you belong to?" "Ah, señor, since you asked me what am I and I was born here, I said Argentine. I am a laborista, with Cipriano Reyes at the head . . . anything else you want to know?" "Yes, señora, why are you a laborista?" "Ay, señor, you are asking me too much, like as if I was asking you why you are the *sub-prefecto*. I am a laborista, you know why? Because we have created the Sindicato de la Carne and now we want to express ourselves in a purely workers' party, do away with all the grievances that we suffer as workers . . . or perhaps we don't have the right to form a party? That's all, señor sub-prefecto, you can do with me what you will, but what I have here in my heart and head, is mine not yours. Anything else?" "Yes señora, I'm going to give you some advice, they have told me that you are an intelligent woman, why don't you get involved in the schools, in something else, not in politics, not in unions, you should leave that sort of thing to the men. You love children I should think, why don't you devote yourself to the schools, in things like that, not unions." I said to him, "No, señor, I am going to tell you something, will you allow me to do that, señor sub-prefecto? In my house there isn't a cent, there's no money, Do you have money to give me? If so then give me it, but spare the advice, at this stage of my life, with three children to support and with the poverty that we suffer, I don't accept advice from anybody." As he remained silent, I asked him again, "Anything else?" Where did he get off giving me advice, when I had to make noises with my pots so that the neighbors would think I had something to give my kids to eat, and I'm supposed to listen to some buffoon with spurs.

It is important to be clear as to the importance of these anecdotes. Their status as historical data is difficult to ascertain. Doña María frequently switches them around, moving them backward and forward in time, or she elides them. Yet their function in the basic plot of her narrative lies in their symbolic assertion of her self-definition as a rebel, as an uppity woman, *la intrusa, la impulsiva, la delegada brava*. Other stories are also added to confirm the plot. Doña María speaks personally with Perón on several occasions. The occasion to which she returns several times in her narrative is when she forms part of a delegation urging on Perón the importance of women's suffrage:

I said to him, "Colonel, I feel wounded many times when my husband on election day says, the people have voted, and I say to him, no the people didn't vote, half the people voted, because a woman is a citizen . . . . We can't allow the situation to exist anymore, Colonel, where alcoholics, madmen, the dead—he started to laugh at this—monks, vote and we have to listen to our husbands, our fiancés, our brothers, and our uncles tell us that the people voted, aren't we the people, too, Colonel? . . ." Perón turned to Reyes and asked him if I was a *doctora.* "No-o-o," replied Reyes with a chuckle, "she's a meatpacker."

The self-portrait contained in these sections, which forms the core of her narrative, also provides the framework for understanding her later actions in politics after she ceased to be a meatpacking worker.

If the plot that Doña María constructs establishes her heretical status as a rare bird, *una mujer atrevida,* whose life history clearly breaks with the conventional script of women's biography, how are we to read the far more conventional themes and more standard forms of self-representation mentioned at the beginning? Is one set of images true and the other false? Does one set merely reflect a formal conformity with the established conventions of working women and their lives while the other represents the authentic woman, the repressed voice normally hidden from history? I think that by looking more closely at the factors in play here, we can start to appreciate what is at stake in oral history, particularly as it relates to issues of consciousness and ideological process. In what follows I will attempt to suggest some of the factors in play in the shaping of Doña María's recounting of her life.

On one level, we certainly need to take account of the impact of Peronist ideology. Many of the themes present in the narrative are clearly taken from and reflected in Peronist discourse as it addressed women. During the crucial decade of 1945–1955, Peronism, through its political and cultural institutions, both mobilized and legitimized women as actors within a newly enlarged public sphere. At the same time, it attempted to redefine appropriate forms of behavior and appropriate divisions between public and private. While the traditional subordination of women to men was denounced, many of the traditional virtues associated with women were reaffirmed within a reworked ideology of domesticity. By the early 1950s, at the height of Evita Perón's influence, women's work outside the home was expressly condemned, and women's political activity was sharply distinguished from that of men. Politics was considered to be an inherently masculine preserve which women were ill-adapted to handle. Women's political activity was taken to derive from their unique virtues as mothers, wives, and guardians of the hearth. They were intrinsically unselfish, capable of self-sacrifice, and communal in nature, not the greedy individualists symbolized by men in politics. Their nurturing role at home was taken, by extension, to be a metaphor for their unique role as guardians of the nation.[8]

Echoes of this ideology are clearly present in Doña María's life story. Indeed, as we have mentioned, sometimes they are drawn directly from political speeches expressing this formal rhetoric. Much of this official rhetoric was reinforced by cultural stereotypes embodied in popular cultural images. Meatpacking had a particular niche in both the popular culture and the official rhetoric of the Perón era. Many novels were written, for example, in a style that might be referred to as "Peronist realism." While the fundamental political purposes of the narratives were to glorify and sentimentalize the struggle of workers and to contrast their conditions of life before and after Perón, these were also strongly gendered texts that established, largely by omission and silence, powerful images of gender relationships and hierarchies in the meatpacking plants and communities.

One of the most famous of these texts, *Pobres habrá siempre,* a book to which Doña María specifically refers in her narrative, was first published in 1943 by the author, Luis Horacio Velázquez.[9] It was republished several times during the Peronist era. The story, based on the case of Berisso itself, concerns conditions in the meatpacking plants prior to Perón, and the emerging consciousness and revolt of the workers, who at the end of the book launch a strike. Women are distinguished by their absence from the main narrative. They appear either as long-suffering mothers or hard-pressed housewives. They are largely absent from the main theme of consciousness raising and union organizing. The images conveyed in this literature are of an overwhelmingly masculine universe.

This is true not simply because of the characters and the formal structuring of the plot, but also because of the presence of what Beatrix Campbell, referring to George Orwell's descriptions of physical labor in *The Road to Wigan Pier,* has called the "cult of the masculine."[10] The physical nature of manual labor is a prominent feature of the genre of popular literature to which we are referring. Muscles ripple, sweat pours, and men are driven to superhuman feats of physical endeavor in images that act as a sort of corollary to the male camaraderie and intimacy celebrated in the text.

The point I wish to suggest by referring to both official Peronist ideology as it addressed women and the set of roles and images, particularly in meatpacking, presented in popular cultural texts is not that they were absorbed and then found direct representation in Doña María's narrative. Rather, I am interested in emphasizing that they should be regarded as one part of the repertoire of roles, conventions, and forms of self-representation that influenced Doña María in her life and that she drew on when reflecting on her life, selecting among her experiences, and constructing her life story. And, if this was the case, we can certainly understand the tension and sense of dissonance engendered among women who had entered the workforce, particularly one who adopted an active role on the public stage of factory and political party like Doña María, when confronted by a discourse that seemed to challenge the legitimacy of the decisions they had made in their lives.

This tension and sense of dissonance is reflected throughout Doña María's narrative and is crucial, I think, to understanding many of its contradictions as far as gender relationships are concerned and the difficulties involved in reading it for gender. Several recent studies of female personal narration have referred to this phenomenon. Faye Ginsburg, referring to the life stories of pro- and anti-abortion activists, speaks of "the dissonance between their experience of changes in their own biographies and the available cultural models for marking them."[11] Her reference to available cultural models points us toward an examination of the limiting, defining—in a word, structuring—role of the cultural vehicles and interpretative devices available to Doña María as she shaped her life story.

The recent "blurring of the genres" has induced an increased sensitivity among historians—perhaps most intensively among oral historians—to the importance of narrative as an ordering, sense-making device at both collective and individual levels:[12] "At the individual level, people make sense of their lives through the stories that are available to them, and they attempt to fit their lives into the available stories. People live by stories."[13] At a more general level, communities, too, adopt narratives which serve to inculcate and confirm their integrity and coherence over time. These communal stories are created and accepted by the participants in a constant process of negotiation among different versions. This indicates the essentially practical function of this sort of narrative counting, serving to draw the community together and enabling it to formulate action in the present and future based on a common understanding of the past. The "collective memory" thus formulated is constructed on the basis of a variety of devices: public myths, founding stories, crucial transforming events, evil and good characters, and the division of the past into the time before and after a "golden age."[14]

In Berisso there were a number of master narratives within whose parameters Doña María could potentially frame her story. I am here referring to local, community narratives rather than those produced at a national institutional and ideological level. These local stories overlap and intersect at many points but can be distinguished for our purposes here.

At a most general level, if Berissenses have a "story they tell themselves about themselves," it is that of the immigrant. This story has official legitimation since Berisso was officially designated "the capital of the immigrant" by government decree in 1978. It is symbolically enacted and played out every September on the Day of the Immigrant when the different ethnic associations parade through the center of the city in their traditional costumes and later perform dances and hold other cultural events. Woven into this story, indeed the crucial core of it, is a morality tale about the hardness of life, the dedication of Berisso's founding generation, and the virtues of hard work as a vehicle for bestowing a better life on one's children. It also speaks of the beneficence of the host country and its embrace of the poor of all countries. As such, Berisso's story is emblematic of Argentina's history—the city's official history is titled *Berisso: Un reflejo de la evolución argentina*.[15] This is a theme that forms a dominant part of the history produced by Berisso's native historians.

A related story—though one with a more polemical, divisive, and class-based character—is centered on the emergence of unions in the meatpacking plants and the role of Berisso in the founding and later history of the Peronist movement. This is a narrative centered on a number of epic themes: the repression of the strike of 1917, the toughness of working in the plants, the appearance of Perón, the great strike of ninety-six days in 1945, Berisso's role in the events of October 1945, the changes in work conditions brought about by the union, the golden era of 1945–1955, the long and bitter decline of the meatpacking industry, Berisso's fall from its former glory, and Berisso's keeping faith with Peronism, living up to the legacy implied in its claim to be *la cuna del peronismo* (the cradle of Peronism).

Many of the elements of these communal stories are to be found in Doña María's life story. She uses them to shape her life story, to express her sense of some of its meaning. The point I wish to make is that, while on one level they are adequate vehicles, like all narratives they also attempt to impose their own closure, employing their specific strategies of containment. Women are either marginalized or allotted certain stereotypical roles. The communal story of the strike of 1945, for example, leaves little room for Doña María to express the extent of her role or that of other women in the strike. While there is a formal recognition of the support of the women workers for the strike, the crucial "heroic" figures are male in all the versions of this story: Cipriano

Reyes with his typewriter and clandestine press, holed up in the *monte,* controlling and directing the strike; his male lieutenants running the gauntlet of police repression, taking on the strikebreakers, trying to deal with the government.[16] There is little room within these dominant narrative conventions for Doña María to develop an account of her leadership of groups of women pickets, of tarring and feathering, of the humiliation of strikebreakers, of her striding the streets with other women to force shopkeepers to close up in sympathy with the strike. These were elements that were difficult for Doña María to openly avow, to integrate as a central part of her life story.

A similar closure is present, I think, if we look at the representation of work in her narrative. Factory life and work in the meatpacking plants are an important part of the union story, and it is very much a masculine story. Stories of the plant abound in tales of the physicality of labor, the appalling work conditions, the latent violence, the presence of a sheer mass of men subject to an inhuman work system. This male universe had its roots in the very structure of the workforce and work process with its strongly gendered hierarchy. Men dominated the higher-skilled and higher-paid positions. The crucial figures in packing-house folklore are men drawn from all-male sections such as the killing floor and the stevedore gangs. Anecdotes told by male packing-house workers of their time in the plants make frequent reference to this folklore and certain mythical figures. Women, on the other hand, confined to inferior positions within the work process, rarely figure in the lore of the plants. The killing floor was the source of the most recounted stories, with the *matambrero*—a sort of meatpacking equivalent of the "great hewer" of mining legend—as the key mythical figure. A close second in status was the leader of the stevedore gangs, who could fill the hold of a ship with carcasses with no room to spare and in record time. These tales are elaborated by male storytellers around themes of physical endurance, skill, work conditions, confrontations with foremen, and jokes.[17]

As a narrative, then, the story of the meatpacking plant leaves women only a marginal space within which to express themselves. Indeed, to the extent that women are represented in the folklore of the plant, they tend to appear as the polar opposite of the public myth of woman as maternal, nurturing, pure, and home-bound—that is, as the morally weak woman corrupted by the dominant male ambience. Once more I wish to emphasize that this story is not unusable for Doña María, but rather that it is inherently limiting, and that its limits have to do with the dissonance between the parameters found in such stories and their representative figures, and the meaning and richness of an individual life that bursts the parameters and violates the stereotypes.

The ambivalence and tension resulting from this dissonance are clearly evident in Doña María's handling of the theme of gender and work in her life story. It is clear that the workplace, the frigorífico, has both a positive and negative value in her story. In general, of course, it is portrayed as the locus of a work system that sucks people in—Doña María frequently uses the Spanish verb *chupar,* with its connotation of literally sucking in liquid—and uses them before spitting them out. She refers to the plants using various metaphors—"ese infierno negro," "ese monstruo"—and emphasizes the human cost for those who had to go into them, including her husband whose health was destroyed by the work he had to perform.

Within this general evaluation, the plant is portrayed at several stages of her narrative as a potentially hostile environment for women workers, in a tone at times apparently in tune with the masculine universe portrayed in the fictional representation of the meatpacking world:

> I think that all the women who ended up working in the frigorífico felt the same . . . because it is a place, well it's like a monster when you go in there, in that darkness, that dampness, in that situation of lines of men with knives in their hands, I don't think that was very nice, you felt bad, but necessity made you get used to it.

Yet despite the recognition in her narrative of a virulently masculine shop-floor culture, which was related to the brutality of the work systems and the celebration of physical prowess that was an intrinsic part of that, Doña María's story does not simply draw the moral explicit in the reworked ideology of domesticity propagated by official Peronism. She recognizes the special problems entry into this world involved for women, both in terms of the world inside the plants and in terms of women's role as mothers. Commenting on how her children had to stay inside and help prepare the food when she was at work, she says: "Only someone who has worked outside the home, the mother of the family who has worked outside knows what it is like." At other times, too, she laments the sacrifices she had to make in fulfilling her role as a mother owing to her union and political work.

Nevertheless, the conflict between work and nurturance is juxtaposed with a more positive evaluation. In a basic sense entry into the meatpacking plant is the fundamental step which makes the plot of Doña María's story possible, for all the sacrifices it implies—and to the end of her story there are times when one is never sure that she thought the sacrifices were worth the price. It is this work that gives her the right to demand a little more from life, to break with some of the conventions of a working-class woman's biography, to be true to her rebellious self-image. This is very far from being, as Doña María tells it, an affirmation of work outside the home as a liberating experience. In her story it is always first and foremost a material necessity, and it is always ultimately defined by her vision of work in the plants—for both men and women—as simply awful:

> Blood on the floor, bits of grease . . . you're continually in contact with the blood of the animal, with the fat, with the nerves, with the bones, and it's a continual contact with something that is cold, the meat is always cold, in addition there was also the frozen meat, do you know what it is like to try and cut frozen meat with a knife?

But work and its pain are mediated by perhaps the crucial institution in Doña María's story, the union. The union does not simply function to mitigate the conditions of work in general; more specifically, it is seen implicitly as a means of lessening the vulnerable position of women in the plants and limiting masculine power and authority over women.

In addition, at various stages of her narrative, Doña María refers to the way in which her entry into the workplace brought about changes in the performance of domestic labor in her household. She emphasizes that her husband helped out with the domestic chores, and she generalizes that women who work are entitled to expect equality in the division of household labor. Once more, however, the way this principle is framed in the narrative demonstrates the ambivalence and tension she feels over this issue, for she couples it with a reaffirmation of the traditional domestic role of women: "Woman has been born to be in the home with her children, to raise her children, to take care of the house, clean it."

The themes of matrimony and abortion, similarly, reflect the tension and dissonance that accompany the issue of gender in Doña María's narrative. Again, one of the consistent roles she adopts for herself, one of the most persistent forms of self-representation that she projects, is that of the good mother and wife. Through these self-images she expresses ideas about marriage and abortion that apparently reflect official Peronism's discourse (though this of course was not her only influence), including hostility toward divorce, birth control, and abortion. Yet close attention to the way in which she handles these themes shows that the formal enunciation of these principles is mediated by a rich subtext that relates them to the stern realities of working-class women's lives and the painful choices of everyday existence in a community like Berisso.

In the case of abortion, for example, after a brief comment that she is against it "because of my religion," she goes on to describe without any censure the common practice of illegal abortion among the women of Berisso. She describes the desperation of women who could not afford to have children, and she states quite clearly that it was routine in the meatpacking plants for the women to take up a collection on payday to help a compañera pay for an abortion. In the case of both abortion and divorce, an attention to the context in which Doña María places her criticisms shows that the influence of the dominant ideology is mediated, relativized, and ultimately minimized by her own sympathy and understanding of the limited options open to women in the real world.

Moreover, it is also clear that her opposition is not primarily an ethical one. Her constant concern when she talks of divorce and separation is expressed in terms of children, which at one level is clearly consistent, within her story, with her stated concern for the future and care of children in modern society. Beyond that, we may suggest that it is also a way of talking about the vulnerability of women in Argentine society. Separating male sexuality from childrearing and marriage through either divorce or abortion would seem to make worse the burden that women already bear in this area. When speaking of her own compañeras in the picada section who had abortions, she refers to a typical case where "the man abandons them with a child in their bellies." Faced with the reality of women's unequal status and power in a society with profoundly hierarchical gender relations, the adoption and valorization of elements of an ideology of nurturing and domesticity may well be seen as a rational option.

Confronted with the power of available communal stories, public myths, and formal ideologies to shape contexts and set the parameters within which life stories such as Doña María's are constructed, how can we approach the problem of using such stories to better understand the issue of gender in working-class history? Is there a way of reconciling the two different sets of stereotypes about gender present in her narrative? One solution, which is certainly prevalent in much feminist scholarship, is to emphasize the presence of counterdiscourses expressive of oppressed and repressed women's voices in these sorts of texts. Faye Ginsburg argues, for example, that pro- and antiabortion activists use their testimonies "to reframe experiences they originally felt were dissonant with social expectations by constituting them as new cultural possibilities."[18] In this way she suggests that their life stories articulate a counterdiscourse which legitimizes their adoption of alternative life-scripts and leads to a new-found harmony in their visions of themselves. In a similar vein Laurel Richardson has suggested that women can overcome the "textual disenfranchisement" embodied in cultural stories that are inadequate to their needs and experiences by creating new "collective stories" with new roles, stereotypes, and resolutions.[19] At the other extreme, a recent study by Spanish feminist historians found that the dominant public myth of the ideal woman as mother and homemaker had succeeded in obliterating the memory of women's role as fighters and production workers during the Spanish Civil War among the very women who had adopted such roles.[20]

It is possible to read important elements in Doña María's life story as a form of counterdiscourse challenging the authority of a dominant set of images about working-class women and their lives. It seems to me, however, that this plot, and the tensions it engenders and expresses, does not lead to a final resolution in favor of a new life-script, a newly found harmony that blends personal history and socially legitimized roles. This seems to me to be too neat a resolution for Doña María's story, failing, among other things, to take into account the power and efficacy of communal and class narratives in working-class communities like Berisso. More helpful it seems to me is Carolyn Steedman's evocation of her mother's working-class story "told by tension and ambiguity, out on the borderlands"; a story that was a disruption of the central one but that was not simply available in ready-to-use form, waiting to be appropriated.[21]

Such stories, told out on the borderlands, inevitably involve unresolved contradictions, silences, erasures, and conflicting themes. Within the conventions of written autobiography, such lapses are often tidied up. Oral testimony is messier, more paradoxical, more contradiction laden, and perhaps, because of this, more faithful to the complexity of working-class lives and working-class memory. It would be possible to see the existence of contradictory versions of gender in Doña María's story in terms of the problems of memory, and this may certainly be the case. It equally reflects, I think, the existence of a genuinely unresolved tension between an official discourse concerning gender relations and one that is far less palatable and legitimate within the terms in which Doña María had to live out her life.

At some stage the oral historian has to make the leap of faith that direct historical experience will break through and find expression in an individual's testimony. This is the basis for any belief in a "referential pact" at the root of any distinction oral history might wish to claim for itself from, say, literary criticism.[22] Within this perspective, then, I think that we must pay Doña María the respect of assuming that her recounting of her life faithfully reflects—mediated as her telling is by existing narratives and dominant ideologies—the way in which a working-class woman experienced gender and class relations in a particular historical era. Her adoption of forms of self-representation drawn from stereotypes of traditional female roles found in official discourse should not simply be taken at face value. Such "story markers" reflect both the power of dominant ideologies and the capacity of the storyteller to imbue these forms with her own meanings, her own subjectivity.

Notes

1   Doña María's testimony is reproduced and analyzed in Daniel James, *Doña María's Story: Life-History, Memory, and Political Identity* (Durham, N.C.: Duke University Press, forthcoming).

2   The basic work on the subject of the labor process in the meatpacking industry is Mirta Zaida Lobato, *El "taylorismo" en la gran indústria exportadora argentina, 1907–1945* (Buenos Aires: Centro Editor de América Latina 1988).

3   One of the earliest, and still one of the most effective, uses of the life-history approach is Sidney Mintz, *Worker in the Cane: A Puerto Rican Life History* (New York: W. W. Norton, 1974). By the 1970s the use of oral sources had become a common recourse of scholars studying Latin American workers and peasants. See especially June Nash, *We Eat the Mines and the Mines Eat Us: Dependency and Exploitation in Bolivian Tin Mines* (New York: Columbia University Press, 1979). In addition, the genre of testimonial literature had begun to broaden the array of voices heard; see especially Elisabeth Burgos-Debray, ed., *I, Rigoberta Menchu: An Indian Woman in Guatemala* (New York: Verso, 1984); and Domitila Barrios de Chungara, *Let Me Speak! Testimony of Domitila, A Woman of the Bolivian Mines* (New York: Monthly Review Press, 1978). An early fundamental work on memory and oral testimony in Latin America is Ecléa Bosi, *Memória e sociedade: Lembranças de velhos* (São Paulo: T. A. Quieroz, 1973).

4   The phrase comes from Raphael Samuel and Paul Thompson, introduction to *The Myths We Live By,* ed. Raphael Samuel and Paul Thompson (London: Routledge, 1990), pp. 1–21.

5   The fundamental texts are James Clifford and George Marcus, *Writing Culture: The Poetics and Politics of Ethnography* (Berkeley: University of California Press, 1986); and George E. Marcus and Michael M. J. Fischer, *Anthropology as Cultural Critique: An Experimental Moment in the Human Sciences* (Chicago: University of Chicago Press, 1986).

6   Luisa Passerini, *Fascism in Popular Memory: The Cultural Experience of the Turin Working Class* (Cambridge: Cambridge University Press, 1987); and Ronald Grele, "Listen to Their Voices: Two Case Studies in the Interpretation of Oral History Interviews," *Oral History* 7, no. 1 (1979): pp. 33–42. Also of interest is Alessandro

Portelli, *The Death of Luigi Trastulli and Other Stories: Form and Meaning in Oral History* (Albany: State University of New York Press, 1991).

7   Samuel and Thompson, introduction, p. 2.

8   For an analysis of the nature of Peronist discourse directed at women see Susana Bianchi and Norma Sánchez, *El partido peronista feminino,* 2 vols. (Buenos Aires: Centro Editor de América Latina 1987).

9   Luis Horacio Velázquez, *Pobres habrá siempre* (Buenos Aires: Editorial Guillermo Kraft, 1943). A film version was made in the last years of the Peronist regime.

10 See Beatrix Campbell, *Wigan Pier Revisited: Poverty and Politics in the 80s* (London: Virago, 1984).

11 Faye Ginsburg, "Dissonance and Harmony: The Symbolic Function of Abortion in Activists' Life Stories," in *Interpreting Women's Lives: Feminist Theory and Personal Narratives,* ed. the Personal Narratives Group (Bloomington: Indiana University Press, 1989).

12 *Blurred genres* is Clifford Geertz's phrase ("Blurred Genres: The Refiguration of Social Thought," in *Local Knowledge: Further Essays in Interpretative Anthropology* [New York: Basic Books, 1983], pp. 19–36).

13 David Carr, *Time, Narrative and History* (Bloomington: Indiana University Press, 1986). On the construction and functioning of community narratives see also Henry Glassie, *Passing the Time in Ballymenone* (Philadelphia: University of Pennsylvania Press, 1982). On the essential narrative quality of human experience see Alex Callinicos, *Theories and Narratives: Reflections on the Philosophy of History* (Durham, N.C.: Duke University Press, 1995).

14 See Carr, *Time;* and Barbara Johnstone, *Stories, Community, and Place: Narratives from Middle America* (Bloomington: Indiana University Press, 1990).

15 Lia Sanucci, *Berisso: Un reflejo de la evolución argentina* (La Plata: n.p., 1983).

16 For the dominant narrative of the strike see Cipriano Reyes, *Yo hice el diecisiete de octubre* (Buenos Aires: GS Editorial 1973).

17 For many of these male-centered narratives of packing-house life see the interviews collected as part of the project "Berisso Obrero: Class, Ethnicity and the Construction of Identity in an Argentine Meatpacking Community, 1900–1990," codirected by Daniel James and Mirta Zaida Lobato.

18 Ginsburg, "Dissonance and Harmony."

19 Laurel Richardson, "Narrative and Sociology," *Journal of Contemporary Ethnography* 2, no. 1 (1990): pp. 117–35.

20 Elena Cabezali, Matilde Cuevas, and María Teresa Chicote, "Myth as Suppression: Motherhood and the Historical Consciousness of the Women of Madrid, 1936–39," in Samuel and Thompson, pp. 161–74.

21 Carolyn Steedman, *Landscape for a Good Woman* (New Brunswick, N.J.: Rutgers University Press, 1989).

22 I take the term *referential pact* from Phillipe Lejeune, *The Autobiographical Pact* (Minneapolis: University of Minnesota Press, 1989).

Women Workers in the "Cathedrals of Corned Beef"

Structure and Subjectivity in the Argentine Meatpacking Industry

MIRTA ZAIDA LOBATO

To enter the factory was to be saved. — María, a packing-plant worker

When the Armour meatpacking company opened its plant in Berisso in mid-1915, Argentina had already acquired the basic features of modern-twentieth-century life: an economy integrated into the world market, a complex and cosmopolitan society, and a political life centered on political parties and a representative electoral system. All these developments were the outward signs of the profound transformations that had altered the traditional underpinnings of the young nation. These changes modified forms of life in Argentina as well as the places occupied by different social groups and by men and women within those groups.

The participation of women in economic activities had declined toward the end of the nineteenth century, according to census figures, and was concentrated in areas of employment, such as domestic labor, that were defined as specifically female. This general observation, however, obscures the new ways in which women were being incorporated into the urban labor market. When the economic crisis of 1890 erupted, the fledgling industrial sector was restructured based on a greater concentration of capital investment. Some firms were transformed into solid enterprises whose expanded activities generated a strong demand for labor. And large-scale enterprises such as the Companía General de Fosforos, Alpargatas la Argentina, la Tejeduria Dell'Acqua, Bagley Galletitas, and the meatpacking plants of Zarate and Berisso were marked by a high concentration of female employees.[1]

The most important industrial sector in Argentina was the meatpacking industry, which provided one of the country's principal exports. In this sector the percentage of women workers rose from 6 percent in 1914 to 25 percent

in 1935, where it remained over the following decades. Yet these overall figures hide the importance of female workers in the largest packing houses like
Swift and Armour, where they represented 30 percent of the total workforce;
up to 50 percent in some sections, such as *conserva* (elaboration of meat products); and the majority in sections such as *bolsa* (net making) and *tripería* (tripe).

In this chapter, I will examine a number of issues regarding female labor
in the Armour meatpacking plant of Berisso in the province of Buenos Aires.[2]
In global terms, I will examine how female life cycles interact with labor demand in a pattern through which periods of paid labor alternate with periods
of domestic labor. I will also examine *who* does what jobs, *how* and *where* within
the factory. I begin by establishing a general profile of who these women
workers were in order to add precision to the homogenizing term "women
workers." This is followed by a section dealing with discourses about women's
work, which generated tensions both inside the factory and within women
workers themselves.

Finally, we will examine female working-class reactions to the experience
of work in the meatpacking plants. I will do so, in part, through the individual and collective memories of those who experienced these transformations in the forms of work and in daily life in the home. Taking my lead from
Paul Thompson, who argues that individual experience embodies social processes, I organized oral history workshops in which men and women took
on the task of remaking, reconstructing, and rethinking, with the images of
today, the experiences of the past.[3] In this way, I build on Ecléa Bosi's observation that "memory is not a dream, it is work."[4]

Who Worked in the "Cathedrals of Corned Beef"?

The Armour plant was one of two North American meatpacking factories
installed in Berisso on the outskirts of the city of La Plata, the capital of
the province of Buenos Aires. This immense industrial establishment, utiliz-
ing all the technological advances of the era, was a true industrial complex
which carried out all the tasks involved in the slaughter of animals and the
preparation of meat products as well as those ancillary activities central to the
process. As one of the "big five" of the international meatpacking industry,
Armour symbolized the growth of oligopolistic capitalism both in the United
States and in Argentina. It embodied modern industrial work in its most efficient and rational form in an Argentina dominated by the "agrarian utopia."

Armour was one of the "cathedrals of corned beef" that drew thousands
of workers, men and women, Argentines and immigrants, to Berisso. As a

Workers leaving the Armour plant in Berisso, circa 1955.
Courtesy of *El Día*.

cultural icon, the packing plant was the site where the dramas of the poor
were woven; where the passions and tragedies of society were played out;
where men showed their strength, their skill, and their masculinity; and where
women could only be victims of the infernal machines, of the squalor, and
of evil.

However, the large-scale factories, among them the packing plants, were
also a valued source of paid employment for both immigrant women and
women migrating from the interior of Argentina. More than half the female
working population was foreign during the early expansion of the meatpacking industry, which lasted until the crisis of 1930. Poles, Russians, Italians,
and Spaniards made up the majority of a heterogeneous workforce that also
included Armenians, Bulgarians, and Syrian-Lebanese in addition to native-
born workers who came mainly from the area surrounding the capital of
Buenos Aires province.

The relative weight of different national groups fluctuated across the decades. From the 1930s to the mid-1940s, Lithuanian women workers displaced
"Russians," while Italians were more characteristic of the post–World War II
immigration, the last great wave of transatlantic migration to Argentina. It

was in this period, too, that immigrants from Argentina's neighbors such as Uruguay and Brazil increased their presence.

Oral testimonies reveal the complex mixture of individual motives and factors of a structural and contingent nature that led certain individuals and families to move. It is clear that the majority of these women were from the families of peasants or the rural unemployed, whether in the Balkans, Lebanon, the Ukraine, or Lithuania, who spontaneously or because of the urging of a relative, news from a neighbor, or the attractions of state propaganda, made the decision to leave the lands of their birth.

The coming together in the Armour plant of people from distant regions, with different ways of life, reminds us of the impact of immigration on working-class formation in Argentina, where each new cohort of migrants added to, or reinforced, the lack of homogeneity among workers. This helped generate an internal divergence between those who had only recently arrived and older groups, who were largely concentrated in more permanent economic activities and possessed some degree of skill.

The evidence from Berisso also suggests that although most women migrated because of their family situations, following fathers or husbands, there was a considerable number who migrated independently of what their family group had done. "I came alone, alone, I didn't know anybody," said Anastasia, a Lithuanian, who added, "I endured many things because I didn't have anyone to help me . . . but I didn't give up. . . . They weren't going to mess me up with anything . . . because I have a strong woman's character."[5] We still do not know enough about this surprising dimension of women's migration history.

As for our sample of the female workforce as a whole, more than three-quarters of these women, whether native-born or foreign, were between eighteen and thirty-seven, an age group characterized by a dual role, both economic and domestic.[6] Overall, 50 percent were unmarried and 46 percent were married. The high percentage of single women is borne out by other studies that have shown that women's workforce participation is secondary to their role as housewives and mothers.[7] In other words, the fewer the domestic obligations women had, especially if single, the more likely they were to end up in the paid production of goods and services outside the home.

Yet this pattern varied strikingly between Argentine and foreign-born women workers. While an average of 67 percent of foreign women workers were married in the period up to 1945, only 35 percent of Argentine women workers were married. The percentage of married foreign-born women workers declined to 50 percent between 1946 and 1958 and returned to 70 percent between 1959 and 1969. Yet the figures for Argentine women workers in the same period were 34 percent (1946–1958) and 39 percent (1959–1969).

The high percentage of married immigrant women—an average of 64 percent for the entire period—together with the fact that they were in age brackets that implied a larger domestic burden and greater family responsibilities, was related to their status as immigrants who were seeking to improve their economic situation. The multiple "necessities" of families made up of foreigners encouraged women to become wage earners, and this coincided with the stages of greatest immigration. Moreover, the force of necessity also became part of the discourse of a population that was increasingly Argentine-born. This process was the result of both the decline of immigrant flows and the growth of economic problems that affected diverse regions of the country after 1930.

The low educational levels of these women workers clearly suggest the un-skilled nature of the work process in the meatpacking industry. Although 88 percent of the women stated that they could read and write, the signatures in the records suggest that they had only barely learned to do so. This is not surprising since only 32 percent of the sample claimed to have finished even one grade of primary school, while 68 percent had not done even this.

Asked their prior occupations upon entry to the plant, 70 percent of Argentine-born women did not claim any profession at all, while 24 percent said they were day laborers (*obreras jornaleras*), and the rest declared themselves dressmakers (*modistas*), domestic workers (perhaps domestic servants), or garment workers (*costureras, bordadoras, pantaloneras,* or *planchadores*). Among foreign-born women, by contrast, 50 percent said that they had no profession, while 48 percent defined themselves as day laborers, with a few from the garment industry.

Among the women who did declare a prior occupation, most had worked at Swift, the other meatpacking plant in Berisso, and a smaller number had worked at local textile firms, in some smaller food-processing factories, or as public employees or domestic servants in the nearby city of La Plata. As for the large number of women who declared no prior occupational experience outside the home, it may be, in part, that prior paid employment was under-reported since it was irrelevant to obtaining a job in the plant. It may also be true that some women who did not declare a formal occupation may already have been working for money in their homes (sewing, washing, or ironing). For this group, entry to the plant would represent the first step toward incorporation into a distinct labor discipline.

There is little doubt that housework was the most important prior experience that women workers drew upon when they entered the factory. The work of the housewife, as E. P. Thompson has pointed out, is largely "oriented towards chores," and the line between working and passing the time is less defined since not all tasks are adapted to clock measurements.[8] The fact that an orientation to chores was of great importance for women as they entered the world of the factory may well have heightened tensions between the two types of work experiences.

Overall for all groups of women, the extradomestic work trajectory was marked by occupational mobility and employment instability. Many women not only moved back and forth between occupations but moved repeatedly in and out of the wage labor force even in meatpacking. Thus these women could be said to respond "flexibly" to the variations in labor demand characteristic of the industry.

Wage Labor as "Necessity"

When and why did women decide to present themselves at the factory gate in search of work? The most commonly stated motives in the oral testimonies were to own a home, to send children to school, to buy furniture, or to build up the savings needed to face the threat of illness or unemployment in the family. "I decided to go back to work," said one woman worker, "because we wanted to get our own house. We were renting." Or as another suggested, "I went to the factory because we needed things. The kids had to study, there was the rent, and tomorrow we wanted to get our own little home, and to expect it all from him wasn't possible, so I said—I'm going to help him, I'm going to the factory."[9]

This aspiration to attain a certain desired standard of living was crucial in encouraging women's work in the plants. The concept of the "standard of living" in workers' families, however, was far from fixed. It was constantly being redefined through changes in customs and models of consumption and need. Yet the notion of "necessity," as presented in the discourse of working women, was also a crucial site of conflict. On the one hand, it helped to underpin the notion that "men did not want their wives to work," which was viewed as "a good thing." But at the same time, we also find women making the decision to enter the factory in spite of their husbands' opposition, while justifying this transgression in terms of dire "economic straits." "To enter the factory was to be saved," says María, from poverty, adversity, hunger, and the impossibility of "getting on" (progresar) in the world as symbolized by the education of children or the purchase of a home.

The tensions present in the discourses of working women are related to this idea of family "necessity" and its relation to a discourse about gender that postulated an ideal model, located in an indeterminate past, in which women did not and should not work outside the home.[10] Designed to show that things were "always this way," tradition was invoked to legitimate certain roles ascribed to women (and to men) by making them seem universal and unchanging. Viewed in this context, women's entry into the workforce generated tension because it constituted a transgression, since, in "normal" times, men would not allow such a thing to occur.

In the discourse of working women, one encounters the full weight of tradition, with its associated images that were constructed around the ideals of motherhood, the family, and the home. As such, women workers were inserted into a wider debate about what came to be called the "family question" in turn-of-the-century Argentina.[11] In the discourses of intellectuals, professionals, and government officials, women were said to fulfill themselves in motherhood while the working woman was viewed as a degenerate hybrid capable of corrupting others.[12] Indeed, work outside the home in general was considered to be the most important factor contributing to the moral and physical degeneration of women, and factory labor in particular was seen as the most insidious of all forms of work. The working woman seeking a wage to help herself and her family was condemned for disrupting the unity of the home. The figure of the mother ever present in her home, by contrast, was presented as both a requisite for the healthy functioning of society and a moral obligation for individual women.

This ideal of motherhood had become part of common sense by the 1930s. Thus, women who began their careers in the packing plants did so in a context in which a woman was seen to be quintessentially a mother. And the mother was, in the words of the popular press, "a love forged to withstand all forms of suffering and types of ingratitude. A heart which never tires of suffering. A soul which never ceases for a moment to love."[13] Parallel to this construction of the maternal ideal, fatherhood was identified with the economic support of the family. The image of the male breadwinner who supported himself, his woman, and his children was constructed around the idea that he had a broader sphere of action and that his obligation was to provide for them through the energy he expended outside the home.

These representations of male and female roles allowed for women's work outside the home *only* when there was no other alternative but poverty and misery. The idea of "necessity" within working women's discourse thus served to legitimate their apparent disregard of maternal duties and family obligations. Thus, female labor was an alternative to be considered only in very exceptional circumstances. It could only be conceptualized as a "help" to make up for the insufficiency or absence of the male wage. In the words of a female packing-house worker, "I went to the factory because we had needs (*necesitamos*) . . . and expecting everything from him wasn't enough, so I said—I am going to *help* him," thus expressing the notion of complementarity associated with women's labor.

This representation justifies the transgression involved with women's waged work by linking *help* and *necessity* and illustrates again the conflictive nature of the decision to send women into an arena considered unfit for them. This tension is intensified if one bears in mind the violence and marginality associated with low-status work in the meatpacking industry. The packing plants were considered, above all else, as a space for real men (*machos*), where the use of knives was common, and where repugnant smells penetrated a woman's body and even produced male rejection. An old textile worker said of his wife who worked in the plants, "Ay . . . poor thing, when she'd come out of the tripería she had a smell that was awful, I remember her hands, nails, because however much she'd wash and perfume it was a smell that penetrated the skin." A woman worker recalled that "we used to come out of the tripería with a smell that was so bad you couldn't even travel on a bus." Yet she immediately hastened to suggest, with a certain defensiveness, that "the tripería seemed to be a dirty place, but the work is important and delicate and *you have to have women's hands doing the work*" (emphasis added).

For a woman to enter the meatpacking plant not only implied abandoning her home and family duties and obligations, but it even threatened her sense of herself as a woman. One woman, commenting on the uniforms worn, spoke about the loss of her very appearance as a woman: "It was clothing that disfigured you, the hat down to here," she said, pointing to her forehead, "and white square overalls." [14] Man or woman: In the end, which were they?

The loss of femininity was not only a ghost conjured up in the imaginary of women workers, especially those who started in the plants in the 1950s. It was a motif present long before in the discourses emanating from a variety of public and private institutions. Already in the 1930s fears about the consequences of wage labor for women can be found: "As she daily crosses the threshold of the factory, she leaves there a scrap of her abandoned home," declared a medical journal that also took pains to emphasize that "the female of the species . . . has shaped the woman. The woman [in turn] the mother. The mother will perhaps create a superior type. *But we cannot remain impassive faced with this new type of [working] woman, an uncertain mix of both sexes.* Woman has for humankind a role of unique and exceptional importance. Everything that hinders or violates this mission, will end up harming society and the species."[15]

Working-class women living in Berisso had to "work to live," and yet their possibilities of finding work were primarily limited to the two meatpacking giants. But the packing plants were considered male territory, where strength was a sign of virility. And when work opportunities expanded in the 1920s with the installation of the Patent Knitting Company in Berisso, clear contrasts were drawn between the two work settings. The textile mill was the inverse of the packing houses, because it was constructed discursively as a delicate and feminine sector, an appropriate place where young women could earn a living. "My father didn't want me to go into the plants, he thought that the mill was better work for a woman," said a woman textile worker, who added that "it was a lot cleaner [t]here, in the [meatpacking] plants you had to be in the middle of muck and blood."

Practices and Representations: The Production Process and the Place of Women

Representations of the place of men and women in society shaped the experience of work in the factories. Women worked in a limited number of sections (tripería, picada [meat cutting], conserva, pintura [painting], embalaje [packaging], salchichería [sausage], and bolsas) in tasks that involved cutting, cleaning, and preserving meat and tripe. Unlike men's unskilled jobs in the plant, women's jobs were characterized by the fact that they were based on skills developed in the home. To cut meat into pieces, to take off the fat, to tie, to wash did not require special training but rather was linked to the type of tasks young girls were given from an early age.

Women's descriptions of work in the various sections of the plant are similar to those reported in the company's time and motion studies. Most of the tasks were not complex, although a short training period was needed to learn to perform them. Piling up empty boxes, wrapping up meat products, putting on labels, feeding assembly lines, and cleaning jars were among the most common work tasks. "I started in the oil section where they filled barrels of oil and sealed them," recalled one worker whose job was to clean "the barrels when they were full and sealed."[16] In other cases, the apprenticeship could be somewhat more prolonged. The job of classifying tripe or wool or testing livers required several weeks to master. After this training period, they could generally meet the company's production norms, although this required good eyesight and optimal motor coordination.

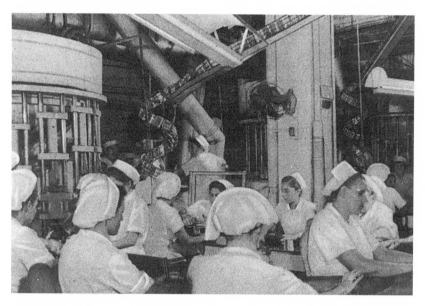

Women in the *conserva* (canning) section of the Swift plant, circa 1945.
Courtesy of *Swiftlandia*.

I used to classify tripe. When they killed the animal, they took the tripe out, they washed it, and there is a table with a hose, with a work mate in front and at the side of the other one they fit the tripe on and run pressurized water through it to see its size. Some were small, others bigger, and each worker had a box and they'd put the tripe in the box. Then a woman would come round and take them out—whoever had more would get a bonus. The more kilos you had the more bonus you'd get . . . you needed practice to do this . . . you had to know what you were doing to classify tripe.[17]

I started in the tanning section, classifying wool. They put the hides in the washer, then they put the instruments on them, later they go to the shearing section where the men take all the wool off, weigh it, dry it, and we classify it, because a sheep has many kinds of wool, so you had to separate it and weight it.[18]

Work tasks were related to a gendered skill structure that was tightly linked to wage scales. In no case did women reach the highest levels, exclusively filled by men, which were usually defined by skill in the use of a knife. Even where women did work with a knife, as in the *despostada* (deboning) section where meat was separated from the bone and cut into chunks, the men received higher pay for separating the meat from bone than the equally skilled women who cut the meat up.

Female tasks usually required less physical force. Men's work in the chilling chambers, the boiler rooms, the fertilizer section, and on the killing floors was extremely arduous. Women's jobs, on the other hand, were characterized by manual dexterity, by a delicate touch that avoided breaking materials, and by the fact that they were more sedentary than those of men.

The valuing of physical force as an attribute superior to dexterity or a light touch can be found in many work settings. In the packing plants, however, such an evaluation not only forms part of a dominant mind-set but is also reinforced by those jobs where masculine attributes (strength, roughness, endurance) are prominent. "A weak man cannot enter a packing plant," said a male worker and union leader from the 1960s. To kill animals, to stack the quarter sections of cows, or simply to keep up with the rhythm of the assembly line called for machos. In this context, the self-image of women workers was formed in contrast with these masculine qualities. As a woman from the tripe section said, "It had to be women's hands" to do that work, and it mattered little that considerable physical strength was needed to degrease tripe without breaking them, to stay seated for hours classifying wool, or to remain standing for hours on end cutting meat.

In their recollections, men and women recognized the existence of male/female differences on the job and accounted for them in terms of biology. These notions about work and its division among the sexes was linked to the triad women/motherhood/home. The basic notion was that women were intrinsically weaker than men because they were smaller or more vulnerable. Thus the presumed differences between men and women naturalized the division of labor and reaffirmed the juxtaposition of strength (male) and dexterity (female). Within this dyad, strength and virility were connoted positively and were used to justify a differentiated skill structure with marked wage disparities between men and women.

Jobs, skills, and wages were also related to the fixing of hours of work. Men worked during the day and sometimes at night. Women were excluded from night shifts, as labor legislation since 1907 had prohibited the employment of minors and women during these hours. Although the labor legislation was not always applied, it remains the case that few if any women did work night shifts in the packing plants.

The disparities in skills, differences in wages, and restrictions on when women could work were based on assumptions about the different roles of men and women. If women's primordial function was motherhood and care of the home, their wage labor could only be understood as something they were condemned to, a fatality whose negative consequences had to be forestalled. To guard women's physical and moral health meant that they were only fit for certain tasks and that they should work on shifts where the light of day provided a mantle of protection of their virtue. Daily work experience reinforced these images about the tasks, conditions, and spaces that men and women could and should occupy. And these images were in turn translated into a consensus about the behavior, places, and powers that were attributed to male and female workers. This field of representations stemmed from and reinforced the unequal power relations between men and women. In the authority structures of the plants, women were subordinated to men, and even in the unions they rarely occupied positions of importance.

The Organization of Work

We rarely find evidence in the Armour archives that personal recommendations or family ties played a key role in hiring workers. Those looking for work, whether male or female, would present themselves at the factory entrance, where an employee from the hiring office selected them according to their proximity in the crowd and his assessment of their physical strength. Once within the plant, workers had to undergo a medical examination that weeded out those with obvious illnesses or physical disabilities, such as hernias, varicose veins, or missing fingers. Once they were in and assigned to a section, those hired stayed in the factory as long as "there was work," and the possibility of being rehired later depended on how well they had adapted to the pace of work and on their skill in carrying it out.

Women were concentrated in sections of the plant that were primarily female, and were continually transferred from section to section according to the company's needs. It was very rare for a woman worker to remain in the same department for any length of time. "I entered the sewing department," said a Polish worker, "from sewing they sent me to meat cutting, from there to caning, from there to oil, later I returned to caning, and finally I stayed put there." This practice of rotating women among sections continued at least until the signing of the first collective bargaining agreements under Juan Perón, which finally limited this management prerogative.[19]

Working conditions varied greatly among departments. In the tripe sections, jobs were performed in a very humid environment, with floors covered with water, and in constant contact with raw materials that impregnated clothes, shoes, and even bodies with a strong odor. In conserva, where they diced the meat, workers frequently cut their hands and contracted infections. Some women worked in conditions of great heat; the women in the hides section who classified wool were subjected to acids. "It was unpleasant work. Do you know why? Because the wool had poison in it that irritated your skin. Often I couldn't even wash the dishes because of the pain."[20]

The differences in forms of work organization were also reflected in payment systems. In some departments, women were paid a piece rate based on production, while in others their pay was calculated on an hourly rate. In those departments where production incentives were incorporated into wage systems (*etiquetada, charqueada*), workers' responses were not uniform, since some women accepted production quotas more readily than others. This often divided native-born workers from immigrants, and younger workers from older ones. The native-born and the young, no matter where they came from, were more resistant to meeting production quotas. They often left if faced with an unacceptably intense pace of work, excessively long workdays, or intolerably dirty or humid working conditions. Yet a woman's place of birth or age did not automatically determine her response. Those women of any origin who were particularly anxious to keep their jobs were more likely to fulfill production targets or to passively accept poor work conditions.

Employment Stability and Instability:
Structural and Subjective Factors

Armour's employment records show that women were moving in and out of paid employment on a regular basis. In the entire sample from 1915–1969, 64 percent of Armour's female employees stayed less than a year. The short duration of their employment was common to both men and women, although, in general, the percentage of women staying under one year was twice that of men and changed in accordance with their age. Overall, 60 percent of women workers worked only once in the company, with the rest signing on between two and ten times. Why did such a high percentage of women join the workforce only once or for such a short time? Did this primarily reflect the production needs of the company? Or are the comings and goings of women workers a reflection of larger cultural patterns? And how is this pattern linked to the notion of "necessity" we have found in women's oral histories?

An analysis of the reasons for leaving noted in the employment records provides us with some answers to these questions. Until 1950, half of women workers who left were listed as doing so "of their own accord" or "for personal reasons." After that point, however, "for lack of work" was the most common recorded explanation. For the post-1950 period, Armour personnel records show that jobs were often defined as temporary, thus revealing the company's resort to a legal loophole that could be used to dismiss "unnecessary" workers who in theory were protected by Perón-era labor legislation. Starting at the end of the 1950s, labor stability declined even further as part of the general deterioration of labor conditions that came with the growing economic crisis of the industry.

The relatively high degree of instability in women's employment reflects structural features of the meatpacking industry in general. The industry was always characterized by variations in seasonal supply and demand for meat, which led in turn to wide fluctuations in labor demand. However, until the crisis of 1930, favorable market conditions led to a sustained expansion that allowed broad sections of the population who had no trade to find employment, even if its duration was uncertain.

The crisis of 1930 led to a decline in exports, increasing layoffs, and a shift in attitudes on the part of those who remained. Women and men who remained employed during the 1930s despite layoffs paradoxically enjoyed somewhat greater stability until the phantom of unemployment was lifted by the outbreak of World War II. Employment instability returned, however, with the end of the war, at the very moment when Colonel Juan Perón rose to power with the prominent support of meatpacking workers. To ameliorate this threat, Perón's government offered compensation to companies that offered severance pay to workers who left voluntarily. Some workers—especially women—took advantage of this benefit and used the money received to escape manual labor altogether, by setting up small businesses that enabled them to remain at home while continuing to bring in money. Alternatively, the severance pay could be used to buy things, after which workers returned to the plant in search of work.

After 1950, however, the industry did little to adapt to changes in technology and in the demand for meat products and failed to carry out the sizable capital investment needed to restructure the companies. Delays in making these decisions were combined with a tendency to seek short-term profits and then get out of the market. This led to an extremely precarious employment structure leading up to the closing of the Armour plant in 1969.

Workers in the packing plants were daily confronted with uncertainty and instability. The reasons that led them to remain in the plants varied, however, according to whether they were men or women. Men laid great store in the possibility of working long hours during the upswing of the employment cycle, which assured them of good wages. In addition, they relied on certain forms of self-employment or the possibility of combining packing-house work with other paid work. Women, on the other hand, once more explained their work cycles in terms of family "necessity."

As we have already noted, for the women we interviewed who entered the plants at the beginning of the 1920s the main motives for joining the work-force were to buy a home, to educate their children and, to a lesser extent, to acquire household goods. In no case did we find work outside the home de-fined in terms of a desire for female independence or as a space within which to create a broader network of social relations. Such motives were more com-monly found, however, among the women who entered the industry in the 1950s and, particularly, the 1960s.

We can therefore reiterate that it was "necessity," defined in terms of the domestic budget, that drove women to enter the workforce. The force of "ne-cessity" also provided a convenient way of handling a conflict present in the women's daily life, since they joined the factory workforce at a time when the discourse of domesticity and the ideal of motherhood had already become generally accepted. This line of explanation was all the more important for women packing-house workers who were entering an environment that was considered absolutely unacceptable for a woman.

Women's pattern of labor-market participation produced attitudes about work in which the alternation between periods of paid employment and non-employment was a distinctive feature. For the women of Berisso, the tempo-rary nature of meatpacking labor was not entirely negative, since they sought a source of paid employment to which they could have access as needed. They could work for a time, leave the plant, and go back to it with some assurance of being rehired by the company. This pattern fit well with the complemen-tary role that women themselves assigned to their own work, which was ex-pressed in terms of the "help" that it signified within the household economy.

The possibility of combining work outside the home with the role of mother and housewife reinforced the idea of the complementary contribution women made to meeting the family's daily needs. Changes in the life cycle—marriage, childbirth—presented women workers in the packing plants with the opportunity to perform this double function. These perceptions on the part of the women workers were, therefore, functional to the companies' desire for a largely nonpermanent labor force.

Conclusion

The process of integrating women into factory labor in meatpacking, one of the most important industries in Argentina, was marked by a series of tensions and contradictions. Society as a whole presented the home as a privileged space for women who, it was said, should not engage in paid employment outside the home. But most working-class women did not have this option, and their entrance into the factory violated the socially acceptable role accorded women. Yet women's entry into the factory was not driven just by extreme economic hardship but by a flexible discourse about "necessity." Thus factory work was both accepted and, on another level, rejected by women. For example, women might acquiesce to gendered inequities in skills and wages, yet they often quit or struck when wage scales were lowered. And while they might fatalistically accept the rhythm of work, they also sometimes protested without waiting for the support of their male fellow workers. And although their salary was presented as essential to feed their families, they could also participate in strikes.[21]

Too-few historical studies of workers in Argentina take gender into account as a fundamental factor in the structuring of working-class experience, which is largely viewed within the context of neighborhoods and ethnic communities or in terms of workplace resistance and strikes. Women's experience of work in the meatpacking industry has been shown to be different from men's precisely because of the meaning attributed to their labor by a shared discourse about gender. Even strictly workplace phenomena such as production roles, skills, and the capacity to give and obey orders were all differentially attributed to men and women. As such, these constructs were continually reinforced by the gender representations that sustained them and the practices that reproduced them.

Notes

Translated by Daniel James. All interview quotes translated by Daniel James.
1   Based on the census returns of 1895, Fernando Rocchi has identified this tendency toward high concentrations of capital and of women workers in the city of Buenos Aires ("Concentrations of Women and Capital: Early Industrialization in Buenos Aires," paper presented at the Eighteenth International Conference of the Latin American Studies Association, Atlanta, 1994).
2   For an analysis of the value of factory archives as historical source material see Mirta Zaida Lobato and Fernando Rocchi, "Industria y trabajadores: El valor de los archivos de fábrica como fuente documental," *Entrepasados: Revista de Histo-*

ria, 1, no. 1 (1990). I have worked with the archives of the Berisso plants of both Armour and Swift, although this chapter deals primarily with Armour. In the Armour archive, I have worked with the 64,940 individual employment cards, of which some 12,695 belong to female personnel who entered the plant between 1915 and 1969. Each card contains the information that the company considered useful: name, place of birth, home address, civil state, occupation, dates of entry and departure, reason for leaving, company sanctions, and, at times, illnesses and accidents. Between 1915 and 1947 the register was made up of individual sheets which were later bound into *libros de personal,* which were separated according to sex. After 1947 a new employment register was compiled, separating men and women, which included information about previous employment and incorporated the sheets from the earlier register in those cases where the personnel were still employed by the company.

The female register contains 12,695 files and, while some have been lost, there is no reason to think that this alters the results of the analysis. Because of the size of the universe under study, a random sample was taken—of a little more than 10 percent of the total of women workers—amounting to 1,357 cases. The sample was taken with a technique called simple sampling using a table of random numbers. See Hans Kellerer, *La estadística en la vida económica y social* (Madrid: Alianza Editor, 1967); and Roderick Floud, *Metodos cuantitativos para historiadores* (Madrid: Alianza Editor, 1975).

3   Paul Thompson, *The Voice of the Past: Oral History* (Oxford: Oxford University Press, 1988), and "Problemi di metodo nella storia orale," in *Vida quotidiana e cultura materiale delli classe subalterne,* by Luisa Passerini (Torino: Rosenberg and Sellier, 1978).

Oral history workshops functioned in Berisso between 1985 and 1990 in the Sociedad Bulgara Ivan Vlasov, Club Eslovaco Argentino de Berisso, Union Polaca, Club Zona Nacional, Sociedad de Fomento Dardo Rocha, and Centro de Residentes Santiaguenos. In this essay I only use a small part of this rich documentation. For an analysis of the tensions involved in the discourse-memory of the workers interviewed see Mirta Lobato, "La memoria compartida: Talleres de historia oral y memoria de trabajo," in *La historia oral: Sus temas,* ed. Dora Schwarzstein (Buenos Aires: CEAL, 1994).

4   Ecléa Bosi, *Memória e sociedade: Lembranças de velhos* (São Paulo: T. A. Quieroz, 1973).

5   Anastasia, interview with author, Berisso, October 13 and 20, 1986.

6   The very young, those between fourteen and seventeen, made up only 8 percent of our sample. The small presence of legal minors in the factory registry is striking. It may be explained in part by the policies of the meatpacking companies, since other firms did use child labor, particularly boys. It may also, in part, be due to the tendency of at least some parents to forge documents and thus secure entry for their children into the world of factory labor.

7   Elizabeth Jelín, *La mujer y el mercado de trabajo urbano* (Buenos Aires: CEDES, 1978); and Zulma de Recchini de Lattes, *La dinámica de la fuerza de trabajo feminina en Argentina* (n.p.: UNESCO, 1983).

8   E. P. Thompson, "Time, Work-Discipline, and Industrial Capitalism," *Past and Present,* no. 28 (1967).

9   Interviews with Angela and Teresa, both packing-plant workers, during the Oral History Workshop, Club Eslovaco Argentino de Berisso, November 25, 1986.

10 Only a very few Berisso women could easily combine wage earning with household duties, as in the case of those who worked at home sewing for the bagging and netting department. Yet the extremely low wages for this sort of work drove them toward the factory. The Armour archives contain letters and notes sent by these women, who were desperate to enter any section of the factory.

11 See Hugo Vezetti, "Literatura medica: Disciplina científica y moralización ciudadana en el ochenta," in *Historia ideológica del control social (España-Argentina siglos 19–20),* ed. Roberto Bergalli (Barcelona: PPU, 1989).

12 For more on representations of working women see Mirta Zaida Lobato, "Mujeres obreras, protesta y acción gremial en la Argentina: Los casos de la industria frigorífica y textil en Berisso," in *Historia y genero,* ed. Dora Barrancos (Buenos Aires: CEAL, 1993). See also Marcela Nari, "La mujer obrera: Entre la maternidad y el trabajo: Reproducción biológica, familia y trabajo en las vidas de mujeres de la clase obrera de la ciudad de Buenos Aires entre 1890 y 1930" (research report, Facultad de Filosofía y Letras, Universidad de Buenos Aires, 1995).

13 José Selgas, "Sabeis lo que es una madre," in *Madre y Niño,* no. 11 (1936), cited in Nari, "Mujer obrera," p. 16.

14 The testimonies are drawn from a November 1991 interview with a textile unionist from the Patent Knitting Company of Berisso; an interview with a Czech woman at the Oral History Workshop, Club Eslovaco Argentino de Berisso, November 25, 1986; and an April 1991 interview with the Argentine-born worker Norma, conducted by Cristina Mateu.

15 Dardo Rietti, "La mujer y el niño en la fábrica y la función de la escuela," cited in Nari, "Mujer obrera," p. 38.

16 Interview with a packing-house worker, Oral History Workshop, Club Eslovaco Argentino de Berisso, October 13, 1986.

17 Interview in Asociación Mutual 10 de Junio de Berisso, December 21, 1988.

18 Interviews with Angela and Teresa.

19 Interview with a Polish worker, August 13, 1988, in Berisso. A single personnel employment card can serve as an example of this situation: country of birth: Argentina; place of birth: federal capital; date of birth: March 10, 1918; entered plant at 18, unmarried; sixth grade primary education; entered bag department February 18, 1937; transferred to *hojalateria* December 13, 1937; transferred to conserva December 13, 1939; left plant voluntarily February 16, 1940; returned to

edible oils April 1, 1941; went to sausage making July 14, 1941; went to hojalateria March 1, 1947; and retired voluntarily for health reasons March 10, 1948.

The issue of labor mobility within the plants affected both men and women. It was a source of concern for companies under Perón and was the center of demands over productivity that began to take center stage with the Congress of Productivity in 1952. Because it affected stability, salaries, and job categories, it was a source of labor tensions. See Daniel James, "Rationalisation and Working Class Response: Context and Limitations of Shop Floor Activity in Argentina," *Journal of Latin American Studies* 13, no. 2 (1981): pp. 375–402.

20 Oral History Workshop, Club Eslovaco Argentino de Berisso, October 7, 1986.

21 For an analysis of labor conflict in the meatpacking industry see Mirta Zaida Lobato, "Mujeres obreras."

Unskilled Worker, Skilled Housewife

Constructing the Working-Class
Woman in São Paulo, Brazil

Joan Scott, in her widely read *Gender and the Politics of History,* analyzes the construction of the "woman worker" and the gendering of categories of skilled and unskilled work. Perhaps most controversial is her analysis of the notorious Sears Department Stores case, which has the effect of ultimately absolving Sears of any discernible historical responsibility for job discrimination against women, since the category "woman worker," with its limitations and disabilities, had already been formulated long before Sears began gender-typing positions within its workforce.[1] It is an argument that clearly reflects Scott's immersion in poststructuralist, Foucauldian conceptions of power and hierarchy, with their lack of emphasis on agency and direct responsibility.

Certainly the "woman worker," as a separate historical category with specific implications (unskilled, temporary, unconsciously but doubly oppressed), is so ubiquitous as to seem natural, the mark of a successful social construction. But I prefer to stress the process by which such identities are reproduced, reinforced, or reconfigured by powerful human actors who promote specific policies and ideologies of gender. In the case of São Paulo, Brazil's leading industrial center, over time (1910–1950) we see a narrowing of the acceptable work roles for working-class women, until only "housewife" remains as a legitimate goal, and this narrowing is actively promoted by representatives of various professional and business groups. Though paulista employers, union leaders, educators, and social workers did not invent the category "woman worker," they directly contributed to the marginalization of the woman who worked for wages, and to the idealization of the woman who remained at home. And in the case of the industrialists, they played an active role in setting up programs and regulations that served to narrow the definition of working-class women's proper roles, even as they continued to exploit women's low-wage labor.

A full account of the changing images of women workers in São Paulo would have to explore debates over labor legislation, the positions adopted by labor unions and radical activists, the activities of feminist organizations, and women workers' own attempts to represent themselves and their roles in an industrializing society. The following analysis does not pretend to be a full account. In this article I will focus on a particular group of industrialists and their allies in the social and educational professions, who played a significant role in defining and limiting training opportunities for women workers and in formulating programs for working-class housewives. In their pursuit of what they considered a modern, industrializing society, these industrialists and professionals promoted certain normative images that ultimately affected a wide range of programs and policies directed at working-class women and created new boundaries for debates about the role of women in industrial society.

*Early Industry, Vocational Programs, and
the Visible Woman Worker*

The position of women in the industrial labor force of São Paulo during the early decades of industrialization (1890s–1920s) is a familiar one. Textiles, by far the largest branch of manufacturing, and the one most approximating modern industry, heavily employed women and girls.[2] A 1912 study of thirty-one textile mills with a total of 9,500 workers revealed that nearly 72 percent of that workforce was female.[3] Only a quarter of these female workers were over the age of twenty-two, so that the classic image of the woman worker juggling the demands of wage and domestic work may have applied to a relatively small portion of the industrial workforce. At the same time, it was generally recognized that substantial numbers of women circulated in and out of the paid labor force—the number of working-class adult women who *never* worked outside the home was probably quite small.[4]

Discussions (mainly among men) of women and work in São Paulo displayed much the same ambivalence as they did in other contexts. As Susan Besse shows in her study of changing conceptions of gender in industrializing São Paulo, there was a growing acceptance of the need for women, even married women from middle-class families, to work outside the home.[5] In the case of working-class women this might be due to low wages for men, frequent layoffs and shutdowns, and debilitating illnesses or accidents, while women from more "genteel" backgrounds might be moved to work by the need to maintain the household's middle-class lifestyle in the face of inflation and the financial exigencies of urban life. The recourse to paid employment might be regrettable, but it also often seemed unavoidable.

The question, then, was not whether women should work at all, but what type of work was proper or acceptable for women to perform. Excepting prostitutes, perhaps the most stigmatized or problematized female figure in the labor force was the mill hand. While textile manufacturers eagerly employed large numbers of women and children at wages well below those for adult males, reformist politicians, educators, journalists, and labor leaders decried this practice and called for an end to the industrial employment of women.[6] The emerging complications of industrial life in a rapidly developing region produced intense anxieties about class conflict, de-skilling and dislocation, and erosion of the traditional family structure. Whether one approached the "social question" as a middle-class hygienist or a working-class labor leader, women in the factory were a "problem." On the one hand they could be charged with abandoning home and children; on the other hand they were belittled as unskilled, uninterested in organizing, and morally compromised.[7]

These nearly universal condemnations of female employment in factories, however, had no immediate impact on the tendency of factory owners to hire girls or women. The more politically self-conscious industrialists, such as Jorge Street, may have been moved by criticisms of women's employment in industry to emphasize the familial atmosphere of their firms, and to install nurseries and other facilities that demonstrated concern for the "special needs" of women workers.[8] But the negative image of women factory hands did not result in either formal or informal prohibitions on their employment in industry. Instead, it served to marginalize the woman worker professionally, and to deprive her of access to skills and positions in industry that might have made a career in factory work more appealing and materially rewarding.

Deeply implicated in the entire debate over women in industry is the question of skill acquisition. With regard to gender roles in industry, it is especially important to emphasize that the categories of skilled, semiskilled, and unskilled are constructions, rather than simple representations of objective technical criteria. As Joel Wolfe points out in his study of the *paulista* textile industry, the women who dominated the spinning (and more rarely, weaving) sections of the textile plants were quite adept at keeping antiquated and overused machines running, and these skills often proved quite valuable to the employer.[9] But the definition of *skill* that dominated the industrial-education milieu rejected such empirical knowledge in favor of systematic technical expertise. To be sure, both male and female workers were criticized for their empirical approach to the work process, but men's trades were more likely to be seen as susceptible to systematic, theoretical training than women's.

Prior to 1910, skill acquisition for virtually all aspiring craftspeople in paulista industry involved a traditional, if informal, apprenticeship whereby the novice gradually absorbed techniques from older workers. This meant that women had few opportunities to acquire such skills, since the predominantly male skilled workers were unlikely to accept them as apprentices. Still, some women, through considerable effort, learned skills such as weaving by observing other workers, perhaps fathers or brothers. Thus this system tended to exclude women, but not absolutely.[10] In contrast, the more formal institutions for vocational training founded during these early decades of industrialization created rigid and usually impermeable barriers between men's and women's work.

The first major attempt to systematize vocational education in São Paulo began in 1911 with the founding of state-run professional schools. Modernizing engineers and educators throughout Brazil during the years of the Old Republic (1889–1930) sought to combat the traditional Brazilian contempt for manual labor by making professional education a respectable option for urban youths from less privileged backgrounds. Whereas earlier industrial institutes had either been designed for the truly indigent, or had the air of reform schools, these new professional schools were meant to attract the sons and daughters of urban working families of modest means who had the resources to give their children a primary school education, but would not disdain a manual occupation in the industrial sector.[11]

From the outset the state sponsored both an Escola Profissional Masculina (EPM) and an Escola Profissional Feminina (EPF), thereby acknowledging the rapid entrance of women into the labor force and giving this trend some legitimacy. But it is important to note the dramatically different trajectories of the two schools, with the EPM moving in a more and more industrial direction, and the EPF assiduously avoiding any association with industrial training. Even workshops for spinning and weaving were included in the EPM, despite the limited demand from the male students, who preferred the better-paying metallurgical and mechanical trades.[12] Reformist educators acknowledged the need to provide young women of limited means with skills that would allow them to earn a living and avoid the horrors of poverty and prostitution, but for that career to be genuinely respectable, it would have to be pursued outside the factory.

Every effort was made to give the EPF an air of gentility and petit bourgeois respectability. It was located in a former residence rather than in a school building, even though the structure was so dilapidated that it was blamed for outbreaks of tuberculosis among students and employees. Its entirely female staff (save one painting teacher and the director) consisted of normal-school graduates from "good backgrounds" who were often compared favorably with the working-class instructors employed in the EPM. According to the director, the EPF's teaching staff was "composed of ladies from our best society, of elevated culture and character, who bring to the school good domestic habits, polite graces combined with technical competence, acquired and practiced as a complement to the actual education." The classes it initially offered included design, dressmaking, sewing, lace and embroidery, flowers and hats, and home economics (mainly cooking). These were, of course, largely nonindustrial trades. But it is worth stressing that the students themselves seem to have been solely interested in marketable skills—not a single one enrolled in home economics when it was first offered, causing the course to be canceled. It was revived as a requirement in 1912, but lack of interest, complaints, and the problem of greasy hands led to its cancellation again in 1914.[13]

We have very little data to indicate what type of young woman attended the Escola Profissional Feminina.[14] We do know that, throughout the years 1910–1930, the EPF had many more applicants than places; in contrast to the EPM, it had no trouble finding candidates with the educational prerequisites necessary for admission to the middle-school level. In light of this, it seems likely that the EPM drew almost exclusively from the working-class milieu, while the EPF drew girls from the lower middle class as well as from the working class. In the early 1920s the governor of São Paulo argued for doubling the size of the EPF to give women options other than primary-school teaching for employment—a remark that would make no sense if the school had a strictly proletarian student body, since very few working-class women at the time became teachers. And the school's director frequently complained about "dilettantes" coming to the school to take art classes with a handsome and charismatic male instructor. It is unlikely that young ladies from privileged backgrounds would have invaded the school's premises unless they perceived the regular students as being "respectable" (and predominantly white).[15]

The man who directed both the EPM and EPF during their first two decades, Aprígio Gonzaga, vigorously advocated a vocational but nonindustrial identity for the EPF. A staunch defender of male skilled workers, he denounced the presence of women in factories, citing the employment of women and minors as the main explanation for low wages. Treating women and children as interchangeable categories, he called for the "removal of children and women from factory work," which would "redound to the benefit of the race, of society, and of the nation."[16] At the same time, Gonzaga positioned himself as a progressive and modern educator who recognized women's need for self-sufficiency. He claimed that there were crafts appropriate for female employment, especially in small dress shops and ateliers, and he struggled against attempts by government officials and nonvocational educators to expand the role of home economics in the EPF. He noted with annoyance that, in 1920, the state government appointed a woman to the EPF staff to teach home economics without consulting him.[17] (Once again, the cooking course never really got off the ground, and the instructor resigned by 1924.)

Gonzaga was apparently under fire from various quarters for his strong advocacy of vocational education for women. In the early 1920s he published a pamphlet titled "Objectives of Vocational Education for Women," in which he attempted to show that one could reconcile employment for women outside the home with support for the traditional family (or as he put it, the essay showed that he was not "against the family"). Adopting an increasingly common posture, Gonzaga noted that necessity forced some women to work outside the home, but also argued that vocational education could make them more effective housewives. "A woman thus educated will no longer be a mere decoration or a dead weight in the household economy, but rather will be a brave and very noble collaborator."[18] Thus, to maintain support for the idea of women's (nonindustrial) vocational instruction, Gonzaga capitulated on the question of incorporating home economics into the curriculum.

Neither the indifference of the women students nor Gonzaga's criticisms served to discourage the swelling campaign to emphasize domestic skills in vocational schools for women. In 1935 a major educational reform in São Paulo, championed by the advocates of rational organization and scientific management, made the separation of female and male training even more rigid. The new code formally excluded women from industrial courses, including textiles, and even in coeducational institutions, men and women were to be taught in separate classes (except for courses in secretarial skills, a category that tends to be more cross-gender in Brazil than elsewhere). Courses for women included domestic arts; embroidery; flower-, hat-, and glove-making; and similar artisanal crafts. The domestic arts, now obligatory, included hygiene and nutrition, infant care (to reduce the "frightful rate of infant mortality"), home economics (cooking, washing, and cleaning), and *contabilidade doméstica*—domestic accounting.[19] Finally, students in both male and female schools could sell the wares produced in class to the public. In the men's case, half the proceeds went into the school endowment and the other half went directly into their pockets. But in the women's case, the other half went into a *pecúlio,* a nest egg to be made available to them upon graduation, when it could be used to set up a new household with a prospective husband or to finance the opening of a small shop. In short, training young women for domestic life had become as pressing a concern for vocational educators (though not, I suspect, for the students) as training them for a specific form of employment.

Whereas industrial employers openly criticized many reforms during this period as reflecting the unrealistic and uninformed views of government bureaucrats who had never set foot in a factory, they responded to the new educational code with unreserved enthusiasm. This is hardly surprising: among the leading figures in the reform process were men like Roberto Mange, a mechanical engineer and founder of a training center for railroad mechanics, and Horácio da Silveira, an active member of the Institute for Rational Organization of Work (IDORT). Both men had intimate ties to such prominent industrial spokesmen as Roberto Simonsen and Armando de Arruda Pereira, and shared their view of a modernizing Brazil that promised to be more productive, efficient, and rationally organized.[20] Such a vision included female factory workers, but only as temporary, semiskilled operatives. Rather than defending women's employment in industry, these industrial spokesmen treated it as a transitory phenomenon, and professed their belief that women's main role in a modernizing society was the maintenance of an organized household.

The industrialists' position on this issue, to the extent that one can be discerned, was a mixture of opportunism and ideological predilections. It hardly behooved industrialists to denounce women's employment in factories as endangering the family or compromising feminine morality, considering the dependence of the textile sector on female workers. At the same time, the more politically engaged industrialists understood that the high level of female employment in factories made industry vulnerable to attacks by a variety of critics, including agrarian traditionalists, middle-class reformers, and male labor leaders. A more masculine workforce would certainly make industrialization more appealing to those who feared that factory work was eroding traditional family relations and gender roles.

Furthermore, industrialists had their own assumptions about the role of women in industry. When private firms set up apprenticeship or training programs of their own, they virtually always excluded girls from eligibility.[21] Girls and women were thought to have natural abilities—manual dexterity, tolerance for monotony—that suited them for routinized industrial labor. Training, therefore, was unnecessary, and could even have the highly undesirable effect of giving women a claim to better wages. Thus, employers derived a certain economic benefit from the exclusion of women workers from the category of *skilled,* and a degree of ideological legitimacy by emphasizing the temporary nature of female industrial employment.

This endorsement by industrialist spokesmen of the woman worker as a special (if marginal) category is also reflected in their easy acceptance of proposed legislation to protect women workers from night shifts and hazardous conditions, and to provide them with limited maternity benefits. Whereas other labor laws elicited grumblings from the São Paulo industrial employers' federation (FIESP), the proposed law on women's work met with immediate approval. In a 1931 notice to members, FIESP's directors pronounced the proposal "as nearly perfect as possible," and felt obliged to insist that most of its provisions were already standard operating procedure in paulista industry.[22]

Vocational Education and the Semivisible Woman Worker

Many of the educators and technocrats who were involved in formulating vocational education policy in São Paulo, Brazil's leading industrial center, also played a prominent role in debates over worker training at the national level during the Vargas dictatorship (1930–1945).[23] In a 1933 speech, Getúlio Vargas declared that "the education we need to develop to the extreme limits of our possibilities is the vocational and technical kind. Without it, organized work is impossible, especially in an age characterized by the predominance of the machine."[24] Indeed, vocational instruction was a perfect issue for a proto-populist regime seeking to curry favor with (re)organized labor, to champion industrial development, and to forge a nationalist political culture. Brazil, rather than relying on immigrant craftsmen or lagging behind more technically sophisticated nations, would now produce its own corps of skilled and disciplined worker-citizens.

Not surprisingly, the documents produced by the various technical commissions studying the training issue routinely and unfailingly identified the skilled industrial worker as male. Not that women were entirely ignored; as educators and technicians paid more and more attention to vocational training as a means to socialize workers as part of a project for national development, they began to discuss the pressing need for women to become skilled

housewives and childrearers. Typical of this trend was a 1934 report by a leading group of vocational educators that called for obligatory domestic education for women in vocational schools throughout Brazil, "because a woman's
professional life should be considered as merely a transitional phase: destiny
designates her for . . . the role of wife, mother and housewife." [25]

This continuing emphasis on domestic education reflected, in part, the
enthusiasm for "rational organization" in all spheres of modern life. While
scientific management and its correlates are most often associated with the
industrial workplace, organizations like IDORT argued that rational principles
could increase productivity and social harmony in every arena of human
endeavor. Public health officials and hygienists already regarded more rational approaches to infant care and nutrition as a major concern of the state.
Accordingly, new vocational schools that admitted women almost always
boasted a *posto de puericultura* (child welfare center) where the (supposedly)
future mothers could learn the basics of good infant care. And while all Brazilian women could learn to be better wives and mothers, hygienists and educators regarded working-class women as especially in need of guidance given
their class's "low moral and cultural level." Thus, not only was the woman
worker an increasingly marginal figure for whom extensive training would be
a waste, but the role of housewife was seen as one that required tutelage and
rational instruction, rather than as a natural outgrowth of women's experience, at least if the women were from the working class. [26]

One of the most influential documents produced by the Ministry of Education in the 1930s was a 1938 report on "Professional [Vocational] Education
in Germany," by Rodolpho Fuchs, a close ally of Gustavo Capanema, Vargas's
powerful minister of education. Fuchs viewed the Nazi system of in-factory
vocational training as a perfect model for Brazil. He especially extolled the
strict separation of the sexes in German vocational education, both with regard to courses and instructional staff, thus producing "feminine women and
real men." He noted that only in São Paulo were courses for men taught only
by men, a welcome exception that he explained by referring to that state as
the "Prussia of Brazil." He also cited with approval the requirement in Germany that all girls not going on to secondary school attend a domestic arts
school and spend six months in service with an experienced housewife, even
if they wished to work in industry. [27] Fuchs, like many of his contemporaries,
sought to modernize Brazil and the Brazilian worker, while reinforcing "traditional" or "natural" gender roles.

By the early 1940s, negotiations among educators, labor ministry representatives, and industrialists had produced an innovative system for voca-

Home economics class (not a vocational course) in sewing for
female apprentices at the SENAI school in Campinas, 1946.
Courtesy of the Núcleo de Memória, SENAI–São Paulo.

tional training in Brazil known as the Serviço Nacional de Aprendizagem
Industrial (National Service for Industrial Training), or SENAI.[28] Funded and
controlled by the industrialist associations, the training service emphasized
both proper socialization and the labor requirements of specific industrial
sectors. This relatively pragmatic orientation meant that SENAI, in contrast
to many state vocational schools, did not completely exclude women from
industrial education. Rapid (two-month) courses to produce semiskilled textile workers were almost entirely composed of young women, and such
courses as paper making, also regarded as semiskilled, admitted female apprentices. A North American visitor from the United States Bureau of Labor
Statistics, Mary Cannon, noted that "the program is geared chiefly to boys,
though theoretically there are opportunities for girls."[29] These opportunities
remained largely theoretical, however. Despite the increasing employment of
women during the wartime production boom, SENAI early on concentrated
its resources in apprenticeship programs for the metallurgical trades—an entirely masculine preserve. And in some cases women's exclusion was formal-
ized: SENAI courses for training textile-factory supervisors (a position held by
women in some all-female sections) were officially closed to women.[30]

Physical education classes for boys and girls at the SENAI school
in Brás, 1946. Courtesy of the Núcleo de Memória, SENAI–São
Paulo.

The industrialists and technocrats who founded SENAI also demonstrated
that proper socialization meant different things for girls than for boys. However small in number, the girls enrolled in SENAI courses routinely received
special treatment. The SENAI school in Campinas, São Paulo, proudly announced that it had cut back on math and Portuguese classes for its female
students and had substituted domestic education, including sewing classes.
Furthermore, the account boasted that the girls regularly prepared meals for
the entire student body. SENAI made sure that it could not be accused of
ignoring women's "true" domestic vocation.[31]

While SENAI recognized females as an important presence in the industrial
milieu (girls consistently accounted for well over half the industrial workers
under the age of eighteen), it reinforced women's "natural" role as semiskilled
and temporary workers, as well as generally rigidifying the distinction between skilled and semiskilled. Young women were well suited to the role of
machine tender; furthermore, their future roles as wives and mother, or mere
supplementers of male incomes, made it economically unwise to provide
girls with extensive vocational training. Just two years before the founding
of SENAI, the FIESP leadership had argued in favor of a lower minimum wage

for women based on their "inferior physiological conditions" due to maternity and menstruation.[32] Obviously, the immediate concern was to ensure a continuous supply of cheap industrial labor, but whatever the purpose, such arguments made it highly unlikely that employer associations would then turn around and provide women with elaborate new training opportunities.

In a 1946 article on industrial fatigue, industrialist-intellectual A. C. Pacheco e Silva was unusually blunt about the proper role for women in industry. Arguing that too much training could create discontent among workers performing the monotonous tasks typical of the modern industrial workplace, he suggested that women, since they were less negatively affected by monotony, should be hired as "machine tenders"—after all, "look how they can knit for hours on end without feeling the slightest fatigue."[33] In other words, repetitious domestic tasks prepared women for the role of semiskilled worker, and vice versa.

Aside from its shameless recourse to the most banal sorts of stereotypes, Pacheco e Silva's article is remarkable for its unreserved endorsement of a certain form of female factory employment. This was, I would argue, indicative of a larger trend. As Brazilian manufacturing shifted from its earlier emphasis on textiles to new metallurgical and mechanical products, the rate of male employment in industry rose steadily. Throughout the late 1940s and 1950s, the proportion of women in paulista industry steadily dropped, easing fears that industrialization would lead to a feminized workforce and would undermine the male-headed household. Whereas women accounted for over 40 percent of industrial workers in São Paulo during World War II, by 1955 less than a quarter of the workforce was female. At the same time, girls continued to constitute well over half the minors employed in industry, and their relative numbers remained fairly steady.[34] In effect, it had become "natural" for a working-class girl to take a semiskilled factory job with few prospects for advancement, and it had also become "natural" for her to give up factory work once she reached marriageable age. There was, after all, a place for women in Brazilian industry, but few working-class women were likely to choose a permanent place as a semiskilled worker over the role of skilled domestic manager.

The Skilled Housewife and the Invisible Woman Worker

Whereas working-class women were only marginally involved in the operations of SENAI, they were a central object of concern for another, more elaborate service set up by industrialists during this period. Created by a 1946 government decree, the Industrial Social Service (SESI) had the same administrative and funding structure as SENAI, and the activities of both agencies were thoroughly imbued with an ideology of rationalization based on the innovations of Frederick Taylor, Henry Ford, and industrial psychology. But SESI had a much broader mission than SENAI. Rapidly responding to the unexpected wave of postwar labor protests, the industrialist leadership founded SESI as a means to provide a wide range of social services to industrial workers and their families, and thereby secure social peace. SESI was not intended as a philanthropic organization but as a vehicle to improve workers' standard of living, hygiene, and culture through rational forms of assistance, guidance, recreation, and instruction.[35]

The very structure of SESI in São Paulo revealed a highly gendered view of the urban working class. The Division of Social Orientation, which was responsible for courses and publications related to workplace issues and organized labor, always identified workers as men. Moreover, it developed special programs to train middle-class men as "social educators," a male counterpart to the usually female social workers, who could then visit factories and fraternize with the presumably male workforce.[36] In contrast, the Subdivision for Assistance to the Family had a largely female staff, identified its clientele as female, and tended to issues related to health and home life. Completely omitted was any venue for directly addressing issues of interest to women workers (as opposed to working-class housewives). Even if SESI had been inclined to discuss, for example, harassment of women workers by workmates or supervisors, there was no institutional space within which to explore such an issue. SESI not only assumed that working-class women were housewives; it effectively erased the woman worker from its representation of industrial life.

Flanked by a small army of hygienists, psychologists, social workers, and educators, the industrialists who founded SESI proposed to ensure social peace both by offering workers material benefits and by creating new norms of behavior among workers on the job and at home. According to SESI, workers on the shop floor could increase productivity and social harmony and decrease occupational hazards if properly instructed in everything from rational organization to labor legislation. Similarly, working-class Brazilians could actively combat such problems as infectious diseases, malnutrition, and disruptive behavior by improving personal hygiene, observing stricter morality, and reorganizing the domestic sphere.[37]

SESI's messages about proper morality and hygiene were, in the abstract, directed at both men and women, both in the workplace and in the home. But SESI officials in São Paulo increasingly treated cultural respectability and good health practices as the domain of the working-class wife and mother. From the outset, SESI had focused some attention on women; the sewing courses were among its first, and most popular, instructional programs. SESI's social workers also sought every opportunity to visit workers' homes, survey conditions, and make suggestions for improving the domestic sphere. Typically, when a worker sought SESI's medical services but could not make the modest payments, a social worker paid a home visit to determine if the financial problems were a matter of poor household management. Or as SESI president Antônio Devisate revealingly put it, the social worker would investigate "to see why the workers' wives were not able to make their husbands' wages go as far as they should."[38] Often, after this initial contact or an encounter at a SESI social center, the social worker tried to organize a group of women in the neighborhood to meet and discuss their personal and financial problems, with the SESI representative gently guiding the course of the conversation and suggesting solutions to domestic dilemmas. One SESI social worker described such gatherings as an incentive for the working-class woman to clean and decorate the house, "since this is not the customary condition of their homes."[39] SESI's Subdivision for Assistance to the Family, meanwhile, began offering various courses in child care, home economics, and cooking.

By the early 1950s SESI–São Paulo had decided to concentrate these various courses for working-class women in Centros de Aprendizado Doméstico (Centers for Domestic Instruction), or CADS; by 1954 the organization had inaugurated twenty-five such centers throughout the state (seven in the capi-tal and the rest in the suburbs and the interior). The centers regularly offered three different cooking courses, as well as courses in child care, house-hold management, domestic hygiene, and preparation for marriage. Sewing courses, previously offered only in factories or union headquarters, were now also available at many of the centers. And to complement the activities of these centers, SESI began publishing two monthly magazines—the short-lived *Dona de Casa,* and the more enduring *SESI-Higiene.*[40]

The centers offered instruction for women of all ages, with the courses for *mãezinhas* (little mothers) aimed at nine- to fourteen-year-olds, the prepara-tion-for-marriage courses aimed at young women, and all other courses open to anyone sixteen or older. The centers also reached out to the families of its students; for example, many parents with daughters in the mãezinha pro-gram attended monthly meetings with the center's staff to be informed of their child's progress and to discuss domestic matters.[41] Students, especially in the cooking courses, frequently organized parties and contests that in-volved friends and family, and every certification ceremony was an occasion for centerwide celebration. The women associated with the centers also par-ticipated prominently in other SESI activities, such as the May Day parade and the Spring Ball. And once having completed the courses, an ex-student could maintain social contacts through the alumnae association formed in each center.

Again, all of these courses operated on the assumption that working-class women were, first and foremost, wives and mothers, or future wives and mothers. Women might work before marriage, or work outside the home intermittently after marriage to alleviate financial distress, but their major pecuniary contribution to the household would come in the form of a ratio-nally organized budget, a healthful atmosphere, and well-brought-up chil-dren. As the premier issue of *Dona de Casa* (housewife) put it, referring to the magazine's title, "Here you have, in just three words, the golden dream of almost every young woman." And it was not just her dream but her biologi-cal destiny. In answer to the question "Is the masculine sex superior to the feminine?" the magazine's editors claimed that it was not a matter of superior and inferior, but of difference, grounded in hormonal activity. "As a result women are capable of noting the small details, while men only see the big picture." Continuing this emphasis on separate spheres, the magazine con-cluded that, "while the man has his victories at work . . . the woman has the compensation of raising strong children."[42]

With varying degrees of subtlety, the home economics courses taught their students that housewives, though not wage earners, were largely responsible for the standard of living and quality of life in their homes. Thus *Dona de Casa* roused its readers with a call to initiate, "by any means possible, a campaign against poor nutrition and the neglect of Brazilian homes." Similarly, an account of a cooking contest among students from the CADS in Santo André and São Caetano assured readers of the *SESI Journal* that "if all future housewives acquired knowledge of the culinary arts, nutrition and diet as administered in the centers for domestic instruction, soon there would no longer be problems resulting from nutritional deficiency."[43] Speaking at this same contest, SESI president Antônio Devisate informed his audience that ignorance about domestic tasks on the part of working-class women was a major cause of marital disputes. Indeed, he claimed that some 90 percent of the separation cases brought to the attention of SESI's legal aid service had such domestic incompetence at their roots.[44] Thus, the competent housewife could not only provide a comfortable home and balanced diet for her family, but could also save her marriage. As if to underline this point, Anita Devisate, SESI's "first lady," regularly handed out prizes such as blenders, dishes, and knife sharpeners at special events.

Much of the cooking and housekeeping advice dispensed by the SESI courses amounted to routine information that could be extracted from the home economics courses offered in São Paulo's vocational schools for women since the early twentieth century. But SESI infused its courses with its own preoccupations, emphasizing the rationalization of housework and adherence to a code of proper moral conduct. An early issue of *Dona de Casa* asked its readers, "Did you know that our organism is similar to a machine?" It also informed current and future housewives that "each twenty-four hours should be divided in three 'eights' so as to be better utilized."[45] In contrast with home economics literature in wealthier societies, the SESI publications did not emphasize the acquisition of modern, labor-saving household devices; most home appliances were beyond the financial reach of SESI's audience. But precisely because of this, the Brazilian working-class household had to be very carefully organized and managed.[46]

SESI courses and publications also advised young women to be "modest, simple and sweet," claiming that men might go out with boisterous, flirtatious, and heavily made-up women, but chose more demure types to be their wives. Dona Nicota, the fictional advice columnist for *Dona de Casa,* warned young women away from any form of premarital sexual activity, and urged them to think less about love and marriage, and more about domestic tasks.[47]

The issue of proper morality emerged even more conspicuously in the discussion of health matters, both in *Dona de Casa* and *SESI-Higiene*. The latter publication, issued by SESI's Industrial Health and Safety Service, clearly targeted women, since the vast majority of its articles dealt with marital, domestic, and childrearing matters. Only on rare occasions did the magazine raise the question of industrial accidents, and it usually did so in relation to some domestic practice that contributed to their incidence. And like much of the organization's literature, *SESI-Higiene* treated good health as a function of knowledge about hygiene and proper morality, regarded as two sides of the same precious coin.

The close association of hygiene and morality is best illustrated by the extensive attention SESI paid to the problem of syphilis. Since its founding the organization had devoted a sizable portion of its resources to testing hundreds of thousands of factory workers for the disease. This campaign may well have been inspired by SESI founder Roberto Simonsen's claim, based on a supposedly scientific survey he sponsored in the 1920s, that 45 percent of Brazilian-born workers were infected with syphilis. The actual results of massive testing in the late 1940s and early 1950s revealed a much lower rate of infection—3.5 percent—among industrial workers, a rate that was lower, in fact, than that found in many industrialized nations.[48] Despite this heartening discovery, SESI continued to treat syphilis as a major health risk for the Brazilian working class and a major concern for working-class women. Indeed, publications aimed at workers—that is, male workers—rarely made any mention of syphilis or other contagious diseases, whereas the women-oriented magazines obsessively discussed the menace of venereal infection. The debut of *SESI-Higiene,* for example, included two separate articles on the subject, one of which informed its readers that you could contract syphilis from a mere kiss.[49]

Given SESI's identification of venereal disease as a major social problem for women, it is not surprising that a large portion of the material in the "preparation for marriage" course dealt with syphilis testing and prevention. Instructors advised the prospective bride to choose her husband carefully and to give special attention to her future mate's physical condition. A premarital examination was a must, as was constant vigilance for signs of disease. Much emphasis was also given to the impact on future offspring; SESI literature told students about the large number of infants who died from the effects of syphilis, claiming that these tiny victims had been "murdered" by their parents. To illustrate this point further, *SESI-Higiene* devoted an entire issue to the hypothetical tale of Lili and Maricota. The former decides to marry the first man she meets, fails to have a prenuptial exam, contracts syphilis, has only one child who dies in infancy, and ends up ill, abandoned, and childless. The latter, in contrast, patiently seeks the proper mate, has a prenuptial exam, and becomes the perfect wife and mother—as verified by the accompanying illustration, showing Maricota holding an infant in her arms and surrounded by six other children. It seems that nobody at SESI found any irony in the idyllic portrayal of a working-class housewife with seven young children, a situation that would almost certainly have spelled poverty for her household.[50]

Syphilis was not the only contagious illness that received attention in the domestic arts courses. Tuberculosis—a disease spread by poor living conditions, and a real scourge of the paulista working class—was a matter of similar concern. During its first ten years of existence, SESI tested over a million factory workers and their families for tuberculosis, and also provided treatment centers and a sanatorium. Yet the SESI literature paid less attention to this disease than it did to syphilis, perhaps because the contraction of tuberculosis could not be so easily attributed to a moral failing. Indeed, SESI appears to have been most enlightened in its attitude toward those diseases that claimed "innocent" victims. It denounced irrational prejudices about leprosy; *SESI-Higiene* reported the case of a woman who, contracting the disease, postponed marriage, went for treatment, and, on being cured, married happily and had healthy children.[51] The organization's obsessive attitude about syphilis, a relatively minor health concern for paulista workers, had less to do with the incidence or severity of the disease, and more to do with the means of transmission.

Another major preoccupation of the SESI domestic arts instructors, and the related publications, was to steer women away from midwives and home births, and toward doctors and hospitals. *SESI-Higiene* and *Dona de Casa* portrayed the midwife as "Dona Ignorância's inseparable friend," and regarded the advice of doctors, especially when it conflicted with traditional midwife practices, as unimpeachable. In its discussions of high infant mortality rates, *SESI-Higiene* cited widely recognized factors such as lack of medical attention during pregnancy and infancy, but, in typical fashion, assigned culpability for the problem to the parents: "It is necessary that the parents understand that they themselves are the most responsible for this high mortality."[52]

While much of the literature produced by SESI in this vein reflected strong North American influences—bolstered by frequent internships by SESI technicians in the United States—SESI displayed more traditional Brazilian attitudes with regard to ideal family size. Unlike North American social workers, who increasingly considered large families to be a major factor in household impoverishment, SESI's personnel and publications portrayed the ideal family as consisting of numerous children—seven in the case of the fortunate Mari-cota. This tendency can be attributed, at least in part, to SESI's strong ties to Catholic organizations, which precluded any overt reference to family planning. Indeed, the only published allusion to this subject during the early 1950s can be found in an article titled "Crime and Punishment" that stridently denounced the alleged increase in abortions. Claiming that the high cost of living was driving women to commit "actual murders," *SESI-Higiene* accused lay abortionists, midwives, and "even unscrupulous physicians who dishonor the noble title that they use," of "tremendous barbarities." The article reminded its readers that the "cost" of abortion, aside from the sin of "killing a human being," included considerable physical risk for the woman. Not only did a perforated uterus "invariably lead to death," but also "sterility and uterine cancer have their origins, most of the time, in these hideous acts that are, unfortunately, so common amongst us."[53]

Another "vice" that SESI's courses and publications routinely condemned was alcohol consumption, treating even recreational drinking as undesirable. According to *SESI-Higiene,* "alcohol destroys the happiness of the home, causes the degeneration of the race, and disturbs social tranquility." And even though the SESI literature regarded excessive drinking as a predominantly male activity, it delegated to the woman the responsibility for discerning signs of such vices in a prospective mate, and for creating a domestic environment that would be conducive to clean living. In its only (oblique) reference to domestic violence, *SESI-Higiene* cited the constant headlines in daily papers about murders and suicides, which it blamed on the victims who "ignore the grave responsibility that is marriage."[54] In short, it was the woman's role to stretch the family budget, give birth to healthy children, create a wholesome home environment, defeat the spread of syphilis, and avoid circumstances conducive to vice and violence. No wonder SESI scolded women who sought to marry as a way to stop working, reminding them that after marriage "their labors will be greater and their responsibilities greatly enlarged."[55] Ironically, the young woman's interlude in the factory was now being portrayed as relatively carefree, whereas the real work and responsibilities would begin once she became a *dona de casa.*

One might expect such daunting prescriptions for competence as a wife and mother to discourage working-class women from enrolling in the SESI courses, but the centers proved to be among the most popular of SESI's programs. From 1948, when the domestic arts courses first started functioning, to 1959, the centers granted nearly 200,000 certificates of completion to paulista women, and another 14,000 certificates to women who completed courses by correspondence.[56] To be sure, some women took multiple courses, reducing the total number of individuals represented in these figures. However, the statistics probably underestimate the centers' impact, since they exclude women who attended classes but failed to complete a course, relatives who participated in the centers' activities, and the 51,000 graduates of the sewing courses.

We can only speculate about the appeal of these courses, since the occasional remark or letter cited by SESI hardly amounts to a random sample of student opinion. In the case of the sewing courses, which SESI portrayed as vehicles for social education and for reducing household expenses, it is evident that many women enrolled for other reasons. Virtually every comment about these courses by former students mentions the value of learning a skill that allowed them to earn extra income and supplement their husbands' salaries. SESI may have denied that these were professionalizing courses, but the women who enrolled in them insistently disagreed. The same explanation could not apply to most of the other courses, however. Except for the most advanced phase, the cooking classes were too rudimentary to provide a means to earn additional income, and the other courses were only relevant for unpaid work in the domestic sphere.[57]

Why, then, did thousands of women flock to these courses on cooking, child care, and other domestic arts? Perhaps the center attracted them as a place for women only, where they could congregate with other working-class women and discuss problems that were genuinely relevant to their everyday lives. After all, what institution offered urban, working-class women a similar meeting place or forum? Certainly not the male-oriented union headquarters, the priest-centered church, or the typically masculine neighborhood bar. And while SESI's approach to the problems of working-class women may appear to us overly moralistic and often unrealistic, it did treat matters central to most women's lives—cleaning, shopping, cooking, childrearing—as serious responsibilities that deserved thoughtful consideration. In a society that barely took notice of women's unpaid labor, SESI's careful attention to these activities, whatever the ideological underpinnings, probably provided a refreshing contrast.

It is also likely that SESI accurately assumed that most working-class women aspired to the role of housewife and mother. Of course, this was not simply a "natural" inclination. In a society that had long conceptualized the female industrial worker as an unskilled operative with little opportunity for vocational education, professional advancement, or active participation in her union, few women could regard lifetime factory employment as a desirable alternative.[58] And the burdens of the notorious double shift, going from paid work in the plant to unpaid work in the home, widely discouraged women from combining a factory job with homemaking except in cases of dire necessity. A SENAI study of students' families, while not necessarily based on typical working-class households, revealed that the students' mothers, on average, contributed less than 4 percent of the total household income.[59]

Again, SESI made every effort to give its women students a sense of accomplishment and importance (as well as a sense of gratitude to the organization's sponsors) when granting the certificates of completion. The prominent role of SESI "first lady" Anita Devisate at such ceremonies, and the presence of political and religious officials, may smack of noblesse oblige, but their participation undoubtedly heightened the solemnity of the occasion. This was surely an unusual experience for working-class girls and women accustomed to having their considerable domestic labors go unacknowledged.[60] Similarly, the various festive events promoted by SESI offered rare opportunities for these women to wear formal dresses—often sewn in SESI courses—and emulate a lifestyle normally inaccessible to them. Whereas working-class men had access to an industrial work culture that created attainable images of masculinity—emphasizing strength, skill, and wage earning—working-class women were constantly bombarded with images of femininity and sexuality that normally were beyond the reach of the financially constrained and overworked housewife.[61] SESI took every opportunity to reinforce those aspects of its programs that addressed working-class women's needs in this vein. Its gala New Year's Eve celebration included the crowning of a Queen of the Workers, and its spring ball also climaxed with the crowning of a Queen of Spring and the presentation of working-class *brotinhos* (teenage girls). Apparently, such activities had considerable appeal among working-class women.[62]

SESI, in its particular fashion, celebrated women's future or current roles as wives and mothers, while downplaying their status as members of the working class and virtually ignoring the idea that they might be workers as well. The goal of the working-class housewife was to cultivate an elegant appearance, stretch the budget, decorate the home, and organize the domestic sphere so that it approximated, as much as possible, the ideal middle-class household—goals that surely led to frustration for many graduates. An article instructing housewives to wax their floors on a weekly basis must have seemed, at best, ironic to the many working-class women who lived in makeshift housing with earthen floors. But the SESI staff took considerable pleasure in the perceived transformation wrought by the CADs. As one female social educator, surveying a graduation ceremony, remarked: "Look at how these young ladies, with very rare exceptions, are now free of embarrassment and proudly hold their heads up high. *They don't even seem like women workers.*" [63]

The Woman Worker as Oxymoron

To the extent that it is possible to discern a coherent pattern in these different arenas of education, training, and services for women, we can observe a persistent emphasis on marginalizing the woman factory worker and on transforming working-class women into models of bourgeois respectability (as defined by the relevant employers, educators, and professionals). It is as if the goal was to make *woman worker* and even *working-class woman* oxymorons. A woman might formally belong to the working class by virtue of her husband's place of employment and her limited financial resources, but her outlook, values, and aspirations, oriented toward her roles as housewife and consumer, would not reflect those SESI traditionally associated with that class.

The widespread acceptance of this identification of working-class women with the domestic sphere is exemplified by the labor press during this period. Union newspapers that subjected male-oriented SESI programs to vigorous criticism, even withering sarcasm, would blithely devote their women's pages to long, SESI-authored tracts on how to manage a household, or how to produce more economical, nutritious meals. [64] These union newspapers not only echoed the notion that women's concerns were domestic in nature, but also treated the domestic or private sphere as beyond political or ideological considerations. Thus, SESI's courses in labor legislation or human relations in the workplace might be incompatible with the development of a militant, class-conscious labor movement, but what harm could classes in household management do?

This consistent identification of working-class women with domestic concerns was made possible, in large part, by emptying the category *woman worker* of all positive connotations. The woman worker became an unfortunate creature who worked only out of necessity. Laboring at lower wages, she undermined men's earning power while exposing herself to sexual abuse. [65] On entering the factory, she faced a monotonous work routine in a dead-end job. A teenage girl might accept such a situation as a brief hiatus on the way to a marriage and family, but what adult woman would eagerly embrace such a fate? For most, the promise of success as a skilled, efficient household manager must have been much more appealing.

Once out of the factory and into the home, how did society measure success for a housewife? Models for domestic achievement and proper personal appearance typically reflected a middle-class ideal of a clean, comfortable, orderly home presided over by a competent, fashionably dressed wife and mother. While working-class men could draw on traditions of craft, organization, masculine strength, and earning power to constitute a viable working-class identity (that is, viable both among themselves and in the larger social context), women's association with the domestic sphere provided them with few resources with which to shape an alternative to the SESI ideal. This is not to imply that working-class women uncritically accepted every aspect of the SESI prescription for femininity, respectability, and efficiency. But the evidence of women's enthusiastic participation in SESI courses and festivities, on an entirely voluntary basis, indicates that there was no strong counterweight to SESI's appeal, or a serious aversion to SESI's claims that skilled housewives could resolve such social problems as low wages, infant mortality, and malnutrition.

Throughout the industrializing world, social workers, educators, physicians, and hygienists have intruded themselves into the daily routines of working-class families; São Paulo is by no means unique in this regard. What is especially interesting, however, is the active and salient role played by leading paulista industrialists in conceptualizing and funding the agencies that energetically sought to redefine the working-class woman as, first and foremost, a wife and mother, even as many of these same industrial employers continued to hire women workers in substantial numbers. Several factors help explain this apparent contradiction. First, the circle of industrialists and engineers who dominated São Paulo's employer associations in the 1940s, and who invented SENAI and SESI, had a project for industrial development that went beyond purely economic concerns. SESI took as its motto "For Social Peace in Brazil," and its founders construed social peace as requiring both harmonious relations with (predominantly male) labor unions, and the cultivation of robust, responsible worker-citizens. The masculinization of the workforce on the one hand, and the training of better housewives and mothers on the other, suited both objectives.

At the same time, the marginalization of the woman worker meant little economic sacrifice for industrial employers, since they could still count on a steady supply of girls and young women who quickly acquired the abilities necessary to perform low-wage, semiskilled jobs. The brief training required for these jobs meant that few resources would be wasted when a young woman decided to retire from factory life, and her temporary status made it unlikely that she would make a fuss about low wages or poor working conditions.[66] Furthermore, the fact that these women tended to exit the factory (by force or by choice) once they began their own families meant that employers did not have to face the added expense of providing maternity leave or child-care facilities.

Again, the industrialists and educators involved in the programs and institutions described above could hardly take credit for inventing the category *woman worker*. Well before the founding of the Escola Feminina, SENAI, or SESI, the woman worker had already been constructed as a subset of the working class, and was regarded as such by both workers and employers. My argument is not that these organizations *imposed* an image of the woman worker on a working-class population that had no prior gender constructions. But I argue that they served to elaborate, formalize, and institutionalize difference—first between female workers and male workers, and then between working-class men/workers and working-class women/housewives—so that social norms became more rigid. It is one thing for a working-class husband to discourage his wife from keeping her job in the factory, or to expect her to do the domestic tasks. It is quite another for an employer-run organization, whose backers routinely hired thousands of women to do factory work, to deny her access to skilled industrial occupations while offering her courses in cooking, sewing, and child care, and delegating to her the responsibility for resolving a host of serious social problems.

Notes

All translations by author.

1   Joan W. Scott, *Gender and the Politics of History* (New York: Columbia University Press, 1988), esp. pp. 167–77. Elsewhere Scott has urged historians to examine the way state policies have actively shaped gender relations. See Joan W. Scott, "Rewriting History," in *Behind the Lines: Gender and the Two World Wars,* ed. Margaret Higonnet et al. (New Haven: Yale University Press, 1987), pp. 21–30.

2   On the role of women in early Brazilian industry see Esmeralda Blanco Bolsonaro de Moura, *Mulheres e menores no trabalho industrial: Os fatores sexo e idade no dinâmica do capital* (Petrópolis: Vozes, 1982); Maria Valéria Junho Pena, *Mulheres e trabalhadoras: Presença feminina na constituição do sistema fabril* (Rio de Janeiro: Paz e Terra, 1981); and Joel Wolfe, *Working Women, Working Men: São Paulo and the Rise of Brazil's Industrial Working Class, 1900–1955* (Durham, N.C.: Duke University Press, 1993).

3   Cited in Wolfe, *Working Women,* pp. 7–8.

4   Theresa R. Veccia, "'My Duty as a Woman': Gender Ideology, Work, and Working-Class Women's Lives in São Paulo, Brazil, 1900–1950," in this volume.

5   Susan K. Besse, *Restructuring Patriarchy: The Modernization of Gender Inequality in Brazil, 1914–1940* (Chapel Hill: University of North Carolina Press, 1996), chap. 6.

6 See, for example, the remarks by Aprígio de Almeida Gonzaga in Escola Profissional Masculina, *Relatório* (São Paulo, 1920), p. 6.

7 On the woman worker as a "social problem" in this era see Margareth Rago, *Do cabaré ao lar: A utopia da cidade disciplinar, Brasil, 1890–1930* (Rio de Janeiro: Paz e Terra, 1985). For a discussion of similar themes in the Argentine context see Donna Guy, *Sex and Danger in Buenos Aires: Prostitution, Family, and Nation in Argentina* (Lincoln: University of Nebraska Press, 1991).

8 On Street's textile mill and *vila operária*, see Palmira Petratti Teixeira, *A Fábrica do sonho: Trajetoria do industrial Jorge Street* (Rio de Janeiro: Paz e Terra, 1990).

9 Wolfe, *Working Women,* chap. 1.

10 On the exceptional women who attained skilled positions within industry see Veccia, " 'My Duty as a Woman.' "

11 For a more extensive discussion of this trend see Barbara Weinstein, *For Social Peace in Brazil: Industrialists and the Remaking of the Working Class in São Paulo, 1920–1964* (Chapel Hill: University of North Carolina Press, 1996), pp. 28–37.

12 Escola Profissional Masculina, *Relatório dos trabalhos* (São Paulo, 1914), p. 12; Carmen S. Vidigal Moraes, "A socialização da força de trabalho: Instrução popular e qualificação profissional no estado de São Paulo, 1873–1934" (Ph.D. diss., University of São Paulo, 1990).

13 Escola Profissional Feminina, *Relatório dos trabalhos* (São Paulo, 1922), p. 11.

14 For a contemporary account see "A Escola Profissional Feminina de São Paulo," *Revista Feminina* 6, no. 66 (November 1919), cited in Besse, *Restructuring Patriarchy,* p. 121.

15 Ibid.; Carlos de Campos (governor of São Paulo), *Mensagem à Assembléa Legislativa,* July 14, 1925, pp. 18–23. Susan Besse (*Restructuring Patriarchy*) came across some letters written to advice columns in women's magazines by students from the Escola Feminina. Since *Revista Feminina* was decidedly *not* proletarian in orientation, this seems to support my supposition.

16 EPM, *Relatório* (1920), p. 6.

17 EPF, *Relatório* (1922), p. 11.

18 Cited in Moraes, "A socialização," p. 221. See also Afrânio Peixoto, "A educação nacional: Aspectos femininos," *Revista Feminina* 7, no. 79 (December 1920), cited in Besse, *Restructuring Patriarchy,* p. 122.

19 Horácio da Silveira, *O ensino technico-profissional e doméstico em São Paulo* (São Paulo: Imprensa do Estado de São Paulo, 1935), p. 21. On the relationship between the enthusiasm for rational organization and educational reform see Weinstein, *For Social Peace in Brazil,* pp. 74–75.

20 On the Simonsen circle, IDORT, and the shift in industrialist discourse see Weinstein, *For Social Peace in Brazil,* chaps. 1–2.

21 While it is hardly surprising that the apprenticeship courses set up by São Paulo Light and Power in the years 1910–1919 recruited only boys, given the extreme

rarity of women mechanics and electricians, it is more telling that a privately run course for textile workers also confined itself to a male clientele (Arquivo do Centros dos Industriaes de Fiação e Tecelagem de São Paulo, circular no. 779, May 10, 1928).

22   FIESP, circular no. 212, November 5, 1931, Biblioteca Roberto Simonsen.

23   On the efforts to create a national vocational training system during the regime of Getúlio Vargas see Barbara Weinstein, "The Industrialists, the State, and the Issues of Worker Training and Social Services in Brazil, 1930–1950," *Hispanic American Historical Review* 70, no. 3 (August 1990): pp. 379–404.

24   Getúlio Vargas, *A nova política do Brasil,* vol. 2 (Rio de Janeiro: José Olympio, 1938), pp. 121–22.

25   "Organização geral do ensino profissional," CPDOC, GC/g 34.11.28, Fundação Getúlio Vargas (FGV), Rio de Janeiro.

26   For a discussion of women's role in the rational organization of all spheres of Brazilian life see Noêmia Nascimento Gama, "Desperdício do elemento humano," *Revista IDORT* 85 (January 1939): p. 18.

27   Rodolpho Fuchs, "O ensino profissional na Alemanha (Berlin, 1938)," CPDOC, GC/g 35.12.00, doc. I-10, FGV. On the training system in Nazi Germany see John Gillingham, "The 'Deproletarianization' of German Society: Vocational Training in the Third Reich," *Journal of Social History* 19, no. 3 (spring 1986): pp. 423–32.

28   On the founding of SENAI see Weinstein, "Industrialists," pp. 393–94.

29   Cited in Wolfe, *Working Women,* p. 103.

30   *Informativo SENAI* (São Paulo) 6, no. 60 (January 1951): p. 2.

31   SENAI–São Paulo, *Relatório pelo ano 1945* (São Paulo: TK, 1946), p. 29.

32   Edgard Carone, *O Pensamento Industrial no Brasil* (Rio de Janeiro: Difel, 1977), pp. 497–98.

33   A. C. Pacheco e Silva, "A fádiga industrial," *Boletim SENAI* (Rio) 2, no. 16 (November 1946): pp. 11–13.

34   On the changing composition of the paulista workforce see Weinstein, *For Social Peace in Brazil,* pp. 193–94.

35   On the founding of SESI see Weinstein, "The Industrialists," pp. 397–98.

36   SESI sponsored scholarships for prospective employees to attend a school of social work, but candidates for funding had to be men. Exceptions were made only if no male candidates were available. SESI–São Paulo, Atas do Conselho Regional, Oct. 18, 1949.

37   For an extended discussion of SESI's mission see Weinstein, *For Social Peace in Brazil,* chap. 4.

38   Transcripts of interviews with Antônio Devisate, president of FIESP, São Paulo, April 12, 1956, and María José Serra, SESI Social Worker, São Paulo, April 16, 1956, Robert Alexander Archive, Rutgers University, New Brunswick, N.J.

39   *Educador Social* (São Paulo) 2, no. 3 (March 1953): p. 4; transcript of interview with Hugo Guimarães Malheiros, chief of SESI Social Service Subdivision, April 13, 1956, Robert Alexander Archive.

40   Because of the broad overlap in the material they covered, SESI decided in 1955 to merge the two magazines under the name *SESI-Higiene.*

41   T'.ie mãezinha courses did acknowledge, if only indirectly, that some adult women worked outside the home, since these girls were being trained to take the place of the working mother in the household.

42   *Dona de Casa,* August 1951, p. 4.

43   *SESI Jornal* (São Paulo) 8, no. 93 (December 31, 1955).

44   Ibid. The president of FIESP automatically became president of SESI.

45   *Dona de Casa,* March 1950, p. 4, and April 1950, p. 4; *SESI-Higiene,* January 1956, p. 16.

46   For a discussion of a similar approach to home economics for working-class women in Weimar Germany see Mary Nolan, " 'Housework Made Easy': The Taylorized Housewife in Weimar Germany's Rationalized Economy," *Feminist Studies* 16, no. 3 (fall 1990): pp. 549–77.

47   *Dona de Casa,* May 1950, p. 4, and July 1950, p. 4.

48   Roberto Simonsen, *Ordem econômica, padrão de vida* (São Paulo: São Paulo Editorial Limitada, 1934), p. 28; SESI–São Paulo, *Relatório* (São Paulo: SESI-SP, 1953). This preoccupation with syphilis also reflects the influence of the eugenics movement in Brazil during the 1920s and 1930s. See Nancy Leys Stepan, *"The Hour of Eugenics": Race, Gender, and Nation in Latin America* (Ithaca: Cornell University Press, 1991).

49   *SESI-Higiene,* May 1950, pp. 2–3.

50   *SESI-Higiene,* May 1954.

51   *SESI-Higiene,* January 1955, pp. 3–4.

52   *SESI-Higiene,* January 1951, p. 4, and November 1953, p. 1.

53   *SESI-Higiene,* July 1953, p. 3.

54   *SESI-Higiene,* May 1953, p. 1.

55   *SESI-Higiene,* October 1951, p. 1.

56   SESI–São Paulo, *Relatório* (São Paulo, 1959).

57   The cooking courses might have been professionally useful for women employed as domestic servants, but they certainly were not geared toward that end, or toward that clientele. On the relative exclusion of Afro-Brazilians from industrial occupations and their concentration in domestic service see George Reid Andrews, *Blacks and Whites in São Paulo, Brazil, 1888–1988* (Madison: University of Wisconsin Press, 1991), pp. 79–80, 101.

58   Of course, those women who had no choice but to work often preferred factory work to domestic service (that is, working as someone else's maid). Elza Teixeira Nunes da Silva, interview with author, Nadir Figueiredo glass factory, São Paulo, June 2, 1986.

59 SENAI-Departamento Nacional, "Evasão Escolar" 3, São Paulo, 1952, pp. 7–9.

60 For example, the mayor of Santo André, one of the capital's oldest and largest suburbs, served as patron (*paraninfo*) for a class of sewing-course graduates. In São Carlos, the inauguration of a CAD was presided over by the president of the municipal council and a bishop (*SESI Jornal* 4, no. 37 [April 30, 1951]).

61 For a similar discussion of masculinity reinforcing worker identities (in contrast to femininity) see Deborah Levenson-Estrada, "The Loneliness of Working-Class Feminism: Women in the 'Male World' of Labor Unions, Guatemala City, 1970s," in this volume.

62 *SESI Jornal* 1, no. 10 (January 31, 1949): p. 1.

63 *SESI Jornal* 4, no. 38 (May 31, 1951), emphasis added.

64 See, for example, the paper of the São Paulo printers' union, *O Trabalhador Gráfico,* March 1960, p. 6. This case is especially remarkable since, on every other matter, the printers' union was very critical of SESI's programs and policies.

65 There is a growing literature, in Brazil and elsewhere, on the notion of the factory as a sexually threatening space for women, a construction that both sought to protect women from sexual danger, and tainted women who persisted in industrial employment. See Rago, *Do cabaré ao lar,* pp. 95–116; Theresa Veccia, "Redefining Women's Roles in Twentieth-Century Brazil: Impressions from the São Paulo Anarchist Press, 1900–1930" (unpublished paper); and Guy, *Sex and Danger.*

66 Joel Wolfe (*Working Women*) argues that women were the true vanguard of the labor movement despite their marginalization by unions. Some women surely played prominent roles in labor protests, but I doubt that such sporadic activism formed a significant counterpoint to the dominant view of working-class women.

"My Duty as a Woman"

Gender Ideology, Work, and Working-Class
Women's Lives in São Paulo, Brazil, 1900–1950

THERESA R. VECCIA

A daughter of Spanish immigrants who came to work the coffee groves at the turn of the century, dona Cinta Ramos was born in Sorocaba, a town in the interior of the state of São Paulo, in 1909. I first met dona Cinta in the state's capital in 1987, in the Villa Maria Zélia, a former *vila operária* (workers' villa), where she has lived since 1919. When the industrialist Jorge Street first built the collection of bungalows in the self-contained neighborhood in the Zona Leste, the eastern part of the city, back in the midteens, its purpose was to house the families of workers employed in the adjacent Maria Zélia cotton mill.

Seven decades later, the vila appeared to have endured the passage of time with remarkable resilience. Indeed, except for the crowded row of parked cars lining its nine narrow streets, the Villa Maria Zélia seemed a world removed from the frenetic intensity of life in the chaotic and congested urban sprawl that is present-day metropolitan São Paulo. A rare vestige from an era in the city's history that has long since passed, it also seemed like a promising place to begin my search for anyone who might have worked in Street's cotton factory before it closed in the late 1920s. An inquiry at the small *lanchonete* in the vila led me to Maria Zélia's Sociedade Amigos do Bairro (Friends of the Neighborhood Society), a community organization with branches in neighborhoods throughout the city. Without hestitating, the group's director suggested that I look up dona Cinta, a resident since the vila's initial founding. As I would later learn, dona Cinta was something of a historical figure in her own right. Having been approached by journalists and scholars on several prior occasions, dona Cinta took evident pride in her reputation as a purveyor of knowledge about the history of the Villa Maria Zélia and the cotton mill for which it originally had been built. An affable person and an engaging storyteller, dona Cinta agreed to talk with me about her life.[1]

Dona Cinta's story and the life stories of several other women whom I interviewed in São Paulo are the focus of this essay.[2] Using oral testimony, the discussion that follows examines the role of gender in the processes of class and identity formation during a period in Brazilian history that was molded by sweeping forces of social and economic change. At the level of the individual, gender defined in fundamental ways the essential terms of one's basic obligations and rights in life, as the opening phrase of the title of this essay suggests.[3] Gender also informed the meanings infused in the concept of work. For at a time when the rapid advance of industrial capitalism drew considerable numbers of women into the billowing textile mills scattered along São Paulo's diversifying cityscape, it is perhaps no less significant that gender norms establishing women's proper role in terms of their identity as daughters, wives, and mothers continued to remain deeply entrenched in society. The resultant incongruence between culturally sanctioned ideals of femininity and the glaring exigencies of material reality generated tensions and contradictions that colored the dynamics of interpersonal social relations, shaping the texture of everyday working-class life.

Dona Cinta's story connects with those of more than 1.5 million Europeans who crossed the Atlantic between 1882 and 1914 in search of jobs and the chance at a better life. Like the Ramoses, many families were lured onto coffee plantations by the promise of free ocean passage, the centerpiece of an ambitious immigrant recruitment program launched by *paulista* coffee planters during the 1880s with strong support from the state government. The abolition of slavery in 1888 cleared the path to begin the importation of foreign workers on a truly massive scale. In the ensuing transition to "free" labor, São Paulo's Afro-Brazilians found themselves increasingly pushed to the margins of society as immigrant families from southern Europe flooded the paulista countryside. The official immigrant subsidy scheme continued to finance the influx of European agricultural workers until its dissolution in 1927.[4]

Many in the immigrant wave, like the family of dona Cinta Ramos, were quick to abandon their jobs in the coffee sector, sometimes migrating between different towns in the interior before succumbing to the greatest magnet of all, the state capital. Mass immigration and the onset of industrialization, both spurred by the spectacular success of the coffee culture, fueled the rapid urbanization of the city of São Paulo. From 1890 to 1900 its population ballooned from 65,000 to 240,000. When dona Cinta arrived in the São Paulo capital in 1919, the city counted more than a half million inhabitants. Over half its residents were Italian-born.

The capital was also home to sizable communities of Spanish and Portuguese immigrants. The Mediterranean newcomers put down roots in various pockets of the city, which grew into the vibrant ethnic enclaves of Brás, Moóca, Ipiranga, and Belém. Also concentrated in these neighborhoods was a diverse and expanding network of factories both large and small, which together were transforming the city of São Paulo into the leading industrial center of a still predominantly agricultural nation.[5]

The earliest industrial establishments in the city produced light consumer goods. The most important of these were devoted to the manufacture of textiles, the sector that remained the motor of Brazilian industry until the 1940s. As in many other parts of the world, women and children dominated the labor force in São Paulo textile mills, a pattern that continued until midcentury. Gender ideology was central to Paulista textile manufacturers in their recruitment of workers and in their construction of the occupational hierarchy of the textile mill. Equally important to the strategies of the *patrões* (employers) were the survival strategies employed by working-class families, organized under the concept of the family wage economy.

Working Children in the Family Wage Economy

Throughout the teeming immigrant neighborhoods in the city of São Paulo, the need to earn one's keep manifested itself at an early age. So, like many of her peers, dona Cinta went out to work when she was ten years old. Yet despite the widespread reliance on multiple wage earners, the struggle to make ends meet still presented an ongoing challenge for working-class families. A 1934 survey of working-class living standards in the city of São Paulo found that although more than half of a household's combined income went toward buying food, this was still not enough to provide adequate nutrition. The average working-class diet was heavy in starch and low in protein, while fresh vegetables, eggs, and milk were among the items considered unaffordable luxuries.[6] The study ended on a sardonic note: "Marie Antoinette would hardly lose her head for telling Brazilian workers to eat cake. They wouldn't understand what she was talking about for they have never tasted cake. Even *goiabada* [a guava sweet], the so-called national dessert of Brazil, was on the tables of only twenty-five families."[7]

Although children who managed to finish primary school considered themselves lucky, most, like dona Ermínia Albertini, the daughter of Portuguese produce vendors and one of eight children, left school before completing the fourth grade. "I started working very young, very, very young. In those days there was so much misery. There was terrible misery. Once you were ten years old, you had to go to work. We were hungry. There were so many mouths to feed, so many of us to dress. So, it was as simple as this: You quit school and you went to work."[8]

Two main factors influenced parental decisions regarding their children's education. At bottom was the driving force of economic necessity, and its pressures were felt most strongly by those who were the oldest. "We, the first ones, we had to sacrifice the most," explained senhor Ignácio Picasso, a textile worker for forty years and the eldest of six siblings. Sr. Ignácio took his first mill job in 1924, when he was nine years old. He went to work at Votorantim, a large textile factory on the outskirts of Sorocaba, a city, ninety kilometers to the west of the capital, that used to be known as Manchester Paulista because of its many textile mills.[9] His sister entered Votorantim at thirteen, after four years of babysitting and doing work around the house while their mother worked full-time in the mill. Neither of them finished grade school. "As our family grew, we had to help my father to support the household. It also got to the point where my mother couldn't work in the factory any longer, so we were the ones who had to work."[10]

Gender also figured into parental decisions regarding education and work. Operating in tandem with the bourgeois ideal of the chief male breadwinner were cultural beliefs that defined marriage and motherhood as the feminine ideal, an equivalent to an occupational pursuit for women. Because domestic work required no formal preparation, when working-class parents could afford vocational training for their children, it was a male privilege. Dona Beatriz Nieto, a lifetime textile worker from Spain who had migrated as a child with her family to France, Panama, and the United States before settling permanently in São Paulo in 1927, explained her father's views on the subject of female education. They were typical of the times.

> My father always used to say that he thought it was very beautiful for a girl to play the violin. But the poor man, he was always moving around and never was lucky enough to find his niche in the world. So, it never worked out for me to go to school to learn. . . . I was already working before I turned fifteen. Now, he sent my brothers to learn a trade because he thought it was more important for men than it was for women. . . . For example, my father used to say, "A woman would get married, so why did she need an education? Or even before marrying, why did she

need to know how to read and write? So that she could send letters to her boyfriend?"[11]

Fathers were not alone in voicing disparaging attitudes about education for women. Such beliefs were commonplace in the working-class community. Zélia Gattai, the daughter of Italian immigrants, repeated the popular refrain echoed in the admonitions of a neighbor and friend, also from Italy, who kept her three daughters out of school altogether. "A woman's place is in the home! What a daughter of mine needs to learn is how to take care of her husband and her house. Now that is what she needs, not school. Schools are not for women. Women need to know how to read? Why? To send letters to their boyfriends?"[12]

Parents sometimes pulled children out of school before they entered the paid labor force, so that they could contribute to the upkeep of the household. Daughters, in particular, grew into valuable home helpers. Dona Odette Alves de Almeida "didn't have time to study," because her stepmother needed her for babysitting, to deliver her father's lunch pail, and for other errands and chores, all of which took precedence over attending school.[13] Born in 1916 in Belemzinho, dona Odette lost her mother two years later, as well as an uncle and a grandfather, all victims of the *grippe espanhola* (Spanish flu), which took the highest toll in the crowded working-class neighborhoods of the city. In the following passage, dona Odette describes the circumstances that interrupted her schooling.

> After my stepmother married my father, she became pregnant right away, and soon she took me out of school to take care of the baby. . . . Once the boy started walking, she put me back in school. But it wasn't long before she was pregnant again, and then she took me out of school once more. So, I never got past the second grade. The last time I went back to school, I passed up to the third grade, but then my stepmother took me out again. I cried so much, but she wouldn't let me stay. . . . That's when I went to work. I was just a girl, thirteen years old. I started to work to help out, because my father had fallen on hard times. Back then, life was difficult. Life is good for the rich, but for the poor it's always been hard.[14]

With a neighbor's help, dona Odette got her first job at the Linhas Corrente textile factory, a large British-owned firm located in the Ipiranga neighborhood.[15]

Even before dona Giorgina Nascimento Martins entered the textile mills where she would spend twenty-six years of her life, financial pressures pushed her out of school in 1924, at the age of seven. In that year dona Giorgina's mother, a Portuguese immigrant and longtime textile worker, saw her earnings plummet when an electricity shortage forced factories to limit their schedule of operations to just two or three days per week.[16] To compensate for the loss in income, she put dona Giorgina and her brother, the two sole survivors of eight children, to work as street vendors. They sold a variety of items, including produce grown on a garden plot near their home in the Villa Maria Zélia, located in the Belemzinho neighborhood:

> We'd go to the entrance of the soccer field, set up a twenty-liter can of water, and boil up corn on the cob. I don't remember how much we sold it for anymore. . . . I also sold lettuce, my brother sold eggs. The two of us would go down to the Rua Rio Bonito and buy *sonhos* [cream puffs] and go selling door-to-door here in the villa. If I wanted to go to the movies, I'd try to sell a lot to please my mother so she'd let me go to the Cinema Melita.[17]

After a few years of vending, dona Giorgina found work in Simão and Cia., a cardboard box factory across town. She and a neighborhood friend named Marina used to walk to work together, leaving at six in the morning in order to reach the factory in the Cambuci district by seven o'clock.

> Once a large caldron of glue spilled on top of me, and they had to give me a bath right there in the factory. I don't like to think back on how much I suffered in there. My hair was really long at the time, because my mother wouldn't let me cut it. One of those strict customs of the Portuguese. . . . In those days, a woman who cut her hair short was a *mulher vagabunda* [tramp]. That's what they used to think, that she had no morals, no shame. I wore my hair in a long ponytail or in a braid. I hated my childhood because of that hairstyle and everything else. My mother wouldn't let me go with girls who wore short skirts. Marina used to wear a short skirt, her parents were German. My skirt was long, down to my ankles.
>
> So, the two of us used to go to work together *no fim de Judas* [at the ends of the earth]. They used to hit us over the head with the boxes. Nowadays people complain. Back then, if you carried too many boxes, the man didn't like it. If you didn't carry enough, he said you didn't want to work and BOOM! [he came down] on your head with a cardboard box.[18]

In 1928, when dona Giorgina turned twelve, her mother asked a nephew who worked as a supervisor in a textile mill in Cambuci to get her daughter a job as an apprentice weaver.

> If you knew how much I suffered there, too. It was far, far, far away. . . . And I said, dear God in heaven, is that where I have to go to go to work? How I used to cry. When I hear someone say that they don't like to work in such and such a factory, I can understand what they mean. Because I used to cry, I didn't like to work there. But I had to, right? You had to work.[19]

Dona Giorgina was subsequently relieved to find a job closer to home. Along with a Hungarian friend, she went to work for Fumagalli, a small operation that started out with just eight weaving looms.

> The man [the owner] used to come to my house looking for me if I didn't go to work. It was shift work there. If someone didn't show up, he would come and get me. If I was on from 2 P.M. to 10 P.M., I was at home in the morning. So if someone was absent, he used to come to get me. That's how much he needed [workers]. . . . We really helped him a lot. We used to work sixteen and even twenty hours a day. My mother would send me my food. As the factory expanded, and everything got organized, then we worked less, only eight hours a day.[20]

Like dona Giorgina Nascimento, the early occupational trajectory of dona Ermínia Albertini also began outside the textile industry. She took her first job in a cracker factory, the Fábrica de Biscoitos São Luis, in 1933, when she was eleven years old. From her house in Belém it was a long commute to the factory in Villa Mariana.

> Imagine, at eleven years of age, I was getting up at four o'clock in the morning, so that I could get to my job by seven. . . . All I had for breakfast was coffee and bread with butter, and I would bring a lunch. My poor mother used to get up before dawn to go get bread, so that we could bring it nice and fresh, because that's when the bakery opened, too. While the water [for coffee] was coming to a boil, she went out to get the bread. I worked from seven to eleven, and then took lunch between eleven and twelve. The wife of the factory owner used to make us a plate of soup, but after a while she ended up forgetting to do that. During the winter months, we used to freeze to death. . . . Once we went to ask for some help to cover the transportation costs, in view of what we were

doing for him, and he refused to give it to us. . . . I worked there for a year and then I was fired. Because one night it rained, it rained for the entire night. The kind of rain that makes you think the sky is coming down. My mother didn't wake me or my sister, and the others didn't go either.

And the next day, when we got to work, our pay stubs were all ready. He didn't even want to hear the reason why [we hadn't gone to work]. He showed no consideration for the fact that it took us two hours to get there, to help, to teach the other girls. . . . There were ten to twelve young girls working there. All the same age. That's what he wanted, young girls. We used to talk among ourselves, we just weren't allowed to eat. The *patrão* didn't allow anyone to eat the crackers. When you ate, you had to eat in secret. And we ate. We were hungry. I used to get up at four in the morning, had my coffee, and when I got to the factory at seven I was dying of hunger. I used to eat, I never gave it a second thought. I hid and ate. It's just that they were hard crackers, they were difficult to swallow, but I ate them. The patrão didn't like it. Sometimes he would say to the foreman, "What is this, everybody in here chewing?" The foreman would tell him, "Oh, let the girls eat a couple of crackers." The foreman was good to us. "Ah, let them eat, the poor things."

At Christmas time, the baker used to make a *panettone* [fruit cake] for us on the sly. He made a panettone for himself, for his own consumption, he used to ask permission to do that. He made sure to leave some extra dough, and then with the leftovers, he made a panettone for us. This was all done secretly, we hid it under the shelf that was there, and everyone ate so that no one would see. Incredible, isn't it, just to eat a piece of panettone? All young girls, twelve or thirteen years old. When I think about it, I get very angry about these things. At the time, I didn't see it. I was a young girl. I wasn't aware of what was going on. I wanted to have fun, right? That's what I wanted, to have fun.[21]

After being fired from Biscoitos São Luis, dona Ermínia got a job in the Cristalaria Aliança, a glass-blowing factory where her brothers worked. It was on the Rua Cezário Alvim, only five minutes away from her house, which offered distinct advantages.

At that point my life had improved a little, my life as a young girl, right? Because I really enjoyed playing with dolls, and when I was working in the cracker factory, there was no time for playing *com aquela a minha luta* [with that struggle of mine]. So then after that, I could play dolls, play my games. I had more freedom to do my own things.[22]

In the textile industry it was common for children to work alongside their parents, and younger siblings often followed their older brothers and sisters into the mills. "One sister would bring along another," explained dona Ermínia, who left her job at the Cristalaria at fourteen, when she was hired by the textile firm where her sister worked.

> In general, if there was one sister in a factory, there would soon be two, because as soon as a job would open up, she would get her sister to take it. . . . It was also important to get a job close to home, so that you didn't have to rely on public transportation. You made a point of finding something nearby. And if you had someone from your family in the same factory, you felt more secure.[23]

While personal contacts were a valuable resource for initiates to industrial work, parents who were consigned to send their daughters into the mills also counted family and neighborhood connections on the factory shop floor among the advantages that textile work had to offer. The wages, though modest, were still higher than what was paid in food-processing plants or in domestic service, the two other most common occupations for working-class women.[24] And for struggling *colono* (tenant) families living on coffee plantations in the paulista interior, the hope of sending their children, especially daughters, into the textile mills could motivate migration to the capital, a move unequivocally described as representing a step up in life. Dona Assunta Bianchi recounted how her parents, Italian immigrants who had grown up working on coffee plantations in Espírito Santo do Pinhal, decided to head for the city of São Paulo with their three sons and three daughters in 1924. "We were three women," dona Assunta explained, referring to her sisters and herself:

> So people began telling my father that factory girls in São Paulo earned a lot of money. That it didn't make sense for my dad to remain in the countryside, sending his girls out to weed the coffee groves, now that we had become young women. When we came to São Paulo, my sister was seventeen, I was sixteen, and the other fifteen. So we were all grown up and able to work in the mills. Besides, a factory was cleaner than the fields. You didn't have to work outside under the hot sun, or get soaked working in the rain.[25]

Besides ranking factory work above agricultural work, and in addition to the material incentive of higher wages, São Paulo's southern European immigrants found another reason to prefer textile employment for their daughters, particularly over domestic service, a sector that mainly employed women of color. Because domestic servants worked in isolation behind the closed doors of another man's private residence, the risks for sexual exploitation at the hands of the employer were perceived to be greater than in industry, although women working in factories were similarly subjected to various forms of sexual abuse.[26] Yet in an interesting twist on the public/private dichotomy, it was the public aspect of industrial employment that made the textile mills appear safer, a perception buttressed by the wide prevalence of kinship networks in the factories.[27] Such beliefs, moreover, ultimately found common ground in the thinking of employers, who in turn manipulated gender ideology in ways that would serve their own particular interests.

Labor Recruitment in the Textile Industry and the Mill Job Hierarchy

The hierarchical ordering of the textile production process was fundamentally rooted in differences of age and gender. To support their heavy reliance on female and child labor, paulista textile manufacturers were drawn to familiar explanations that turned on stereotyped definitions of gender differences that deemed women, especially young women, "naturally" suited for the rhythms and demands of textile work. Following the kind of logic that has resonated in the views of employers across time and in a variety of settings in order to rationalize socially constructed labor hierarchies, they clung to the notion that women possessed innate emotional, physical, and intellectual characteristics that supposedly harmonized well with particular aspects of the textile production process.

Nimble fingers, a skillful eye, and patient diligence were feminine attributes that allegedly matched neatly with the requirements of most machine-tending jobs in the weaving room. Similar arguments were advanced about the spinning section, where, with the exception of supervisory personnel, the labor force was largely if not entirely female. And although the tasks involved were exacting and extremely repetitive, and the pace of production was unrelenting, textile manufacturers categorically described the work as light and easy, requiring little effort. In short, this was work fit for women. As one industrialist put it, "Jobs in textile factories are easy, so easy, in fact, that women and minors of both sexes dominate the labor force."[28] The spinning room was the particular reserve of young women, and offered the lowest-

Women working cocoon-reeling machines in a silk factory, Campinas, São Paulo, circa 1925. Courtesy of the photographs collection, library of the Ministry of Labor, Brasília, Brazil.

paid positions in the industry, jobs that the factory owners likened to "child's play," and that, they argued further, were beneath the dignity of any self-respecting man.[29]

The top textile positions were in machine repair and supervision, both areas that generally employed men only, although women were sometimes hired to supervise the work of other women. And while the textile workforce remained predominantly female, women were excluded from industry-sponsored training programs and from vocational schools subsequently founded by the government for working-class youth. The courses open to women focused not on training them for paid employment, but instead on perfecting their domestic skills, so that when the time came, they might better fulfill the proper female wife/mother role.[30]

That the large-scale entry of women into industrial occupations threatened the very foundations of the gendered social order was not entirely lost on paulista textile manufacturers, the employers responsible for hiring the bulk of women working in Brazilian factories. Perhaps partially in response, their attempts to resolve the cultural paradox of the woman worker were focused on defusing the perceived threats to the coherence of family life, and

Workers in the spinning room of a São Paulo cotton mill, circa
1925. Courtesy of the photographs collection, library of the
Ministry of Labor, Brasília, Brazil.

Men supervised the work of girls and women employed in the
winding room of this silk mill, Campinas, São Paulo, circa 1925.
Courtesy of the photographs collection, library of the Ministry
of Labor, Brasília, Brazil.

more specifically, the female sexuality that had emerged as a negative social consequence of rapid industrialization.[31] Thus, it was precisely because of its familial character that the industrialist Jorge Street defended factory employment as a safe and socially acceptable wage-earning activity for working-class women. In a well-known 1917 interview from which the following excerpt is taken, Street justified hiring young women workers by positing the "safe" moral environment of the textile mill, while implicitly questioning the moral "safety" of working-class homes and neighborhoods:

> In São Paulo, where I employ almost 3,000 workers, more than 1,100 are young women between the ages of fifteen and eighteen. Physically, they are as strong as their older *companheiras,* and they produce and earn equivalent salaries. I must also say that among them [the women aged fifteen to eighteen] are to be found the best women workers there are, rivaling many of the male workers. These young women belong to groups of families who work in the factories I run in São Paulo.
>
> These families are often comprised of four or five members: father, mother, and one, two, or even three teenage daughters, or one or two children. There are families earning 400$000 [milreis] and 500$000 per month, and some earn as much as 600$000. What is the problem [with this type of arrangement]? This is also common in all the other factories as well. Is a young woman of sixteen or seventeen safer at home, better protected from *qualquer mau passo* [any moral transgression] than she would be working in a factory? Certainly not.[32]

While a heavy reliance on categories of workers whose tenure for employment was defined as auxiliary and/or temporary exerted a downward pressure on wages in the industry overall, paulista textile manufacturers justified their hiring preferences on the grounds that employers in the city faced a chronic shortage of labor.[33] "Scarcity and extremely high wages are the realities, in spite of theoretical or opportunistic fictions of labor surplus and low pay," declared the industrialist Eduardo Jafet, in a statement typical of the manufacturing class during the 1920s.[34] It thus followed that employing women and children was nothing less than a virtual necessity if the aim of advancing industrial progress was indeed to come to fruition.

Despite the manufacturers' persistent claims to the contary, unemployment continued to be a nagging feature of the industrializing economy of São Paulo throughout the first decades of the century.[35] Rather than facing a shortage of workers, employers were actually able to draw from an unskilled labor pool glutted with men, women, and children. Except for a temporary hiatus during World War I, the labor market remained saturated with the ongoing influx of immigrant workers from overseas, and with the chronic attrition of colono families from coffee plantations in the São Paulo country-side. Because racism largely closed industrial employment opportunities to Afro-Brazilians living in the city of São Paulo during the early decades of the twentieth century, the competition for industrial jobs was played out mainly within the southern European immigrant community, and it divided along lines of age and gender.[36]

What paulista manufacturers labeled a labor shortage might have been more aptly called an undesirable incidence of labor mobility. Job abandon-ment, one of the few recourses available to dissatisfied workers, in turn had a detrimental impact on levels of productivity.[37] Some employers responded by providing subsidized worker housing. They built vilas operárias, a model with roots dating back to the founding of the first modern textile factories in northeastern Brazil during the early nineteenth century.[38]

By connecting workers to their jobs through the provision of low-rent housing, employers institutionalized a family-based labor system that in prac-tice tended to operate more informally throughout the industry. On the one hand a fundamental working-class survival strategy, such a system also held obvious benefits for patrões who, even in the absence of vilas operárias, as-sumed that working-class households depended on multiple wage-earners. That assumption was used to justify the failure to pay a living wage to indi-vidual workers. Complaints about low wages that surfaced during a wave of textile strikes in 1924, for example, elicited the following response from the industrialist Octávio Pupo Nogueira:

> Fanfulla [an Italian newspaper in São Paulo] alleges that according to payroll records of a certain textile factory [in the capital], salaries paid to male heads of households do not exceed 262$000 per month. But as a rule, their wives and children also work in the same factory. These workers are members of the same family, and obviously, they are not working for free.[39]

Mill owners who provided low-rent housing sometimes extended addi-tional social welfare benefits to their workers, and others funded leisure ac-tivities as well. Described by one contemporary observer as part of a laudable effort to "help to ease somewhat the wearisome monotony of the worker's life," factory-sponsored recreation was also aimed at persuading workers to steer clear of "bars, taverns, and other places of vice, and particularly, to keep them away from alcohol and gambling."[40] These activities were considered especially undesirable because of their potential for undermining the work ethic, and for disrupting harmony in the working-class family, the unit that formed the basic building block on which rested the stability of the entire factory labor force.[41]

Under the vila operária plan, families served as the primary mechanism for the recruitment of labor. As a result, employers enjoyed direct and easy access to child workers like dona Ernestina Maniasse Gonçalves who, along with three older sisters, took her first job at the Maria Zélia cotton mill when she was very young, working from seven o'clock in the morning until five in the afternoon with a ninety-minute lunch break. "The boss used to pick me up and carry me in his arms, that is how very small I was," recalled the former textile worker, a resident of the Villa Maria Zélia since 1919.[42]

As in other workers' villas around the city of São Paulo, the size of the house allocated to residents of the Villa Maria Zélia depended on how many family members worked in the factory. Two workers were required to rent the smallest house, three or four workers could rent a two-bedroom house, and at least five family members had to be employed in the factory in order to rent the three-bedroom house, the largest model on the site. Rents ranged from 20$000 to 50$000 milreis per month. According to one contemporary account, that was considerably lower than rental rates outside the villa, where the average adult (male) worker, who earned between 200$000 and 300$000 milreis per month, paid between 100$000 and 120$000 milreis for housing.[43]

The story of dona Cinta Ramos, the woman introduced in the opening paragraphs of this essay, provides one example of the vila operária system at work, while also illustrating the extraordinary geographic mobility characteristic of the European immigrant population in São Paulo during the early decades of this century. For the Ramos family, their arrival in the Villa Maria Zélia in 1919 represented the final stop on a lengthy trek in search of work and financial security. They had immigrated from Cádiz to São Paulo in 1905, and after a brief and unsuccessful stay in the capital city, the family took to the rails, bound initially for coffee country, where they settled in Jaú, located in west-central São Paulo in the region known as the Planalto Paulista Occidental. Shortly thereafter, the Ramoses abandoned the coffee groves to seek factory work for the oldest boys. Heading back south, they went to Jundiaí, a small town with several textile mills. In 1909 they moved again, this time to Sorocaba, the city where dona Cinta, one of nine children to survive out of twenty, was born. In Sorocaba, three of her brothers took jobs as weavers in Votorantim. However, in the mass firings that followed in the wake of a great strike at the factory in 1919, the boys lost their jobs and the Ramos family lost their home.[44]

On the road once more, the Ramoses made their final move, to the nearby capital city. Learning through the grapevine about the recent opening of Jorge Street's new cotton mill with worker housing, they went to the Villa Maria Zélia. Three sons and a daughter took mill jobs, while their aged father continued to eke out a marginal living as a *bicheiro,* a bookmaker for the popular form of street gambling called *jogo de bicho.* Later, the *prefeito* (mayor) of the workers' villa, Dr. Luiz Torres, who was married to a niece of the factory owner's wife, Zélia Street, approached senhora Ramos with instructions that, in order to remain in the three-bedroom home that they had begun renting, it would be necessary to send another child into the mill.[45] In the following passage, dona Cinta relates her memory of that conversation.

> "You'll have to put another one of your girls to work," he told my mother. "But I can't," she explained, "because my twelve-year-old is very sick, and I can't send her to work in the condition she's in. And my other, she's not yet eleven." "Send her anyway," urged the mayor. "We'll give her an easy little job, and that way you'll have the number of workers you need to stay in your house."[46]

So, rather than choosing employment for the older of the two girls, a victim of the devastating 1918 Spanish flu epidemic, who was still recuperating from the effects of the illness that nearly claimed her life, ten-year-old Cinta went to work. Dona Cinta started out as a helper in the spinning section of the mill, a low-paying entry job typically assigned to the youngest female employees. Dona Cinta guessed that she earned about 120$000 a month for sweeping floors in the spinning room.

> I used to get a *vale* [voucher] for 50$000 milreis. We had the company store here, and everyone took out vouchers on the first day of each month, so that they could go do their shopping. At the end of every month, all the vouchers were sent up to the main office, and on the fourteenth, that was payday, whatever was left over, you received in cash.[47]

With four older siblings also employed in the mill, dona Cinta occupied the lowest rung on the family totem pole, and her mother arranged for the monthly rent to be subtracted from her wages: "They [the factory] deducted the house from my pay, 50$000 milreis, and I received the voucher for 50$000 milreis. I never brought money home. My pay packet always came back empty. They subtracted for the house, for the vouchers. And so my pay envelope, it was always empty."[48] By pooling the wages, or, perhaps more accurately, the vouchers that their children earned in exchange for working in the cotton mill, the Ramoses were able to feed their family.

> On the first day of each month, my mother used to buy four or five pieces of dried salt cod. We put them to hang in the kitchen. We always had enough to eat in our house. We bought everything at the company store, parmesan cheese—all good stuff—wine, and on Fridays and Saturdays, we'd pick up some beer and soda.
>
> My mother also bought cigarettes there by the carton, and fabric, remnants that they sold by the kilo at a cheap price, only to the workers. When we finished something, my mother would say, "Go over to the *armazém* [store], ask Oliveira if there's enough left on the voucher to bring some more home."[49]

"My mother used to buy nine kilos, a can, of butter at the beginning of the month," dona Cinta continued,

> But it wouldn't last all month. We used to run out about three days before the next month when we'd get another voucher. So I'd go over to the armazém. "Go ahead, take the can," he'd tell me, "when the new voucher gets here, I'll subtract from that one."
>
> Here in the villa, we were the ones who spent the most money. Anytime something new came in, we used to like to try it. Oliveira used to say, "Hey Ramos, *tem novidade aqui* [we've got something new here]." Those drinks, *licores,* like *rum negrita,* they were so delicious! Then at the end of the month, we would go down to see how much was left on the voucher, and maybe tell him "give me so much of this or so much of that" in order to use up the little that remained. Or if we wanted to make the most of it, we'd tighten our belts a bit and hold back to wait until the new voucher came in.[50]

"So, we earned enough to make it through the month," dona Cinta explained in conclusion. "But never did we earn enough to put any money aside, to save anything. But it was enough to go from month to month, to get by like that. However, as far as for putting food on the table, that much we were able to do. We always had enough to eat and drink."[51]

From the standpoint of unmarried children who worked in São Paulo's textile factories, employment did not confer much in the way of individual autonomy. Rather, both sons and daughters put their wages in the *caixinha,* as the common household fund was called, which was administered by mothers. "In my house we always had a common purse," explained senhor Giácomo Ordóñez, who labored in the São Paulo textile mills along with his mother, father, six sisters, and three brothers.

> Each of us who earned a salary, we gave it to my mother. She was the one in charge of the money. Even to buy a pair of shoes, anything like that, you needed to talk to her. But she always took good care of us, too. It was up to her to decide whether our shoes needed fixing, we didn't see to that. Our responsibility was to go out to work and to bring home the money we earned, and she was the one who decided if our shoes needed shining or not, if they needed to be repaired, or when it was time to buy a new pair.[52]

Since factory wages were not sufficiently high to support economic independence, working sons and daughters usually continued to reside with relatives or with *compadres* (godparents), people who were like family, while the boarding houses in working-class districts attracted renters from the pool of new arrivals without any personal connections in the city. At twenty-eight, textile worker dona Odette Alves de Almeida still surrendered her pay packet to her stepmother, the envelope *fechadinho* (sealed tight).

> After work, if the other girls bought an ice cream, I made up some excuse—that my throat was bothering me and I'd catch cold if I ate ice cream. . . . Until the day I got married, I never had money. It all went into my stepmother's hands. I wasn't even allowed to open up my pay packet to check that my pay was right. . . . All I ever had was bus fare, and when I didn't bring food along with me to work, I was given 400 reis for lunch. A roll cost 200 reis, and with what was left I bought either a bit of cheese or a few slices of mortadella. It was one or the other, there wasn't enough money for both. . . . I didn't want to fight about it. If you fight, you live fighting, and that is hell. But things weren't like they are today, where girls leave home to live alone, with friends. If they have *juízo* [good sense], nothing happens to them. I couldn't move out, because in those days, if a girl left her parents and her home, people would talk. Any girl who left was considered a *moça perdida* [fallen woman]. She would be gossiped about, and her chances for getting married would be ruined. I could have gone to live with my grandmother or my grandfather, but I decided against it because I didn't want to start a big fight in the family. I gave it a lot of thought, but in the end I decided not to go.[53]

Some daughters, however, like dona Assunta Bianchi, eventually challenged parental control over their earnings. Thirty-eight years old in 1947, dona Assunta had never married and was still living at home with her parents and a younger unmarried brother. For over twenty years, ever since her family had moved from the countryside to the capital in 1924 and she had taken her first textile job at the age of sixteen, dona Assunta had been turning over all the wages she earned as a weaver to the common family purse. The decision to begin paying room and board came when her parents and a younger brother started up a small cheese factory adjacent to their home.

> All of us who lived at home, we had always handed our pay over to our mother. But once they opened the cheese factory, my mother began plowing all the money into the factory, everything into the factory. So then I started thinking about what would happen to me if my parents died, or if my younger brother got married. . . . My parents' house was in my brother's name. I'd be left with nothing. And I didn't want to end up having to depend on my brothers to support me. I needed to start saving my own money, so that I'd be able to have something for myself, somewhere to live, when I retired.[54]

Above and beyond the obligation to earn wages, parents also expected daughters to shoulder a share of the domestic work. For dona Odette Alves de Almeida, her weekdays began at 4 A.M. First there was the trip to the bakery for bread, then the preparation of the morning coffee and other chores before leaving in time for the seven o'clock shift at the factory. The shift ended at 5 P.M., but dona Odette normally put in a couple of hours of overtime before returning home, where it would be time to help with the evening meal.[55] Weekends, as dona Assunta Bianchi explained, were spent finishing the household chores that had accumulated during the week. "On Saturday afternoons and Sundays, I washed down the house, cleaned the yard. I saw to all the work that needed to be done. You didn't have to tell me what to do. I knew what had to be done and I did it."[56] Like dona Assunta, dona Cinta Ramos took pride in the help she gave her mother around the house.

> The house had to be washed. Washing made it very white. Every Saturday or Sunday, or on a holiday, we washed the whole house. Because our house wasn't made of tile, we had to wash all the walls and the floors with soap powder. You know, my mother didn't have to tell me what to do. I took the initiative. As soon as we finished dinner—we used to eat in the

living room because the kitchen was small, too small to accommodate nine people—I cleared off the table and came through to the kitchen. I never went out to see my *para namorar* [boyfriend] until the dishes and the kitchen were cleaned up. My mother only had to wash the lunch dishes, because we just had an hour and a half for lunch. I ironed at night. On Sunday mornings we washed clothes. But the big things, sheets and tablecloths, we sent to a washerwoman here in the villa. . . . Every week we scoured the aluminum pots and pans. Because we had a shelf up on the wall where we put them for everyone to see. They looked so pretty, the aluminum shined so bright that the pans looked like they were made of silver.[57]

Haim Grünspun evoked similar images of lustrous cookware in his vivid reminiscences of his childhood years growing up in the largely Italian enclave of Bexiga. In an intimate portrayal of everyday life in the immigrant neighborhood, Grünspun writes that well-scoured pots and pans were everywhere a familiar sight. Prominently displayed by bairro residents, they served as a yardstick for measuring a woman's housekeeping abilities.[58]

Just as daughters learned from an early age to value their domestic talents, some also spoke of the satisfaction they derived from their factory jobs, work more commonly associated with feelings of alienation. Weavers expressed particular pride in their ability to master the skills their job demanded. Dona Odette Alves de Almeida described why she became a weaver in 1931, at the age of fifteen, after a few years in the spinning section of the Linhas Corrente factory.

I was determined to learn how to weave. In those days, people used to say that a weaver earned more than a schoolteacher. And it was the truth. Back when I learned how to weave, weavers who earned 500$000 milreis per month did earn more than a teacher. Where I had been working, I earned 100$000 to 115$000 milreis every two weeks. It didn't amount to 300$000 in a month. But I was earning okay. It wasn't bad. But I wanted to earn more. . . . What I really liked were the looms. I always liked weaving. I adored it and I wanted to learn. Once I did, I liked it even more. I had a knack for it. . . . Back then, a weaver was an artist. We made beautiful cloth, fabric with lovely designs.[59]

Dona Odette returned to the theme of skill, using the verb *tocar* (to play, as in a musical instrument) when she described working as a weaver in 1946 at the Ítalo-Brasileira factory on the Rua Joly in Brás.

The weaver who worked two looms in that factory was an artist. You couldn't work more than that. [Não pôde tocar mais, não.] You made well-finished cloth, fabric that was ready to be sold. It wasn't washed or dyed, it went straight to the customer. Tailors would buy directly from that factory. It was a beautiful kind of work.[60]

Dona Cinta Ramos, also a weaver, depicted the work process in a similar way:

To see the loom at work was a beautiful thing to watch. Everything going at once, all the spools turning around at the same time. It was beautiful. . . . Working those machines was not something that just anyone could do. You needed to be an artist, really. You had to have the will to work and the skill to work. The machine is kind of dangerous, you know, and when you're just learning, you're afraid to stop the spool. It's frightening to put your finger on it while it's spinning around.[61]

In another description of the artistry in weaving (prior to the de-skilling wrought by the introduction of machinery requiring workers to tend an ever-increasing number of looms), dona Giorgina Nascimento Martins displayed a competitiveness echoed by other weavers of her generation:

At Fumagalli, I worked with Patrícia on a Jacquard loom. It was satisfying work. I also worked at weaving *pano xadrez* (checkered cloth). That was very complicated. But if I were to go back to work today, I think that if I spent a few hours there, it would all come back to me. Even with all the years I have on my back. Sometimes when I am in bed, I start to think, let me see, what was it like to be at the loom? And I remember how I enjoyed it. When it came to working, I was ambitious. I wanted to work by the piece: the more you produced, the more you earned. It's not to brag, but I used to beat any partner I had. All of my partners lost to me. When I was on the night shift, another woman came and worked on my machine during the day. I always earned more than they did. Always. I was like this, I didn't want anyone to do better than I did on my loom. If it was someone else's loom, it didn't matter. But on mine, I had to be the winner. And I used to win, I don't know why. I would win. As soon as I got [to work], I would go to see how much she had done. Then I had to go and produce more![62]

Dona Cinta Ramos displayed a similarly irrepressible spirit of self-confidence in discussing her work. When I asked her if she had ever been fined on the job, she answered: "No, not me. Poor them if they had dared to try to fine me. [Coitado deles se me multassem.] Not me. I wove cloth that was very well made. That time that I made that defect I hadn't seen, that was the only time anything like that happened. I was always careful in watching [my work]."[63] The defect dona Cinta referred to occurred when she worked at the Ítalo-Brasileira mill, owned by manufacturer António de Camillis. In her description of that incident, dona Cinta used her pride in her weaving skill as a weapon of self-defense against what she considered to be an unjust criticism of her work:

> I hadn't seen what was on the underside [of the material], my eyes were there on top, not underneath. I was called in to the quality control room. The patrão was there. He was an old man, his hair was all white, *coitadinho*. I walked in, with my head held high. I said to the foreman, "What's going on here? Why have you all called me in here?"
>
> "Well, look here," he said, pointing to the defect.
>
> "Oh, really?" I said back to him. "But listen, Sr. Martim, I am not underneath the loom. My eyes are on top of the loom. Am I right or am I wrong, Sr. António? How was I supposed to see that? I only noticed it when I turned the piece of cloth over. What was I supposed to do about it then? Why don't you take that piece off? Use it as a remnant. *Puxa, porra,* my cloth comes in cleaner than anyone else's here."
>
> "Now, why is this happening—because the *cerzideiras* [darners] pointed me out?" I turned to them [the darners] and I said, "What do you want? Are you coming to work expecting to do nothing here? Do you want all the cloth in perfect condition? If they don't want to darn the cloth, then you don't need cerzideiras."
>
> I always spoke my mind. [Eu sempre tinha voz ativa para falar.] That's why I always tell my daughters to do a good job, to show care in what they do, to keep their desks clean. Some people are very messy, with papers everywhere. So that when you speak out you feel that you are justified. People who are disorganized can't talk. Sr. António said that everything was okay, and that I was free to go. I worked very hard, I produced a lot, but when it came time to defend myself, I wasn't afraid. I had a voice. [Eu tinha voz.][64]

Even though they valued their skills at the loom, factory work was not something that weavers like dona Cinta, dona Giorgina, or dona Odette wished for their own daughters. Indeed, they felt fortunate to have seen their girls grow up to take white-collar jobs in the city, working in clerical positions or as schoolteachers. Dona Ermínia Albertini was similarly thankful that her daughter, an only child who became a primary-school teacher, was able to take advantage of educational opportunities that had been beyond the reach of women of her own class and generation. For at the same time that dona Ermínia took pride in the contributions she had made to the material support of her family as a child, she still regretted not having received an education.

> I wanted to study so much, but there never was enough money. Never. . . . I wanted to become a typist. That was a beautiful job in those days. I wanted to learn how to make artificial flowers, hats. I thought all those things were beautiful. I wanted to be a seamstress, a hairdresser. I wanted to be all these things, and I became nothing. . . . Besides, your mother thought you should go to work. That was how you were raised. What could you do about it? This was just like the way your mother told you that you were born to get married. And that's what our mothers told us, of course. That you're a girl, that you'd been born to be a housewife. They didn't think that it made sense for a girl to study. Why should a girl need to study so much? . . . These were the kinds of things your parents drummed into your head ever since you were little . . . things that your parents forced on you.[65]

A daughter's wage work thus tended to be seen as a temporary stepping stone toward marriage and motherhood, ideals that figured prominently in the upbringing of young working-class women. And indeed for many, getting married was the rite of passage to adulthood. Still, whether they married for love or other reasons, women harbored few illusions about what lay in store after marriage vows were exchanged. As dona Ermínia put it:

> When I was single, I had as much fun as I could, because I knew that things change so much after you get married. I always went to all the parties and dances. I'd be the first to arrive and the last to leave, so people used to call me the *arroz da festa* [the life of the party]. As long as the band kept playing, I was there. You should take advantage of everything you could while you were still single, that's what I thought. That way, after you got married, if you could still go out and do things that would be fine, but if not, well then, at least you would already have had your fun.[66]

Years of helping with the housework provided working-class women with valuable training for married life. However, because the subject of sexuality was taboo, women were not as well informed about their own bodies. Consequently, whether they desired it or not, pregnancy often followed on the heels of marriage. Given the countervailing pressures in their lives, women evinced mixed feelings about motherhood. Dona Odette Alves de Almeida explained that she had "wanted children more than anything."[67] Married at the age of thirty, dona Odette soon thereafter gave birth to a son, and then to a daughter, but when the infant girl died of pneumonia one month later, she explained: "I thought I wouldn't be able to have any more children. Well, it's not that it wasn't possible for me to have more, but my situation was so bad, my financial situation, that I really needed to go back to work. So, how was I going to be able to stay at home and raise another baby?"[68]

Economic realities and the need to seek employment made women want to limit family size, but this depended on cooperation from their partners, something that was not always forthcoming. Condoms were the only contraceptive available at the time, and they were disliked by many. After discovering that she had become pregnant yet again, one woman remembered confronting her husband with the news. "You drink your pinga, and I pay the price," was how she put it. Faced with an unwanted pregnancy, a woman had few alternatives. It was common knowledge that the doctors people called *matadouros* (butchers) performed illegal abortions, with potentially fatal results. More often, women turned to midwives for homemade remedies that were supposed to induce miscarriage. Such remedies did not always work, and, at worst, they too could be fatal.[69]

The lack of safe and effective means of family planning meant that women lacked the tools they needed to control their fertility, despite their desires to do so. Although statistics for São Paulo during the first half of the twentieth century are sparse, the available evidence suggests that the urban birth rate did not register any significant decrease until the 1940s.[70] But even if women were not able to prevent conception, some attested to having decided to terminate a pregnancy, despite opposition from male partners, or as in one case, from a father who disapproved of a decision made by a married couple.

In other instances, the financial burden of numerous offspring could actually become too much to bear, as the experience of dona Maria Cubero makes painfully clear. A daughter of Spanish colonos, and one of five children, dona Maria grew up in the interior of São Paulo. Unable to make ends meet, dona Maria's parents made the heart-wrenching decision to part with two of their children before migrating to the capital.[71] While parents who found themselves in equally dire straits sometimes relinquished their children to Catholic orphanages, dona Maria's parents decided instead on a private arrangement.[72] They gave a son and a daughter to the wealthy wife of a coffee planter. Shortly after arriving in the city of São Paulo, however, dona Maria's mother died of a sudden illness. Saddled with three young children who were all still too young to work, dona Maria's father got a job in the Jafet textile factory. Three months later, on payday, he vanished, abandoning his children to the care of relatives. He was never seen or heard from again, nor was dona Maria ever able to locate her siblings who had been entrusted to the *fazendeiro*'s wife.[73]

Domestic Work and Paid Work: Reconciling Conflicting Demands

Whether or not women continued to work in the textile mills after marriage or after they became mothers essentially boiled down to a matter of money. Financial pressures often loomed largest before children were old enough to work. As children grew into young wage earners, it became easier for mothers to withdraw from the paid labor force. Although contemporary sources acknowledge the presence of married women as a long-standing feature of the textile industry, we lack the comprehensive data that would be necessary to reconstruct employment patterns based on age, gender, and marital status.[74] Information drawn from one cotton mill in the capital, the Sociedade Anónima Cotonifício Paulista, sheds new light on the subject, though its restricted nature necessarily limits the scope of our conclusions.[75]

Established by Italian immigrant Giovanni Baptista Scuracchio, the Sociedade Anónima Cotonifício Paulista was founded with a capital base of 500:000$000.[76] Located on the Avenida Celso Garcia, in the heart of the working-class factory district of Brás, the Cotonifício Paulista first opened its doors in 1922. In 1935, the medium-sized cotton mill employed 473 workers. The proportion of men and women in its labor force, indicated in Figure 1, conformed to the general pattern existing in the industry as a whole during the period 1900 to 1950.[77]

Similarly, the age distribution of female workers in the Cotonifício Paulista in 1935, illustrated in Figure 2, also reflected an industrywide pattern, one that remained relatively unchanged throughout the first half of the twentieth century.[78]

As the Cotonifício Paulista records show, the majority of women workers in 1935 were under thirty years of age. More specifically, of the total number of women working in the factory in 1935, 32 percent were aged fourteen to nineteen, and 23 percent were between the ages of twenty and twenty-nine. Women in the thirty- to thirty-nine-year age bracket represented 21 percent of the total female labor force. Thereafter the figures drop dramatically. Women aged forty to forty-nine represented 10 percent, and those between fifty and fifty-nine, just 3 percent of all the women who were employed in the factory in 1935. It is significant that one-third of all the women working in the mill

Figure 1. Numbers of Men and Women Workers in S.A.
Cotonifício Paulista, 1927–1949

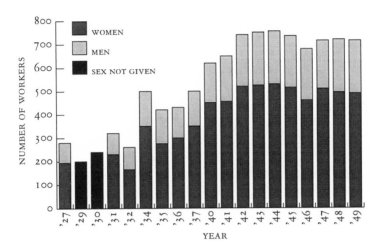

Source: S.A. Cotonifício Paulista, *Relações dos empregados* (personnel rosters) for the years 1927 to
1949. In the archive of the S.A. Cotonifício Paulista.

Figure 2. Age Distribution and Marital Status of Women
Workers in S.A. Cotonifício Paulista, 1935

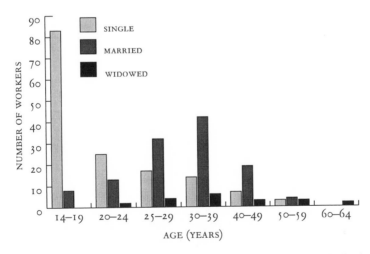

Source: S.A. Cotonifício Paulista, *Fichas de registro dos empregados* (personnel records) for the year
1935. In the archive of the S.A. Cotonifício Paulista.

Figure 3. Length of Employment and Marital Status of Women
Workers in S.A. Cotonifício Paulista, 1935

Source: S.A. Cotonifício Paulista, *Fichas de registro dos empregados* (personnel records) for the year
1935. In the archive of the S.A. Cotonifício Paulista.

in 1935 were over thirty years of age. The vast majority of these women were
married.

The relative proportion of single and married women in the labor force
varied according to age group. Not surprisingly, single women accounted for
90 percent of workers under twenty, while they comprised 46 percent of the
group of women aged twenty to twenty-nine. Married women predominated
among workers over thirty, accounting for 64 percent of workers between
thirty and thirty-nine, and 70 percent of those aged forty to forty-nine. Married women and widows each represented one-third of the small group of
women over fifty.[79]

Clearly the most striking feature to emerge from the records of the Cotonifício Paulista is the remarkable number of women who worked in the factory
for what can be described as long periods of time. As illustrated in Figure 3,
three-fourths of the 278 women employed in 1935 spent more than four years
in the factory. Of this group, 73 women worked between five and ten years,
46 between eleven and fourteen years, and 28 between fifteen and nineteen
years. Thirty-six women worked in the factory for twenty years or longer.

Even though it is not possible to weigh the representativeness of this particular factory with regard to the textile manufacturing sector in the city as a
whole, the long-term employment patterns shown in the Cotonifício Pauli-

sta factory records stand in stark contrast to existing conceptions about the high degree of labor turnover normally associated with the industry. A case study of another textile factory in the capital that was of comparable size to the Cotonifício Paulista, meanwhile, provides an interesting counterpoint to the findings presented above.[80] Using archival materials of the firm Ferrabino e Giaccaglini Ltda., a spinning mill that was founded in 1921 in the Moóca neighborhood, Chiara Vangelista offers a statistical analysis of the quantitative data contained in that factory's personnel records.[81] Compared with the Cotonifício Paulista, Ferrabino e Giaccaglini favored younger workers. Of the 285 workers admitted for employment between 1936 and 1940, 82 percent were between the ages of fourteen and twenty-seven (88 percent of the women who were hired fell into this category, as compared with 75 percent of the men).[82] The youthful workforce is likely explained by the fact that this mill engaged only in spinning operations, a sector that tended to employ the youngest women textile operatives and that also paid the lowest wage rates in the industry.[83]

A more significant contrast distinguishing Ferrabino e Giaccaglini from the Cotonifício Paulista during this period centers on the differing trends in the length of employment registered at the two firms. At Ferrabino and Giaccaglini, more than half the employees who were hired between 1936 and 1940 ended up working in the mill for less than one year, a pattern reflecting the high level of mobility generally associated with the textile labor force. In addition, Vangelista discovered that not a single woman was recorded as having worked in Ferrabino e Giaccaglini for more than fifteen years.[84]

Although Vangelista does not differentiate between married and single women in her study, an examination of the marital status of women workers at the Cotonifício Paulista in conjunction with their employment tenure reveals that three-quarters of the women who worked in the cotton mill for four years or less were single. This may have indicated a greater willingness among younger women to leave the Cotonifício in pursuit of better opportunities in other factories in the city, while older women, because of their different position in the family wage economy, may have been financially less able to risk the uncertainties of a job search and the attendant potential for unemployment. Or, as one longtime millworker suggested, the desire to settle down in one place tended to come with age because workers who moved frequently from one textile factory to another could lose years when the time came to calculate the terms of their retirement benefits. The physical limitations brought by aging, she went on, also made it desirable for older women to stay put, where they could continue working at looms that they knew.[85] The important role that married, older women played in the workforce of the Cotonifício Paulista in 1935 may have also reflected the overall expansion of opportunities for textile employment in the city, as the industry began to emerge from the throes of the worldwide depression. Indeed, it was precisely during this period of economic recovery that São Paulo textile employers first began to actively recruit workers from the city's Afro-Brazilian population.[86]

While a reconstruction of worker employment patterns and a comprehensive demographic profile of the textile labor force must await further research, oral testimonies from former workers open a window on the varied constellations of family circumstances that helped to shape the choices women made regarding factory employment. Certainly there were many reasons for quitting industrial work. Whether male or female, or young or old, all who entered the São Paulo textile mills encountered the harsh conditions that were basic features of factory life. Workers toiled in the searing summer heat, their bodies drenched in sweat, and they endured the penetrating cold and damp of the São Paulo winters. The torrential February rains brought floods to the factories, leaving some to stand knee-deep in water and filth as they tended their machines. In the spinning and weaving rooms, the cotton lint that filled the air also covered the workers' bodies and faces. It stuck in their ears and, worse, it entered their lungs. The continual inhalation of cotton dust over a prolonged period could eventually lead to brown-lung disease. Tuberculosis was another common ailment afflicting workers in the industry, and many also suffered ill effects from the *chuveirinho,* the sprinkler system that spewed a steady, fine mist into the air to prevent threads from becoming dry and brittle.[87] In the weaving room, employees labored under the deafening clamor of the power loom, a noise that, as one weaver described it, "was enough to make you crazy."[88] Looking back, dona Cinta Ramos said, "I was used to the noise at the time, but if I were to enter [a mill] now, I don't think that I could stand it. It would make me deaf. Good God! [Pelo amor de Deus!] When you're young, everything is good. Not now. Every little noise bothers me."[89]

Work in textile factories also posed more immediate dangers. The failure of manufacturers to provide adequately for worker safety, a shortcoming frequently noted by contemporary observers, contributed to hazardous conditions on the shop floor, where job-related accidents caused untold injuries and loss of life.[90] Besides leaving the mills to protect their own health, in a city where one-sixth of all infants died before their first birthday and a quarter did not survive beyond their second year, some women may have quit their factory jobs with the welfare of their young children in mind.[91] Others who could afford to, dropped out of the workforce with marriage. Dona Ermínia Albertini stopped working after fourteen years in the textile industry several months before she got married, in order to allow time for wedding preparations which included hand-embroidering the linens for her bridal trousseau. She quit her job at her fiancé Vicente's behest and probably not without evincing a sigh of relief herself. Senhor Vicente's mother had spent most of her life working in the textile industry, dona Ermínia explained, and her new husband "didn't want his children to grow up on the streets like he had done."[92] Even though economic constraints precluded widespread conformity among the working class to the bourgeois gender ideals of the male provider and the female housewife/mother, for millworkers like dona Ermínia, giving up a factory job significantly lessened the daily work burden that automatically came with marriage. However, like other working-class wives who left industrial employment, dona Ermínia still continued to make direct economic contributions to her household after she married. Finding ways to earn money that were more compatible with housekeeping and childrearing, women often sewed for others or took in homework from local factories. In dona Ermínia's case, she turned to sewing out of her home in order to "help out," establishing her clientele at the bank where her husband worked.[93]

Idealized portraits of domestic life, a central feature of prevailing gender ideology, failed to acknowledge the actual work in housework. And while the elite depicted São Paulo's working-class districts as filthy and disease-ridden repositories of uncultured people, working-class wives actually devoted much of their lives to the daily struggle against dirt. An adult woman's sense of identity was, in fact, intimately linked to the way she executed the domestic labor that was culturally defined as women's work. Dona Cinta Ramos spoke for the women of her class and her generation when she said with evident pride, "Mine is the house of a poor woman, but cleanliness is the one thing we have never lacked."[94]

Living up to rigorous standards of housekeeping presented working-class women with a formidable challenge. The work entailed in keeping households clean and running efficiently was labor-intensive and time-consuming, especially before children were old enough to help. Clothes were washed by hand, hung out to dry, and then pressed with a heavy iron that was heated on a coal-burning stove, which remained the standard until the 1940s brought the advent of the gas range. Cooking with coal required long hours, forcing women to rise well before daybreak to get the fire going, in order to allow time for the coals to become hot enough to make the early morning coffee. Coal also generated a lot of soot, which compounded the daily chores of sweeping and scrubbing. Because food was purchased in small quantities for daily consumption, shopping was another of the day's many chores.[95]

Even though industrialization in large part had moved production out of the household and into the factory, certain types of home production traditionally performed by women persisted. Ready-made clothing did not become widely affordable until the 1940s, and so even though women had long ceased to weave cloth at home, they still made virtually everything their families wore, from undergarments to the tailored shirts and fancy dresses that were carefully guarded for special occasions. Millworkers sewed using fabric purchased at a discount from city factories, and they remade clothing for work and everyday wear from hand-me-downs, patching and piecing many times over until the original article was no longer recognizable. Some women fashioned children's outfits from flour sacks acquired at the bakery for pennies. They also sewed bedsheets and towels, and knit sweaters, scarves, and blankets, and sometimes they made their own bath soap.[96] Those fortunate enough to escape crowded tenement buildings grew vegetables on small garden plots and maybe raised a few chickens or goats for their own consumption. Sometimes they sold surplus produce to their neighbors or on street corners. Women also cultivated herbs and plants, like *língua-de-vaca* (Chaptalia integerrima), *erva-cidreira* (Melissa officinalis), and *losna* (Artemisia arborescens), that were used for medicinal purposes to treat common ailments. In some cases, usually in the outlying suburban districts, workers built their own houses, gradually adding on, room by room, as financial circumstances allowed.[97]

The various forms of household production that persisted well into the twentieth century aided women in their efforts to make what little cash there was in hand go as far as possible, thereby lessening the need to buy from local shops on credit, or to accept cash advances from the mill. By minimizing their dependence on wages however they could, working-class families struggled to avoid the chronic indebtedness that plagued many poor urban households. While it was not possible to garden or raise animals in the capital's densely populated working-class neighborhoods, it was not that uncommon in the more far-flung suburbs of the Zona Leste. Families living there were able to curtail outlays on food and costly medical treatment and at the same time add nutrition and variety to their meals.[98]

Along with the domestic work, husbands seem generally to have left the job of managing household finances to their wives. The way dona Ernestina

Maniasse Gonçalves described these arrangements was typical. When I asked her how such decisions were made in her household, we had the following exchange:

> DONA ERNESTINA: I resolved everything, about money, the house. I took care of everything. Eeh . . . My husband didn't want to bother himself with such things. He thought that the house was a woman's affair and that the street was for men. [Achava que a casa era da mulher e a rua do homen.]
>
> THERESA: Did he used to go out?
>
> DONA ERNESTINA: Sometimes, more on the weekends.
>
> THERESA: Where did he go?
>
> DONA ERNESTINA: [Laughter] To bars, to dance halls. Eeh . . . He had a good life. [Se passou bem a vida dele.] So much so that it's been thirteen years since he died, and he's been more of a help to me since he died. I have a wonderful son who isn't married. I have a house. I have everything I need.
>
> THERESA: Was it common for men to go out like your husband did?
>
> DONA ERNESTINA: Oh no, no, it wasn't. The majority of husbands were *bem direitos* [good]. Good husbands. Mine wasn't.
>
> THERESA: Did you argue with him?
>
> DONA ERNESTINA: No, it didn't make sense to argue. He'd come home drunk. [Com as pingas dele.] When they drink pinga, they become aggressive, no? It's better to keep quiet. So much so that when he died, I found him dead in the morning. He lived alone and he died alone. [Viveu isolado e morreu isolado.] He died over there [pointing] in the living room, on the sofabed where my son sleeps.[99]

While dona Ernestina relied on the normative ideal of a good husband to criticize her own husband's behavior during nonworking hours, she stressed, however, that he had been a good worker:

> Now as for being a worker, *um trabalhador,* that he was. That's one thing I can't hold against him. He could go to bed at two in the morning, and at six o'clock he was on his feet. And he didn't want anyone to say he was, he used to say, "What is it? What's the matter? What do you think I am, a bum? [Cê pensa que sou vagabundo?]" He retired for disability. He had varicose veins. But he died working. On Saturday he worked until four o'clock, and at four o'clock on Sunday was when the funeral procession left [from our house].[100]

Although control of the family purse strings could be a source of power for married women, it also came with limitations. Since wives were responsible for putting food on the table, when money ran out, the problem was theirs to resolve. Wives also depended on their husbands to surrender their wages to the common household fund, after they skimmed off a portion for personal spending. Ultimately, however, husbands held discretionary power over their earnings. Married women, especially those who were not also earning wages, found themselves therefore in a vulnerable position, their economic security resting on the continued goodwill of their husbands.

Women also took responsibility for nursing the sick in their families and caring for elderly relatives. In addition, some women continued to help their mothers with domestic work even after they had married and had families of their own to take care of. For dona Cinta Ramos, her factory work schedule facilitated her ability to fulfill that obligation. "When I worked in a cashmere factory, I worked only one loom. So whenever the yarn ran out, I'd get a day or two off. Then I would go on a cleaning spree. I'd clean my mother's house, wash her laundry, iron. I'd clean our house, air out the mattresses, leave everything in order for when I went back to work." [101]

Although women received help from their daughters with housework and child care, men in the household remained exempt from most aspects of domestic work, because it was defined as women's work. As dona Cinta put it, "My husband never helped around the house, not even to hold the baby. I'd ask him, 'Please hold her for a little while, while I do this or that.' 'Ah,' he'd say, 'Sit her in the highchair.' And off he'd go. As soon as he finished lunch, he left for the club." [102] However, just as men were socialized into viewing housework as a woman's job, women shared the same view themselves, as dona Cinta indicated when she described the division of labor in her household:

> My husband never did anything around the house. He didn't even know how to make a cup of coffee. It's that we women have this feeling, this feeling deep down that it is our job. So it didn't make sense for me to say to my husband, "Do this, do that." I never said "Do this," or "Do that" to him. It didn't make sense, because I thought that that was my obligation, my obligation as a woman. . . . After he ate dinner, he went to the club. . . . By the same token, I never liked my children to do housework. I never made them do housework. Never. I did everything. Because it just wasn't worth it. They don't do it right, you get nervous. You end up having to do it over yourself, you get upset, and that is even worse. . . .

But when my daughters got married, they became outstanding housewives, all the neighbors tell me, they are good housewives, great in the
kitchen, they know how to cook and to make sweets.[103]

Wives who continued to work in factories after they married and had children were likely to have been married to men who held low-paying industrial
jobs or who worked as day laborers, while other husbands may have simply
existed on the margins of the workforce, drifting in and out of unemployment. Members of the lower classes lived life so close to the edge that family
emergencies were commonplace. Illness, unemployment, or the premature
death of a spouse were all reasons for women to return to the mills. The financial pressures that pushed women into factory work weighed most heavily on
single mothers, abandoned wives, and widows. As a group they headed one-
third of working-class households, according to a 1944 estimate.[104]

One wife who worked for almost two decades in the textile industry took
her first job when the unemployment crisis of the early 1930s threw her husband out of work for a period that lasted several years. During this time, his
contribution to supporting the household consisted of catching fish in the
clear waters of the Tietê River, while she earned wages tending looms in the
Mariângela factory. Even after her husband found a job in the Antártica beer
factory, this woman stayed on at Mariângela "in order to help out."[105] She
worked there for another twenty years until she retired, at the age of sixty.

Some married women moved in and out of the textile workforce whenever they "needed the money." Such was the case of dona Eulina de Oliveira's
mother, who also worked in the Mariângela factory. Over the course of two
decades, she returned periodically to that same factory, working for brief
stints that could last anywhere from a few months to a year at a time.[106]

For long-term employees with young children, an immediate problem was
to arrange for child care. Some women put their infants in on-site nurseries,
provided by large factories in order to minimize the disruption of production. Others turned to female relatives to take care of their children while
they worked. Dona Beatriz Nieto, who was married to a trolley conductor
for the São Paulo Light Company, bore five daughters over the course of
the thirty years she spent employed in the textile industry. The Nieto family
shared a house with dona Beatriz's parents, and her mother looked after the
girls while she worked. Dona Beatriz withdrew from the textile workforce
only for a monthlong maternity leave with each birth, and once for a two-
year period when her daughters were very young in order to give her mother
a rest. Dona Beatriz, like other working mothers, preferred to work in textile

factories that operated with two shifts, one from 5 A.M. to 2 P.M. and another from 2 P.M. to 10 P.M. Such a schedule, which sometimes alternated weekly, gave women a sizable chunk of time during the day in which to get their domestic work done.[107]

Not all women, however, managed to achieve such a neat balance among the conflicting demands of factory work, housework, and childrearing. Under certain circumstances, as illustrated in dona Odette Alves de Almeida's story, the choice to go back to work was no choice at all, but rather a bare-bones question of survival. In 1946, after working fifteen years in the textile industry, dona Odette quit her job at the Santa Teresinha factory in the working-class neighborhood of Moóca, when she married at the age of thirty. Early in her marriage, her life proceeded on a fairly even keel. Although her husband drank heavily at times, he still worked hard as a shoemaker. He owned a small workshop specializing in high-styled men's footwear with a partner and earned enough to afford the rent on a *quarto e cozinha* (a room and a kitchen), a typical two-room dwelling, in Moóca. "I fulfilled my obligations as a woman," dona Odette said, "that is, by washing the clothes, cooking, keeping the house in order."[108] But as a new wife, dona Odette also brought money into the household. Like many of her peers, she bought a sewing machine and learned how to sew. "To help my husband, I earned money by sewing clothes," she explained.[109]

Dona Odette scrimped and saved, and after a year, they bought a small plot of land in what was then a vast, unpopulated expanse of forest and brush. "Mato, mato, mato mesmo" was the way she described Itaim Paulista, an outlying district in the Zona Leste.[110] Two months before the birth of their first child, dona Odette and her husband moved out to Itaim, where "there was not another soul in sight."[111] They put up a *barraquinho* (small hut), and the two of them started building a house, a quarto e cozinha without running water or indoor plumbing. After they had finished building and were well settled in, dona Odette's husband suggested that they move back to the capital. "He wanted to sell and I didn't," she explained:

> I will not leave this place. [Daqui não saio.] I had never had *um canto meu* [a place to call my own], because my stepmother always used to say to me, "you are a foundling [*uma enjeitada*]." She was the one who married my father. I already existed, so I was no foundling. I wanted my own place. There was a large *quintal* [garden], I raised chickens, goats, pigeons, rabbits. I sold a lot of stuff, even after the children came, I kept on selling. There was so much we weren't able to eat it all.[112]

Dona Odette's position eventually won out, and the family stayed living in Itaim, while her husband continued running the shoemaking business in the capital. With the passing years, however, he slipped deeper and deeper into alcoholism, and as his drinking problem worsened, so did the family's economic situation. Eventually dona Odette's husband stopped bringing in money altogether, returning home only to sleep. It became increasingly difficult for dona Odette to buy corn feed for her goats and to purchase other staples. She began selling off her animals to get the money she needed to survive. "Then I started to know hunger, to feel hunger. Have you ever been hungry in your life?" she asked me before continuing her story:

> There wasn't any bread, I had sweet potatoes instead. . . . All there was to eat was *almeirão* [wild chicory] and tomatoes. I washed them and ate them with salt. Water and salt, there wasn't any oil to put on them. I'd get a tiny piece of meat that was called *coxão duro,* that had a sliver of fat around it, and make a pot of soup. . . . I ate whatever was in the quintal, sweet peppers—not fried, but roasted over the fire. Tomatoes and almeirão, and that was it. Nothing else. . . . I needed to have money to buy things, for the children, for the chickens, and there just wasn't enough money to go around. There was so little left over. I felt that I shouldn't even take one of the eggs from my chickens, or one of the chickens to eat. I needed the money.[113]

After dona Odette's last sixty chickens were stolen and there were no animals left to sell, she was forced back into the textile mills in 1955 to keep her family from starving.

Because bus service between Itaim and the capital was irregular and inefficient, the journey was a difficult one that could take more than two hours. On her way into the city, dona Odette encountered some women she had worked with years before when she was still single. They told her about a factory on the Rua Cachoeira that was hiring, and dona Odette got a job there that very day. Physically isolated and far away from the support network she had left behind in the capital, dona Odette had no choice but to leave her children, aged nine, five, and thirteen months, to fend for themselves while she worked in the factory.

> I left the baby in the hammock, with a pan of *mingau* [cassava cereal] by his side. His older brother fed him throughout the day. When I got home late at night, I fixed the baby's dinner. Many times I arrived to find the baby's bottle shattered in pieces on the floor. This was before we had

plastic bottles. How he never fell on the glass, I'll never know. God must have watched over him.[114]

Dona Odette worked in the textile industry for eighteen more years, until she had put in enough time to collect retirement benefits. When she retired in 1973, she was fifty-seven.[115]

Even after retiring from the mills, women often continued to find ways of bringing money into their households, some until they were well advanced in years. In 1945 dona Cinta Ramos quit the loom after twenty-six years, at the age of thirty-six, when her aging mother was no longer able to babysit for her three daughters while she worked. She then tried her hand at earning money in various ways. First she bought a used sewing machine and started to take in homework from a garment factory in Moóca, sewing while her youngest either napped or sat strapped in a highchair. Then, after a few years, dona Cinta "became her own boss," designing and sewing children's clothing that she sold through a friend who had a small shop near St. Rita's Church.[116]

Work was a theme woven throughout dona Cinta's story. "I had a method for working," she said, referring to the loom.

> I don't know how to explain it, I don't mess around. I work and my hands are quick. Even at home, if I am cooking, cleaning, I stop one thing, start another, do two or three things at once, I keep working, and by noon everything is done. That's why I used to sew. I earned a lot by sewing. I'd sit down at the machine and it was full speed ahead. I used to enjoy it.[117]

For years she marketed her handsewn goods through another friend who sold clothes out of her home, a common strategy used by working-class women who sewed for a living, to avoid the taxation that came along with formally setting up shop. In addition, dona Cinta sewed for people in her neighborhood, and she also made arrangements with the principal at the high school her daughters attended on the Avenida Tiradente to sew and sell winter jackets to the rest of the students there.

Along with earning money at her sewing machine, dona Cinta also took in washing. "I had a very good clientele," she told me. "I got the laundry spotless. . . . One of my customers always said, 'As long as you wash for me, I'll never buy a washing machine.' I used to wash everything, even curtains."[118] Another customer, who lived in a cramped apartment where there was no space to hang sheets and towels out to dry, paid dona Cinta to do her laundry for seven years, until she, too, moved to the Villa Maria Zélia. During the years that dona Cinta worked as a washerwoman, it was her responsibility to pick up and deliver the heavy loads of laundry to and from each of her customers, a burden that grew more onerous as she got older. After an operation for varicose veins when she was sixty-eight years old, dona Cinta stopped taking in laundry and turned to her last money-making activity:

> One day, with a little money, I bought some dishtowels and tablecloths, bathtowels and washcloths, and then I began selling. I bought the towels there on the Rua Bresser and the Rua Oriente, and sold them to my neighbors here in the villa. I didn't have to leave the villa, they came to my house to buy them. But after a while, I started having pains in my legs, and I couldn't walk over to the Rua Bresser. I wasn't even able to make it on the bus, so then I stopped selling. I had always walked to the Rua Bresser, but sometimes on the way home I'd catch a bus on Rubino de Oliveira. It's pretty far away. I just couldn't do it anymore, especially not in the heat.[119]

With that, dona Cinta's lifelong struggle to earn her keep was finally over, at the age of seventy-three.

As the oral testimonies presented in this essay have shown, working-class women made many and varied contributions to the economic support of their households throughout their lives. Those who quit their factory jobs after marriage and/or motherhood often earned money working in informal market activities, while others made a longtime commitment to millwork, completing the thirty years' employment required for the collection of retirement benefits. The existence of this latter group, in particular older women who labored in the mills for the better part of their lives, challenges standing preconceptions about female employment patterns among the working class. With greater specificity, the picture to emerge from the data taken from the Cotonifício Paulista cotton factory records similarly belies stereotyped images of women textile workers.

The oral testimonies, more generally, yield a subjective portrait of gender. How beliefs about gender and cultural expectations for behavior were internalized and transmitted from one generation to the next, as well as women's multifaceted responses to those beliefs and expectations, are recurring themes in the stories told here. In the formation of women's identities, the primacy of gender remains clear. Although the women I interviewed had been workers in their own right, all persisted in defining themselves through the prism of their familial roles. It is equally significant that they defined their paid work in a helping capacity, using maternalist terms to defend their transgression of prescribed gender norms. In their self-representations, moreover, these women also gave a tacit nod to the (ideal) masculine breadwinning role, although it was one that in actuality found scant expression in their everyday lives.

Like the masculine role of economic provider, the feminine role of housewife and mother often remained far beyond the grasp of São Paulo's working class. Indeed, few women were free to devote themselves solely to fulfilling the unpaid role of housewife/mother. But this ideal resonated in their lives nevertheless, serving as a fundamental reference point in an ideology of gender that cut across the social spectrum and permeated the cultural fabric. When coupled with the need to earn money to support the household, the responsibility to perform all the domestic labor that the expression *obrigação de mulher* necessarily implied produced separate sets of competing demands. Working-class women devoted much of their time over the course of their lives trying to reconcile the two.

Within the broader social relations of gender, the control of female sexuality remained an integral aspect of the system of paternalistic dominance in working-class families. For daughters, it meant the continuance of that system even after marriage, whereas sons gained their independence from paternal authority with adulthood. For women, the eclipse of the childbearing years eventually signaled a certain emancipation, and the aging process itself also brought them added, welcome freedoms. Sometimes this came hand in hand with widowhood. To provide a concluding example, I will return to one of this essay's central protagonists, dona Odette Alves de Almeida.

Dona Odette, whose childhood years were overshadowed by her stepmother's cruelty and whose marriage ultimately fell casualty to her husband's alcoholism, found in her old age opportunities she had never had before. A lively and energetic woman of seventy-one when I interviewed her in 1987, dona Odette enjoyed good health and still lived in the house that she and her husband built in the 1940s. When she retired from the textile industry in 1973, the same year that her husband died, she gained the time to pursue her own interests. She attended a school for senior citizens in her neighborhood, finishing the equivalent of the third and fourth years of primary school in one year. A member of the São Paulo Textile Workers Union since 1934, dona Odette had participated in strike marches ever since she was a young girl delivering lunch pails to her father at work. But only since she retired did she have the time to become active in day-to-day union operations. Also a founding member of the *sindicato*'s association for retired textile workers, established in 1975, dona Odette described with pleasure her freedom to come and go to a degree that had not been possible earlier in her life:

DONA ODETTE: I'm always here [in the union] now. My children tell me I should bring my bed here, that one day I'll sleep here. I'm always coming here, sometimes I go out for a beer with the people from the sindicato. When I had a husband I couldn't do that.

THERESA: Why?

DONA ODETTE: He was *um homem esquisito* [a peculiar man]. I couldn't even smile at anyone. He wouldn't let me greet people.

THERESA: Why?

DONA ODETTE: He didn't like it.

THERESA: Was he jealous?

DONA ODETTE: I think it was more a sickness than jealousy. It was stupidity and *cachaça*. [Era burrice aguda e cachaça mesmo.] A lot of pinga. Now I have to try to make up for everything and do it fast. I have to take advantage of all that I can.[120]

Looking back on the past, dona Odette summarized her hopes for the future in the passage that follows:

My life was like this. I didn't have a childhood and I didn't have the chance to be a teenager, or a young adult, because by then I was married. Now I have everything, you know. I have my childhood, my youth, my old age. That's where I am now, in my old age, right? If I don't do everything that I can right now, I'll never get another chance. Now is the time for everything. It's all or nothing now.[121]

Notes

I would like to thank Susan K. Besse, Deborah Levenson-Estrada, Florencia E. Mallon, Steve J. Stern, and Barbara Weinstein, as well as John D. French and Daniel James, the editors of this volume, for their insightful comments on earlier versions of this essay. In addition, I extend my deepest thanks to all the people whose stories appear here. Without their help and kindness, this project would not have been possible.

1   Dona Cinta quickly produced a collection of news clips and other relevant materials she has stored over the years, including a commemorative album about the cotton factory, published in 1927. Our initial interview, which took place in her kitchen over *cafezinhos* and *mantecales* (Spanish crescent cookies made from her mother's recipe), spilled over into three sessions.

2   As part of the research for a larger project, I conducted taped interviews with twenty-three people. I located some of them through the São Paulo Textile Workers' Union and conducted a number of interviews there as well. I also

interviewed several individuals affiliated with the anarchist Centro de Cultura Social (Center of Social Culture), an organization first established in the city of São Paulo in 1933. I found a few people through churches in working-class neighborhoods and several more by knocking on doors. I took notes in a dozen additional interviews with union officials, textile workers, factory owners, and relatives of Jorge Street and Lindolfo Collor. The taped interviews lasted from two to three hours, with the exception of six people with whom I conducted multiple interviews. All translations are my own.

3   The phrase *my duty as a woman* is taken from Odette Alves de Almeida, interview with author, São Paulo, June 17, July 3, and July 6, 1987; and Cinta Ramos, interview with author, São Paulo, May 6–8, 1987.

4   Thomas H. Holloway, *Immigrants on the Land: Coffee and Society in São Paulo, 1886–1934* (Chapel Hill: University of North Carolina Press, 1980), pp. 42–55; George Reid Andrews, *Blacks and Whites in São Paulo, Brazil, 1888–1988* (Madison: University of Wisconsin Press, 1991), p. 83.

5   Maria Célia Paoli, "Working-Class São Paulo and Its Representations, 1900–1940," *Latin American Perspectives* 14, no. 2 (spring 1987): p. 205; Giorgio Mortara, "A imigração italiana no Brasil e algumas características demográficas do grupo italiano de São Paulo," *Revista Brasileira de Estatística* 2 (1950): p. 326.

6   Horace B. Davis, "Padrão de vida dos operários da cidade de São Paulo," *Revista do Arquivo Municipal de São Paulo,* vol. 13, ano 2, 1935, pp. 126–28, 137–38, 142. The survey, conducted by the Education Institute of the University of São Paulo and the São Paulo Institute of Hygiene, studied 221 families selected at random, with an average household size of 5.42. Each household contained at least two wage earners.

7   Ibid., p. 165.

8   Ermínia Albertini, interview with author, São Paulo, May 21, June 12, and June 16, 1987.

9   Ignácio Picasso, interview with author, São Paulo, September 17, 1987.

10 Ibid.

11 Centro de Memória Sindical, *Depoimento de Beatriz Nieto,* São Paulo, June 12, 1984, pp. 46–47.

12 Zélia Gattai, *Anarquistas, graças a Deus* (Rio de Janeiro: Record, 1979), p. 45.

13 Odette Alves de Almeida, interview.

14 Ibid.

15 Ibid.

16 Centro dos Industriais de Fiação e Tecelagem de São Paulo (CIFT-SP), Circulars 405 (January 16, 1925), 423 (February 14, 1925), 435 (March 4, 1925), 436 (March 9, 1925), 437 (March 12, 1925), 469 (May 28, 1925); 471 (May 28, 1925), 478 (June 8, 1925), and 513 (August 24, 1925); CIFT-SP, *Acta da Assembléia Geral Extraordinária de 7 de março de 1925.*

17 Giorgina Nascimento Martins, interview with author, São Paulo, June 18, 1987.

18   Ibid.

19   Ibid.

20   Ibid.

21   Ermínia Albertini, interview.

22   Ibid.

23   Ibid.

24   Andrews, *Blacks and Whites,* pp. 69–70, 101; June E. Hahner, *Emancipating the Female Sex: The Struggle for Women's Rights in Brazil,* 1850–1940 (Durham, N.C.: Duke University Press, 1990), pp. 97–101.

25   Assunta Bianchi, interview with author, São Paulo, August 17, 1987.

26   "Fabbriche e officine," *La Battaglia* (São Paulo), July 7, 1907; "Guerra social, Brasil: O 'lock-out' da 'Fábrica Confiança,' " *A Voz do Trabalhador* (Rio de Janeiro), April 17, 1909; Hahner, *Emancipating the Female,* p. 221.

27   Ermínia Albertini, interview; and Ignácio Picasso, interview.

28   Octávio Pupo Nogueira, "Carta ao 'Piccolo,' " *Boletim Algodoeiro* 48 (February 18, 1924): p. 825.

29   CIFT-SP, *Memorial apresentado ao Dr. Júlio Prestes de Albuquerque, Presidente do Estado de São Paulo, 27 de abril de 1927.*

30   São Paulo (state), *Mensagem apresentada ao Congresso Legislativo, em 14 de julho de 1920, pelo Dr. Washington Luis Pereira de Sousa, Presidente do Estado de São Paulo;* Maria Valéria Junho Pena, *Mulheres e trabalhadoras: Presença feminina na constituição do sistema fabril* (Rio de Janeiro: Paz e Terra, 1981), pp. 136–38; João Baptista Scuracchio Neto, interview with author, São Paulo, July 19, 1986; Ignácio Picasso, interview; Cinta Ramos, interview; and António Chamorro, interview with author, São Paulo, August 3–4, 1987.

31   I borrow here from Ann Farnsworth-Alvear's formulation of the woman/worker as a cultural paradox, in "Gender and the Limits of Industrial Discipline: Textile Work in Medellín, Colombia, 1905–1960" (Ph.D. diss., Duke University, 1994), p. 206.

32   "Código do Trabalho," extract from "Gazetilha" of *Jornal do Commércio,* September 10, 1917. In Brazil, Congresso, *Documentos Parlamentares, Legislação social,* vol. 1 (Rio de Janeiro: Typ. do Jornal de Commércio, de Rodrigues e Cia., 1919), p. 838. On the "safer" moral environment of the textile factory see also CIFT-SP, *Memorial apresentado ao Dr. Júlio Prestes de Albuquerque.*

33   Esmeralda Blanco Bolsonaro de Moura, *Mulheres e menores no trabalho industrial: Os fatores sexo e idade na dinâmica do capital* (Petrópolis: Vozes, 1982), p. 54; Wilson Cano, *Raízes da concentração industrial em São Paulo* (Rio de Janeiro: Difel, 1977), p. 129.

34   Quoted in Warren Dean, *The Industrialization of São Paulo, 1880–1945* (Austin: University of Texas Press, 1969), p. 152. In a 1927 report to the São Paulo state governor, CIFT-SP alleged that a scarcity of weavers was paralyzing 7 percent of the looms in the industry in 1927 (CIFT-SP, *Memorial apresentado ao Dr. Júlio Prestes*

de Albuquerque; see also CIFT-SP, Circular 779 [May 10, 1928], and *Memorial apresentado ao Exmo. Sr. Presidente da Câmara dos Deputados, 1927*).

35   São Paulo (state), *Mensagem enviada ao Congresso do Estado, a 14 de julho de 1915, pelo Dr. Francisco Alves, Presidente do Estado de São Paulo,* and *Mensagem apresentada ao Congresso Legislativo, em 14 de julho de 1928, pelo Dr. Júlio Prestes de Albuquerque, Presidente do Estado de São Paulo;* São Paulo (state), *Boletim do Departamento Estadual do Trabalho* 23 (1917): p. 288; Joel William Wolfe, "The Rise of Brazil's Industrial Working Class: Community, Work and Politics" (Ph.D. diss., University of Wisconsin—Madison, 1990), pp. 43–44.

36   According to Andrews, the color barrier to industrial employment was most impenetrable in the period before 1930, although it was not effectively overcome for another decade (*Blacks and Whites,* pp. 98–102).

37   In one instance, the manufacturer Eduardo Jafet blamed low productivity on a lack of training and on the absence of a professional attitude on the part of workers (Dean, *Industrialization of São Paulo,* p. 152).

38   Stanley J. Stein, *The Brazilian Cotton Manufacture: Textile Enterprise in an Underdeveloped Area, 1850–1950* (Cambridge: Harvard University Press, 1957), pp. 50–57.

39   Nogueira, "Carta ao 'Piccolo,'" p. 824.

40   Alfredo Cusano, *Il Brasile, l'Italia e la guerra* (Roma: Editrice l'Italo-Sudamericana, 1921), p. 268.

41   Ibid.

42   Ernestina Maniasse Gonçalves, interview with author, São Paulo, May 14, 1987. Dona Ernestina was born in Brás in 1915, a daughter of Italian immigrants who had seven other children. Initially, her family had settled in the interior of São Paulo, near São Pedro, where they purchased a small piece of land with savings that dona Ernestina's grandfather had brought over from Italy. Unable to make a living in farming and hoping to improve their economic situation, the extended family migrated to the capital city, arriving shortly before dona Ernestina was born. She was unable to remember how old she was when she first began working in the factory. After the Maria Zélia factory closed down, dona Ernestina worked in the textile industry until her first child was born in 1937. After that, she did industrial homework until her second child turned four in 1948. Her return to the textile mills was cut short a few years later by a serious illness. Dona Ernestina's oldest child then went out to work to contribute to the support of the household.

43   Cusano, *Il Brasile,* p. 274; and Cinta Ramos, interview.

44   Cinta Ramos, interview.

45   Rosaura Street, interview with author, São Paulo, May 8, 1986.

46   Cinta Ramos, interview.

47   Ibid.

48   Ibid.

49   Ibid.

50 Ibid.

51 Ibid.

52 Giácomo Ordóñez, interview with author, São Paulo, August 10, 1987.

53 Odette Alves de Almeida, interview.

54 Assunta Bianchi, interview.

55 Odette Alves de Almeida, interview.

56 Assunta Bianchi, interview.

57 Cinta Ramos, interview.

58 Haim Grünspun, *O Bexiga: Anatomia de um bairro* (São Paulo: Livraria Cultura, 1979), p. 68.

59 Odette Alves de Almeida, interview.

60 Ibid.

61 Cinta Ramos, interview.

62 Giorgina Nascimento Martins, interview.

63 Cinta Ramos, interview.

64 Ibid.

65 Ermínia Albertini, interview.

66 Ibid.

67 Odette Alves de Almeida, interview.

68 Ibid.

69 Ofélia Bordini, interview with author, São Paulo, August 27, 1987; and Odette Alves de Almeida, interview.

70 In 1927 the average birth rate for the state of São Paulo was 32.51. In 1940 the city of São Paulo registered an average birth rate of 26.30, while the national average was 43.0 (São Paulo [state], *Mensagem apresentada ao Congresso Legislativo na 2a Sessão da 14a Legislatura, em 14 de julho de 1929, pelo Dr. Júlio Prestes de Albuquerque, Presidente do Estado de São Paulo;* Mortara, "A imigracão," pp. 468–69).

71 Jayme Cubero, interview with author, São Paulo, September 8 and 16, 1987.

72 Regarding child relinquishment see "Il mistero della Idalina svelato," *La Battaglia* (São Paulo), October 21, 1910; and "L'Orfanotrofio Cristoforo Colombo," *La Battaglia* (São Paulo), January 8, 1911.

73 Jayme Cubero, interview.

74 CIFT-SP, circular 311 (April 7, 1924); CIFT-SP, *Memorial apresentado ao Dr. Júlio Prestes de Albuquerque.*

75 Figures 1, 2, and 3 are based on data drawn from personnel records from the company archive of the Sociedade Anómina Cotonifício Paulista. Included in the information on workers were dates of entry and termination, birthdate, place of birth, parents' nationality, address, and job position. Of the women I interviewed, only two had ever worked in this factory. Dona Olga Sacchi, who was employed in the Cotonifício Paulista from 1935 to 1963, didn't volunteer much information about her experiences in the mill, which she described in a word as having been "terrible." Dona Cinta Ramos worked there only very

briefly in the late 1920s or early 1930s. When I asked her about it, she said, "I don't even think I worked for a week at the Cotonifício Paulista. I didn't like it there. You know what I didn't like, it was that I had gotten used to working in Maria Zélia, working there for so many years. You developed affection for the work, for the loom. . . . You became attached to a factory, to the work [*A gente foi pegando amor naquela fábrica, no serviço.*]." After leaving the Cotonifício Paulista, dona Cinta found a job that she liked better in another mill in the city.

76   CIFT-SP, *Boletim de Informações* (August 31–September 2, 1922).

77   Brazil, *Recenseamento Geral do Brasil, realizado em 1 de setembro de 1920,* vol. 5 (part 1), book 2, Indústria, pp. vi–vii, 786–87; Brazil, *Recenseamento Geral do Brasil, realizado em 1 de setembro de 1940* (part 7), book 3, pp. 472–73; Brazil, Instituto Brasileiro de Geografia e Estatística, Conselho Nacional de Estatística, *Anuário Estatístico do Brasil,* ano 7 (1946), p. 135; and *Anuário Estatístico do Brasil,* ano 12 (1951), p. 120.

78   Ibid.

79   The personnel department probably did not record all changes of marital status; nor would the records reflect the presence of men and women living in consensual unions.

80   Chiara Vangelista, "Per una ricerca sul mercato del lavoro: La mobilità della manodopera in una filatura paulista," *Nova Americana,* no. 3 (1978): pp. 215–30.

81   Vangelista's database consists of four hundred workers' *fichas de registro* for the period 1923 to 1940. Because the registry was begun in 1936, records pertaining to workers hired between 1923 and 1936 exist only for those workers still employed by the firm as of 1936 (Vangelista, "per una ricerca," p. 216).

82   Ibid., pp. 218–19.

83   São Paulo (state), "Condições do trabalho na indústria textil do Estado de São Paulo," *Boletim do Departamento Estadual do Trabalho* 1 (1912): pp. 1–2. Reprinted in Paulo Sérgio Pinheiro and Michael M. Hall, *A classe operária no Brasil, 1889–1930, documentos,* vol. 2, *Condições de vida e de trabalho, relações com os empresários e o estado* (São Paulo: Alfa-Omega, 1979), pp. 87–88.

84   Vangelista, "per un ricerca," pp. 220, 222. From a comparative Latin American perspective, Farnsworth-Alvear's findings on length of employment among textile workers in Antioquia, Colombia, indicate high turnover rates, with similar patterns for men and women workers. Forty-one percent of women and 49 percent of men in her sample worked less than two years; 34 percent of women and 27 percent of men worked between two and five years; 13 percent of women and 8 percent of men worked between six and ten years; 4 percent of women and 3 percent of men worked between eleven and twenty years; and 5 percent of women and 11 percent of men worked for more than twenty years (Farnsworth-Alvear, "Gender and the Limits," p. 51).

85   Assunta Bianchi, interview; and Giorgina Nascimento Martins, interview. It should be noted that the Cotonifício Paulista records do not provide the length

of employment for three women workers employed there in the year 1935. According to data on the number of workers in the factory in that year, published in the *Estatística Industrial do Estado de São Paulo* in 1935, forty-seven workers are missing from the personnel records of the Cotonifício Paulista archive. It is likely that these were workers who were employed in the factory for less than one year.

86   Andrews, *Blacks and Whites,* pp. 98–102.

87   José R. Oliveira Netto, "Profilaxia das causa diretas de insalubridade das fábricas de fiar, tecer e tingir algodão: Comentários à situação das fábricas paulistas em face destas causas," *Boletim da Sociedade de Medicina e Cirurgia de São Paulo* 5 (1922): pp. 179–81.

88   Ignácio Picasso, interview.

89   Cinta Ramos, interview.

90   Ibid.; Ermínia Albertini, interview; Eunice Longo, interview with author, São Paulo, August 3, 1987; and "Attraverso uno stabilimento di tessitura," *Avanti!* (São Paulo), May 24, 25, and 28, 1907 (reprinted in Pinheiro and Hall, *A classe operária,* vol. 2, pp. 162–68).

91   CIFT-SP, *Boletim de Informações* (July 23–26, 1922); see also Arthur Moncorvo Filho, *Histórico da protecção da infância no Brasil, 1500–1922* (Rio de Janeiro: Empreza Gráphica, 1926).

92   Ermínia Albertini, interview.

93   Ibid.

94   Cinta Ramos, interview.

95   Ermínia Albertini, interview; Odette Alves de Almeida, interview; and Cinta Ramos, interview.

96   Ofélia Bordini, interview; Juan Martínez, interview with author, São Paulo, September 16, 1987; and Isabel Ruis, interview with author, São Paulo, September 10, 1987.

97   Giorgina Nascimento Martins, interview; Ignácio Picasso, interview; and Giácomo Ordóñez, interview.

98   Davis, "Padrão de vida," p. 151. The 1934 survey showed that out of 204 respondents, 15 cultivated gardens and 48 raised chickens.

99   Ernestina Maniasse Gonçalves, interview.

100 Ibid.

101 Cinta Ramos, interview.

102 Ibid.

103 Ibid. Dona Cinta explained that when her daughters were growing up, they took turns working part-time after school at the company store in the Villa Maria Zélia, working under an informal arrangement with the shopkeeper. The girls didn't earn wages but instead were given items like food and soft drinks to bring home in exchange for their labor.

104 Olga Sacchi, interview with author, São Paulo, June 19, 1987. Although we lack

data on female-headed households during this period, a 1944 survey of one hundred families of different occupational backgrounds residing in working-class neighborhoods found that 29 percent were headed by women (Donald Pierson, "Hábitos alimentares em São Paulo," *Revista do Arquivo Municipal de São Paulo,* ano 10, vol. 97 [September–October 1944]: pp. 45–79).

105   Ermínia Albertini, interview.

106   Eulina de Oliveira, interview with author, São Paulo, August 5, 1987.

107   Beatriz Nieto, interview with author, São Paulo, August 13, 1987.

108   Odette Alves de Almeida, interview.

109   Ibid.

110   Ibid.

111   Ibid.

112   Ibid.

113   Ibid.

114   Ibid.

115   Ibid.

116   Cinta Ramos, interview.

117   Ibid.

118   Ibid.

119   Ibid.

120   Odette Alves de Almeida, interview. Dona Odette estimated that there were 730 members in the union retirees' association in 1987.

121   Ibid.

Talking, Fighting, Flirting

Workers' Sociability in Medellín
Textile Mills, 1935–1950

ANN FARNSWORTH-ALVEAR

It was a family, it's like, look, you would get there with problems, one would be sick a lot of the time, down in the mouth, with problems, a lot of the time without a cent and needing something bad at home, and you'd get there and someone would say, "Ehhh, didn't you wake up *pissed* [*verraca*] today! What happened to you?" And so you'd forget that you'd left problems at home, because there was this camaraderie [*compañerismo*] . . . the compañerismo of the people here, of those of us that were workers. — Susana Osorio, retired from the Rosellón Mill in Envigado, a suburb of Medellín

By choosing the word *family* to describe the cotton mill where she'd worked from the age of fifteen until retirement, Susana Osorio both accepted and wholly reappropriated the metaphor preferred by Colombia's industrial bourgeoisie.[1] Her employers were Echavarrías, sons of Medellín's most powerful family, and they regularly used the language of fatherly protection and filial piety to reinforce a paternalistic system of factory discipline. In company ceremonies at Rosellón and at Coltejer, their largest mill, the Echavarrías cast workers as their dependents; they handed out prizes and baskets of food, judged beauty contests, and sponsored spiritual exercises for employees. For workers, however, the language of family provided an alternative category: that of siblings. Susana and other retirees used the analogy to describe not their dependence on a paternalistic boss but rather their complex relationships with one another.[2] More importantly, the stories they told about mill work were often stories about *compañeros,* boy- or girlfriends, arguments, and fights. These stories challenge a feminist historian to think about the meaning of personal exchanges in the political world of work.

Like Susana, labor historians have generally relied on the category *family* to emphasize workers' solidarity; we write about brotherhood and (less often)

sisterhood, about comradeship and community. But both the metaphor and the relationships it describes deserve more scrutiny. Almost by definition, a family is an involuntary grouping. One doesn't choose one's parents, siblings, or cousins; one is stuck with them. Similarly, although less permanently, one is stuck with one's coworkers. In Medellín, as elsewhere, industrial work required spending long hours with companions not of one's choosing, and whether one made friends, fought, or tried to keep to oneself, relationships with coworkers could determine the quality of life at work. This essay treats workplace sociability as a fragmented process by which workers remade the disciplinary space of the factory into a space of intimate reciprocity. At issue is the concept of resistance. Does shoving a workmate somehow transgress against the constraints of factory labor? Does flirting resist industrial discipline? These are "sideways" questions; they cut against the grain of both "top-down" and "bottom-up" perspectives on labor history.

Women's memories of mill work fit but awkwardly into a bottom-up view of the factory as a place split between workers and management. Medellín's paternalistic industrialists required female employees to be "good girls," chaste and well-mannered, which makes gender discipline and factory hierarchy hard to disentangle. Arguing loudly, picking a fight, flirting too much, using foul language: these challenged public codes of femininity as much as they challenged work rules. Women's stories about such behavior can be contradictory. Talking and laughing about remembered fights, for example, provides an avenue for self-expression, yet such boisterous sociability—and the disobedience it implies—often conflicts with workingwomen's definitions of self. Listening for the silences and contradictions that shape women's oral narratives is thus as important as hearing their stories about what they did at work.

Paternalistic Discipline in Medellín

Talking, arguing with a workmate, teasing a friend: these may seem such everyday, universal activities as to be outside the domain of labor history. In Medellín's cotton mills, however, shop floor sociability acquired new meanings over time, as industrialists pursued more and more control over time spent at work. Understanding workers' interactions thus requires an overview of the city's industrial history, not as a context for the story, but rather as *part* of the process of sociability.

In 1902, immediately after the resolution of Colombia's longest civil war, commercial investors set about building factories in Medellín.[3] Hoping to profit from an expanding national market for cheap textiles, they pressured the government to establish protective tariffs, began importing looms, and visited cotton mills in Britain and the United States, pens in hand. Along with their new looms, Colombian capitalists imported a set of understandings about how to organize the working time of the women, children, and men they hired. The factory ideal required not only spatial enclosure but also the manipulation of human bodies.[4] It required that workers be individually partitioned and that managers be able to guarantee their positions in time and space. Operatives must not move around to chat or take other unauthorized breaks. As in Europe and the United States, however, local practices added layers to this supervisory ideal. Industrial discipline arrived not as a block of practices but rather as a piecemeal process, with workers contesting managers' control in organized and unorganized ways. Additionally, local debates about factory labor and "the social question," especially with regard to women, determined which kinds of circulation and coagulation would be defined as "dangerous."

At the outset, Colombian industrialists contended with a young workforce unused to factory discipline. Through the 1920s, mill administrators struggled to ensure that workers arrived day after day, that they returned after lunch, and that they didn't give themselves vacation without notice. If a worker was "chatty with the men" or "a fighter," the administrator might make a note of it, but would generally take no concrete action.[5] After a series of strikes in the mid-1930s, however, the focus of control shifted from making sure workers showed up to seeing that they were "at work" while at the mill.[6] Factory owners began to apply more sophisticated forms of labor control: they employed more supervisors, set up a paternalistic system of benefits, kept more careful records of workers' behavior and productivity, and posted formal rules and regulations. They also suppressed independent unions, by methods both legal and illegal, and different industrialists worked together to develop a network of anticommunist, church-sponsored company unions.[7] One's words and actions were now as important as one's ability to do a job well. At the same time, a person was now more likely to be sent home for talking, arguing, or taking a break with a friend. Workers' relations with one another thus became more closely bound to the disciplinary relationship between worker and overseer.

Medellín's textile mills changed significantly in the period 1935–1950. The percentage of women among textile workers stood at about 70 percent through the 1920s, dropped steadily through the 1930s, and reached 50 percent in 1940–1949.[8] By 1955–1960, women made up only 8 percent of new hires,

Figure 1. Percentage of workers entering Medellín's mills
between 1918 and 1960 who were cited or suspended during their
employment.

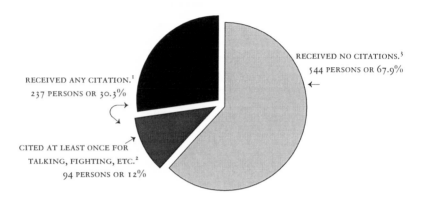

RECEIVED NO CITATIONS.[3]
544 PERSONS OR 67.9%
←

RECEIVED ANY CITATION.[1]
237 PERSONS OR 30.3%

CITED AT LEAST ONCE FOR
TALKING, FIGHTING, ETC.[2]
94 PERSONS OR 12%

Based on a sample of 781 personnel records (see note 14).
[1] Includes persons written up for poor work, absenteeism, insubordination, tardiness, and
other infractions.
[2] Includes persons written up for talking, fighting, arguments, and gossip (see figure 2).
[3] Includes 181 persons who stayed at their jobs for less than one year, a group that generally left
or were dismissed without formal citations.

and as older women retired, the workforce became almost entirely male. The
shift did not occur in discrete stages, with men employed at specific jobs
and women being replaced room by room. Rather, women and men worked
alongside one another. This was especially true in the weaving rooms, which
were thoroughly mixed-sex by the late 1930s and through the 1940s.

Controlling sociability had an explicitly moralistic edge in Medellín. Since
the second decade of the century, Catholic reformers had denounced the
intermingling of women and men in the textile mills. A 1918 ordinance, for
example, required factory owners to hire matrons, or *vigilantas,* often widows,
to oversee "morality" in the mills. In practice, this meant policing workingwomen's interactions with male coworkers, from supervisors to loom oilers.
Gradually, the city's industrialists incorporated the reformers' moral vision—
as exemplified by the ordinance—into their own systems of discipline. By the
mid-1930s, the city's textile companies were defining themselves as Catholic institutions and promoters of public morality. At Fabricato, owned by

another branch of Echavarrías, a dormitory built in 1936 provided subsidized housing for single women from the countryside; nuns monitored the women's leisure hours, measured their hemlines, and watched over boyfriends' visits. Such behavioral proscription was widespread, and most of the city's textile companies undertook to ban "immoral" women. Through the 1950s, being seen in the wrong part of town, using "bad" language, or talking too much to a male worker got a working girl in trouble; getting pregnant got her fired.[9] It is this pretension to total control that shapes any discussion of workers' sociability in Medellín. With such strict rules and so rigid a definition of morality, almost any form of self-expression appears as a form of resistance to industrial discipline.

In their drive to purify the city's mills, reformers and industrialists equated morality and control with silence.[10] In 1922, for example, the official charged with enforcing the 1918 ordinance made a special visit to one factory upon hearing "that the matron, through her pusillanimity, authorized chatting between men and women workers."[11] At another mill he praised the "strict vigilance" that reigned, specifically noting that "conversations among workers are not permitted, that is to say, between men and women workers. Morality thus proceeds very well."[12] By the 1930s, when factory managers began posting formal regulations, they too focused on silencing workers. In 1936, for example, the Fábrica de Bello printed up its first list of formal regulations; these forbade "conversations between the male and female personnel, within the factory, whether during work or rest hours."[13] Other mills adopted similar rules, and supervisors enforced these by combining verbal reminders (impossible to quantify) with formal disciplinary procedures, as described in figure 1.[14] Apart from moral concerns occasioned by gender mixing, managers in the 1930s and 1940s hoped that rules about speech would limit the disruptive potential of talk. Coltejer, for example, required new workers to sign a warning against the kind of talk that might cause fights: "I have been informed that all gossip or ridicule of any worker, on or off company property, will be grounds for immediate dismissal." Controlling workers' verbal exchanges was the most obvious way to regulate sociability, both to ensure that workplace interactions conformed to bourgeois standards of morality and to limit work hours to the activity of production.

Disciplinary procedures varied among the different mills. A worker at Coltejer, for example, had a better chance of getting away with talking to a workmate or settling a quarrel without calling attention to her- or himself than did a worker at Fabricato or Tejicondor. Yet certain patterns held across mills (see figure 2). Women were somewhat more likely to be repeatedly writ-

Figure 2. Persons written up for behavior involving coworkers,
as a percentage of those cited or suspended.

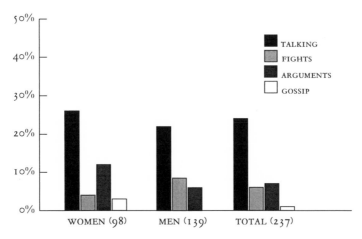

Based on a sample of 781 personnel records (see note 14).

ten up for conversation, but receiving at least one such citation was fairly
common for both women and men. More women were written up for "arguments" (*disgustos*) than for "fights" (*peleas*), although different comments may
reflect supervisors' attitudes as much as actual behaviors. If fighting and arguing are considered together, however, women and men got into trouble over
altercations with workmates at about the same rate. Again, personnel records
provide evidence about managers' preoccupations and about how their approaches varied by a worker's gender and from mill to mill; they reveal less
about workers' behavior itself and nothing of the subjective experience of
sharing a workplace with so many others. Addressing that level of complexity
requires listening to retired people's stories.

Compañerismo and Talk

Despite the rules against talking, workers' productivity—from their first day
in the mill—depended on the help and advice they got from one another.
Employers knew this, and they encouraged some forms of compañerismo
while outlawing others. Old-timers trained new workers, many of whom were
only recently arrived from the countryside, and most of whom had no experience with industrial work. Once they were on their own, the bewildered
newcomers relied on their immediate coworkers for guidance. María Cris-

tina Restrepo vividly described her adjustment to Fabricato's spinning room, which she entered in 1944; here *friends* is my word, which Cristina expands to *girls* and *compañeras*.

> CRISTINA: I was scared to death, to see those machines, plus this roll—so immense—I said, "I'll die of fright . . . horrible, dreadful, that terrible heat, all that cotton. . . . I said, "Ayii, but I won't quit, I won't quit, I won't quit." . . . And then after a week I felt all right, the girls, the compañeras, perfect.
>
> ANN: Really good friends?
>
> CRISTINA: Really good friends, really good compañeras, the first three days one doesn't know where to put one's clothes [laughs], I didn't know where the bathroom was, nothing. . . . One girl, really nice, very polite, she really stuck by me."[15]

Compañerismo emerges in retired workers' accounts as a category of friendship, a neighborliness that grew out of relations of mutual aid in the workplace. Despite working conditions designed to isolate operatives from one another, including loud machines, physical separation, rules of silence, and piece rates, workers depended on one another's help. Providing that help identified one as a good workmate; refusing to do so fueled vicious fights and long-standing enmities.

In interviews, retired workers often illustrated the meaning of compañerismo, with either a positive reference to their own behavior or a negative evaluation of others'. María Rosa Lalinde, for example, contrasted what she described as the snobbishness of the girls in loom preparation with the mutuality of the weavers.

> Picture this, that if a girl [in preparation] was ill, and the other one got there and she said, "Hey, go'on to weaving and bring me the rack 'cause I feel really sick," [the other would say] "Umph, no, they sent you." Very bad compañerismo. But in weaving, one would go to breakfast—"don't worry, Rosita, go ahead, go ahead"—whether it was a man or a woman . . . a lot of compañerismo; not in *pasa-lizos* [part of preparation], nope.[16]

Helping a newcomer or fellow worker keep up, relieving a sick friend of an onerous task, swapping shifts: such daily relations of mutuality cemented friendships and were in themselves a source of pride, a way of defining oneself as a good compañero/a. Beyond strengthening bonds between workers, however, such acts of goodwill maintained the rhythm of industrial output. From recruiting new workers to training them to compensating for occasional lapses, relations of compañerismo were themselves necessary to the process of production.

At the same time, some forms of compañerismo reflected not so much relations of mutuality as patterns of stratification among workers. Younger workers and newcomers to the mills were assistants, apprentices, bobbin carriers, and lubricators. Operatives sought to increase their production by maintaining good relations with these ancillary workers, as well as with the mechanics. Estanislao Bedoya, for example, remembered the tips the weavers gave him when he was fourteen and a bobbin carrier:

> There was one detail: they were all on contract, and so they [the weavers] would motivate you. . . . "Don't let me run out of weft 'cause then the machine stops and I lose money." . . . And so I'd hop to it [*ponerme las pilas*], and I wouldn't even take breaks or go to the snack bar, and this was like go and go and go so they wouldn't run out, all of them, every week they'd give me a tip of ten or fifteen pesos, *a tip,* and I'd get more money and so I was all motivated.[17]

Similarly, María de los Angeles Estrada described with evident pride how she made friends among the weavers (*tejedores*) while working as a cleaner. In describing her popularity María linked her willingness to help out, her good looks, and the friendly way she interacted with coworkers. Throughout the interview she returned to this theme, emphasizing the esteem in which other, more skilled, workers held her. (She made no references to other janitors or cleaners, only to weavers, mechanics, and supervisors.)

> ANN: And what was your relationship with them [the weavers] like?
> MARÍA: Well, like always, you know that you yourself are the one that makes friendship and fondness [*cariño*] happen. Depending on how they treat you, you also return that gratefulness, right? Oh! no, no, I got along really well, really well, the mechanics all had a special liking for me, the operatives [*las obreras*], everybody. They'd go, we'd go to breakfast in shifts . . . so that the personnel that stayed in the workrooms would take over the machines, so's not to turn them off, so's it wouldn't be lost, so's there would be enough production, because if they stopped the machines for fifteen minutes, then the tejedor wouldn't make anything, or the tejedora.
>
> Anyway, seeing then that I was so willing to help out, which I shouldn't say because one shouldn't sing one's own praises and I'm singing them, right? You're not going to say, "Oh! I'm so pretty! I'm so,

how wonderful! No. Anyway, the obreras, the tejedoras liked it if I went over to help them, because then I'd get the machine to go around again and I'd fill the bobbins with yarn; "come, come here," they'd call me over, some of them called me Tiny [*la chiquita*], others Blondie [*la monita*], others Anita, but anyway I always understood, right? Yes and the fondness, I saw that there was this fondness for me.[18]

Yet she also felt, and keenly, her inferior position, explaining that:

If you go to a factory and they put you to work cleaning bathrooms and you see another compañera who's handling a machine or who's handling a telephone, aren't you going to feel like kind of empty? But hey, look, we came in the same and look what they've got her doing and look at the job they gave me, I, you feel very empty inside, right?[19]

In addition to one's personal style, it seems, one's assigned place in the hierarchy of textile production influenced one's standing among coworkers.

If María claimed a general acceptance and popularity, many other women remembered feeling excluded from daily expressions of camaraderie because shyness or a strict demeanor kept them from socializing freely. Ofelia Gómez, for example, described her sister and herself as "very retiring" (*muy recojidas*), and said that "in the factory they called us 'fussbudgets' [*sismáticas*], because we were standoffish, almost obnoxious."[20] Another woman explained that she had been a loner and thought it best to study people before trusting them, but she made sure to pay some attention to her coworkers: "They could also call you selfish there, right?"[21]

Some women remembered being made fun of for maintaining a reserve with men and for refusing to flirt. Employing the third person to repeat "what others said" about her and her sister, Gumercinda Baez explained,

One's attitude was, like, serious. "The Baez sisters sure are serious aren't they?" . . . and they'd criticize like always in life, there's a lot of criticism, "That old maid over there, dressing up saints because she couldn't undress drunks."[22]

Similarly, Bárbara Alzate de López described her earlier self as having been "very serious," and recounted the jibes of a coworker who competed with her for a certain mechanic's affections (later Bárbara's husband). "She would make fun of me. . . . We'd run into each other and she'd say . . . like 'Blessed *Saint Bárbara*!' [Laughter.]"[23]

Many women described themselves, as did Ofelia, Bárbara, and Gumercinda, as different from their coworkers, more shy, more straitlaced, less fractious. In part, this reflects the way women shape their own narratives to fit culturally sanctioned images of femininity. It is also a matter of who was interviewed. Although some had worked only a few years or had left early to marry, most of the people I interviewed were women and men who had reached retirement in the mills. They represent those who remained at their jobs for more than twenty years, just 5 percent of the women and 10 percent of the men.[24] The women, especially, had been among those careful not to offend against mill rules either by being too friendly or fighting too readily.

Yet even loyal and long-term workers, those adept at staying out of trouble, told stories of suspensions and altercations with supervisors that disrupted their own narratives of obedience. Often, these stories were told with indignation at the injustice of a suspension or reprimand. María Cristina Restrepo, for example, recounted being suspended for talking when "talking" had been necessary to her work:

> They suspended me one day because the girl that had to clean showed up . . . and I told her, "Don't go and clean [the machine] now, because the spool [*carreta*] is very full and you won't be able to hold it and you'll bust it open." And so the foreman saw us and said, "No, send them home, one day each one" . . . and the conversation wasn't any more than that.

However, many retired workers were explicit about the amount of talking, bickering, and flirting that went on behind supervisors' backs. Lucía Jiménez, for example, readily acknowledged the gap between work rules and daily realities:

> ANN: And how were your relationships with your compañeras?
> LUCÍA: Very good, we had very good compañeras, horribly, horribly good compañeras.
> ANN: Yes? Could one talk during work hours?
> LUCÍA: No, not during work hours, but we had compañeras, that some of us helped each other out, it's like we can't talk during work hours? We were all there together—but yes, we could.[25]

Although they tell different kinds of stories, both María Cristina and Lucía remember talking as normal and, more importantly, legitimate behavior. Mundane as these examples may be, they attest to a larger truth: that prescriptions are not descriptions.

Zoila Rosa Valencia made this point subtly, by telling a story that contrasted the strict obedience of a coworker with her own ability to do the work without obeying all the rules.

ZOILA: I really like to talk and everything, I talked but I was working.
ANN: And this wasn't against the rules?
ZOILA: There was one there who said it was, but her mouth would get stuck here, she had to keep a bottle of water there to touch to it, and she scolded me because I talked a lot, I talk but I work.

A few minutes later, still confused, I asked:

ANN: What do you mean her mouth would get stuck?
ZOILA: It was that she wouldn't open her mouth so as not to talk, because she was very strict always and so it would stick [shut] purely from— you're working horrible, with plenty of heat, plenty of cotton rags? And you won't open your mouth? And so she kept a bottle of water here and she would touch her [mouth] with water. She scolded me a lot because I talked a lot, and I'd say, "Look, they can fire me or whatever, but I, I work but I talk too, because that's also part of it." . . . And look, they fired her, and left me there [laughter]. Do you see? Her instead of me— I shouldn't say it, I was very good at classifying the cloth.

As she developed it, the story became a fable of moral economy; the obedient woman, who scolded the others for talking, ended up fired. By telling a story about how they were required to destroy scrap pieces of cloth, Zoila uses the firing to reinforce a narrative argument against obeying too strictly, against losing one's ability to make moral judgments.

ANN: Why [did they fire her]?
ZOILA: Because, I don't know, because look, she was very strict, so you see that too much of anything is bad, poor her, they fired her.
ANN: Why?
ZOILA: Because she'd grab a piece of cloth and she wouldn't know what to do with it, and she'd run over to the office to ask this gentleman, those high-level employees over there, every few minutes with a rag, and I'd say to her . . . "Look, it's what your conscience tells you, it's you. This is what you live. You figure out where you should put it. *Do* something with it; don't ruin it."

And I never did cut them up [the cloth scraps], and I would say, "Oh God! Let it fall to a really poor person and let them make some clothes for their little child." I never did cut them and cutting them was *required*.

I never did cut them, I would feel such remorse to see a good big piece, that someone could use, and to cut it: Don't you think it's a sin?[26]

Having argued thus for a moral economy separate from work rules, and having presented the silent, obedient one as a woman without the conscience to disobey the rules about cutting fabric scraps, Zoila then explained that they were sent to different work stations, and the woman was eventually fired for refusing to clean a bathroom.[27] That is, the other woman was fired not for unthinking obedience but for prideful disobedience. This apparent contradiction underscores the extent to which this is a *story* that Zoila manipulates to make a point. In her recounting, the anecdote serves to attach transcendent value to her own disobedience; "talking" is equated with refusing to cut fabric that a poor person needs (perhaps to make clothes for a child), and both are opposed to unthinking obedience. Silent obedience is thus revealed to be inadequate by the very system that demands it; the other woman is fired and Zoila's own worth is recognized: "I was very good at classifying the cloth." Other women adopted the same roundabout strategy to tell stories of conflict and disobedience. Like Zoila, they framed accounts of disagreements with their coworkers with references to their skill as workers. They also used comedy to resolve some of the tension between having been both "good girls" and strong-minded women.

Fighting

For both women and men, an altercation with a coworker was a serious breach of factory discipline and could result in a fine, suspension, or firing. For women, however, fighting also transgressed gender boundaries separating anger, strength, and self-defense from images of femininity. One of the men I interviewed, the mechanic Enrique López, stated the contradiction between femininity and fighting explicitly: he observed that "women don't fight, and if they fight, they fight with their fingernails and nothing more."[28] Different definitions of *fighting* applied to women and men; by men's standards, he implies, women simply didn't fight. Yet at the same time he recognizes that, yes, women fought, but their ways of fighting were specifically female and thus insignificant.

Women's own stories about conflicts at work turned on the contradictions between fighting and having been good workers in an industry that valued a feminine demeanor. Part of the difficulty, for women, is that stories about fights are primarily narratives of pride: pride in one's work and in one's ability

Coltejer's twenty-fifth anniversary party in 1932. Women workers
pose for a photograph before sitting down to a festive brunch.
Courtesy of Fundación Antioqueña de Estudios Sociales.

to stand up for oneself. Talking about fights often allowed a retired worker to
present herself as a person who didn't let herself be pushed around. Genivera
García, for example, responded to a question about altercations among coworkers by saying, "No, of course there might be some problem every once
in a while, and I haven't been a person that stays quiet or someone who hangs
her head; I did have my disputes." [29] Proud of both their moments of intran-
sigence and their reputations as loyal workers and good compañeras, most
women told their stories in a double voice. They made their stories about
work, attributing the trouble to coworkers' refusal to do their fair share. They
also made the stories funny and laughed at themselves in the telling.

Concha Bohórquez, for example, recounted her refusal to sweep (after a
year of doing janitorial work without a promotion to weaving) more as an
altercation with fellow workers than as a breach of mill discipline, and she
presented her victory, when the supervisor changed the rules to make the
others sweep, as their comeuppance.

CONCHA: And so I got angry and I sat down, and I didn't want to sweep;
so then the supervisor says to me, "Look, Concha, what's this? What's
this horrible dustheap?" And I said, "It's 'cause there's no one to sweep."

Tejidos Hernández, 1917. Although workers pose facing the
camera, the space is clearly one of constant social interaction.
Different machines and work areas are in close proximity, and no
physical boundary separates female, male, or child workers.
Photograph by Benjamín de la Calle. Courtesy of Fundación
Antioqueña de Estudios Sociales.

"And what are you doing?" And I said, "Nothing, but I won't sweep by
myself, I won't sweep by myself."

ANN: [Laughter.] And what did he say?

CONCHA: Ah! "And so there's no one who sweeps here?" It was that there
were some who made fun of me, because I swept, and one, Oh! I can
just see her, one Matilde Velásquez, she would say to me, "Concha, you
didn't come here to do anything but clean?" . . . And so they made fun
of me, and so I said to myself, "I am really dumb," and there was one,
a few, a few who said, "and I've been working here *so long,* so long now
and they've never made me sweep."

Only after having established that the others had made fun of her does she
go on to describe denouncing them to the supervisor:

CONCHA: And so I said to him, "What do you mean there's no one to
sweep? Look here Don Aníbal, there are almost a hundred old women
there, *sitting* in circles . . . talking, talking behind people's backs, gossip-

Packing and finishing, Coltejer, circa 1940. Both men and
women sit at the sewing machines in the background. Note also
that folding and packaging was relatively clean, quiet work,
more conducive to talk than weaving or spinning. Photograph
by Francisco Mejía. Courtesy of Fundación Antioqueña de
Estudios Sociales.

ing, and they don't work *at all*. . . . What's wrong with them that they
can't grab a broom and sweep?"

I told him, "I don't know, but anyway I won't keep on sweeping, do
what you want with me, but I won't sweep," and so he went off to laugh.
. . . In a bit he passes by and says, "Go on, all of you, all of you," the whole
workroom, the workroom was very big . . . "All of you go read that."

ANN: And what did it say?

CONCHA: The list of everyone in the workroom, the days it was their turn
to sweep. . . . He made every single little one of them sweep.

ANN: And did they get mad?

CONCHA: Oh! They got mad! They almost beat me up, look, they insulted
me and shouted the ugliest things at me.

ANN: I guess so [laughter].

CONCHA: They were furious, furious, and me: happy, lucky, happy-go-
lucky. [More laughter.][30]

Ceremony for retired workers, Fabricato, 1953. Everybody
I interviewed had reached retirement in the mills, and many
people cherished the awards they received at such ceremonies.
For long-term workers, the rhetoric of family also brought a
public recognition of their worth. Photograph by Carlos
Rodríguez. Courtesy of Fundación Antioqueña de Estudios
Sociales.

In choosing this story to present her younger self and her relationship to both
the factory and her coworkers, Concha navigated between the conventional
signposts of compañerismo, obedience, and rebelliousness. She presented a
multilayered, self-aware persona and turned the interview itself into a place
for fun.

In pointing to her compañeras' bad work habits as the source of the
conflict, Concha employed a common narrative strategy—one that enabled
women to transgress accepted boundaries of femininity while emphasizing
their worth as workers. María Concepción López, for example, recounted
with gusto a fight with a coworker nicknamed the Butterfly, but she framed
the anecdote with a reference to the woman's negligence in cleaning the loom
they shared.

> ANN: Did you sometimes have like fights with the women, with compa-
> ñeras? And what were they like?
> MARÍA CONCEPCIÓN: Of course! Over there in the Leticia factory I fought

[laughter], one time I had this compañera—because there were two shifts—and there was this one, from here, also from Bello, she kept after me; they called her the Butterfly.

ANN: And why?

MARÍA CONCEPCIÓN: . . . I don't know, because she looked like it [laughter]. OK, and what do you think, every day she'd be coming out, and I'd be going in, and she would say, "Hey, you, look, you left the selvages on the floor"; and I'd tell her, "Not hardly, I picked them all up, it's you that leaves them for me," and we fought, hear? And we grabbed each other there in the bus, I was shoving her between the wheels of the bus—because I was sure strong then . . . and me hanging on her hair.

This story of María's strength and combativeness doubles as testimony that she was a good worker. She not only presents her adversary as negligent, but also calls management as a witness to her own worth.

I went to Don Samuel. "Look, Don Samuel, I just got in a fight with the Butterfly on the way in, because it's a pain in the neck [*fregancia*] every day, saying that I leave the selvages on the floor, and I don't leave her the selvages, I don't leave bad looms for my compañeras; you decide if you're going to give me a pink slip"; [and he said] "I won't fire you, María, you're very useful to me here." Ah! What do you think, she was left hoping. Oh well![31]

Bringing in management seems to provide women with a protective cover for stories involving outrageous or unladylike behavior. Even when understood as a narrative strategy, however, the appeal to authority complicates the question of resistance still further. On the one hand, Don Samuel's willingness to overlook the incident is important only because María's behavior might have gotten her fired. He appears in her story precisely because fighting interfered with the factory ideal of disciplined production. On the other hand, his appearance is incidental to the conflict between the two women. More tellingly, the story provoked laughter (hers and mine), not because her behavior transgressed against factory rules, but rather because women's fights clash with more general social norms.

Although told within the framework of an interview "about work," women's stories about their friendships and conflicts were often comments on femininity in the most general sense. Cristina Monsalve, for example, used the story of a vigilanta's malicious gossip to emphasize the three themes around which she structured the interview: a widow's precarious position in the factory and in society, her own reputation as a moral woman, and her ability to defend herself in a hostile world.[32] Placed in this context, Cristina's sharp tongue becomes a heroic asset.

To begin, she explained that the vigilanta of the women's restroom, whose job it was to make sure that women neither conversed nor tarried too long, didn't like her and began to spread a rumor that Cristina, who had gained weight, was pregnant. A coworker informed Cristina:

> She told me, "Girl, look what she's saying . . . that you're pregnant." And I said: "Yeah? And they're going to be twins, one for her and the other one for you," I answered her like that. When I told myself: "Keep quiet? No. Wait and see," and I went to the office.

Rather than confront the other woman immediately, Cristina, like María Concepción, sought redress from a supervisor. Unlike María Concepción, however, she claimed a moral legitimacy in refusing to press the issue with higher management, saying that she did not wish for the other woman to lose her job.[33]

> CRISTINA: I went to the office, and I told Don Antonio, "Look, Don Antonio, I'm very sorry, but do me the favor of calling the, the, the bathroom monitor, because she's telling my compañeras that I'm in a compromised state." And I took off my apron—you had to wear an apron there, right?—and I told him: "You are a married man, go right ahead, check me, because it's easily known," I told him. And he said, "What's this, Doña Cristina?" And I told him, "That's right sir, what you heard"; and so he had her [the friend who had told her] called in, and he said to her, "What did that lady tell you about Doña Cristina?" And she said, "Uh, yes she said that Doña Cristina almost seemed to be in a compromised state."
>
> ANN: Uhmm, so outrageous.
>
> CRISTINA: Ay! What a sin.
>
> ANN: Some people are like malicious.
>
> CRISTINA: And so he said to me, "This is very serious, so that you know. . . . I authorize you to go to the administration office." And I told him, "No, Don Antonio, I won't go to the administration, because she is the mother of five children, as am I, and perhaps they'd fire her, and that would pain me a lot, not for her but for the children."
>
> ANN: She was also a widow?
>
> CRISTINA: Hmmm. I left it to God to take care of her.

Cristina did not, however, leave it to God or anyone else. Rather, as she de-scribed it, she used the occasion of her next menstrual period to humiliate the vigilanta in a pointed way:

> And I said to her, look, uh, when I got sick? I left the toilet full and I told her, "Look, I left them there for you to baptize, and watch how you talk," . . . and I tormented her with that until, until they fired her. . . . "Look, there they are for you to baptize and watch how you talk," . . . and look, I left with my retirement and she left fired.

This seems to be an oft-repeated anecdote, consciously remembered and structured to say certain things about factory life, society's prejudices, and Cristina herself. With the punch line, the speaker has finished a story; it is a completed fable, and like Zoila Rosa's story about talking, it ends with the moral reminder that the other woman ended up fired. Yet her firing stands not as testimony to the importance of working hard, but rather as a reminder of people's maliciousness and the importance of upholding one's reputation. Significantly, the supervisor can arbitrate the conflict because he stands apart from it; the quarrel is not about work, at least not as he defines it.

Fighting constituted resistance only in an indirect and contingent sense. Fights marked a community of equals, in that they were reciprocal in nature. While one might talk back to or even physically challenge a class superior, one did not generally "fight" with him or her. Like other forms of nonwork inter-action at work, moments of conflict defined an autonomous cultural space within the factory walls. Factory owners defined fighting, with talking, as an affront to discipline and thus made it so, but operatives' daily struggles were as much with one another as with management. In pursuit of companionship and self-expression, Medellín's workers created a culture of reciprocity within the mills; naming all aspects of that culture "resistance" would render one-dimensional workers' creative interactions.

Flirting

Workers not only talked and argued, but also flirted, paired up, and pursued courtship during work hours, despite the concerted efforts of factory man-agers and moral reformers. To do so, they broke rules, tricked vigilantas, and risked disciplinary action—all of which resisted the industrial order. As with fighting, however, ambiguities arose; resistance was more a strategy for flirt-ing than vice-versa. Additionally, understanding flirting requires balancing an analysis of its function as "resistance" with an exploration of the ways it both buttressed and challenged gender ideology.

Flirting, more than fighting or talking, challenged the local ideology of industrial discipline; it defied the moral pretensions of industrialists and moral reformers. In interviews, I tended to ask questions about the gap between factory rules and the reality of daily interactions. Most people responded that, yes, the vigilantas were strict: one couldn't talk or visit with a boy- or girlfriend, but they had found ways to get around the rules. Concha Bohórquez, for example, explained that, no, talking was not allowed, but conversations between *novios* happened "on the run, on the wing." A married couple described how they managed to see each other while working in different sections of the mill:

ANN: And how did you meet each other?
EUGENIO MÁRQUEZ: Well right there in the same factory, she would pass by and look, and I would pass by and look—
ESTER GÓMEZ DE MÁRQUEZ: In the shifts . . . I had to pass by his section, [it was] a walk way.
ANN: Yes. And so it was like you kept an eye out for each other?
EUGENIO: An electric eye![34]

Like Ester and Eugenio, most retired people described both how rigid the rules had been and how easily they'd gotten around them. If the vigilanta was strict, they met their novios during official breaks or between shifts. Bárbara Alzate de López explained that Enrique, who worked as a mechanic, would meet her during lunch and between shifts but not during work hours. "That's what the signs said, you can talk all you want when you leave, but inside the factory, nothing!" she recalled.

We'd go out in shifts, and, and we'd go out and so he like, it was like weaving over here and spinning over there, and so he'd come out of weaving, and I'd meet him here and he'd meet me over here, and so we'd go on talking while we ate lunch, he'd go to lunch and I'd be coming back, and they'd sound the siren and all that, and we would talk.

Luis Castrillón remembered meeting his girlfriend between shifts, for which he was penalized with a shift change: "They changed my shift, I remember really well that they changed one of my shifts, because, well, they saw me with her. . . . I would go in a little bit before she left and we would talk a bit watching out for the vigilanta, ah yes, that was what life was like."[35] Workplace flirtations were sometimes risky and opportunities fleeting, but the many interstices of the working day, from lunch breaks to shift changes to the physical passageways between factory buildings, provided spaces for courtship.

In social/sexual terms, factory space was different from both home and street. Precisely because Medellín's textile industrialists developed and carefully guarded a reputation for moral policing, parents and older relatives sent their girls off to work with less fear of sexual danger than was generally the case in other industrial regions. Although some retired women remembered family disapproval about their seeking a mill job, most of those who worked at Coltejer or Fabricato reported that local residents, and even people in outlying villages, recognized the "morality" of these aggressively Christian workplaces. For young women particularly, this may have allowed freedoms (for whispered conversations and unchaperoned moments) not available in their parents' houses, but in an environment that was safer than the street. On the other hand, workplace interactions may have merged easily with other opportunities for flirtation and courtship. Young people met each other at work and then pursued socially sanctioned means of getting to know each other. Luis Castrillón, for example, also waited beneath his girlfriends' windows and visited them in their parents' living rooms. As María Cristina Restrepo put it, "It was very simple, because then you would meet in the factory; and over there's the house, and there's the street."

Mixed-sex interaction at work, however, may have allowed for more informality than the conventional patterns of visiting or courting. Many women enjoyed the easy, teasing compañerismo of male workers without involving themselves in the negotiations of courtship and marriage, negotiations that would have meant leaving their jobs. María Cristina, who remained single and reached retirement at Fabricato, remembered her various beaux with fond amusement. She used a comic anecdote to describe her popularity with both male coworkers and the supervisors at Fabricato.

> Working one Sunday, some guys, workers, came over to talk to me; and then the supervisor saw us and so I said, "the *supervisor,* the *supervisor;* but don't you move." And so he came over and [said], "Come," all four, it was four guys, compañeros from right there, the same workroom, "Come here, I am going to ask you a question." All of us shaking; yes [laughter]. . . . And so he said, "Tell me, what [perfume] does Cristina wear that everybody hangs around her machines all the time?"
>
> And so one of them was more bold, and he said to him . . . "Look, it's simple. I went to ask her if since we were working on Sunday and we didn't go to mass, if it was a sin. . . . Do you think it is?" And so he said,

"You all always win, that's what," the supervisor said. And so I said, "Ave María, it's not like it's won," I said.

But we did say, "They're going to suspend us." Fine, and so he said, "Fine, you all like to talk to Cristina, on Sunday we're going to work, but I'm going to put her to work whitewashing, who wants to hold the ladder for her?"; so they all jumped up, "I'll hold the ladder!" [Laughter.] That was a whole conversation there too.

The snatches of dialogue Cristina uses to illustrate her story contribute to a reconstruction of mixed-sex relations in Medellín's mills. First, despite the vigilanta system, men and women congregated, talked, and flirted. Second, it seems that supervisors, too, could participate in the kind of teasing jocularity that enlivened the workday and went unrecorded in the disciplinary record. Third, Cristina's story shows how the enforced piety of a mill like Fabricato, where religion and *la moral* were supposed to occupy workers' hearts and minds at all times, could be undercut by joking irreverence, as when her friend used Sunday mass to distract the supervisor from disciplining them for talking.

If workplace familiarity created opportunities for stolen conversations, romance, and simple teasing, it also prepared the ground for petty jealousies. In describing her courtship with Enrique, for example, Bárbara Alzate de López emphasized, in a lighthearted way, his inconstancy and the recriminations she suffered at the hands of his other girlfriends. "They did me a lot of wrong," she remembered, saying that they stole the yarn from her spinning machine so that she would have to stop and refill, thus losing money. But, Bárbara maintained, she ignored the rumors she heard at work—until he took up with a certain girl in the weaving section, "which like made me a little bit mad. . . . He left me to go out with her. . . . She worked in weaving with him, so when I would be going out and waiting for him, he had already left with her, and so, tell me who would put up with that?" For her, the social world of the factory transformed a personal rejection into public humiliation.

As a loom fixer, Enrique enjoyed an ease of movement within the factory that allowed him opportunities for conversation and flirtation not available to operatives. As he recalled, "the men talked a lot, chatted with the obreras. . . . To talk with an obrera while you were fixing her loom? This was very common." He added, however, that many vigilantas had been quick to suspend an obrera for talking to a mechanic, even if she was only responding to his questions.[36] Daily relations between loom fixers and female operatives were colored by inequalities of status: mechanics escaped the petty authority of vigilantas or room supervisors. They were considered highly skilled workers and were well paid; they also derived advantage from masculine privilege, as only men could be mechanics.

Within the gendered hierarchy of textile workplaces, in which both women and men worked as spinners and weavers but technicians and higher-level supervisors were invariably male, sexual harassment happened between workers, as well as between supervisors and female operatives. In fact, working-women in Medellín were probably less vulnerable than factory women elsewhere, at least after the imposition of Catholic paternalism in the 1930s. But that protection, bought with acute surveillance, was only a relative protection. Committed to the ideology of moral reform, Antioqueño industrialists routinely fired male workers, including supervisors and mechanics, who "disrespected" female coworkers. Indeed, their willingness to fire men as well as women for lapses of morality was what set Medellín's paternalists apart from their counterparts abroad. Nevertheless, many of the women I interviewed described male workers' unwelcome advances and their own discomfort in the face of ribald comments or open propositions.

Women had struck to protest sexual exploitation at the Fábrica de Bello in 1920, and retired women, remembering the 1930s and 1940s, employed their own language of censure.[37] They remembered with distaste the innuendos of some male coworkers, and they staked a claim to self-respect on the distinction between mutual flirtation and sexual intimidation. When recounting unwelcome advances, for example, women often emphasized their ability to defend themselves, and thus rescued a sense of honor from a dishonorable situation. As part of an extended lecture on the trials of being a widow, Cristina Monsalve recalled an altercation with a mechanic:

ANN: And wasn't there, what was it you told me, like about a mechanic?
CRISTINA: No, it was that one day a mechanic thought that I looked like very good—
HER DAUGHTER: Or he thought you looked easy, he thought you looked easy.
CRISTINA: ¡Ay! [He said to me] "How good you look, you haven't got a single bad piece [of breastmeat], you're like a chicken!" [No tiene presa mala, ¡está como la gallina!]
ANN: ¡Ay!
CRISTINA: "I'd throw away four hundred pesos on you tonight," and I said, "and why don't you throw them away on your mother, you *scoundrel!* What have I done to you for you to say such things to me? Look, I'm

not going to the office to tell what you said to me because they'll fire you and you have children, but I know how to defend myself from you." And look, and he's still alive . . . and I won't speak to him—he's old, old, but I won't speak to him.

Other women employed different strategies of defense: María Cristina Restrepo, for example, convinced a male coworker to leave her alone by persuading her brother to pose as a boyfriend. And Ofelia Gómez, who worked at Coltejer in the 1940s, adopted a more intransigent position. "I carried a pocketknife," she explained,

> And a compañero told me, "Look out when the electricity goes out, they're going to grab you." I took out the pocketknife and I had it open, and the lights were about to come back on when [a guy] grabbed me, and I cut him—right then and there they took him to the emergency room. And that one got fired, that one got fired.

Her sister added that "she was very sought-after . . . but she defended herself very well." [38]

Ana Palacios de Montoya, who used the nickname Nena, related her interactions with a mechanic, a man I had also interviewed, in a somewhat lighter vein. She maintained a clandestine but long-term relationship with another worker, whom she married in 1961, after Coltejer eased its restrictions on married women, and this stability may have enabled her to counter and laugh off other men's banter more easily than most workingwomen. Nevertheless, she underscored her satisfaction at informing the mechanic, finally, that she was married.

> NENA: That one hassled me a lot. . . . He'd say why couldn't we go out on Sunday,
> ANN: [Laughter.]
> NENA: That we should go out to the country and take a bottle of *aguardiente* with us. . . . So I'd say, "take a blanket too," and, "So at one o'clock?"; "No, one is really late, I'll be there at twelve," and me a married woman, such things, and when he realized, I told him, "Now I'm going to tell you; because I'm going to retire now, with God's help I'll leave this next year, and I'm going to tell you: don't hassle me *for anything,* I am married." And he said, "Nena, I'm going to fall over."
> ANN: [Laughter.]
> NENA: And he's a good friend of mine, he comes over, he's a good friend of mine. [39]

Nena countered and joked with the mechanic, emphasizing their friendship, but simultaneously presented their workplace interaction as a problem that it was incumbent on her to resolve. The boundary between flirtation and harassment was drawn and redrawn by different women in different ways, and one suspects that workingwomen in Medellín attempted as many varying forms of pursuit, concession, and defense as other urban women in this century. Rather than providing easy generalizations, women's stories about mixed-sex interactions sketch an ambiguity. The factory allowed women the pleasures of an easy camaraderie with male coworkers, but it also housed certain risks, to one's reputation and to one's person.

Conclusion

Like their stories about talking and fighting, workers' accounts of sexualized interactions were only tangentially about the factory as a site of industrial production. Although some people described getting in trouble for socializing or arguing, their stories were about one another, not about management. Similarly, women directed their frustration with men who overstepped the boundaries of sociability against the men themselves, not against supervisors or vigilantas who failed to guarantee civility. Workers' relations with one another, whether jovial or nasty, existed separately from the disciplinary apparatus of the factory.

It is this separateness that so confuses the question of resistance. By playing around, talking, and bickering, workers combated the very basis of industrial discipline. They refused the idea that waged time must always be work time, that they should be as silent and fixed in position as their machines, and that their coworkers were interchangeable parts. That said, however, daily patterns of sociability presupposed no organic links of the kind labor historians call "solidarity." Workers' conviviality challenged the industrial order, but it also generated enmities and, for women, imposed normative constraints.

Because Medellín's workers succeeded in evading industrialists' attempts to control all aspects of their working time, their interactions acquired an aspect of resistance. Yet precisely by so often evading managers' eyes, workingwomen and -men took their mutual exchanges quite outside the two-dimensional realm of resistance and accommodation. Attending to the creative ways they reconstructed their lives in the factories requires not finding a middle ground between the two, but rather refusing to accept this opposition. Resistance is not a concept that will help labor historians understand informal work cultures.[40] Instead of flattening working people's interactions into meanings derived from their subaltern status as workers, labor historians might do more to explore the contradictions inherent in their being human beings even while at work.

Notes

1   Susana Osorio, interview with author, Envigado (Rosellón), July 24, 1991. Susana Osorio is a pseudonym, at her request. This was an informal interview, taped while Susana and two friends waited in line for their pension checks. All other cited interviews were conducted in workers' homes; names given are pseudonyms except where the person interviewed specifically requested that his or her name appear. I interviewed weavers, spinners, and people who had worked at a variety of other tasks, as well as a factory matron (*vigilanta*) and men who had worked their way up to become supervisors. All translations are my own.

2   Workers in company towns have reappropriated the language of family in a variety of national settings. For an excellent discussion of this language as used in the southern United States see Jacquelyn Dowd Hall, James Lelondis, Robert Korstad, Mary Murphy, LuAnn Jones, and Christopher B. Daly, *Like a Family: The Making of a Southern Cotton Mill World* (Chapel Hill: University of North Carolina Press, 1987), p. xvii.

3   Medellín has long been seen as an unusual case of local entrepreneurship, and the city's industrialization has sparked debates about patterns of capital formation, regional markets, and the Antioqueño personality. The best new work argues that the capital for early industrial ventures came from import/export firms and holders of urban real estate rather than from mining fortunes or coffee planters. See Fernando Botero Herrera, *La industrialización en Antioquia: Génesis y consolidación 1900–1930* (Medellín: Centro de Investigaciones Económicas, 1984); Ann Twinam, *Merchants, Miners, and Farmers in Colonial Colombia,* Latin American Monographs, no. 57 (Austin: University of Texas Press, 1982); and Juan José Echavarría, "External Shocks and Industrialization: Colombia, 1920–1950," (D.Phil. diss., Oxford, 1989).

4   See, for example, Michel Foucault, *Discipline and Punish* (New York: Vintage Books, 1979), p. 143.

5   Comments of this sort fill a 1918–1934 personnel log from Coltejer, held at the company's *hemeroteca* in Itagüí.

6   For an extended discussion of this process see Luz Gabriela Arango, *Mujer, religion, e industria* (Medellín: Universidad de Antioquia, 1991); Ann Farnsworth-Alvear, "Gender and the Limits of Industrial Discipline: Textile Work in Medellín, Colombia, 1905–1960" (Ph.D. diss., Duke University, 1994); and Alberto Mayor Mora, *Etica, trabajo y productividad en Antioquia* (Bogotá: Tercer Mundo, 1984).

7   Textile workers' often-suppressed attempts to form unions or negotiate mean-
     ingful compromises with management are not discussed here, but see Mauricio
     Archila Neira, *Cultura e Identidad: Colombia, 1910–1945* (Bogotá: Cinep, 1991); and
     Ivan Darío Osorio, *Historia del Sindicalismo Antioqueño, 1900–1986* (Medellín: Insti-
     tuto Popular de Capitación, 1988).

8   See *Informe de Hacienda de 1916,* as cited by Montenegro, "Breve historia de las
     principales empresas textileras," *Revista de Extensión Cultural* (de la universidad
     nacional de Colombia, seccional de Medellín), p. 62; as well as Montenegro, "La
     industria textil en Colombia, 1900–1945," *Desarrollo y Sociedad,* no. 8 (May 1982):
     p. 133. See also the *Anuario estadístico de Medellín, 1923,* to which have been added
     the available figures for Fabricato (Arango, p. 301) and for Montoya Hermanos y
     Cia (Inspector de Fábricas, Acta no. 1362, April 10, 1922, Signatura 8934, Archivo
     Histórico de Antioquia [AHA]). See also Botero, *La industrialización en Antioquia,*
     p. 174; and Dawn Keremitsis, "Latin American Women Workers in Transition:
     Sexual Division of the Labor Force in Mexico and Colombia in the Textile In-
     dustry," *The Americas* 40 (1984): p. 497.

9   This was true of the city's largest and most established mills, but there were two
     important exceptions: Tejidos Leticia, whose Jewish owners paid little mind to
     the ideology of Catholic paternalism, and Tejicondor, founded in 1935 and thus a
     relative latecomer. Workers from other mills referred to these as factories of tol-
     erance (*fábricas alcahuetas*), because the owners hired unmarried mothers as well
     as married women. Nevertheless, there seem to have been rather arbitrary limits:
     women who retired from Tejidos Leticia and Tejicondor remember a limit of
     three births—with a fourth pregnancy, a woman would be fired.

10   See Mary Roldán, "Purifying the Factory, Demonizing the 'Public Service Sec-
     tor': The Role of Ethnic and Cultural Difference in Determining Perceptions of
     Working Class Militancy in Colombia, 1940–1955" (paper presented at the Eighth
     Latin American Labor History Conference, Princeton University, April 1991).

11   Acta no. 1533, "Libro de Actas del Inspector de Fábricas," August 9, 1922, Signa-
     tura 8934, AHA.

12   Acta no. 427, August 18, 1927, Signatura 8949, AHA. See also Acta no. 1476,
     July 7, 1922, Signatura 8934, which editorializes that talking "is prejudicial for
     the maintenance of morality; it wounds the interests of the firm and prejudices
     the women workers, who obtain a lower salary if they neglect their labors."

13   Tejidos de Bello, "Reglamento de la Fábrica," vol. 881, Archivo Fabricato, Au-
     gust 1935.

14   Figures are based on a simple random sample of 781 personnel records from six
     mills. Based on the estimates of company archivists, I calculated that the mill ar-
     chives held 65,000 records for the years under study; aiming for a sample of 1,000
     people, I entered the data from one in every sixty-five records (after a random
     start). Their estimates were low, and the finished sample contained 781. Thanks

to George Farnsworth and Stephen Pyne for their statistical help, and to Christa Avampato for her work on this project.

15   María Cristina Restrepo, interview with author, Bello (Fabricato), October 23, 1990.

16   *Pasa-lizos,* or drawing in, refers to the process of threading the loom harness with the warp yarn. It was seated work and relatively clean (Ana María Jaramillo, interview with María Rosa Lalinde, Medellín [Fabricato], 1987). I have added some punctuation marks for clarity. I thank Ana María Jaramillo for her friendship and for sharing the transcripts of interviews she and Jorge Bernal conducted in 1986–1987; thanks are also due to Maurício Archila and the Instituto Popular de Capacitación in Medellín.

17   Estanislao Bedoya, interview with author, Medellín (Coltejer), October 25, 1990. Another man who had worked as a *repartidor* when he was fifteen remembered being pampered by the women weavers: "They really liked me because I was the person—the youngest, and so they really like me there . . . they'd give me snacks." Fabio Garcés, interview with author, Medellín (Coltejer), October 25, 1990.

18   María de los Angeles Estrada, interview with author, Medellín (Tejicondor), July 16, 1991.

19   Ibid.

20   Ofelia and Clara Gómez, unrecorded interview with author, Medellín (Coltejer), July 18, 1991. This and other comments by the Gómez sisters are taken from my notes of this conversation.

21   Martha Franco, interview with Ana María Jaramillo, Medellín (Fabricato), 1987.

22   Gumercinda Baez Amado, interview with author, Bello (Tejidos Leticia), February 22, 1991.

23   Bárbara Alzate de López, interview with author, Envigado (Rosellón), August 2, 1991.

24   Percentages are based on the statistical sample described in note 8.

25   Lucía Jiménez, interview with author, Envigado (Rosellón), May 21, 1991.

26   Zoila Rosa Valencia, interview with author, Bello (Fabricato), October 8, 1990.

27   After explaining that all the women in the section were moved elsewhere, Zoila said, "The one that I told you about, that her mouth would get stuck from not talking, one day they sent her to replace the woman who did the cleaning, in the bathrooms, and she didn't want to go, and so they fired her."

28   Enrique López, interview with author, Envigado (Rosellón), July 30, 1991.

29   Genivera García, interview with Jorge Bernal and Ana María Jaramillo, Medellín (Fabricato), 1987. For a discussion of remembered fights as narratives of pride see Alessandro Portelli, "The Best Garbage-Can Wiper in Town," in *The Death of Luigi Trastulli and Other Stories* (Albany: State University of New York Press, 1991).

30   Concha Bohórquez, interview with author, Bello (Fabricato), October 23, 1991.

31   María Concepción López, interview with author, Bello (Tejidos Leticia), May 22, 1991.

32   Cristina returned repeatedly to these themes, constructing her narrative around the stock phrase that a young widow "has to fight the world, the devil, and the flesh." Throughout two interviews, however, she developed a subtext of resistance, a story of her successful fight against the many obstacles in a widow's life. Key anecdotes serve to tell that story: (1) she confronts the company's general manager to get her job back after her husband's death, traveling to Medellín to do so; (2) she struggles to raise three children on her miserable wages, recounting the pain of leaving them each morning; and (3) she defends herself from male workers who see a young widow as fair game for sexual harrassment, reconstructing conversations in which she is always ready with a sharp retort (Cristina Monsalve, interview with author, Envigado [Rosellón], July 30, 1992).

33   Unlike María Concepción, who claimed that she had informed on fellow workers who sought to organize a union, Cristina insisted at several points that "yo no era sapa," a colloquialism akin to "I never squawked." She claimed, for example, that management had asked her to be a vigilanta but that she would not do it: "No! What a horrible thing! To be a vigilanta? Ay! So that everyone who went by would say: 'that damned old tattletale?'"

34   Eugenio Márquez and Ester Gómez de Márquez, interview with author, Bello, October 16, 1990.

35   Luis Castrillón, interview with author, Envigado (Rosellón), July 24, 1991.

36   Enrique López, interview with author, Envigado (Rosellón), July 30, 1991.

37   On the Bello strike see Ann Farnsworth-Alvear, "The Mysterious Case of the Missing Men," *International Labor and Working Class History* 49 (1996): pp. 73–92.

38   See note 20.

39   Ana Palacios de Montoya, interview with author, Medellín (Coltejer), November 8, 1990.

40   For a thoughtful argument to the contrary see Alf Lüdkte, "Cash, Coffee-Breaks, Horseplay: *Eigensinn* among Factory Workers in Germany circa 1900," in *Confrontation, Class Consciousness, and the Labor Process,* ed. Michael Hanagan and Charles Stephenson, *Contributions in Labor Studies,* no. 18 (New York: Greenwood Press, 1986); as well as Lüdkte, "Organizational Order or *Eigensinn?* Workers' Privacy and Workers' Politics in Germany," in *Rites of Power: Symbolism, Ritual, and Politics since the Middle Ages,* ed. Sean Wilentz (Philadelphia: University of Pennsylvania Press, 1985).

Women and Working-Class Mobilization in Postwar São Paulo, 1945–1948

JOHN D. FRENCH WITH MARY LYNN PEDERSEN CLUFF

It has often been observed that "where power is, women are not." Noting women's virtual absence from the realm of conventional politics, Jane Jaquette urged scholars in 1980 to look beyond elections in studying female political participation in Latin America. Arguing for an "expanded notion of the political," she called for research on female participation within different social classes, especially their role in "informal networks . . . clientele linkages, . . . strike activities, urban land seizures and barrio politics."[1] This chapter employs a community study method to investigate women's grassroots participation in politics and labor mobilization following World War II in the region of greater São Paulo known as ABC (named after the *municípios* of Santo André, São Bernardo do Campo, and São Caetano).

One of Latin America's preeminent industrial centers, the ABC region has expanded at an accelerating pace since its first factories were established at the turn of the century. From a population of 10,000 in 1900 (including 1,000 industrial workers), the ABC region grew to a population of 216,000 by 1950 (including 46,000 industrial workers). Brazil's fourth-largest industrial center, the socially homogeneous factory districts of Santo André and São Caetano represented one of the most dramatic concentrations of modern, large-scale industrial production in postwar Brazil.[2]

This chapter will focus on the role of women during the extraordinary political and trade union mobilizations that began in 1945.[3] This postwar upsurge was vigorously repressed after 1947, however, and was soon forgotten, its significance largely ignored by later historians and activists. While some scholars have dealt schematically with working-class activism during this period, no one has seriously examined the role of working-class women, neighborhood agitation, and electoral politics.[4]

Between 1945 and 1948, workers in Brazil were drawn into public and political activity on an unprecedented scale. During such periods of popular ferment, the dynamics of women's sociopolitical participation emerge more clearly than in normal times. This broad generalization about such unusual periods holds true for Santo André and São Caetano: the greater the extent, depth, and intensity of working-class mobilization, the greater the involvement and visibility of working-class women, housewives as well as women workers.[5] This article is thus intended to fill two lacunae in recent research on women in Latin America: the scarcity of historical studies of women and politics,[6] and the lack of detailed examinations of women's participation in trade unions.[7]

Working-Class Consciousness and Gender Ideology

Although women have long been assumed to be irrelevant to "real" (that is, male) class politics,[8] Brazilian researchers in the last twenty years have published a number of fine empirical investigations into the lives of women workers and working-class housewives.[9] Yet these dimensions of female working-class life have not yet been successfully integrated into an understanding of the broader dynamics of working-class struggle.[10] Moreover, the "snapshot" nature of most of this sociological fieldwork has obscured patterns of development over time.

Observers of Brazilian working-class life have repeatedly emphasized the influence of patriarchal family ideology, with its biological determinism and stereotypical assertion that women's rightful place is in the home. Researchers have also linked the prevailing gender ideology to women's greater passivity at work and to their lesser participation in unions and politics. Unfortunately, the assumption that a given social class necessarily has or should have a particular type of consciousness has led some scholars to adopt a crude typology of "class-conscious" or "non-class-conscious" workers, the latter being a residual category to which women and other "failed" or "backward" workers are relegated. For example, one study asserted that working women did not "identify with their work," failed to maintain "any identification as a worker," and behaved "much more like passive and dependent housewives than militant workers, which they are not."[11]

Luiz Pereira's excellent sociological investigation in Santo André in 1958 suggested the importance of a nuanced understanding of the relationship between gender ideology and behavior. The industrial working-class families he studied believed that "women — mothers and daughters — should live as much as possible within the household" and restrict themselves to domestic activities. In keeping with these patriarchal ideals, he found clear notions of male and female spheres, and less family interest in educating daughters than sons.[12]

Although male supremacist ideology is deeply entrenched in all social classes, it is also a class-specific phenomenon that is shaped to fit differing economic realities, in this case the needs of a wage-dependent, urban, working-class household. Pereira found that community residents "highly value the wife who works outside the home for pay, to 'help the husband' . . . [even as they] value more highly the situation of the wife who does not have to do so because the husband earns a good living or because the sons 'already have a wage.' "[13] While by no means eliminating gender conflict, the interdependent nature of the household unit nonetheless has important implications for working-class behavior.[14]

The persistence of such attitudes in the ABC region was confirmed in Carmen Macedo's impressive study of eighty-two families of São Caetano ceramic workers in 1974. She found that women's work outside the home, whether that of wives or daughters, was viewed as a woman's duty rather than her right. "It is not," she concluded, "an ideology of equality of the sexes that impels the woman toward the labor market. . . . [Rather, she does so] *despite* an ideology of inequality between the sexes" (emphasis in original). Macedo cautioned that this gap between the ideal of female domesticity and the reality of women's work outside the home does not necessarily imply "the abandonment of the ideal of different roles" for men and women. Instead, women's work outside the home is viewed as an exception stemming from economic difficulties or the family's desire for upward social mobility.[15]

Other observers have cited working-class women's partial or sporadic participation in the workforce, explaining that "they tend to see work outside the home as something compulsory and, hence, undesirable."[16] But this apparent female acceptance of patriarchal norms also contains an element of protest and class feeling. As Carmen Macedo and Jessita Rodrigues have suggested, it is incorrect to say that working-class women reject work outside the home per se. Rather, in using the widely accepted conventions of patriarchal discourse, they are implicitly criticizing the employment opportunities open to them and the actual conditions of labor that they experience in the industrial workplace.[17]

Despite the seemingly unambiguous patriarchal language invoking separate spheres, working-class women's expressed distaste for work outside the home actually conceals a distinctly feminine reflection of their consciousness of class. Moreover, their expressed desire not to enter into social production can also be interpreted as a desire to avoid women's double workday, as has been suggested by Rosalina de Santa Cruz Leite. Her interviews with twenty-two activist female metalworkers in São Paulo revealed these women's awareness that "the woman who works is more the master of her own nose." Yet her interviewees were also aware of the unequal division of domestic tasks between working wives and husbands, arguing that "there's no advantage to getting married if all it means is double work."[18]

Women Workers, Housewives, and Voters in Santo André and São Caetano

Industrial employment in the ABC region grew rapidly after the establishment of the first large textile factories in 1900. By 1920 some forty-three hundred workers were employed in the ABC region, with at least 15 percent of local laborers being women (see table 1). Employed in several large local textile factories, women workers actively participated in the 1919 Ipiranguinha textile strike in Santo André. As part of the broader labor upsurge that swept male and female workers in São Paulo between 1917 and 1919, the strikers paraded through the streets in an effort to call out workers at other factories. At the strike's dramatic climax, a vocal nineteen-year-old male weaver named Constantino Castellani was killed by a policeman protecting a local factory.[19]

Female participation in industrial employment among local residents stood at one-quarter of the total resident workforce in 1940 and 1950, with some women employed in neighboring São Paulo. Census statistics documenting female employment in factories located in the ABC region (whose workforces have typically included commuters from São Paulo) would be far more revealing than this demographic data on local residents. Unfortunately, only the industrial census of 1940 broke down the total industrial workforce by gender. But we do have unpublished statistical data from the municipal archives that allow analysis of factory workforces by gender in Santo André and São Caetano for 1938, 1942, and 1947 (see table 2).

Significant changes in women's participation in the labor force in Santo André and São Caetano occurred between 1938 and 1947. While the absolute number of women working increased substantially, their relative share of the total factory workforce declined moderately (see table 3). Yet disaggregated analysis reveals that women were by no means tangential to the factory proletariat, because of their overwhelming concentration in larger enterprises with significant female workforces (see table 3).

Table 1. Female Participation in Industry among Residents of
the ABC Region of Brazil, 1920–1950

YEAR	TOTAL RESIDENT WORKERS	RESIDENT WOMEN WORKING	WOMEN WORKERS (%)
1920	2,648	388	15
1940	23,190	5,372	23
1950	59,550	14,591	25

Sources: Instituto Brasileiro de Geografia e Estatística (IBGE), *Recenseamento . . . 1920, Censo
Demográfico*, vol. 4, pt. 5, no. 2, pp. 776–77; IBGE, *Recenseamento . . . 1940, Censo Demográfico*,
vol. 25, no. 1, pp. 130–31.

Table 2. Female Participation in Industrial Workforce Employed
in Santo André and São Caetano, 1938–1947

WORKERS IN SANTO ANDRÉ[a]	1938	1942	1947
Total workforce	17,125	22,914	44,350
Women workers	6,120	6,124	11,908
Percentage of women workers	36	27	27

Sources: Prefeitura Municipal de Santo André (PMSA), unpublished documents, "Estatística
Industrial" for 1938, 1942, and 1947.
[a] Figures for Santo André include the districts of Paranapiacaba and Utinga.

In 1947, 47 percent of all women workers in Santo André and São Caetano were found in ten enterprises employing three hundred or more women
workers (see table 4). The average total workforce of all enterprises employing forty-nine or more women had increased from 544 in 1938 to 926 by 1947
(see table 3). Women were also present in significant numbers in certain metalworking, chemical, and rubber factories (see table 5). Moreover, the largest
employers of women in 1947 were two enormous, ultramodern rayon-fiber
factories that ranked among the largest enterprises in the region. Although
classified as textile plants, the Rhodiaceta factory (with 1,879 workers) and
the plant operated by Indústrias Reunidas Francisco Matarrazo (with 2,619
workers) differed radically from the spinning and weaving sector of the textile industry that had traditionally employed large numbers of women.

As might be expected from the literature, women's industrial employment
was concentrated disproportionately in two stages of the family life cycle: the
teenage years and, to a lesser extent, the years of early family constitution.[20]
While 27 percent of all industrial workers in the ABC region were between
the ages of ten and nineteen, fully 54 percent of all women who worked in fac-

tories were teenagers. Indeed, women comprised 47 percent of all industrial workers between ten and nineteen years of age. In all, more than two-thirds of the women working in industry were under twenty-nine years of age.[21]

These female factory workers experienced far higher rates of turnover than did their male counterparts due to such life-cycle events as marriage and childbirth. These realities have led many industrial sociologists to talk of women's "incomplete commitment" to industrial labor. Yet the age-specific concentration and high turnover rates also document the ubiquity of the factory-labor experience among local working-class women. Few families would have lacked a mother, daughter, sister, or aunt who had worked in a factory, which undoubtedly contributed to women's understanding of the demands and problems of factory life.

The enormous increase in industrial employment in the ABC region between 1938 and 1950 was paralleled in other big cities. On contemplating the spectacular growth of the nation's industrial working class, Brazilian dictator Getúlio Vargas (who had first enfranchised women in 1932) framed electoral legislation in 1945 designed to favor urban areas over rural areas. Moreover, an ex officio group-registration procedure was established to enfranchise indus-

Table 3. Industrial Enterprises in Santo André and São Caetano
Employing Forty-nine or More Women in 1938 and 1947

CATEGORY	1938	1947
Enterprises employing 49 or more women	22	27
Total number of employees	11,970	25,015
Women employees	5,487	8,305
Percentage of all women employees	90	70
Average number of employees per enterprise	544	926
Average number of women employees per enterprise	249	308

Sources: PMSA, unpublished documents, "Estatística Industrial" for 1938 and 1947.

Table 4. Industrial Enterprises in Santo André and São Caetano
Employing Three Hundred or More Women in 1938 and 1947

CATEGORY	1938	1947
Enterprises employing 300 or more women	6	10
Total number of employees	6,740	14,173
Women Employees	3,761	5,601
Percentage of all women employees	61	47

Sources: PMSA, unpublished documents, "Estatística Industrial" for 1938 and 1947.

Table 5. Workforces and Strike Activity at Enterprises in Postwar
Santo André and São Caetano Employing Three Hundred
or More Women

ENTERPRISE (ACTIVITY)	WORKFORCE			STRIKES IN 1946–47
	TOTAL	WOMEN	% WOMEN	
Rhodiaceta (rayon fiber)	1,879	1,176	63	yes
Indústrias Reunidas Francisco Matarazzo (rayon fiber)	2,619	823	31	no
Sociedade Anónima Moinho Santista (textiles)	1,266	766	61	yes
Pirelli (electrical cable, tires)	3,268	623	19	yes
Companhia Brasileira de Cartuchos (munitions)	832	408	49	yes
Lanifício Kowarick (spinning and weaving wool)	692	431	62	no
Justifício Maria Luisa (spinning and weaving wool)	488	342	70	no
Indústrias Reunidas Francisco Matarazzo (ceramic dishes)	947	334	35	no
Compania Química Rhodia (chemical products)	1,737	306	18	yes
Valisere (textiles)	445	392	88	no
TOTALS	14,173	5,601	40	

Sources: PMSA, unpublished documents, "Estatística Industrial" for 1938 and 1947.

trial workers disproportionately through factory payroll lists. Although Vargas's reasons need not concern this discussion, the dramatic events of 1945 marked the moment of effective mass enfranchisement of the urban working class in Brazil. The impact of Vargas's electoral legislation was direct and striking. Electoral participation in the ABC region jumped fivefold from six thousand voters in 1936 to twenty-eight thousand in December 1945, with women comprising a third of the total electorate.[22]

The results of a large-scale statistical investigation of women's electoral participation are not yet available.[23] But several provisions of the 1945 electoral legislation bore directly on women. Although retaining the literacy requirement favored urban potential voters over rural potential voters, it also affected women's participation negatively because of their higher rate of illiteracy. More important was the fact that the legislation made voting obligatory by imposing fines for nonparticipation on all but one major group: women who did not work outside the home could vote but were not required to do so.[24]

Although the reasons for adopting the housewives' provision remain unclear, this feature of the legislation gave wage-earning women disproportionate weight in the female electorate. According to the local electorate's occupational breakdown in 1948, women made up 33 percent of all registered voters, split almost evenly between housewives (17 percent) and working women (16 percent). The ABC region's most industrialized district, with the largest number of working women, also had the most voters per population and the largest percentage of registered women voters. While the ex officio registration procedure made the electoral inscription of female factory workers automatic, the fact that fifty-six hundred housewives went individually to their local electoral notaries to register suggests something of the general ferment and excitement during 1945.

In the three elections between 1945 and November 1947, the Santo André electorate split into three parts: one-third voted for Vargas's Partido Trabalhista Brasileiro (PTB), one-third voted for the Partido Comunista do Brasil (PCB) of Luis Carlos Prestes, and one-third voted for various middle-class parties on the Right. Brazilian electoral findings, unlike those in some European countries with strong traditions of popular religiosity, show absolutely no evidence that women workers voted disproportionately for conservative or rightist parties.[25]

The most widespread unifying sentiment among men and women workers and residents in the ABC region during these years was a positive assessment of Getúlio Vargas, or what I have called *popular getulismo* (in 1950 Vargas received an astonishing 84 percent of the total vote in the município of Santo André). Although verging on the speculative at this point, some evidence suggests that women may have been especially strong supporters of Vargas and the populist Labor Party in preference to the more radical communists. Less support for the far left has been found among women working-class voters in a number of European and Latin American countries.[26]

Women can be shown to have been disproportionately mobilized for the presidential contests of 1945 and 1950, in which Getúlio Vargas played a major role. These two elections attracted a far higher voter turnout in the ABC region than did state or municipal elections. It is possible to calculate the minimum number of women who must have voted by assuming an unrealistically high turnout of 100 percent of registered male voters. This approach allows the conclusion that at least 50 percent of all registered women turned out for these presidential contests (compared with a minimum of 28 percent in the state and municipal elections in 1947).[27]

Some evidence suggests that working-class women may have benefited more from Vargas's social and labor legislation than men did. The 1943 labor law codification included many provisions of interest to women, including protective legislation, equal pay for equal work, and mandatory day care centers in large factories, even though most of these provisos lacked enforcement.[28] Especially relevant to women was the effective establishment of a minimum wage in 1939–1940. Although it was set far below the level sought by the unions, the 1940 minimum wage did not depress industrial wage levels as some have believed.[29] While largely irrelevant for male workers in the region's most modern, highly mechanized, and profitable factories, the new minimum wage represented a dramatic improvement for poorly paid women workers at many large enterprises like the Pirelli metalworking plant.[30]

If urban women supported Vargas disproportionately, it seems peculiar that the 1945 electoral law exempted housewives from compulsory voting. That provision might have been adopted to further decrease the vote in rural areas, where few women worked outside the home. Or perhaps, as Asunción Lavrin suggests, Vargas "was leaving the housewives and their husbands one option to 'decently' preserve patriarchal norms" by giving these traditional, nonmobilized women "an option of rejecting a change on which they (and possibly their husbands) would not agree."[31]

Women, the Family, and the Community

The end of World War II represented a hopeful moment for working-class men and women in Brazil, with nearly full employment and the government's campaign to promote union membership since 1943. The lessening of workers' fears that union or political participation might lead to dismissal was joined with the widespread belief that Getúlio Vargas's populist rhetoric and social and labor legislation represented promises that would be fulfilled after the war.

Under these conditions, the ouster of Vargas in October 1945 by "the rich" and the military prompted anger and protest among workers. Casting their votes for the first time in December 1945, local workers experienced a heady feeling of political success that enhanced the sense of self-confidence already flowing from relatively favorable labor-market conditions. The results—71 percent of the total vote cast for the informally allied PTB and PCB parties— amply confirmed the workers' sense of common identity and soaring hope.

Within working-class families, these conditions created a lessening of the disincentives to struggle that prevailed in normal times.

Local workers did not restrict their activism to the voting booth, however. Working-class anger, protest, and hope also revitalized the trade unions and spurred an early 1946 strike wave that involved one hundred thousand workers in metropolitan São Paulo. Strikes in February and March of 1946 proved a baptism of fire for the emerging left-center trade union movement. A third of the local workers participated in some form of mobilization, and at least one-fifth of all workers joined in the strikes sweeping greater São Paulo.[32] While workers were exercising their "rights," the streets of Santo André and São Caetano were taken over by mass picketing and occasional, usually nonviolent, confrontations with the police.

Strikes were generally observed in the factories affected. Many workers struck for reasons of "solidarity" with other workers, and nonstrikers were quickly organized to contribute funds to support the major stoppages, which lasted an average of two weeks. During these strikes, a new locus of identity emerged among local workers. For working-class housewives, this new extrafamilial, nonprivatized interest reinforced their bonds with their husbands while opening a window on the wider world. If housewives did no more than prepare family meals on smaller rations, they were nevertheless contributing in their own way to the workers' victory. Thus many women who were conservative about matters of gender roles could still feel comfortable with this small expansion of their family role as wives "loyal" to their husbands.

For other, less traditional housewives, the years 1946 and 1947 offered opportunities to expand their "traditional" responsibilities beyond the boundaries of the family. In normal times, the family's subsistence problems were dealt with individually through the wife's small triumphs at getting a "good deal" or knowing the "right connections" to acquire a scarce product. But during these years, hours of standing in line and constant bargain-hunting emphasized that these problems were now common to all. Yet no opportunities existed to deal with these problems collectively until the first neighborhood Comités Democráticos Progressistas (CDPs) were formed by the Communist Party in October 1945.

Phenomenally successful, these officially nonpartisan neighborhood organizations were designed to serve as the community analogue of the workplace-based trade union mobilizations of the day. From the outset, the CDPs were aimed at providing the unemployed, the young, and especially housewives with an outlet for their desire to participate.[33] With the support of many women, these committees dealt with the high cost of living (*carestia*) and other consumer problems, such as diluted milk, inedible bread, and shortages of sugar and cooking oil. By organizing picket lines and petitions, the CDPs demanded government action while trying to oversee local shopkeepers.[34]

The Communist Party's top women leaders explicitly expressed their goal of mobilizing more and more women through such practical, close-to-home concerns. As Communist Deputy Zuleika Alambert told the São Paulo State Assembly in 1947, the days were gone when Brazilian women lived "exclusively for their home and their children without directly participating in political, social, and economic life." Beset by carestia in their homes and exploitation on the job, women were now demanding their rights as a matter of justice, not charity.[35]

Yet as a visiting communist city councilwoman from Rio de Janeiro complained, many Brazilians still insisted that "women shouldn't participate in the political life of the country . . . [and] that woman's place is in the home." Emphasizing this point at a women's election rally in São Caetano, Arcelina Mochel argued that every time a woman "waits in long lines for her tiny ration of meat, oil or bread and protests, . . . she is making politics of the highest sort."[36]

In discussing the PCB's postwar effort to organize women, one scholar has criticized the communists for considering "demands linked to carestia as typically female" and the basis for "women's political action." She argued that in doing so, the PCB took "the sexual division of labor in the interior of the family [as a given]: the men fight for better salaries, the women fight against carestia."[37] A more sympathetic scholar, however, has defended this emphasis on carestia, which she believes provided the strongest incentive for working-class housewives to mobilize.[38]

Yet it would be wrong to assume that the PCB's neighborhood and women's organizations were exclusively concerned with carestia. They would have failed miserably had they concentrated primarily on problems of inflation and scarcity that were virtually unsolvable at the local, much less neighborhood, level. Examination of CDP activity suggests instead that far more energy was devoted to a range of "doable" activities that could produce small victories that would encourage group participants. For example, one committee in Vila Guiomar reported success in modestly reducing municipal water and sewer rates and establishing better garbage pickups. Elsewhere, the municipal CDP in Santo André collected five thousand signatures and got the São Paulo Railway to agree to restore train service that had been reduced during the war.[39]

Other CDPs worked actively to register voters, especially housewives, and they organized neighborhood literacy classes to help residents meet the legal requirements for voting. Everywhere, these committees focused attention on the problems of children and petitioned for the establishment of primary schools in ill-served neighborhoods. In São Caetano, they proposed the establishment of a hospital as well as a night school for local residents over fourteen who had never had an opportunity to attend school. They also organized Christmas parties for neighborhood children and held educational celebrations of events like the birthday of independence hero Tiradentes and the centenary of the abolitionist poet Castro Alves.[40] In this sense, the postwar emphasis on carestia may be more accurately interpreted as the opening wedge of a far more ambitious and multifaceted drive to raise "diversified demands, based on local problems."[41]

Women, the Workplace, and the Union

However they visualized their work experience, female factory workers in Santo André and São Caetano faced difficulties and problems that were specific to women in the workplace. Although community norms sanctioned "necessary" work outside the home, women still faced many discriminatory attitudes and behaviors in this consciously male domain. Women were completely absent from many workplaces, and when they were employed in local factories, they were segregated into lower-paying, less-skilled, and inferior industrial jobs.

Women also faced deprecatory male supremacist attitudes from some of their fellow workers, as well as from factory managers and foremen. Even men who did not express overt prejudice were influenced by implicit comparisons of male and female workers. The common wisdom held that women were not serious or real workers, that they worked only to supplement family income, that they were willing to work for less, that they took more abuse from foremen than any man would, and so on.

Male workers even expressed concern over the danger of exposing women to immodesty. One of the complaints of 950 strikers at the Companhia Brasileira de Metalúrgia e Mineração (which was 2 percent female) was that workers were forced to eat lunch in an uncomfortable area that doubled as a locker room. They demanded a proper lunchroom, complaining that their wives and daughters were often embarrassed by the sight of undressed men when they arrived at lunchtime with their husbands' or fathers' *marmitas* (tin pails for hot lunches).[42]

The male workers' factory life also affected the world of home and family in other ways. Strikers at one textile plant complained that wages were so low that they had to work twelve hours a day in order to earn enough to support their families, which deprived them of time with their families. The metalworking firm of Fichet and Schwartz Hautmont (o percent female) won union praise for humane treatment when it rehired a male worker dismissed for absenteeism due to a family situation.[43] Nevertheless, male prejudice and belief in notions like "proper spheres" must be placed in the larger context of substantively discriminatory employer policies.

The largest postwar strike involving women in the ABC region took place in March 1947 among the 1,879 workers (58 percent of them women) at the French-owned Rhodiaceta rayon-fiber factory. The workers' negotiating committee cited a number of specific demands and complaints by women. The committee reported that women in general were paid even less than the inadequate wages paid to men. In one factory section, women were having difficulty meeting the base piece-rate quota, because management was running the machines at too fast a pace. Moreover, women were constantly threatened with suspension by foremen for failing to meet quotas and were criticized for not being able to carry out the heavy work demanded. According to the committee, the plant had even failed to provide a sufficient number of dressing rooms for women employees.[44]

In advancing these demands, Rhodiaceta's male and female negotiating committee was undoubtedly seeking to guarantee women's support for the strike. Yet scholars' understanding of male-female workplace and union dynamics would be fatally flawed if they failed to perceive the interdependence of male and female interests vis-à-vis management. Whatever prejudice existed among workers, every male worker in the shop would also benefit from these "women's demands." Establishing equal pay for equal work would lessen the downward pressure on male wage levels. Also, adjustments in piece-rate quotas for women would lessen on-the-job production pressure throughout the plant. Indeed, another strike complaint at Rhodia was a recent doubling of the number of machines that a single worker was expected to tend.

Finally, both male and female Rhodia workers stood to benefit from increasing wages, improving bad working conditions, or providing time for those in dirty departments to wash up. Who could disagree with the demand that more bathrooms should be installed (and kept clean) to prevent disagreeable backups? Shared grievances also included a twenty-minute lunch break and management's castelike maintenance of the division of white- and blue-collar personnel. For example, the strikers complained that office workers had recently been provided with a shower, while manual workers who needed showers had none.

Thus attention to women's specific grievances at Rhodia by no means conflicted with male working-class interests. Moreover, the prevailing gender ideology also gave working-class men a special "responsibility" for their women (and other weaker groups within their class).[45] Women were indeed subject to special abuses because they were women—especially sexual harassment by foremen—and were less able and willing to speak up in their own defense. With fewer long-term job prospects, a working-class woman's chance to earn real money (as opposed to washing clothes) came only once in life. The fact that women worked outside the home due to family necessity also meant that their wages were used to meet specific household financial exigencies and obligations, whether to parents or to husbands.[46]

Although verging on paternalism at times, this sense of *companheirismo* and men's special responsibilities had worked to the benefit of wage-earning women in the past. In 1934 the Pirelli metalworking plant was closed in a strike that included as a major demand an end to the *beliscão,* or pinching, of the female workers by foremen supposedly seeking to increase production. The strike also set limits on foremen's prerogatives that benefited all Pirelli workers.[47]

Demands focusing on the differences in the workplace interests of male and female workers could also have been formulated in 1947. For example, women could have demanded equal hiring in the better-paying jobs and skilled positions that were predominantly male. Such zero-sum demands for access to male occupations or professions have played a crucial historical role in middle-class women's movements in the United States and Europe. Yet such a challenge to the sexual division of labor within the factory made no real sense for workers in the ABC region in the 1940s. Without established negotiating power, even a united Rhodia workforce had a doubtful capacity to force agreement on an intransigent management.

In fact, the success of any group of workers depended on the unity of all workers. Whatever the diverging interests within the working class, all subgroups were forced to confront the need for unity at the moment when they exercised their ultimate bargaining chip: the withdrawal of labor power. Especially in the male-female workplace, a strike situation emphasized the essential and very practical equality of men and women. Even a group of viciously misogynist males, who were moved to strike strictly in defense of their own interests, quickly realize that the women they despised could defeat the work stoppage by nonparticipation as easily as any men.

In this regard, the mixed male and female workplace was potentially at the forefront of change in gender relations within the labor movement.[48] Whether motivated by pragmatism or principle, Brazilian labor leaders recognized the need for women's support in their conduct of strikes during 1946 and 1947. Whether consciously or not, local left-center union leaders applied the principles of working-class unity in order to maximize workers' leverage vis-à-vis the employers and their powerful allies. Thus every effort was made to incorporate women into strike activities on a large scale. Where women comprised a significant portion of the workforce, women strikers were always found among the speakers at local rallies.

At the mass level, the broader assertion of a common class identity served to lessen resistance to innovation and changes in consciousness, including ideas about gender. The Firestone factory in Santo André, with twelve hundred workers (13 percent female), was one of the first to be struck. From the outset, Lúzia de Lourdes Gonçalves emerged as one of the three most active rank-and-file leaders of the striking rubber workers. In the excitement of the strike, acceptance of leadership from a woman *companheira* was not inconceivable to her male compatriots.[49]

A passionate orator, Gonçalves was given the honor of welcoming the legendary *cavaleiro de esperança,* communist Senator Luis Carlos Prestes, to Santo André in February 1946. In denouncing the police, she told her audience of perhaps twenty thousand that striking was supposed to be a crime. She then cited police statements that the PCB had taught the workers to strike and defiantly declared that if this were true, she would join the Communist Party forthwith. Hailing the solidarity of the workers, she concluded, "This fight is forging the unity of the working class . . . so that, from now on, we will march more united than ever" in the fight against misery.[50]

Substantial unity of purpose did characterize the one hundred thousand strikers in greater São Paulo in February and March of 1946. Unlike the strikes during the First Republic (1889–1930), no laments were heard about the abject behavior of women in refusing to strike. Nor was the likelihood of a work stoppage tied to the percentage of women employed in a given factory, as is indicated by the fact that four of the five largest factories employing women struck in 1946 and 1947 (see table 5). Only one enterprise, the Swift meatpacking plant, was reported to have tried to operate with strikebreakers, which led to a number of clashes with police. In denouncing the "traitors," how-

Luis Carlos Prestes during a post–World War II campaign rally
in São Paulo. Courtesy of Iconografia.

ever, labor leaders did not single out the female sex from among the "girls,
women, and men" still going to work. Moreover, at least one woman was
among the dozen Swift strikers arrested by the local police. In response to a
union appeal, the police released the woman before her male compatriots.[51]

During and after the strike, union and PCB leaders consciously sought to
foster a general companheirismo among local workers. Actively implement-
ing a system of union factory commissions in the workplace, they also created
an elaborate recreational and social life for male and female workers. On at
least two different occasions, groups of more than one thousand workers and
their families participated in union-sponsored trips to the beaches in nearby
Santos. During the strike and afterward, large-scale dances, picnics, and bar-
becues were organized to celebrate particular victories and general working-
class togetherness.[52]

In an effort to unite every group within the workforce as the strikes ebbed
in March 1946, an ad hoc committee was established to crown the "Queen of
the Santo André Workers." Modeled after a similar effort in São Paulo, this
contest was aimed at the beauty-conscious "proletarian girls" who worked

in local factories. The "queen" was chosen based on ballots cast by workers from among the nominated "princesses" (one to a factory) and was awarded a permanent, a manicure, perfume, and similar prizes. Articles during the contest published photographs of the candidates and described their hair and eye color, age (between seventeen and twenty-one years), and popularity with fellow workers.[53]

While the aim of the union contest was to promote working-class togetherness, little evidence suggests that the workers' contest replaced the employer-sponsored beauty contests with their more lucrative prizes. Moreover, none of the names of the ten or so nominees appeared in any political or union context then or later. Activist women workers like Lúzia Gonçalves apparently did not take such efforts very seriously. Indeed, not a single female trade-union or political activist in Santo André or São Caetano was ever mentioned in relationship to the contest, which might indicate an informal boycott of what activist women might have viewed as an insulting or "frivolous" activity.

Policy and Leadership in the Leftist Women's Movement in São Paulo

After World War II, the Communist Party and its female leaders, members, and sympathizers created Brazil's first sustained mass organizations of working-class women. Unlike what occurred among radical labor groups in the First Republic, women not only participated actively in major strikes in 1946 and 1947 but created ongoing women's organizations of a kind that were "almost non-existent" before 1930.[54] Moreover, the social base of this leftist women's movement differed from that of the women's suffrage movement of the 1920s and 1930s, which was "exclusively composed of women of the middle class and bourgeoisie."[55]

Far too little is known about the policies of this radical postwar women's movement or the individuals who founded and led the numerous organizations that created the Federação de Mulheres Brasileiras in 1949.[56] The movement has been generally criticized for organizing women "primarily around political events, against the high cost of living, and only secondarily, in favor of women's rights." Women are said to have been mobilized between 1945 and 1950 "not around their position in the family or in society but in terms of political objectives" defined by men.[57]

Such criticisms, however, risk the danger of historical anachronism in judging the efforts of four decades ago according to the ideas of the feminist "second wave" since the 1960s. Indeed, examination of this postwar ferment provides evidence that these women's organizations were conceived in a broader and more autonomous sense than has been commonly thought. Although these women were far from advancing a feminist critique of sex roles, they nonetheless represented a profound challenge to prevailing cultural mores and gender ideologies.[58]

The objectives of this movement were set forth in a 1947 inaugural speech to the São Paulo State Assembly by Zuleika Alambert, the leading woman Communist in São Paulo, who later served as a longtime member of the PCB Central Committee.[59] A twenty-five-year-old store clerk in 1947, Alambert hailed from the radical port city of Santos, the only jurisdiction in São Paulo where the Communist presidential candidate came in first in December 1945. Alambert explained that the União de Mulheres Democráticas organized in Santo André and in other São Paulo cities in 1946 were intended to "develop a peaceful but intransigent fight to conquer women's rights in all sectors of human life" and to resolve their vital problems such as carestia and equal pay for equal work.[60]

Alambert defined the relationship between working-class men and women exclusively in cooperative terms: women stood "shoulder to shoulder with their companheiros . . . [in] daily struggle." Framed within a context of male-female interdependence among workers, this approach also coincided with aspects of prevailing gender ideology at the mass level. For example, a female salesclerk from Santo André interviewed at a gigantic Prestes rally in São Paulo asserted, "I'm going without lunch to be here . . . and [although I'm pleased with the turnout], I'm even happier because I see so many women, which is to say that the Brazilian woman is at man's side in the fight for our demands."[61]

At the same time, women PCB leaders like Alambert were capable of enunciating a broad and ambitious definition of the responsibilities they sought to assume. Not satisfied with separate women's organizations, Alambert also spoke of women organizing "in their neighborhoods, in women's commissions in cultural and recreational associations, in anti-carestia leagues, in their workplace, [and] in the women's division of their unions." At this point, however, a male fellow deputy jeeringly interrupted to inquire, "And in cooking schools too?" The same deputy had complained earlier in the speech that "the mouth of a woman is a weapon far worse than firearms."[62]

This expansive jurisdictional definition of women's work seems to have created tensions with some male PCB and labor leaders, especially regarding the demand for separate women's divisions in trade unions. Speaking to a meeting of the local União de Mulheres Democráticas, Santo André's Communist state deputy, Armando Mazzo (a former furniture maker), offered a different definition in which male and female workers joined together in their male-led unions, which in turn engaged in joint struggle with women organized in their own groups.[63]

Analysis of the biographies of leftist women active in Santo André and São Caetano during the period from 1945 to 1948 sheds light not only on leftist ideas and praxis but also on the slow process of change in gender ideologies at the individual level. These activists were mainly young working women in their mid-twenties who seized on the new opportunities of the day more quickly than did their elders. Most were single, reflecting the fact that a full political life placed demands on individuals that were hard for married women with children to fulfill—especially when their husbands expected meals on time when arriving home from work.

It has also been noted that women workers were often discouraged from participating in political and trade union activities by disapproving parents, husbands, or boyfriends. Yet the family did not serve solely as a drag on female political participation.[64] According to ideology (if not conviction), PCB leaders and many male trade unionists in this period professed to believe in the equality of women and sought to mobilize them in workers' struggles. This approach opened the way for another avenue of recruiting female activists—from among the wives and daughters of militant workers. Indeed, at least five key female activists were wives of worker leaders, and another five were daughters of such families. As Leite noted about the 1980s, "It is hard to find a married woman who is a union activist whose husband is not [also an activist]."[65]

Carmen Edwiges Savietto (1922–1956) stood at the center of communist activism and PCB-led women's organization in postwar Santo André. Then in her mid-twenties, this lifelong communist had been born to a working-class family in the ABC district of Ribeirão Pires, the center of anarchist radicalism among local stonecutters before 1930. Carmen Savietto emerged from a remarkable family of activists. Her father Claudio was a Communist Party member, and her uncle Augusto Savietto had served as president of the metalworkers' union in Santo André during the difficult years between 1938 and 1942. Augusto Savietto was succeeded in this position by his son Euclydes (who served 1942–1945), a teenage enthusiast of Prestes in 1935, who received 5,600 votes in December 1945 in Santo André and barely missed being elected to serve as a Communist federal deputy. The succeeding president of the metalworkers' union was Carmen Savietto's brother, Victor Gentil Savietto (serving 1945–1947).[66]

Communist leader Carmen
Edwiges Savietto (1922–1956) in
a photo taken from a campaign
leaflet for her successful 1947
municipal campaign in Santo
André. Courtesy of John French.

Trained as a bookkeeper, Carmen Savietto became actively involved in the
metalworkers' union during the war, as a volunteer who kept track of dues
payments in an institution without money. Her sister Mercedes served as
secretary for the 685-member consumers' cooperative of unionized workers
headed by local Communist Party leader Rolando Fratti, who later married
Carmen.[67] If family connections aided Carmen Savietto in establishing her
credentials, her rise to political prominence within the PCB resulted from her
own individual talents, dedication, and audacity. In mid-1945 she was the only
publicly identified speaker at the PCB's first small rally of sixty in Santo André,
which tested the apparent legalization of the Communist Party. Heavily involved in supporting strikes in early 1946, she led many of the women's
delegations that visited her brother and other union leaders when they were
arrested later in the year.[68]

Carmen Savietto was also deeply committed to organizing women as
women, a task she undertook in October 1945 that led to the founding of
the União de Mulheres Democráticas (UMD) in Santo André in 1946. As UMD
president, she experienced her share of police harassment. For example, in
August 1946, the vigorously repressive local police chief raided a Vila Guiomar house where a UMD meeting was taking place. While the police were
arresting Carmen and the woman of the house, the forty women assembled

joined in a shouting match with the police until they were allowed to send a ten-person delegation to accompany the prisoners to the jail. The latter were subsequently released without being charged.[69]

A leader of her cell and a member of the PCB Municipal Committee, Carmen Savietto was the party's official representative in negotiating with the police in May 1947, when they closed six local headquarters after the Communist Party was outlawed. Nevertheless, as Santo André's largest single party, the PCB participated actively in the municipal election campaign of November 1947 under a different party label. When communists won the office of mayor and thirteen of thirty council seats in November 1947, Carmen Savietto was one of only two women on the PCB slate, but she received the fourth-highest number of votes of all the thirty-three PCB nominees.[70]

Carmen Savietto's recognized leadership is suggested by the manifesto distributed in the name of the thirteen victorious communist candidates. She was one of three named signatories, along with Armando Mazzo, the former state deputy and newly elected mayor, and Marcos Andreotti, the founding president of the metalworkers' union in the 1930s.[71] If the government had allowed the winners to assume office, Carmen Savietto would have been the first woman in the history of Santo André and São Caetano to serve in an elected post.[72]

Despite such accomplishments, it is clear that the rise of outstanding individuals like Alambert and Savietto to PCB leadership and elective office did not take place without resistance. In fact, neither the party nor the labor movement followed a conscious policy of female inclusion in leadership. In December 1945, only two out of thirty-five PCB candidates for federal deputy in São Paulo were women. Again, in January 1947, only four of seventy-four PCB candidates for state deputy were women, including Carmen Savietto and Zuleika Alambert (who was elected *suplente* and served in that capacity).[73] Again, some discontent among women communists was expressed in this regard. In her speeches in the ABC region, Rio's communist councilwoman Arcelina Mochel stressed the importance of nominating women for office at all levels.[74]

Conclusion

Scholars in the past have failed to understand the enormous political significance of the exceptional years between 1945 and 1948, which gave birth to the Populist Republic that lasted until the military coup of 1964. The sustained mobilizations that occurred in Brazil's urban-industrial regions unleashed new social forces that included the working class and women, and set in motion a series of fundamental changes in the nature of politics and the interests represented in the political arena.

Although women had been formally enfranchised since 1932, few of them, especially in the popular classes, had ever voted prior to 1945. Female interest in politics in the 1940s was unusually high given the larger society's relatively rigid gender roles and patriarchal cultural norms, and this interest thus represented a decisive break with the past. Extensive mass participation during these years led to important changes in popular behavior and mass consciousness. New notions of "rights" emerged; new ideas of what was and was not "acceptable" became widespread; and workers and women came to a new understanding of the ballot, neighborhood organizations, and trade unions as means of advancing their interests.[75]

It is evident that the years between 1945 and 1948 resulted in important breakthroughs for women. Individuals like Carmen Savietto and Zuleika Alambert shattered the prevailing stereotypes of gender and class that had denied women, especially working-class women, active political involvement in the broader world outside the home. The working-class Left and its women activists thus made a decisive contribution to defining the terrain, tactics, and forms of urban politics, and left an enduring legacy to Brazil's radical, labor, and feminist movements for years to come.[76]

Notes

This chapter is a lightly reworked version of an article that originally appeared in *Latin American Research Review* 24, no. 3 (fall 1989): pp. 99–125. This research was undertaken with grants from the Women and Gender Research Institute of Utah State University, with the help of research assistant Mary Lynn Pederson Cluff. All translations are my own.

1   Jane Jacquette, "Female Political Participation in Latin America," in *Sex and Class in Latin America*, ed. June Nash and Helen I. Safa (South Hadley, Mass.: Bergin, 1980), p. 235.

2   This analysis focuses exclusively on the factory districts of Santo André and São Caetano, leaving aside the largely nonindustrial município of São Bernardo do Campo.

3   John D. French, *The Brazilian Workers' ABC: Class Conflicts and Alliances in Modern São Paulo* (Chapel Hill: University of North Carolina Press, 1992); French, *O ABC dos operários: Lutas e alianças de classe em São Paulo, 1900–1950*, trans. Lólio Lourenço de Oliveira (São Paulo: Hucitec; São Caetano do Sul: Prefeitura Municipal de São Caetano do Sul, 1995).

4 See Francisco Corrêa Weffort, "Origens do sindicalismo populista no Brasil (A conjuntura do após guerra)," *Estudos CEBRAP*, no. 4 (1973): pp. 65–105; and Ricardo Maranhão, *Sindicatos e democratização (Brasil 1945–1950)* (São Paulo: Brasiliense, 1979). For a promising recent treatment see Hélio da Costa, *Em busca da memória: Comissão de fábrica, partido e sindicato no pós-guerra* (São Paulo: Scritta, 1995).

5 Participation by working-class women in the labor movement has been greatest and most visible at moments of intense class mobilizations such as strikes. Conversely, women have been largely absent from the ongoing organizational activities of the workers' movement. Regarding the Brazilian First Republic see Esmeralda Blanco Bolsonaro de Moura, *Mulheres e menores no trabalho industrial: Os fatores sexo e idade na dinâmica do capital* (Petrópolis: Vozes, 1982); for a discussion of contemporary Peru see Maruja Barrig, *Las obreras* (Lima: Mosca Azul/Adec., 1986), and Virginia Guzmán et al., *Dos veces mujer* (Lima: Centro de la Mujer Peruana Flora Tristan/Fondo Voluntario de las Naciones Unidas para el Desarrollo de la Mujer/Mosca Azul, 1985); and regarding Colombia see Cristina Steffen, Magdalena Leon de Leal, and Dora Rothlisberger, *La participación política de la mujer en la clase obrera: Un estudio de caso* (Bogotá: Universidad de los Andes/Asociación Colombiana para el Estudio de la Población, 1978). This widespread pattern of intense yet intermittent participation is not unique to women but rather mirrors in an exaggerated way the ups and downs of male working-class participation as well. Women's diminutive role in union leadership and ongoing labor militancy might be explained as the result of their exclusion by an overwhelmingly male labor leadership. Yet the observations of scholars and activist female workers suggest that such an explanation is too facile; see in this regard Barrig, *Obreras;* Conselho Estadual da Condição Feminina, *Mulheres operárias* (São Paulo: Nobel/Conselho Estadual da Condição Feminina/Centro de Memória Sindical, 1985); Rosalina de Santa Cruz Leite, *A operária metalúrgica: Estudo sobre as condições de vida e trabalho de operárias metalúrgicas na cidade de São Paulo* (São Paulo: Semente, 1982); and Magda de Almeida Neves, *Trabalho e cidadania: As trabalhadoras de Contagem* (Petrópolis: Vozes, 1995). Leite has observed this pattern among contemporary São Paulo metalworkers, where only a small group of female activists participates in union affairs, and the same is true of São Bernardo do Campo, according to Leda Gitahy et al., "Luttes ouvrières et luttes des ouvrières a São Bernardo do Campo," *Cahiers des Amériques Latines* 26 (July–December 1982): pp. 11–38. In explaining the failure of most women to participate, the female activists whom Leite interviewed cited women's greater fear and passivity in the face of authority. Yet these activists also emphasized that once women overcome these obstacles, they become "extremely combative and enter into the fight with passion, with an immediate involvement even greater than that of men." This transition occurs most often during peaks of intense working-class mobilization such as mass strikes. In the aftermath, however, women have been more likely to quickly abandon systematic trade union work than have

men (Leite, *Operária metalúrgica,* pp. 130, 132, 135). An analogous pattern has also been identified in a recent study of female political participation. Women, Lúcia Avelar suggests, are far more likely to be present in ad hoc "political actions of short duration and which involve direct action" and are less likely to participate in ongoing, structured forms of institutional participation (*O segundo eleitorado: Tendências do voto feminino no Brasil* [Campinas: Editora da UNICAMP, 1989], p. 87).

6   June Hahner, "Recent Research on Women in Brazil," *Latin American Research Review* 20, no. 3 (1985): p. 169; Asunción Lavrín, "Women, the Family, and Social Change in Latin America," *World Affairs* 150, no. 2 (1987): pp. 114, 117.

7   K. Lynn Stoner, "Directions in Latin American Women's History, 1977–1985," *Latin American Research Review* 22, no. 2 (1987): p. 115. For an exception see Marysa Navarro, "Hidden, Silent, and Anonymous: Women Workers in the Argentine Trade Union Movement," in *The World of Women's Trade Unionism: Comparative Historical Essays,* ed. Norbert C. Soldon (Westport, Conn.: Greenwood, 1985), pp. 165–98.

8   Marxist views of the "woman question" have been decisively transformed since the late 1960s. In his 1970 book, Brazilian Communist Party leader Moisés Vinhas still judged women workers largely in terms of what they did and did not contribute to the male working class. Although aware of their special situation and potential contribution, Vinhas characterized women as "carriers of conservative ideas and habits" within the working class (Vinhas, *Estudos sôbre o proletariado brasileiro* [Rio de Janeiro: Civilização Brasileira, 1970], p. 171). This definition of the working class as male, with only a secondary role played by women, has been vigorously challenged in the last two decades even within the Partido Comunista Brasileiro (PCB). See the self-critical 1979 PCB resolution on women in Marco Aurélio Nogueira, ed., *PCB: Vinte anos de política* (São Paulo: Livraria Editora Ciências Humanas, 1980), pp. 329–53. For a critique of the invisibility of women in the earlier sociological discourse on Brazilian workers see Elisabeth Souza-Lobo and Elizabeth Higgs, "As operárias, o sindicato, e o discurso sociológico" (paper presented at the Encontro Anual da Associaçao Nacional de Pós Graduação e Pesquisa em Ciências Sociais, Aguas de São Pedro, São Paulo, October 1983); and Elisabeth Souza-Lobo, "Práticas e discursos das operárias, processos de trabalho e lutas sindicais no Brasil: Os anos 1970 e 1980," in *A classe operária tem dois sexos: Trabalho, dominação, e resistência* (São Paulo: Editora Brasiliense/Secretaria Municipal de Cultura, 1991), pp. 17–111.

9   Ecléa Bosi, *Cultura de massa e cultura popular: Leituras de operárias* (Petrópolis: Vozes, 1972); Arakcy Martins Rodrigues, *Operário, operária: Estudo exploratório sobre o operariado industrial de grande São Paulo* (São Paulo: Símbolo, 1978); Elisabete Doria Bilac, *Famílias de trabalhadores: Estratégias de sobrevivência* (São Paulo: Símbolo, 1978); Carmen Cinira Macedo, *A reprodução da desigualdade: O projeto de vida familiar de um grupo operário* (São Paulo: Hucitec, 1979); Jessita Martins Rodrigues, *A mulher operária: Um estudo sobre teçelãs* (São Paulo: Hucitec, 1979); Vera Maria Candido

Pereira, *O coração da fábrica: Estudo de caso entre operários têxteis* (Rio de Janeiro: Editora Campus, 1979); Heleieth I. B. Saffioti, *Do artesanal ao industrial: A exploração da mulher: Um estudo de operárias texteis e de confecçoes no Brasil e nos Estados Unidos* (São Paulo: Hucitec, 1981); Ana Maria Q. Fausto Neto, *Família operária e reproduçao da força do trabalho* (Petrópolis: Vozes, 1982); Heleieth I. B. Saffioti, "Technological Change in Brazil: Its Effects on Men and Women in Two Firms," in *Women and Change in Latin America,* ed. June Nash and Helen I. Safa (South Hadley, Mass.: Bergin and Garvey, 1986), pp. 109–35. For an interesting discussion of the development of feminist studies in Brazil since the 1960s see Heleieth I. B. Saffioti, "Feminismo e seus frutos no Brasil," in *Movimentos sociais na transição democrática,* ed. Emir Sader (São Paulo: Cortez, 1987), pp. 105–58.

10   One of the few exceptions is the 1995 book on women metalworkers in Contagem, Minas Gerais, by Neves, *Trabalho e cidadania.*

11   Heleieth I. B. Saffioti, "Relationships of Sex and Social Class in Brazil," in Nash and Safa, *Sex and Class,* p. 157.

12   Luiz Pereira, *A escola numa área metropolitana: Crise e racionalização de uma empresa pública de serviços* (1965; reprint, São Paulo: Pioneira, 1976), p. 39.

13   Pereira, *Escola numa área metropolitana,* p. 31. Labor economist John Wells notes that "the determinants of labour force participation by 'secondary' family members," such as adolescents and wives, are "quite complex." Summarizing the findings of two surveys of working-class living standards in São Paulo from 1938 and 1941, Wells notes that "married women's labour force participation was considered undesirable . . . and was avoided when household income was adequate" ("Industrial Accumulation and Living-Standards in the Long-Run: The São Paulo Industrial Working Class, 1930–75 [Part 1]," *Journal of Development Studies* 19, no. 2 [1983]: pp. 159, 163).

14   Pereira, *Escola numa área metropolitana;* Marianne Schmink, "Household Economic Strategies: Review and Research Agenda," *Latin American Research Review* 19, no. 3 (1984): pp. 87–101; Marianne Schmink, "Women and Urban Industrial Development in Brazil," in Nash and Safa, *Women and Change,* pp. 136–64; Eleanor Leacock, "Postscript," in *Women's Work: Development and the Division of Labor by Gender,* ed. Eleanor Leacock and Helen I. Safa (South Hadley, Mass.: Bergin and Garvey, 1986), pp. 258–60; Macedo, *Reprodução da desigualdade.* Regarding the United States see David Montgomery, *The Fall of the House of Labor* (Cambridge: Cambridge University Press, 1987), pp. 139–40.

15   Macedo, *Reprodução da desigualdade,* p. 36. See also Eva Alterman Blay, "Trabalho, família, e classes sociais em São Paulo," *Revista do Instituto de Estudos Brasileiros,* no. 13 (1972): pp. 87–99. The prevailing gender ideology among workers in Santo André and São Caetano nevertheless represented an important advance over the profound gender inequalities prevailing in the rural areas from which these workers had migrated. For a brief summary of the relevant findings of five studies of rural communities, see Morris J. Blachman, "Eve in an Adamocracy:

The Politics of Women in Brazil" (Ph.D. diss., New York University, 1976), pp. 38–42; see also Heleieth I. B. Saffioti and Vera Lúcia Silveira Botta Ferrante, "Famílias rurais no estado de São Paulo: Algumas dimensões da vida feminina," in *Trabalhadoras do Brasil*, ed. Maria Cristina A. Bruschini and Fúlvia Rosemberg (São Paulo: Fundação Carlos Chagas/Brasiliense, 1982), pp. 111–33. As has been suggested for Puerto Rico, proletarianization and urbanization do indeed contribute to "the breakdown of patriarchy" (Helen I. Safa, "Female Employment in the Puerto Rican Working Class," in Nash and Safa, *Women and Change*, p. 96).

16 Saffiotti, "Technological Change," p. 121.

17 Macedo, *Reprodução da Desigualdade*, pp. 22, 36; Rodrigues, *Mulher operária*, pp. 119–23, 108.

18 Leite, *Operária metalúrgica*, p. 56.

19 French, *Brazilian Workers' ABC*, pp. 42–43; and *O ABC dos operários*, pp. 40–41.

20 Hélio Zylberstajn, Carmen Silvia Pagotto, and José Pastore, *A mulher e o menor na força de trabalho* (São Paulo: Nobel, 1985); Chiara Vangelista, "Per una ricerca sul mercato del lavoro: La mobilità della manodopera in una filatura paulista," *Nova Americana*, no. 3 (1978): pp. 215–30.

21 See table D-6 in John D. French, "Industrial Workers and the Origin of Populist Politics in the ABC Region of Greater São Paulo, Brazil, 1900–1950" (Ph.D. diss., Yale University, 1985), p. 632.

22 See chapter 4 in French, *Brazilian Workers' ABC* and *O ABC dos operários*.

23 John D. French and Mary Lynn Pedersen Cluff, "Once Women Vote: The Politics of Female Enfranchisement in São Paulo, Brazil, 1932–1982" (paper presented at the Berkshire Conference on the History of Women, New Brunswick, N.J., June 7–10, 1990).

24 Voting was finally made obligatory for all Brazilian women, including housewives, in 1965 (Blachman, "Eve in an Adamocracy," p. 80).

25 Joni Lovenduski and Jill Hills, *The Politics of the Second Electorate: Women and Public Participation* (Boston: Routledge and Kegan Paul, 1981); Brian Peterson, "The Politics of Working Class Women in the Weimar Republic," *Central European History* 10, no. 2 (1977): pp. 87–111.

26 Lovenduski and Hills, *Second Electorate;* Peterson, "Working Class Women"; Paul H. Lewis, "The Female Vote in Argentina, 1958–1965," *Comparative Political Studies* 3, no. 4 (1971): pp. 425–41; Maurice Zeitlin and James Petras, "The Working-Class Vote in Chile: Christian Democracy versus Marxism," *British Journal of Sociology* 21, no. 1 (1970): pp. 16–29; Patricia A. Kyle and Michael J. Francis, "Women at the Polls: The Case of Chile, 1970–1971," *Comparative Political Studies* 11, no. 3 (1978): pp. 291–316.

27 For a discussion of Brazilian survey data dealing with differences in levels of interest and participation in politics by men and women see Blachman, "Eve in an Adamocracy," pp. 64–77; and Avelar, *Segundo eleitorado*, p. 39. For postwar São Paulo, direct evidence of differences in the rate and type of political participa-

tion by men and women can be found in a September 6, 1946, dispatch from American Consul General Cecil M. P. Cross to U.S. Ambassador William D. Pawley (U.S. National Archives and Records Service). "Communist Strength in São Paulo" summarized the results of a poll undertaken with one thousand residents in São Paulo, four hundred in Santos, and three hundred each in Campinas, Ribeirão Preto, Baurú, Botucatú, Itapetininga, and Sorocaba. According to the results, 79 percent of the men and 59 percent of the women reported that they were voters. The gender gap was even greater, however, when the individuals were asked about membership in some political party: 9.4 percent of the men versus only 3.4 percent of the women responded that they were members. Unfortunately, declared party membership was not broken down by gender; for men and women together, however, the Communist Party came in first with 2.4 percent of those polled, followed by the União Democrática Nacional with 2 percent, and the other parties, including the PTB (0.3 percent), all came in at less than one percent. The relatively strong communist showing was of special concern, Cross noted, because "it was under particularly heavy police and Army pressure" which "doubtless" led many fearful individuals to conceal their PCB membership.

28   A. F. Cesarino Júnior, *Direito social brasileiro,* 4th ed., vol. 2 (Rio de Janeiro: Freitas Bastos, 1957), pp. 490–97.

29   Lacking detailed evidence, Maria Valéria Junho Pena links the new minimum wage legislation to a lowering of wage levels and a subsequent increase in women's labor force participation. She also points out that the initial 1940 minimum wage decree allowed a 10 percent discount for women and children, allegedly to compensate employers for the extra costs of required protective measures. But this feature was revoked as unconstitutional in the 1943 labor code (*Mulheres e trabalhadoras: Presença feminina na constituição do sistema fabril* [Rio de Janeiro: Paz e Terra, 1981], pp. 164–65). The charge that the minimum wage legislation of the Estado Novo negatively affected wages should be considered unproven at best (see John Wells, "Industrial Accumulation and Living-Standards in the Long-Run: The São Paulo Industrial Working Class, 1930–75 [Part 2]," *Journal of Development Studies* 19, no. 3 [1983]: pp. 302–5).

30   Augusto Savietto, president of the Santo André metalworkers' union, interview, *Diário do Grande ABC,* November 11, 1979; also see the account by Angelina Jerônimo, a retired seamstress in São Paulo, who offers warm praise for both the minimum wage law and Getúlio Vargas (Conselho Estadual, *Mulheres operárias,* p. 59). Regarding a later period see Russell E. Smith, "Male-Female Wage Differentials and the Minimum Wage in the São Paulo Textile Industry, 1961–1976," in *Status Influences in Third World Labor Markets: Caste, Gender, and Custom,* ed. James G. Scoville (Berlin/New York: Walter de Gruyter), pp. 215–40.

31   Asunción Lavrin, letter to John French, May 13, 1987.

32   See chapter 6 in French, *Brazilian Workers' ABC* and *O ABC dos operários.*

33 See the PCB document on CDPS in Edgard Carone, ed., *O P.C.B. (1943–1964)*, vol. 2 (São Paulo: DIFEL, 1982), pp. 57–59.

34 See "Centenas de mulheres de Santo André dirigem-se ao prefeito," *Hoje*, August 28, 1946; "O pão e o leite estão envenenando," *Hoje*, September 3, 1946; and "São Caetano não recebe oleo nem açúcar," *Hoje*, September 14, 1946.

35 Assembléia Legislativa do Estado de São Paulo (ALESP), *Anais da Assembléia Legislativa do Estado de São Paulo*, vol. 5 (1947), p. 156.

36 "As mulheres de Santo André participarão ativamenta das eleições," *Hoje*, October 21, 1947. For biographical information on Arcelina Mochel see Ana Montenegro, "Notas indicativas para uma memória do movimento feminino no Brasil, 1945–1964," in *Ser ou não ser feminista* (Recife: Guarararapes, 1981). Theresa Veccia kindly provided me with this citation.

37 Pena, *Mulheres e trabalhadoras*, p. 210.

38 Fanny Tabak, *Autoritarismo e participação política da mulher* (Rio de Janeiro: Graal, 1983), p. 119.

39 "Santo André, Comité Democrático de Vila Guiomar," *Hoje*, December 10, 1945; "Congratula-se com a Sociedade Amigos da Cidade o Comité Democrático de São Caetano," *Hoje*, January 23, 1946; and "Comité Democrático Progressista de São Caetano," *Hoje*, December 28, 1945.

40 "Grande comício pró-constituinte realizou-se dia 24 em Santo André," *Hoje*, October 28, 1945; "Noticiário geral dos comités democráticos," *Hoje*, February 22, 1946; "O povo de São Caetano contra a carta de 37," *Hoje*, February 27, 1946; "Voltarão a circular mais dois subúrbios para Santo André," *Hoje*, March 7, 1946; "O povo de São Caetano pede a revogação do ato concessão de serviço de aguas no município," *Hoje*, March 18, 1946; "O 'Dia de Tiradentes' condignamente comemorado em Santo André," *Hoje*, April 23, 1946; and "S. Caetano comemorou o aniversário de Castro Alves," *Hoje*, March 21, 1947.

41 Leite, *Operária metalúrgica*, p. 14.

42 "Greve pacífica dos operários de Cia. Brasileira de Metalúrgia e Mineração," *Hoje*, February 18, 1946.

43 "Atitude louvável da Cia. Fichet and Schwartz," *Hoje*, February 19, 1946.

44 "Unidos, os tecelões S. André levantam suas reivindicações," *Hoje*, March 18, 1947; "Vão ao dessídio [*sic*] coletivo 10 mil operários de 25 fábricas de tecidos de Santo André," *Hoje*, March 19, 1947; "Os donos da 'Rhodiaseta' mandaram parar as máquinas," *Hoje*, March 22, 1947; and "A intransigência da 'Rodiaseta' [*sic*] impede a solução conciliatória do dissídio," *Hoje*, March 25, 1947.

45 In discussing the First Republic, Bolsonaro notes that adult male workers and the organizations that represented them, many of which enrolled women, often assumed this stance as "defenders of the interests of women, minors, and children." This tendency was especially pronounced when championing such groups involved "the defense of their own interest" as understood by male workers (Bolsonaro de Moura, *Mulheres e menores*, pp. 119–20).

46   See Neves, *Trabalho e cidadania,* p. 69.

47   Marcos Andreotti, interview with author, Santo André, September 21, 1982.

48   The proposition that gender dynamics in labor organizations are influenced by the proportion of women in the total workforce can be tested empirically. Male labor leaders in overwhelmingly male industries might be expected to display less sensitivity to such issues than male leaders in predominantly female industries. As proof, consider the example of the autoworkers of São Bernardo do Campo, an industry where women comprised only 9 percent of the total workforce (for an account by a female union activist in São Bernardo see Maria Mendes da Silva and Maria Quartim de Morâes, *Vida de mulher* [São Paulo: Marco Zero, 1981]). Although their militant union leaders created special initiatives to mobilize women metalworkers in 1978, the union newspaper explicitly and repeatedly defined such efforts as a means of "reinforcing the men's struggle" against employers (Gitahy et al., "Luttes ouvrières," p. 26). Indeed, the vigorous masculinity of union president Luis Inácio "Lula" da Silva undoubtedly contributed to his initial popularity among male autoworkers. See the remarkable 1978 interview with Lula on machismo, family, abortion, birth control, and feminism in João Guizzo, ed., *Lula, discursos e entrevistas,* 2d ed. (Guarulhos: O Reporter de Gaurulhos, 1981), pp. 234–42. Lula's views have evolved considerably since then, however.

49   "Movimentada a assembléia dos trabalhadores da Firestone," *Hoje,* February 8, 1946.

50   "Os Alunos de Felinto Defendem a Causa dos Patrões," *Hoje,* February 9, 1946.

51   "Protestam os grevistas da Swift do Brasil S.A.," *Hoje,* March 7, 1946.

52   "Homenagem de Santo André ao proletariado e povo santista," *Hoje,* February 12, 1946; "Solucionada a greve dos trabalhadores de 'Rhodia,'" *Hoje,* February 20, 1946; "Divertem-se os grevistas da Swift," *Hoje,* February 26, 1946; and "Trabalhadores de Santo André em visita de cordialidade aos seus companheiros de Santos," *Hoje,* September 3, 1946.

53   "Santo André tambem terá sua Rainha dos Trabalhadores," *Hoje,* March 26, 1946; "Foi realizada domingo a primeira apuração do concurso 'Rainha dos Trabalhadores de Santo André,'" *Hoje,* April 13, 1946; "A 'Rainha dos Trabalhadores de S. Paulo de 1946' vai ser homenageada pelo trabalhador de Santo André," *Hoje,* July 19, 1946; and "Concurso 'Rainha dos Trabalhadores de Santo André de 1946' desperta grande interesse o certame de Santo André," *Hoje,* June 6, 1947.

54   Bolsonaro de Moura, *Mulheres e menores,* p. 119. For profiles of radical female activists of that era see Antonio Candido, *Teresina etc.* (Rio de Janeiro: Paz e Terra, 1980); and Francisco Correia, "Mulheres libertárias: Um roteiro," in *Libertários no Brasil: Memória, lutas, cultura,* ed. Antonio Arnoni Prado (São Paulo: Brasiliense, 1986). For first-person accounts of the era see Zélia Gattai, *Anarquistas, graças a Deus* (Rio de Janeiro: Record, 1979); and the interview with Elvira Boni in

Angela de Castro Gomes, Dora Rocha Flaksman, and Eduardo Stotz, eds., *Velhos militantes* (Rio de Janeiro: Zahar, 1988), pp. 20–67.

55 Branca Moreira Alves, *Ideologia e feminismo* (Petrópolis: Vozes, 1980), p. 156; see also Tabak, *Autoritarismo*, and Blachman, "Eve in an Adamocracy."

56 Heleieth I. B. Saffioti, *A mulher na sociedade de classes* (São Paulo: Livraria Quatro Artes, 1969), p. 290; Leite, *Operária metalúrgica*, pp. 14–17; Tabak, *Autoritarismo*; and "Notas indicativas," pp. 63–103. For a profile of one important post–World War II activist see Maria Augusta Tibiriça Miranda, *Alice Tibiriça: Luta e ideais* (n.p.: PLG Comunicação, 1980). See also the 1978 interview with Zuleika Alambert (*Memórias das Mulheres do Exílio,* ed. Albertina de Oliveira Costa [Rio de Janeiro: Paz e Terra, 1980], pp. 46–68) and the autobiography of the young communist woman who married Luis Carlos Prestes (Maria Prestes, *Meu companheiro: 40 anos ao lado de Luiz Carlos Prestes,* 2d ed. [Rio de Janeiro: Rocco, 1993]).

57 Saffioti, *A mulher na sociedade,* p. 290; Pena, *Mulheres e trabalhadoras,* p. 209.

58 Challenging the ideology of traditional sex roles was not a priority of the leftist women's movement after 1945 (Leite, *Operária metalúrgica,* p. 17). As Pena points out, the communists' major challenge to patriarchal mores stemmed from their unsuccessful advocacy of legalized divorce during the Constituent Assembly in 1946 (Pena, *Mulheres e trabalhadoras,* pp. 211–13). Divorce was an extremely touchy issue in this overwhelmingly Catholic society, and the PCB's position favoring divorce was not emphasized by the female party leaders like Zuleika Alambert or Carmen Savietto in São Paulo.

59 Zuleika Alambert, *A situação e organizacão da mulher* (São Paulo: Global, 1980).

60 ALESP, *Anais da Assembléia Legislativa do Estado de São Paulo,* vol. 5, pp. 166–67.

61 ALESP, *Anais da Assembléia Legislativa do Estado de São Paulo,* vol. 5, p. 167; "São Paulo unido aclamou Prestes," *Hoje,* April 24, 1946.

62 ALESP, *Anais da Assembléia Legislativa do Estado de São Paulo,* vol. 5, pp. 168–69.

63 "Centenas de mulheres de Santo André dirigem-se ao prefeito," *Hoje,* August 20, 1946. No ABC trade unions at this time maintained separate women's divisions, although such divisions subsequently flourished in the paulista labor movement in the late 1950s and early 1960s. One of the earliest initiatives in this regard was taken by the metalworkers' union of São Paulo ("O que foi a 1.a conferencia das mulheres do setor metalúrgico," "Resoluções da 1.a conferencia," *O Metalúrgico,* May 1956). The female proponents of separate women's divisions within the unions justified them with the argument that different methods than those used for men could mobilize women more successfully (Conselho Estadual, *Mulheres operárias,* pp. 106–10). Creating separate women's divisions in unions remains a controversial idea, however, and was rejected as divisive at the 1978 Congress of Women Metalworkers of São Bernardo do Campo. For more on this meeting, the resolutions adopted, and the ensuing controversy, see Luís Flávio Rainho and Osvaldo Martines Bargas, *As lutas operárias e sindicais dos metalúrgicos em São*

Bernardo (1977–1979) (São Bernardo: Associação Beneficiente e Cultural dos Metalúrgicos de São Bernardo, 1983), pp. 45–48, 184–85; Leite, *Operária metalúrgica,*
p. 142; and Gitahy et al., "Luttes ouvrières," pp. 26–29.

64   Conselho Estadual, *Mulheres operárias,* pp. 93–94, 99, 100.

65   Leite, *Operária metalúrgica,* p. 139.

66   Biographical details about Carmen Savietto can be found in a letter from Rolando Fratti to Ademir Medici, April 16, 1990, included in Ademir Medici, *A
vitória dos candidatos de Prestes* (Santo André: Prefeitura Municipal de Santo André,
1990), pp. 3–5, 100; Marcos Andreotti, interview with author, Santo André, September 27, 1982). For additional information on her family see French, *Brazilian
Workers' ABC,* pp. 92, 145; and *O ABC dos operários,* pp. 86, 134.

67   See "Lista dos trabalhadores sindicalisados inscritos na 'Cooperativea de Con-
sumo dos Trabalhadores Sindicalisados de Santo André, Limitada,'" Prefeitura
Municipal de Santo André, September 4, 1946, processo 6567/46.

68   "Comício comunista," *Borda do Campo,* July 15, 1945; "Visitou os trabalhadores santistas uma comissão de mulheres do município de Santo André," *Hoje,*
June 27, 1946; and "As mulheres de Santo André solidárias com os trabalhadores
presos," *Hoje,* July 19, 1946.

69   "Quis implantar a ditadura fascista em Santo André," *Hoje,* August 13, 1946.

70   Tribunal Regional Eleitoral de São Paulo (TRE SP), processo 6254/174 (1947).

71   French, *Brazilian Workers' ABC,* p. 245; and *O ABC dos operários,* p. 234.

72   After World War II, the ABC region also produced a very different kind of
successful female political leader: the populist Tereza Delta, who was elected
mayor of São Bernardo do Campo and, later, state deputy (see French, *Brazilian
Workers' ABC* and *O ABC dos operários*).

73   The PCB's poor record of nominating women should be placed in the larger
context of the extremely small number of female nominees for public office in
postwar Brazil. Blachman and Toscano both report that only 18 women ran for
federal deputy in 1945 out of 950, and none were elected. Estimates for 1947 vary
between 8 and 17 women among the 1,464 candidates for state assembly posts
nationwide, with either 9 or 5 having been elected (Blachman, "Eve in an Adamocracy," pp. 86, 88; Fanny Tabak and Moema Toscano, *Mulher e Política* [Rio de
Janeiro: Paz e Terra, 1982], p. 78). On the subsequent evolution of female participation in the state and national legislature, see Lúcia Avelar, *Mulheres na Elite
Política Brasileira: Canais de Acesso ao Poder,* Série Pesquisas, no. 6 (São Paulo: Fundação Konrad-Adenauer-Stiftung, 1996), pp. 25–27.

74   See TRE SP, processos 8A (1945) and 8B (1946); and "As mulheres de Santo André
participarão ativamente nas eleições," *Hoje,* October 21, 1947.

75   Since Brazilian electoral studies emerged in the 1950s, Lúcia Avelar notes, male/
female difference has been routinely treated "merely as a background variable,
without taking into account the great transformation in daily life experienced by
women" as a result of the "emergence of urban patterns of life and their greater

integration into the educational and occupational systems." As she notes, "we know little about the impact of these changes in the political orientations of women" (Avelar, *O segundo eleitorado,* pp. 21–22).

76 The Left's rivals for urban popular support in postwar São Paulo openly acknowledged the pioneering role played by the communists; see the remarks by Duke Borges Barreiro, who headed the Departamento Feminino of the party of populist politician Adhemar de Barros (Partido Social Progressista) in the município of São Paulo (Regina Sampaio, *Adhemar de Barros e o PSP* [São Paulo: Global, 1982], p. 142).

The Loneliness of Working-Class Feminism

Women in the "Male World" of Labor Unions, Guatemala City, 1970s

DEBORAH LEVENSON-ESTRADA

It has taken extraordinary courage for workers to join unions in Guatemala, where since 1954 the state's de facto policy has been to literally cut labor activists into pieces. Despite and because of this violence, workers rebuilt trade unionism in the late 1950s and the 1960s, when Guatemala experienced substantial industrial growth for the first time. By the mid-1970s, Guatemala City, where industrial growth was concentrated, had become the site of a large, influential labor movement that supported the call for revolutionary change that swept the region. The state responded by redoubling its terror, and by the end of 1980 most urban working-class leaders were dead or in exile. Subsequently industry has declined, violence has continued, and the labor movement has reemerged only as a pale shadow of its former self.

In addition to the fear and constant danger with which all activists have had to live since the 1954 coup, women activists have also had to live with men, at home or in unions, who have either opposed or tried to control women's participation in unions. During the best and worst of its times and to the present day, the Guatemalan labor movement has been dominated by men who have conceptualized trade unionism and qualities such as militancy and solidarity as masculine. Their strong sense of masculine worth, honor, and courage has helped empower them in a situation of extreme social stress.[1] What has it taken for women to become labor activists? To answer that question and to further explore the connections between gender and activism, this chapter looks at the experience of a 1970s union leader named Sonia Oliva, and at the history of her union at the Japanese-owned ACRICASA thread factory in Guatemala City.

My knowledge of Sonia Oliva's history has been strongly influenced by her account of her life. When I interviewed her in the 1980s in her country of exile, she understood that a vital relationship existed between class action and the social construction of women, and I, singularly concerned with my version of a class analysis, did not.[2] When I initially asked Oliva how she became involved in the ACRICASA union, I anticipated a reply that would focus on changes in production, low wages, mistreatment on the job, and so forth. Instead, she told me a personal story:

> I'm from a small village in Zacapa [eastern Guatemala], where I was born in 1953, and my father is a peasant. My mother did not live with us anymore because my parents had separated, and so, since I was the only woman in the house, I did all that kind of women's work—cooking, cleaning, washing, ironing. I finished elementary school when I was thirteen because I made a big effort. I had to walk six kilometers daily, but I did it! There was no high school in the area and I wanted to keep studying, so I came to live with an aunt in Guatemala City. She found me a job in a supermarket as a cashier, but I couldn't go to school because she made me stay in the house cleaning in the evening. She treated me badly and even hit me. . . . Oh how I wanted to study! But she wouldn't let me because of all the work in the house.
>
> I befriended a girl and I used to cry and tell her my problems. Since she lived alone in a boardinghouse she said, "Look, you are working. You can leave the house, you don't have to put up with this." My father came to the city a few days later. I explained my situation, and he said I was right, and he gave me money to buy the things one needs to live alone, like a bed, so off I went to live with my friend, alone where she lived. Everything went beautifully after that.

Sonia went on to speak of how much she enjoyed studying at night school, which she left after she became involved in the union at her new factory job at ACRICASA. Because I did not look as if I understood the point of her story, she stopped to spell out her narrative strategy: "But you know the reason I told you this tale is to explain *how* I could get involved in the union. There was no one at home to stop me, a woman . . . no husband, mother, father, mother-in-law, father-in-law. I was alone."[3]

Oliva's awareness of the oppressive nature of gender roles and ideologies enabled her to be her own feminist historian. Therefore, she chose to first recount her personal journey in order to explain to me that she had to be "alone," outside of normal gender relations, to be an activist. That was *how* she became an activist.

Besides revealing that the parts often assumed to be played by the Latin

American working-class woman (the *clasista*) and the U.S. female middle-class scholar (the feminist) can be reversed, Oliva's remarks suggest both the stark importance of gender and the gray complexities of real life. She speaks of women's ascribed role in the household as well as its violation (her mother, not her father, left the home; Oliva wanted to and did work), of the view among some women that paid work was liberating in some sense (her friend remarked, "you are working . . . you don't have to put up with this"), and of at least one man who did not always enforce the imprisonment of women within certain domains. Yet even though her father was sympathetic to her desire to study, Oliva understood that she had to live apart from the constraints of gender to join a union.

She grew up in a rural and urban *ladino* (mestizo or non-Indian) Guatemalan world marked by rigid conventions about what constitutes proper male and female being, rights, and obligations, regardless of class. Male obligations have been to protect women and children, and to be the stable breadwinner and public protector of the home. According to popular usage, to be *macho* has meant to defend oneself and one's family, to be brave and bold, to confront, to be capable, to not allow oneself to be stepped on, and to have the final word over women and everyone else. Women have been defined as mothers, homemakers, and emotional caretakers for others, and their arena is supposed to be the home. What women do outside the home remains suspect; they earn status and a sense of worth for what they accomplish within it. Many qualities, such as apoliticism, dependence, and certain types of emotionalism, have been defined as feminine in relation to this household role and in deference to masculine identity. Many fictions are interwoven: the "real" value of women is domestic; domestic work is not real labor; the worlds of work and family are opposites, because real labor is monetarily compensated in contrast with what happens in the home, which is emotionally constituted; it is men who work for wages outside the home, and thus their work has greater social and economic value.

Class has complicated these ideals. The gap between the real and ideal male and female has been wide in the homes of working-class and poor families in Guatemala City, and there exist images regarded as humorous to express this: for example, the "charming," tipsy, can't-keep-a-job, womanizing male, a folkloric neighborhood figure alongside the big, tough wife who kicks him out the door and provides for their many children. Indeed, the "secret" that women and children are breadwinners, and that fathers often abandon the family, has been shared by many, and it is not very secret. Many of the Guatemalan workers whom I interviewed recounted as a central drama of their lives the failure of their fathers to maintain the family and the success of their mothers in doing so. Both in accord with the female ideal and against it, mothers have been a prime force in holding families together in the face of desertion and disaster. They stay with their children and they work hard inside and outside the house, and they are revered for this by their children. In their children's eyes, mothers working outside the home are not suspect. One worker described a typical youth. His father deserted the family, and he recalled, "Everyone but my father did something for the family. I started working in an ice factory when I was ten; my brother sold pots door to door; my sister collected cloth and we used to pull out the thread and sell it. My mother made and sold tortillas. She woke up at four in the morning to work until late at night. She was a dedicated mother. She had no life of her own. It was a restricted life economically, but I was happy with my mother." [4] When this worker remarked that his mother had "no life of her own," he was not happy about that, but he did not expect her to rebel against this suffocation, and he appreciated her self-sacrifice, upon which his family life and happiness depended. In other words, if played out, normative gender roles are inherently inhibiting. If not played out, other problems arise: husbands often oppose women working outside the home; fathers are seen as failures, and their children react against them; and women work far too much. The gender rules are neither overturned nor strictly adhered to. Working-class people have lived in a gray area of gender "imperfection," and although perhaps few men have been "feminine," many women have been "masculine."

By the 1970s when Sonia Oliva went to work at ACRICASA, she was not alone. Many women worked for wages outside their homes. They not only labored as domestic servants and schoolteachers, but they were also employed in the modern, capital-intensive factories that dominated many neighborhoods by the 1970s. [5] Preserving the sense that women really belonged in the home, working-class people usually understood female work for wages outside the home to be temporary labor; this was particularly true of factory work, which, unlike domestic or some service employment, was envisioned as male labor and not as an extension of the female caretaking role. In the home and the workplace, working people did not have a positive sense of male and female that fit the fact of full-time, permanent female labor in factories. This absence plagued the labor movement. Oliva's room of her own made it possible to be nonconventional and join a union, but in the union the problem of conventional ideas about gender reappeared.

Women at Work: The ACRICASA Union

ACRICASA opened in 1973 with state-of-the-art machinery to make acrylic thread for the Central American Common Market. What impressed Sonia Oliva most about the factory when she started to work there in 1974 was the contrast between the treatment given machines and people. She explained that "the machines got everything they needed to function twenty-four hours a day without hitches or failures, but we did not."[6] In 1975 a union drive began among the workers, of whom one hundred were men and three hundred were young women ranging in age from eighteen to twenty-six. These young women were mainly ladinas, and a few were Mayas; almost all of them were new to the industrial workforce, and many were new to the city.

Some of the shop floor realities that angered the workers were not specific to women workers: all workers shared the low pay, twelve-hour shifts, and lack of face masks against the dust. Other problems were of special concern to women: the absence of toilets was particularly troublesome for women; more so was the fact that Japanese supervisors felt entitled to slap women workers! In addition, many women and men were troubled that the company provided no transportation to the plant, which was located at the end of a dirt road about two kilometers from a main road that was serviced by unreliable public transportation. Women on the night shift felt particularly vulnerable, and they argued that at any time of day or night the many pregnant women had to walk excessively.[7]

A group of men workers, most of whom were mechanics, started an organizing drive in early February of 1975. The leadership expanded to include one woman after several of the original men organizers were fired because a spy had infiltrated the presumably secret ad hoc organizing committee. However, this first woman leader resigned the following morning, because, according to Oliva, "when she got to her house and said she was helping to form a union, the mother, the husband, everyone bawled her out, and the next day she came in and said no, she couldn't do it, and it was very dangerous and all that, so they put me up."[8] The genesis of Oliva's official leadership post and the reason her female predecessor was chosen were the same: the Labor Ministry mandated that unions have a nine-person executive committee; women were elected at ACRICASA because there were not nine men willing to risk being union officials. The male trade unionists had not transformed their vision of womanhood, but they were realists. They had to abide by the Labor Ministry's rules, and if they wanted a union at ACRICASA, they had to accept women. Oliva, a charismatic person, was important to them, and so

A woman, hard at work and pregnant, inside the ACRICASA
thread factory, Guatemala City, 1984. Courtesy of Patricia
Goudvis.

was the entrance of women into the union. After the union's lawyer secured
an injunction against the company to prevent further firings, over one hundred workers, most of whom were women, joined the union. This number
was far greater than the men organizers, who had feared that the female composition of the labor force would slow down their efforts, had anticipated.[9]
But there they were, and the union was off and running.

It took almost nine months to win the union legal recognition, and then
fifteen months to win a contract. During those months, the mainly women
workers employed a variety of tactics to pressure management into negotiations. They often crowded into the manager's office to collectively demand
that management meet with the union. They went out on brief illegal strikes.
Typically when they walked off illegally, the company telephoned a labor inspector. But when the labor inspector pulled up at the gate, the workers
rushed to work. After the labor inspector walked through the door only to
find the workers busy at their posts, the workers grabbed him and pointed out
the many violations of the national labor code. They also painted signs such
as "We want bus service" and "We want a wage increase" inside the plant,
and on management's cars. Their fame as persistent trade unionists spread.

When the young women from ACRICASA walked by the many nearby non-union factories where mainly men worked, they taunted the men workers by throwing the link between masculinity and class militancy in their faces: "We are women and *we've* organized. . . . What have you *men* done?"[10]

Trade unionism was Oliva's life by 1977, and it kept her busy day and night. When miners marched 250 miles from a tungsten mine in the western highlands town of Ixtahuacan to Guatemala City to dramatize their fight for a union, Oliva was the only woman in the labor movement to join several men trade unionists and journey up the Pan American Highway to meet the miners. She and the *muchachos* from the well-known and virtually all-male Coca-Cola Workers' Union slept by the edge of the road with the miners and marched into Guatemala City at their side.[11]

Oliva attended all the meetings she could, she thought about the problems Guatemala faced, and she took action whenever she saw the opportunity. Along with many other Guatemalans in the 1970s who had experienced the growth of capitalist industry and agriculture under a terrorist state, she opposed capitalism and the state. The state and national and foreign companies gave urban and rural workers nothing but trouble, and their policies obliged workers to engage in bitter and dangerous struggles to win minimal demands. Even after Oliva's union won a contract in early 1977, workers continually had to pressure the company to abide by it, and in March of 1977 workers on the night shift struck over the company's refusal to pay overtime. Oliva did not work that shift, but she wanted to join the wildcat strike, and to get into the locked compound she scaled an eight-foot wall and then jumped to the ground, despite the fact that she was six months pregnant.

Three months later and a few days after her son Pavel was born, workers seized the factory to force compliance with the union contract. Oliva grabbed her days-old infant and rushed down to the factory. Her companions were glad to see her, but she and others became frightened for the baby when they realized that the Pelotón Modelo (riot police) had surrounded the factory and might enter with tear gas bombs at any moment. Oliva recalled that she "didn't know what to do, confront the Pelotón Modelo or take care of Pavel." At just that moment the worker in charge of the boiler threatened to blow up the entire factory if the police came any closer to the building, and the frightened manager had the police withdrawn. The workers, and Pavel, camped out inside the compound for fifteen days, at which time the company agreed to comply with the contract that it had already signed.[12]

Instead of meeting the demands of motherhood in a conventional manner, Oliva brought Pavel to meetings and demonstrations. Instead of leaving her child in someone else's care, as male trade unionists automatically did, she brought her son into her world of activism. When the company did not implement a provision in the contract for day care, Oliva brought forty-day-old Pavel to work, "to make a point."

> Pavel and I showed up at work one day, me with diapers, bottles, and so forth, and everyone was astonished. At that time I worked in the laboratory with chemicals, so the manager says, "You have to work, you can't have a child here with these chemicals." "Right," I said. There was supposed to be a day care center, and if they wanted to, they could give me a paid holiday until they built one, but until that time I would come with Pavel. They said they'd call a labor inspector. I said, "Great!" Because according to the pact there was supposed to be a day care. I got a box and fixed it up for Pavel, I put the box on my desk. The day was wild. I got up all the time to prepare his bottles. Every time he cried, I'd say, "Ah, my little son," and stopped working to take care of him. I always made him my priority.[13]

After a few days of this, during which time one other woman followed Oliva's example and brought her child to work, the company took a worker off a machine and placed her in a small room with a few cribs and supplies. That was the day care center. But the day care center was closed at night, and many mothers worked the night shift. Oliva, who worked the day shift, left Pavel at work at the conclusion of her shift, again, "to make a point." Her tactic was successful. She explained, "Poor thing [Pavel]! I felt awful but these are the things one must do. I didn't pick him up, so there he stayed. I knew they wouldn't leave him alone, that they would do something. Next day they came and bawled me out. They had to keep the girl there all night and pay her. Finally they gave in."[14] Oliva was hardly a typical mother.

By 1978 the union was strong, and it had succeeded in guaranteeing compliance with a good contract. In addition, the union was involved in helping other workers and in exposing injustices in Guatemala. The union's leaflets spoke of more than unions and workplaces, and the union publicly supported the growing Sandinista struggle against Somoza in nearby Nicaragua.[15] The women from the union helped constitute the dynamic popular movement that dominated the urban landscape in the late 1970s. Oliva was the only woman from her union to "sleep with the Ixtahuacan miners," as she jokingly phrased the fact that she had camped overnight with them by the side of the Pan American Highway, but many of the women from the union went to the massive demonstration that greeted the miners on their arrival in Guatemala City in November 1977.[16] Virtually all the union members went out into the streets to protest after the army killed over one hundred Kekchi Maya villagers in the distant mountain town of Panzos in mid-1978, and by then the union was an active member of a broader labor movement that called for "Revolutionary Popular Government."

The state reacted strongly against the unions in the popular movement. To take just the case of ACRICASA, in July 1978 nine male and twenty-six female union members were seized by police, dragged from the bus won by the union in its 1977 contract, and taken to prison, where they were held on the charge of being "subversive." It took several weeks and hunger strikes by workers at the factory and in prison to get them released.[17] In October, ACRICASA union leader Gonzalo Ac Bin was assassinated. In early 1979, Oliva and Pavel were kidnapped by masked men. Oliva was beaten, and the two of them were held for over fifteen hours before they were released on the condition that Oliva leave the country, which she and Pavel did. On June 21, 1980, two newly elected ACRICASA union leaders, Florencia Xocop and seven-month-pregnant Sara Cabrera, were among twenty-seven union leaders to be kidnapped, never to be seen again. After this, the union retreated from politics.[18]

Working-Class Feminism

Trade unionism demanded a great deal from the women at the ACRICASA thread factory, and they met the challenge. When the women crowded into the manager's office, painted signs, argued with labor inspectors, or occupied the plant, they violated "ideal" female behavior; they also acted on matters that were not gender specific. Interested in Nicaragua, the Guatemalan countryside, and other unions—in short, in all the motion that whirled about them and drew them further into action—their involvement in the union and in the popular movement was rooted in the multiplicity of their being, and not only in matters related to the household and family, or to their sense of self as maternal. Several of the women workers were close to the Mayan peasantry and were anxious about the growing number of conflicts over land titles and the rumors that the army was bombing the highlands. The women union members had a relationship "to the world of reality and not only to the world of men and women."[19] Their activism was not simply an extension of their gender identity as mothers, wives, and daughters, an identity that could propel them into politics to defend kin "vicariously," as one feminist scholar has

Women workers inside their locker room, ACRICASA thread
factory, Guatemala City, 1984. Courtesy of Patricia Goudvis.

called maternal politics, or politics based in one's femaleness, whether that is
understood as a real essence or as a social construction.[20]

Their politics were more than maternal ones; but neither were the women
in the ACRICASA union simply good class-conscious trade unionists whose
specificity as women had been made invisible, as many argue has happened in
Latin American labor movements.[21] Some of their grievances were specific to
women, and in pursuing these claims they violated "proper" female behavior—as they did whenever they protested—but in these cases they did so in
especially dramatic ways. One of ACRICASA's first concessions to the workers
was the installation of indoor toilets, but supervisors clocked workers when
they went to the bathroom. One day a woman who stayed in the bathroom for
four minutes was reported to the manager. She in turn informed the union
representatives, and they accompanied her into the manager's office. There a
quarrel began during which she suddenly became silent. She stood up, left
the room, returned with a soiled sanitary napkin, placed it on the manager's
desk, and, red in the face, stated, "If you want to know why I was in the
bathroom so long, here's why!" and with this the clocking of workers in the
bathroom stopped.

To give another example of this pronounced refusal to bury "private"
matters in "feminine" silence, by law Mother's Day was a paid holiday, and

ACRICASA granted it without question to legally married women. In 1977 the ACRICASA union, with its many single mothers, demanded the same right for single mothers. The company refused. The manager claimed that because these women were not married, they were not mothers. A group of workers argued inside the manager's office—"If you don't give me this holiday because I am not a mother," said one infuriated worker, "I will lie on your desk and you bring a doctor in here to decide in front of everyone whether I am a mother," and management, embarrassed, gave in immediately.[22] Single mothers acknowledged that status, and simultaneously attempted to legitimize it by laying claim to a holiday that glorifies the most conformist style of mothering and womanhood.

In short, the ACRICASA women workers do not fit neatly into the categories sometimes used by scholars to describe women's activism. Theirs were not maternal, "womenist," or "genderless" politics, nor would it be fair to these women to call them "second-wave" feminists who explicitly challenged, rather than accepted, ceded to, or drew strength from, an essentialist vision of womanhood. The tension between accepting and rejecting one's "proper" role, rights, and obligations, as a female remained a largely unresolved matter. It seems easy enough analytically to conceptualize the issue as a choice between nonconformity and conformity, but things do not work out that way in real life. On the one hand it is important to point out that there existed among the women a consciousness savvy about, and critical of, gender constructions. But it also must be made clear that the women in the union did not question many inequalities between men and women. None of them, including Oliva, took issue with the fact that ACRICASA gave men the better-paying jobs, and even though most union members at ACRICASA were women, most of the leaders were men. Only in a few cases, such as that of Oliva and the disappeared Florencia Xocop and Sara Cabrera, did women assume official leadership posts, and this was only when there was no one else willing to take these jobs. Most women union members did not question gender roles to the extent that Oliva did. The fight for day care mentioned earlier in this chapter illustrates the difference between Oliva's views and those of most other women trade unionists at ACRICASA.

Day care is potentially subversive to gender constructions because it can, but does not necessarily, challenge the notion that women should be in the home with children. Care for children of mothers who must work can be the heart of the demand for welfare; but so can freedom for women from the work of constantly overseeing children. The demand tells us little about why it is made. It can be generated by women who wish to protect mothering, it can be made by women and/or men who want to be less concerned with parenting, and it can be made for a combination of these or other reasons.

The origins of day care in Guatemala go back to the beginning of this century, when wealthy women who were concerned with the "social question" sought relief for poor working women through private charity organizations. They wished to protect urban children and society from the ravages to which city life subjected the family. Later, in the 1944–1954 reform period, a strong initiative for day care came from the short-lived middle- and working-class feminist movement, Alianza Feminina. Members of Alianza Feminina, which included many women artisans, wrote extensively about the plight of working mothers who needed to work and were unable to find adequate day care for their children. Because of Alianza Feminina's efforts, day care centers were established, and the 1947 Labor Code required factories with forty or more women workers to provide day care facilities. Alianza Feminina, and most first-wave feminist groups in Latin America, had not departed from the premise that child care was a women's issue. Their thinking reflected both their own views about women's essentially maternal nature and their own realism: it was women who took care of children; whether or not that *should* be the case was not questioned. The demand that factories with a certain number of *parents* have day care facilities was unimaginable to these progressive Guatemalan women in the 1940s.

This legislation remained a part of the labor code after that code was revised in the wake of the 1954 coup. In the post-1954 period, and certainly in the 1970s when the labor movement was relatively powerful and under sharp attack, labor lawyers who sought ways to work within the fragile legal structure raised the issue of day care at plants employing forty or more women because it was a legal demand, and thus a "legitimate" one that could be pursued in court, and not because it was something, like higher wages, for which workers really pressed. In the 1970s male trade unionists actually opposed day care for factories where they worked. Their reasoning was based on their "common sense": their wives gave the authentic care; why substitute anyone for a mother? They (the men) were killing themselves working to have a "normal" family (a wife at home), and what else would wives do? One worker explained to me that he opposed day care in his factory (a factory of men) because he couldn't imagine what his wife would do all day without children to look after.[23]

At ACRICASA the labor lawyers suggested that the union demand day care for tactical reasons: a court battle could result in a rare union victory. Most of the women in the union were uncertain as to whether they really wanted the company to open a day care facility at the plant. Of course, they all routinely supported the demand as good union members, but as good mothers, they had reservations. Many women said that they had relatives at home to take care of their children, and, again, as good mothers, they preferred that. They argued that the home was safer and more loving, and they did not have to drag the child onto dangerous, overcrowded public transportation every morning. Several said that their relatives at home would be shocked at the thought of putting a child in day care when there were female relatives at home for just that purpose (many lived with their mothers). One woman explained that "even though my mother works [making food and selling it in front of the house], I would be rejecting her if I took my children to work with me every day."[24] Women admired Oliva's commitment and audacity when she brought her son Pavel to ACRICASA as a protest, but only one of many mothers followed her example. Several commented that it was dangerous to have a child near chemicals, and many questioned the wisdom of leaving Pavel overnight. These same women risked their lives to protest the murder of Kekchi Mayas in Panzos in July 1978, when the state was killing people who so much as attended demonstrations, and they behaved "outrageously" to win single mothers the right to a day off with pay on Mother's Day, but on the politics of mothering, *those* maternal politics, most parted company with Oliva.

Oliva had no reservations about fighting for day care. What empowered Oliva in this struggle for women's rights was her nonessentialist sort of feminism, rather than the "maternalist" or "womenist" consciousness often attributed to women activists from the laboring classes. It is not only middle-class women who have a feminist consciousness and will.[25] Oliva had the energy to lead an essentially lonely fight for day care because she was an unconventional mother. The truth was that at ACRICASA day care was not a vital necessity for most women, because these women workers, just like the men workers, had women at home to take care of their children. For Oliva it was a vital necessity because she had chosen to break out of relations that would have kept some "domestic" women in her life. Oliva loved Pavel, but she did not bring him with her constantly because she wanted to be with him constantly. She had no choice if she was to remain outside the domestic sphere, as a worker and an activist, and this was very important to her. She wanted day care because she felt that was a benefit her employer should pay for, and because she wanted a life outside of mothering. Oliva took on the sometimes-feminist consciousness, full of ambiguities and never proclaimed, of many ACRICASA militants who both broke the mold of gender constructions and reproduced them, albeit further down the path toward finding "another way to be."[26] Oliva had

Six years after the union won a day care center inside the factory.
The center still exists, but only a handful of workers use it. One
woman brings her child to work on the company-supplied
ACRICASA bus, another benefit the union won for workers.
Guatemala City, 1984. Courtesy of Patricia Goudvis.

stronger feelings than most women about the rules and codes that sorted out
male from female: she did not like them at all. She thought it was ridiculous
that the union movement did not demand day care in factories with working
fathers, and she was alone in her opinion.

Gendered Activism, Gender Troubles

The women at ACRICASA who "gender baited" the male workers at neighboring factories knew what they were talking about. Men workers were far more
concerned with gendering the labor movement than their female counterparts were. Unlike women activists, men commonly linked union participation to their gender. One worker explained, "My children will say with pride,
'My father was a member of the Coca-Cola workers' union.' If I were not in
the union, how could I face them, what kind of man would I be?"[27] Activism demanded extraordinary public heroism, and this sort of courage was a
male-associated character trait, part of the essence of masculinity. No matter
how many publicly heroic women there were, trade unionism was perceived

as a masculine domain wherein the courageous and manly were counted. Union literature sometimes used the adjective *virile* to describe job actions, and a typical editorial in a union newspaper challenged workers whose union activities had been lax: "Don't you have hair on your chests?"[28] In popular imagery, men trade unionists became the city's best breadwinners, the most steadfast defenders of family, and the ultimate fathers, despite the reality that union activity often got them killed, always kept them too busy to spend time with their children, and occasionally endangered their children's lives.

But even though machismo was one of several qualities mentioned by male trade unionists as important to good trade union leadership, many men understood that machismo had limitations, and even a negative side. The term *macho,* for example, because it implied no distinction between collective and individual defense, was sometimes used disparagingly by male workers to refer to a bullheaded worker who took on a boss or supervisor on his own and could only "think with his balls." After several incidents of worker adventurism at the Coca-Cola Bottling Plant, "thinking with one's balls" became a serious criticism within the prestigious Coca-Cola workers' union. This is not to say that men revised their understanding of masculinity and class; on this score their trade unionism remained conservative. What it does suggest is that their gendering of class included some gray areas. Men knew that activism demanded an intellectual and worldly clarity that went beyond mere masculinity. In their eyes this clarity was not gendered, but was "classed" in the sense that workers tended both to look to middle-class men and women lawyers for "brains," and to represent intellectuality as belonging to the middle class, male and female.[29] Masculinity was empowering only up to a point; workers were saddled with a feeling of intellectual inferiority for which their masculine identity did not compensate. Mixed with their view that men were tough by nature was the conception that workers were workers precisely because they were not smart. The working class was gendered as male with pride, but it was also constructed as "dumb." Intertwined with the invigorating sense that "tough," "male," and "worker" went together was the painful notion that physical labor was opposed to mental labor and that workers were short on brains. "Stupid" lurked inside of the "worker," who was connected to "male" and "tough."

Men workers' defense of women workers also illuminates the complex, shifting manner in which masculinity was bound up with class action. At least two of the most important industrial unions in the city were initiated by male workers in response to the sexual abuse of women workers. Efrain Alonso, the cofounder of a union at the Kern's canning factory, explained how that union started: "I remember that there were these managers, these middle-class young guys with their cute little cars. And when the harvest came they needed a lot of extra women to work, so they always picked the prettiest ones, and what they did afterwards [the managers], they took them to drink on Fridays, on the weekend, I don't know what they did, and these poor women had to give in to what they wanted because they needed the job. This was incredible, and the teacher [an ex-teacher in the plant with whom Alonso organized the union] and I discussed it thoroughly, and this is how the whole thing [the union drive at Kern's] started." [30]

A man at the Ray-O-Vac battery factory recalled the genesis of the union at that plant: "There were many abuses, but especially against the women, because in exchange for having a job they had to sleep with the managers, and they used to sit and cry and tell us about it. A committee formed to protest this, and with this the whole procedure of getting a union started." [31]

That women were in these factories in the first place signified a breakdown in male breadwinning capacity in the world of the ideal sexual division of labor. Worse, if managers could sexually harass women with impunity, male workers' masculinity was completely null, stolen. Men rushed to defend women and their own masculinity. Two commentators on an early version of this chapter have suggested that this represents not outrage at sexual abuse, but instead a "matter of messing with 'our' class's women," a class struggle over women's bodies, a question about who gets to sexually abuse. [32] But what did these men at Kern's and Ray-O-Vac do? No doubt the line between "protect" and "possess" is thin, but it is there; and in these two cases male workers did not proceed to harass their female coworkers sexually. Instead they signed them up into the union, which is not to say that sexual harassment did not go on in unions, but why form a union to sexually harass women workers? That would seem a difficult route, particularly after the union had publicly declared itself against sexual harassment, and particularly in Guatemala; why risk your life to sexually harass a woman when one can do it with impunity any day of the week? Outrage at the sexual abuse of women was informed by class machismo, and so was the question of the mode of struggle—the notion that men had to defend women—but it was also influenced by workplace class solidarity, which embraced sympathy for female coworkers.

Of course when men organized women into unions, they did so with mixed feelings, precisely because to do so contradicted their views of male and female; on the other hand, so did reality. Women were in factories. At ACRICASA and elsewhere, men activists were neither blind nor stupid, so they signed women up in unions, and they kept women in their place by simply treating them the way they always had treated women: the men often did not inform women of important meetings, decisions, problems, or gossip. They asked women in unions to do "women's work," such as cooking, cleaning up, and taking notes. This had the effect of making it more difficult for women to assume leadership roles, although they often led informally and, in the case of ACRICASA, they were elected officials. At ACRICASA and elsewhere, when women were notably militant or capable as trade unionists, men masculinized them. Because of class realities men could not reject these women; because of gender concepts they could not accept them as women. "So and so has more pants than most men I know," ran the typical remark about forceful, outspoken, and effective women trade unionists; this was the way men in the ACRICASA union described many of their militant female comembers. In this way men kept trade unionism very masculine—these women were more male than most men!—to maintain unionism as their own, even if it included women. The tension between representing unions, militancy, and class as male and the reality that unions, militancy, and class were both male and female, could not be eradicated. If men really conflated *class* and *male*, if *male* really "constituted" *class*, and if men workers did not on some level recognize the difference between their male coding of class and class reality, they would have excluded women from their unions. Instead, the women who were recognized as important to the labor movement, such as Oliva, were masculinized.[33]

Another way women were accommodated was as followers. No stereotypes were challenged: men "naturally" led, and women followed. The schoolteachers' union provides an example: public school teachers and their large union were overwhelmingly female in the 1970s. The union, which conducted a long and important strike of over 18,000 teachers in 1973, was led by men. The women members were not masculinized, and they were not generally even considered to be *obreros*. They did not need to be *made* maternal, because they were understood to represent the very essence of the maternal: they had made a vocation of the female's natural role of nurturing. During the 1973 strike, activist women schoolteachers were given a religious cast; they became "selfless apostles" fighting "for the children."[34]

Even if male trade unionists could find a way to accommodate women in unions either as "real men" or, as in the case of the schoolteachers, "real women," they rarely permitted their own wives to become involved in unions. Here, sexual possessiveness was at the heart of the matter. Wives were by definition unequivocally sexual, and not just female. They belonged to their husbands, and they could not be regenderized. During no job action was a "wives of trade unionists' support committee" formed, and when wives helped out individually during occupations or strikes, their husbands mediated their participation. Wives were allowed to cook, but not to hang around, and their husbands did not explain what was happening.[35] During the year-long occupation of the Coca-Cola plant in 1984–1985, when the union there included over two hundred men and very few women, a suggestion by a foreign trade union delegation to form a wives' support committee was rejected, because, in the words of one leader, "We decided if the wives were brought into the plant, there would be all kinds of flirting and jealousy, and this would lead to conflicts between workers."[36] The implication was that the wives were not members of the working class, therefore they had no inherent right to be there. Wives—for all the passivity, gentility, and domesticity ascribed to women—had the power to drag the class struggle backward, not impel it forward, because of their sexual allure, which would cause rivalry and betrayal. It was no accident that most women trade unionists were not wives.

While for men trade union activism was associated with their gender identity, for women the situation was the reverse. A schoolteacher might see herself and be seen as a self-sacrificing supermother, but for women factory workers activism contradicted the social ideal of femininity. Because of this, trade unionism demanded personal difference. Leticia Najarro, a textile union bureaucrat long supported by the AFL-CIO, who along with Sonia Oliva has been unique in her status as a female union leader known at the national level, evoked the nonconformist activism demanded of women when she remarked that "it is impossible to be a woman trade unionist and be married."[37] Moving away from men as companions was one type of deep personal change (Oliva did not stay with Pavel's father). Another was being a nontraditional mother. By bringing Pavel into trade unionism, Oliva took the least conventional path: a man would have left the child with a woman, and a female trade unionist could have done the same and "worn pants" in relation to children, by leaving Pavel in the safe hands of feminine women.

To be union activists in Guatemala, women have had to carry on two struggles—one against the company and the state, and another against sanctioned models of gender behavior—while men have had to wage the first and not the second; indeed men inform their trade unionism with their personal identities as men. For some women, class consciousness has sometimes involved the recognition that not only are they more than what is socially defined as a "worker"—a non-self-directed, nonthinking, manual being—but they are more than "women" as well. As Oliva explained, she had to be outside the relations that imprisoned her as a woman in order to live her life as a woman class activist. Helen Safa wrote in a seminal article that because working-class women do not take themselves seriously as workers, their class consciousness will be acquired in other situations, such as the home and the community.[38] We should consider a variation on Safa's thought: when women do take themselves seriously as workers, they begin examining and reshaping the roles into which they are cast at home and in society, where they are not considered "real" workers. It follows from this, and from Oliva's experience, that women are more likely than men to become self-conscious when they became class-conscious.

Thus it is not only overt male attitudes that have made trade unionism difficult for women. The personal nonconformism that trade unionism has demanded threatens an important means whereby women have achieved an identity and have received love and status. It is not easy for a woman to live without a man in Guatemala, even if it is hard to live with one. Oliva did not have a man, or the status of being a man's woman. And while she did not stop being a mother, she was criticized for her mothering. Because of all it entailed on the personal level in terms of revisualizing her female self and her relations to men and other women, few women became leaders of the union movement in the 1970s, and fewer women than men became activists.

On the other hand, when women did become activists, they were em-powered in different ways than men were. Men legitimated their involvement through their gender identity, and they organized around it, as in, "Don't you have hair on your chests?" But did this really help? After all, courage was not really about one's sex, any more than class and militancy were. In specific situations, women activists were more capable of class action, of uniting with workers regardless of sex, than men were, because women did not, and could not, legitimate class in their gender. To give one example of this, a union drive started in the late 1970s at a textile plant called MacGregor's, which employed more women than men. Male workers started the union campaign, and man-agement, playing on gender constructions, responded by organizing an anti-union caucus among women workers. Completely unchallenged by the union, the caucus of antiunion women grew. Despite this, the male trade unionists continued to view the caucus as "a typical phenomenon among older women workers and not serious." Sensing that the union would fail if the caucus was not checked, a handful of pro-union women took it upon themselves to start a campaign of diplomatic counteragitation to break the caucus's hold. They did, and in the process they established themselves as the most democratic, fair-minded, and pro-labor workers, because they had taken the caucus seri-ously and had respected the workers in it enough to parley with them. After the union won and elections for officers were held, these women were among those elected, much to the surprise of the male organizers who feared this represented an antiunion—i.e., feminine—tendency in the union.[39] The men could not see past their conception of female identity to the fact that ex-antiunion women had elected women who had been consistently pro-union; instead men understood this as a ploy by the antiunion caucus, even though that caucus no longer existed. Because the plant employed mainly women, the union would never have taken on any life without these women organizers. This history was cut short by the repression in 1980, when the union was destroyed. The point is that women trade unionists had a different consciousness and they were freer to see what was happening and to act as agents of class unity, because they were less bound by sexist prejudice. Their capacity as trade unionists was greater precisely because they were women, for whom the connection between class and gender differed from that of men. Once they became involved in union activity, once they took that "unfeminine" step, these women had a greater capacity to see beyond gender constructs. They did not glue their union work to gender constructs, as men did.

Conclusion

This chapter has argued that there has been no genderless working-class struggle in Guatemala. The Guatemalan Marxist Left has maintained that women's oppression has been the result of capitalism, and that the struggle for women's rights and liberation, and against machismo, has been secondary in importance to, and even detrimental to, the primary battle between classes. Oliva's history indicates that this is a false dilemma: she had to challenge sexism to be a class activist. There is no "more important" or "prior" issue—class or gender—these are inside one another, and the struggle against gender conventions and sexist ideologies is integral to any project of liberation. A critical consciousness about class needs a critical consciousness about gender, and vice versa.

I have also argued that women and men do not act only out of gender. Activism stems from the multiplicity of their being, of which gender is a part. I am concerned about pigeonholing women's activism into maternal or womenist politics. Much of the scholarly and popular literature about Latin American women in recent years has focused on political activism that stems from women's sense of themselves as women. Groups of relatives of the disappeared, such as the Madres de la Plaza de Mayo in Argentina, and neighborhood women's groups, are often presented from this perspective, and some authors argue that once in politics because of gender identity, women come to develop a critique of gender. But there exists as well women's political participation that, in its origins, is a transgression of the social construction of female, and within that space of transgression grassroots feminism flowers.

I wish to draw attention to this "feminism from below." Oliva was able to both concentrate on issues of womanhood *and* reject "woman" as an identity.[40] Clearly Oliva is exceptional, but feminists have always been the exception, regardless of their social class, time, or place. And certainly Oliva's lonely grassroots feminism has been full of its own ambiguities and contradictions, its lack of fixity, but what feminism has not? In the 1970s Oliva was a nonconformist working-class woman in the thick of things. She did not stay on the margin as a deviant or an outcast. Oliva was simultaneously one of the gang *and* unique in her attempt to elude her "feminine" fate.

There existed no feminist movement in the years 1954–1986 in Guatemala among working-class women.[41] This was not due to an imaginary, "objective," strategic, tactical, or inherent insignificance of feminism, but to other factors such as the strength of prejudices, the fear among women of the personal and social traumas that feminism would provoke, and state terrorism. Normative gender identities have had time, habit, culture, and social structure on their side, and most intensely, emotions, since most affective relations and families have been built around gender roles. Feminism has felt like a threat to love. As if that were not enough, state terrorism has made second-wave feminism seem irrelevant, and womenism, political activism to defend the family, seem relevant. State terrorism has reinforced the family by attacking the family, despite its incessant profamily rhetoric. Under state terrorism, family has been one of the only places where safety and trust can exist. Kidnappings have usually been carried out against family networks precisely because they provide a safe house for relations of confidence. To criticize the family or to separate from it when it has been under barbaric attack, and when it has seemed a last refuge, feels inappropriate even if it has not always been inappropriate.

In sum, the stakes in trade unionism and feminism have been unusually high in Guatemala, and no minimally safe social space has existed for either. In Guatemala, to act as a historical subject has been to stake one's life. But male trade unionists living with the fear of a horrible death also live out lives in the personal realm that, however stressful, do not overturn the familiar customs of gender, while women trade unionists must face the double insecurity of living with intense anxiety while traveling an unfamiliar emotional path alone. And that demands courage that surpasses extraordinary courage.

Notes

All translations are mine.

1 Two organizations were seminal to Guatemalan urban trade unionism. One was the Young Catholic Worker, which argued that women should not be in factories and supported the male breadwinner's project to lift himself out of the conditions of misery created by modernity. The other organization was the Guatemalan Communist Party (PGT). The PGT supported women's suffrage and rights, but it implicitly envisioned female labor as domestic, and it understood domestic labor to be outside the sphere of "real" productive relations that lead both to class consciousness and to the revolution that will change the world. For an interesting discussion of Marxist thought as masculine, "bound up with an ontological habitat that is profoundly masculine," see Christine Di Stefano, "Masculine Marx," in *Feminist Interpretations and Political Theory*, ed. Mary Lydon Shanley and Carole Pateman (University Park: Pennsylvania State University Press, 1991), pp. 146–63.

2 Ideas from Joan Scott that startled scholars (including myself) a few years ago now seem like common sense: "There is no choice between a focus on class or on gender; each is necessarily incomplete without the other" ("On Language, Gender and Working Class History," in *Gender and the Politics of History* [New York: Columbia University Press, 1988], p. 66).

3 Sonia Oliva, interview with author, San José, Costa Rica, March 1985.

4 Rodolfo Robles, interview with author, Guatemala City, August 1984.

5 In the 1970s the presence of women in manufacturing was 17 percent. The majority of these women were concentrated in a few industries: women represented 45 percent of workers in clothing, 53 percent in tobacco, and 30 percent in food. They represented 73 percent of the nation's schoolteachers and 74 percent of the service workers (Guatemala, Dirección de Estadísticas, Censo Poblacional, 1973).

6 Sonia Oliva, interview.

7 *Boletín del Sindicato de Trabajadores ACRICASA*, March 1975; Marta Gloria Torres, interview with author, New York City, December 1984.

8 Sonia Oliva, interview.

9 Marta Gloria Torres, interview.

10 Mercedes Barrios, interview with author, Guatemala City, January 1991.

11 The Coca-Cola union, a virtually all-male union, was famous for its militancy and for its endurance in the face of many death-squad attacks against it; in the 1970s it was the strongest union in the labor movement. The miners marched from San Idelfonso Ixtahuacán to Guatemala City in November 1977. They won legal status for their union, only to see it destroyed by violence. For more about the Coca-Cola workers' union and the post-1954 Guatemalan labor movement in general see Deborah Levenson-Estrada, *Trade Unionists against Terror: Guatemala City, 1954–1985* (Chapel Hill: University of North Carolina Press, 1994).

12   *El Gráfico,* August 12, 1978; *La Nación,* August 12, 1978.

13   Sonia Oliva, interview.

14   Ibid.

15   SITIACASA, communiqué, September 1978.

16   Sonia Oliva, interview.

17   Author interview with union member, Guatemala City, April 1991.

18   The union has managed to maintain its legal status, it has renegotiated its contract several times since 1980, and most ACRICASA workers are still union members. The union has not reentered the political arena with its 1970s vigor, and along with just about every other group in Guatemala City, it has dropped its prorevolutionary stance.

19   Virginia Woolf, *A Room of One's Own* (New York: Harvest/Harcourt Brace, 1989), p. 114.

20   See María del Carmen Feijóo and Mónica Gogna, "Women in the Transition to Democracy," in *Women and Social Change in Latin America,* ed. Elizabeth Jelin (London: Zed Books, 1990); and Marguerite Guzmán Bouvard, *Revolutionizing Motherhood: The Mothers of the Plaza de Mayo* (Washington: Scholarly Resources, 1994), for a discussion of the "maternal politics" of the Madres de la Plaza de Mayo. See María del Carmen Feijóo and Marcela María Alejandra Nari, "Women and Democracy in Argentina," in *The Women's Movement in Latin America,* ed. Jane Jaquette (Boulder, Colo.: Westview, 1994), for a discussion of the problems of "womenist" movements, i.e., those in which women are acting primarily on the basis of their "traditional" roles.

21   For one example, see Thelma Gálvez and Rosaldo Todoro, "Chile: Women and the Unions," in Jelín, *Women and Change.*

22   Author interview with ACRICASA worker, Guatemala City, August 1984.

23   Ricardo Samayoa, interview with author, Guatemala City, August 1984.

24   Mercedes Barrios, interview.

25   In her book *Emancipating the Female Sex: The Struggle for Women's Rights in Brazil, 1850–1940* (Durham, N.C.: Duke University Press, 1990), June Hahner states that movements for women's rights depend on a "class of educated women with some leisure" (p. xiii). Why should this be the case? Day care is a "women's right," and Oliva had little education and no leisure time. The equation of feminism with middle-class women, and womenism with working-class women really takes class constructs too seriously and thus underestimates working-class women. Patricia Chuchryk also points to feminism among working-class women in her article "From Dictatorship to Democracy: the Women's Movement in Chile," in Jaquette, *The Women's Movement in Latin America.*

26   Rosario Castellanos, "Meditación en el Umbral," in *Poesia no eres tú* (Mexico City: Fondo de Cultura Económica, 1975), p. 316; this refers to another way to be that is neither being a woman nor being a man.

27   Author interview with Coca-Cola worker, Guatemala City, August 1984.

28 *Voz y acción: Vocero popular de trabajadores de Coca-Cola,* September 1978.

29 The proportion of female to male lawyers or legal aids advising the urban labor movement was far higher than that of female to male labor leaders. The many women lawyers and legal aids, such as Rosa María Wantland, Marta Gloria Torres, and the disappeared Yolanda Urizar, were taken very seriously by male workers. Their advice was sought and usually heeded.

30 Efraín Alonso, interview with author, New York City, April 1984.

31 Luis Colocho, interview with author, Guatemala City, November 1985.

32 John French and Daniel James, personal letter, 1995.

33 An interesting inversion of this phenomenon is found in Barbara Taylor, *Eve and the New Jerusalem: Socialism and Feminism in the Nineteenth Century* (New York: Pantheon, 1983), where she describes how a positive assessment of the feminine made it possible for women to be members of the Owenite movement.

34 Male trade unionists were not above pointing to the number of women teachers to explain the decline of the teachers' federation.

35 Carmen López Balam and María Quevedo, interview with author, Guatemala City, August 1984.

36 Author interview with Coca-Cola worker, Guatemala City, August 1984.

37 Leticia Najarro, interview with author, Guatemala City, July 1984.

38 Helen Safa, "Class Consciousness among Working Class Women in Latin America: A Case Study in Puerto Rico," in *Sex and Class in Latin America,* ed. June Nash and Helen Safa (New York: Praeger, 1976).

39 Author interview with ex–MacGregor worker, Guatemala City, November 1985; Frank Larrue, interview with author, Washington, D.C., March 1984.

40 Denise Riley, *Am I That Name? Feminism and the Category of Women in History* (London: Macmillan, 1988).

41 The 1980s saw many changes. In the early 1980s, groups of relatives of the disappeared became increasingly active. These groups were composed primarily but not exclusively of women. Also in the 1980s, a small group of women trade unionists started a women's labor organization, although it developed no program independent of the federation to which it was affiliated, UNSITRAGUA. After the return to civilian rule in 1986, a few feminist groups appeared; several of these are led by women who have lived in exile and who have critiqued the Guatemalan Left's sexism. The need to understand the relationship between activism and prejudices about sex only intensifies. The industrial workforce has been "regendered" because the *maquiladora,* the only growing industrial sector, employs mostly women. This sector has had a great deal of trouble organizing due to the violence against organizing efforts, as well as to the kinds of problems discussed in this chapter: many male trade unionists, and many women workers, have trouble conceptualizing the women maquiladora workers both as workers and as trade unionists.

Morality and Good Habits

The Construction of Gender and Class in

the Chilean Copper Mines, 1904–1951

THOMAS MILLER KLUBOCK

In January 1990, the workers of the El Teniente copper mine engaged in Chile's first major strike since Augusto Pinochet had relinquished power to a transition democratic government in 1989. Families of the miners played an active role in the strike, figuring prominently in the many images of marches and demonstrations that filled Chilean newspapers. Miners' wives organized committees of support for their striking husbands, walked picket lines, and marched in protests. In interviews with journalists, women from the mining community eloquently defended the strike, invoking their position as mother and wife to emphasize their "moral authority" and the strike's legitimacy.[1] This active involvement drew on traditions of female participation in strikes that had been built in El Teniente since the 1940s.

Miners around the world are renowned for their combative militancy and have received ample attention from labor historians. Rarely, however, have historians examined the role played by women in miners' communities and movements. In the case of Chile, the copper miners of El Teniente and Chuquicamata have left an indelible mark on Chile's modern history and have attracted social scientists and historians interested in questions of working-class behavior and politics. Writers from a variety of disciplines have viewed miners as the most significant and combative sector of the working class.[2] Despite women's central and visible participation in miners' strikes, their experiences and the role of gender and sexuality in shaping miners' particular forms of class identity and militancy have been largely ignored.[3]

In general, histories of miners have focused on the proletarianization of workers from peasant and rural backgrounds.[4] Historians have described states' and mining companies' strategies for establishing productive and disciplined labor forces as well as peasant communities' resistance to these pres-

sures. However, in describing the process through which peasants are converted to workers, historians have neglected women's role in the process of
proletarianization. They have also ignored the ways in which gender ideologies structured the formation of mining working classes, as well as how that
process transformed relations between men and women, and constructions of
both masculinity and femininity.[5] The mining working class that succumbs to
proletarianization, the peasant communities that resist external economic and
political forces, and the workers who engage in heroic labor actions appear
in most histories as male, or as a homogeneous, ungendered unity. Studies of
miners have tended to celebrate and embrace miners' manliness as central to
their combativeness and to accept their particular formulation of manhood as
natural. This acceptance of a common wisdom about miners' enduring masculinity has served to obfuscate the role of women in mining camps and to
mask the ways in which sexuality and gender are both historically constructed
and contested.[6]

This chapter looks at the articulation of male mine workers' masculinity
and working-class women's femininity as part of the process of class formation in the El Teniente mine. It examines the effects of proletarianization on
a labor force steeped in traditions of mobility, and the ways in which migration to the mining camp, new forms of work, a new sexual division of labor,
and new forms of family and community life transformed gender relations. It
also studies how ideologies of gender and constructions of sexuality shaped
the process of proletarianization and the formation of El Teniente's working-
class community, and looks at the implications of the gendered class identity
elaborated in El Teniente for miners' politics and forms of labor activism.

El Teniente's Early Workforce: Male and Female
Migration and Mobility

The El Teniente copper mine, located roughly one hundred miles southeast of
Santiago, at ten thousand feet above sea level in Chile's Andes, began production in 1904 under the auspices of the U.S.-based Braden Copper Company. It
later came under the control of the Guggenheims, who were expanding their
mining interests both in the United States and abroad, and was finally sold to
the Kennecott Copper Company in 1916. By the early 1920s, as the world demand for copper expanded, El Teniente had become the jewel of Kennecott's
copper empire and one of the world's major producers of copper, employing
close to ten thousand workers and producing eighteen thousand tons of ore
daily—close to 46 percent of Kennecott's total production of copper.[7]

The increase in copper production that developed in order to meet growing world markets during the 1920s encountered serious obstacles in El Teniente. During its first decades of operation, the Braden Copper Company, like the copper industry in other parts of the world, was unable to rely on a steady and trained workforce. Living and working conditions high up in the mountains were extremely difficult and dangerous, and the demands the company placed on its workers and the disciplinary regime it imposed were onerous.[8] Migrants from the countryside, towns, cities, and ports who traveled to the mine, either contracted by company agents or drawn by rumors of high wages, tended to leave after short stints. They returned to the countryside or sought employment in other sectors of the economy. During the 1920s, expanding railroad construction, nitrate mining, new urban industries, and public works projects provided workers with alternatives to copper mining. Often, El Teniente's workers returned to the mine for a short time and then once again departed for other horizons.[9] They also moved from section to section within the mine itself in search of more desirable jobs, working conditions, and wages, and quit when assigned to arduous jobs or abusive bosses.[10] The company's Welfare Department recognized in 1922 that "the enormous mine turnover should be seriously taken into account as something requiring a remedy."[11] The company felt that the workers' transience led to a lack of discipline that crippled production.

Women also participated in the ebb and flow of migration to and from El Teniente. Some women traveled to the mine with their male partners, but most went alone in search of economic opportunities. Single women sought work in petty commerce and services, industries that sprang up around the dynamic economy of the mine. They intended to work in or start bars, brothels, and small businesses. In addition, they looked for jobs as domestic servants in workers' canteens, white-collar workers' and North American administrators' houses, or in laundries and shops in the camps. Most hoped to save a little money, leave the camps, and begin a small business. Few intended to make their lives in El Teniente.

An analysis of judicial records and the records of the civil registry provides some sense of the men's and women's social origins. In 1917, 170 women married El Teniente workers. The vast majority of these women had not accompanied male workers to the mine and did not come from the same towns as the men they married.[12] Many of the women who came with their male partners had met them in major urban centers or ports and had traveled with them to the mine. A number of marriages of men and women who had come to the mine together reveal the transient nature of both the men and the women who wound up in El Teniente. In one case, a woman from the central rural town of San Vicente married a miner from the town of Curicó. The two legitimized their children, who had been born in Santiago and Valparaíso. Although both listed rural origins, they had clearly lived and worked for a number of years in Chile's central port and capital city.[13]

Not all men and women came from the countryside. Many had lived and worked in towns, ports, and cities across the country. Of 155 women listed by the civil registry in 1917, slightly fewer than a third (40) came from cities and ports—not including those women from rural areas who had lived in cities and towns. This is almost identical to the number of men (47) who listed similar nonrural origins. In addition, 25 women, as opposed to 10 men, came from Rancagua, confirming the popular wisdom that many single miners married local women who lived and worked in Rancagua, a booming agricultural/mining town.[14]

Unlike copper miners in southern and south-central Africa and Peru, El Teniente's working class did not have origins in cohesive and enduring peasant communities. Many men and women came from urban centers, ports, or rural towns like Rancagua, which were centers of regional commerce. In addition, many of the men and women who did come from the countryside had spent time working at jobs in different parts of the country. The El Teniente workforce's transience was already well established by the time the mine began production. As studies of nineteenth-century Chile have shown, the *peones,* who constituted a significant part of the rural labor force, were accustomed to mobility. They moved from hacienda to hacienda in search of work, and from region to region following the harvest up and down Chile's southern, central, and northern valleys. During the off-season they traveled to mining centers and ports in search of work.[15]

This mobile labor force also included women. Gabriel Salazar has shown that in the late nineteenth century many women moved independently to rural towns, where they set up their own businesses in petty commerce. Similarly, El Teniente drew many single women who sought to make a living through wage labor or who hoped to open their own businesses. These women participated in the migrations to El Teniente, but they traveled to the mine alone. They composed a parallel migratory workforce that filled jobs in commerce, domestic service, and the informal economy of brothels and bars.

Many women who came to El Teniente listed some form of employment with the civil registry, ranging from tailoress (*modista*) and sewer (*costurera*) to informal storekeeper (*comerciante*) and domestic servant (*empleada*). Frequently, the women who migrated to the mine never made it to the camps or into formal employment by the company. These women found work in the small businesses that lined the railroad to the camp, in Rancagua, or in the informal settlements (*callampas*) near the mine's camps. Many started their own establishments to sell contraband liquor and provide accommodations for prostitutes and their clients. The local court was busy with cases of women arrested for illegally selling liquor and sex from their homes or businesses. Their clients were miners, who on days off and weekends flooded these informal bars in search of entertainment.[16] Other women sold alcohol to miners in the train station or hawked goods in the streets of Rancagua. This was the case of Edelmira Sándoval Garrido, a single woman who sold produce informally in El Teniente's train station. She was arrested for also selling wine. Admitting her crime, Sandoval told the court that she had been driven to violate the company's dry law by her "state of poverty."[17]

Inside the El Teniente camps, women were denied access to employment, and were even refused entrance to the mine, because of their sex. Until the 1950s, the company pursued a policy of hiring only men. The camps did, however, offer jobs for single women as empleadas in canteens and hotels, and many single girls traveled to the mine in search of domestic work. These women worked for low wages that represented less than half of the lowest wage paid to a Braden Copper Company male worker.[18]

Empleadas frequently supplemented their wages by working as prostitutes. Oral sources, court cases, and popular literature describe clandestine prostitution as common among empleadas during the 1930s and 1940s. The miner and writer Baltazar Castro described in the 1940s how single girls "went up to work in the cantinas of Teniente C, the camp next to the mine, where they hoped to earn more money from the passions of the workers than from their work in the pensions."[19] Empleadas often sought to add to their meager wages by establishing sexual relationships with miners in exchange for money or other material goods.

Because of the dearth of women in the camps, empleadas had a large field of potential lovers. Many maintained their independence by entering into semiformal economic arrangements with miners. Men would provide their lovers with presents like clothes or other goods, or would pay them money directly. The twenty-six-year-old *enmaderador* Pedro José Muñoz Muñoz, for example, maintained a sexual relationship with the empleada Rosa Cornejo Martínez. For six months Muñoz "gave her clothes and everything she needed," until he discovered that she had also had similar relationships with other men. When Muñoz confronted Cornejo and slapped her in the face, she told him that her other relationships were no one else's business and that she was "the owner of her own body."[20] Cornejo's attitude toward Muñoz revealed the nature of these kinds of sexual relationships and the degree of autonomy that empleadas enjoyed. Cornejo seemed uninterested in establishing a monogamous relationship and refused to capitulate to Muñoz's insistence that because of his relationship with her he had rights over her body and behavior.[21]

During the first decades of El Teniente's operation, then, both men and women entered the mine and its camps with little intention of staying on. Some hoped to earn money to be invested in land or in a small business. Others simply moved on to other jobs around the country. Both men and women participated in the general transience of the Chilean workforce, often independently of one another. The sexual/romantic relationships they established in El Teniente reflected this fluidity. Many men and women never intended their relationships to end in marriage, despite men's claims of control over women's sexuality and men's indignation at empleadas' assertion of the right to be nonmonogamous.

Proletarianization, Company Paternalism, and the Gender Ideology of Domesticity

During the 1920s it became increasingly important to the Braden Copper Company to maintain a stable, disciplined, and experienced workforce in the mine, in order to increase production to supply rapidly expanding copper markets abroad. The company thus instituted a new series of paternalist labor policies to complement its more authoritarian strategies of labor control. While the major agents of work discipline and social control before the 1920s had been the company's private police force and the Chilean military, coercion and repression had not been entirely effective. Although miners' strikes had been successfully broken and efforts at unionization quashed, the company still could not rely on a constant and productive workforce. In addition, despite the repressive regime in the camps, workers continued to try to build an independent union. By the early 1920s the company realized that it had to provide workers with new inducements to remain at work in the mine. Braden began to give prizes and bonuses for consistent work attendance and efficient production and offered workers high wages relative to those being paid in other areas of the economy.

As part of a new system of labor relations, the company created a Welfare Department; a Center for Education and Social Work; a newspaper, *El Teniente;* and a vocational school. These institutions joined a network of social organizations already set up by the company, including a bowling alley, the Club Social Obrero, and a lengthy list of sports clubs. The goal of these social institutions was to combat high turnover rates and habits like gambling, drinking, and the frequenting of brothels, which were thought to undermine productivity and contribute to labor problems.

The company's social welfare program focused particularly on relations between men and women in the camps and on a gender ideology of domesticity. The Welfare Department felt that workers would tend to remain in the mine and abandon their disruptive habits if they married, lived with their families, and participated in a wide range of social and cultural activities. It thus embarked on a campaign to transform the floating population of single workers and single women in the camps into a permanent and married workforce.

In 1922, the company Welfare Department proposed building more housing for married workers, since married workers who had left families behind usually left the mine after a short time.[22] It also suggested buying a plot of land and constructing houses for workers, so that, according to one company manager, "our workmen would thus become more or less permanent, which is, in the main, what we are trying to arrive at."[23] The company believed that single workers, who composed the bulk of the workforce, tended to drink, gamble, fight, and eventually prove more willing to go out on strike, while married miners, more dependent on their wages and jobs, were seen as more constant and reliable. According to the company, workers who married in El Teniente or who brought their wives and children with them tended to stay on for years, dependent on the job in the mine to support their families. A single worker or a married worker whose family lived elsewhere had more freedom to come and go, to risk unemployment in strikes, and to engage in the vices condemned by the company.

According to the company's logic, single women contributed to unstable domestic arrangements, unhealthy recreational activities, and labor problems. Thus women became the targets of the company's social workers, whose aim was to "educate and form good housewives so that they will not be a burden first on their fathers and then on their husbands." In the vocational school for women, *Escuela Vocacional No. 7,* women could take classes in household cleanliness, clothes making, cooking, household budgeting, and home economics. Trained housewives would help stretch workers' wages. The company consistently attributed workers' families' poverty to women's ignorance of domestic science and their mismanagement of the household.[24]

By providing women with recreational and educational opportunities, as well as attention from social workers, the company hoped to keep them in the camps and to train them to maintain model households with their husbands. The company's concern with the women of the mining camps was reflected in the wide variety of articles in *El Teniente* directed toward a female audience. At times, the company paper seemed solely dedicated to issues concerning miners' wives and daughters, and attempted to inculcate in El Teniente's women the values of domesticity and motherhood.[25] The Welfare Department sought to make life in the camps more attractive to miners' wives, who often abandoned their husbands or refused to live in the camps.[26]

The company's preoccupation with relations between men and women and the transience of the labor force was revealed in regulations it implemented in 1917 requiring workers who lived with women to be married. According to a study of El Teniente written in 1922, many "disorders of diverse kinds" were manifest in the camps, particularly because "the feminine element is not the best."[27] Living or sexual arrangements between men and women outside of matrimony and the presence of prostitutes or a transient population of women in the camps were thought to contribute to the encouragement of other supposed vices like drinking and gambling. Workers were late or missed their shifts, the company felt, because of the "bad" influence of these women.

The company, after studying "the advantages for order and discipline in the mine, ordered in the most resolute and determined manner the legitimization of the civil state of all its employees."[28] The regulation prohibited families or couples without a civil marriage license from occupying company housing. In order to control sexual activity in the camps, police frequently searched workers' lodgings late at night. Until the 1950s, the company implemented a policy of forcing a worker found alone with a woman either to marry her or to leave his job. Women were not consulted to see if they desired such a union. And if they indeed rejected this abrupt end to their independence, they too risked losing their jobs and being kicked out of the camps.[29]

These regulations were greeted with protests by the workers, who, to get around the marriage requirement, began to rent or purchase false marriage licenses in Rancagua. The company's ideal of domesticity clashed with the male workers' own sexual practices and ideas about how relations between men and women should be conducted. The miners' opposition to the company's marriage policy persisted for decades to come. In 1946, for example, Braden rejected the union's petition that the company end its regulation prohibiting nonmarital relationships between men and women.[30]

The company also realized that the children brought up in the camps would provide the next generation of workers. Workers with families would not only themselves provide stable labor, but they would also provide the company's future workforce. Thus a decent education and upbringing were fundamental for El Teniente's children, as well as for its workers. The company created "industrial schools for boys and girls," which had a curriculum, developed by the cultural department of the U.S. embassy, that taught boys mechanics and elements of electrical and civil engineering and taught girls sewing, weaving, secretarial work, domestic science, and home economics. The goal of these educational programs was explicitly stated in a company report:

> If we can train and educate our own people and if we can satisfy the Braden workman and employee, there is a large labor element in Chile which would be contented here and would not continually be after the politicians to enact new laws prejudicial to our interests, and one of the most desirable features would be . . . the education of children throughout the entire property, taking the line of the Catholic Church, Mussolini, and Hitler who always worked on the young people, feeling that if the youth had a proper training there was no need to worry about their later years.[31]

Settled in stable families, workers and their wives would provide the mine's future trained labor force.

Schools sought to prepare workers from nonindustrial backgrounds for the rapidly developing industrial economy. Braden needed a semiskilled workforce, accustomed to the rhythms of industrial labor and integrated into a system of capitalist social relations. While the company's vocational schools aimed to help male workers adjust to work in a modern and industrial capitalist enterprise, its classes for women sought to train them to fulfill a particular ideal of domestic activity as housewives. The kinds of education offered to women by the company were devoted to domestic affairs and home economy.[32] Thus educational opportunities for women and girls in the camps were strictly limited. They were provided one real choice: marry young and marry an El Teniente worker.[33]

The company also established a "family allowance," which became a crucial stimulus for men and women to enter into marriages. The family allowance was a bonus paid to married workers with children. The company intended the allowance to help workers with families meet the challenges of a rapidly rising cost of living and to serve as an inducement to create families. Throughout the 1920s and 1930s male workers and their female partners frequently entered into legal marriages in order to legitimize their children and thus qualify for the bonus. The miner Pedro Antonio Pinto and his partner, for example, married "to legitimize our son because it is necessary so that he can receive the family allowance and so that the conceded benefit be granted and our son's legitimacy be legally accepted."[34] The family allowance provided male workers with the economic resources to maintain their families and domestic arrangements based on the exclusion of women from the labor market.

The family allowance became increasingly important to both men and women, because women enjoyed few possibilities for wage labor and had limited educational opportunities. Women were excluded from high-paying jobs in the mine, and their education prepared them for roles as housewives and mothers. Married women could and did engage in informal labor—taking in boarders, sewing, and laundry, or selling homemade bread and sweets. And single women could work as empleadas. However, the money women earned in these activities was a fraction of male workers' lowest wages and was insufficient to support a family. Women's exclusion from the formal labor market, combined with the bifurcated educational system and the family allowance, served as a considerable encouragement to embrace marriage as one of the only remaining viable strategies for subsistence.

The company also tried to curtail the sexual and social independence of single women in the camps. Canteen and pension empleadas' sexual activity was strictly regulated. The company imposed curfews, fired them if they were caught with boyfriends or lovers, and forbade them to frequent the social clubs where miners gathered to drink and socialize.[35] Empleadas were fired if they became pregnant.[36] In 1943, for example, the copper company dismissed the pregnant empleada Rosa Zuñiga "to demonstrate to these girls that they will always be the victims and that they must observe proper morals."[37] Without such a severe lesson, the company argued, "the number of women who give themselves for money would increase and little by little any notion of morality and good habits would be lost."

In its efforts to reorganize gender relations and form nuclear families in El Teniente, the company received significant help from the state. After 1930, Chilean governments became increasingly involved in the establishment of what could be termed a proto–welfare state. This process accelerated under the governments of the Popular Front (1938–1948), which oversaw the process of import-substitution industrialization and the implementation of social reforms that were intended to benefit the urban middle and working classes. While the state had evinced little interest in either labor or social relations in the copper mining enclave, apart from the periodic dispatch of the armed forces to quell workers' strikes and rebellions, and had left the administration of life and work in the mine largely to the company, beginning in the late 1930s it began to involve itself in the regulation of both labor relations in the mine and gender relations in the camps. After 1938, labor inspectors, the minister of labor, and even the president entered El Teniente's camps to review work and living conditions and to enforce labor and social legislation. Correspondingly, the local court began to play a more interventionist role in working-class family and domestic life.[38]

The local court in the Sewell camp provided important support for the company's policies on gender and family life. Its efforts were particularly aimed at policing women's sexuality. For example, in the late 1930s the court began for the first time to hear cases of women accused of procuring illegal abortions. Before 1930, the court docket registered no abortion cases. Abortion became a significant legal and social transgression for single women, who were castigated by arrest, dismissal, and eviction from the camps.[39] At the same time, women who left their husbands began to be arrested and prosecuted for the crime of "abandonment." While company records show that many men left their wives at will, none were arrested for abandonment. "Abandoning the home," as it was called, became a particularly female crime.[40] Clandestine abortions and leaving husbands were ways for women to exercise some control over their sexuality and their lives: the company and the state perceived these expressions of independence as threats to the community of working-class families they hoped to build.

For the first time, too, domestic violence became an important concern of the company and of the local court. While almost no domestic violence cases appear on the court record before the late 1930s, a large number appear after this time. Domestic violence was not a new legal category. Rather, traditional assault cases or cases of injuries (*lesiones*) now came to be composed frequently of incidents of conjugal violence. The appearance of domestic violence cases reflected the company's and the state's new interest in regulating gender relations and the new social realities of the increasing population of married workers. After all, domestic violence threatened the order of family life. Thus company social workers and the court began to receive women's complaints about their male partners' or husbands' abuses and began to step in to try to restore harmony to miners' households. Domestic violence became an ideological tool in the company's war against "working-class vice" and the "irregularity" of workers' sexual relations. As they sought to stamp out the consumption of alcohol, informal sexual practices, and gambling, so, too, did the company and the state begin to clamp down on husbands' abuse of wives. The policing of domestic violence represented a new front in the larger campaign to regulate and administer working-class men's and women's domestic lives and to shape men into "responsible" heads of household and women into model housewives.

While both men and women tended to reject company and state efforts to regulate their sexuality, these new policies on domestic and family life had different meanings for women than for men. For many men, mandatory marriage restricted their sexual possibilities and threatened their sense of masculinity and manhood. Although they enjoyed the control over women's sexuality and the enforced female monogamy that the institution of marriage established, they rejected imposed marriage and monogamy for themselves. For women, while marriage brought an end to the independence they had working in the camps or in businesses outside the mine, the new policies provided important securities and protections. Married women could draw on a whole series of rights and privileges encoded in company policy and law that were denied to single women, and they owned a social legitimacy that single women could never hope to possess.

The company regulations requiring men and women to formalize their sexual arrangements in marriage provided women with a number of benefits. A company report celebrated the "great triumph" of imposing legal marriages on men and women and pointed out that one of the consequences of the prior "decayed" sexual practices was that women and children were left "without legal support."[41] Marriage removed many of the social and economic vulnerabilities experienced by single women. In marriage, women discovered their new legal rights, enforced by the courts and the company, to their husbands' wages and bonuses, most importantly the family allowance, and the improved situation of legally legitimized children. Thus, the company's and the state's efforts to mold men into heads of household benefited many women even as it served as another arena of conflict between the company and its workers.

Married women drew on the ideology of domesticity, and the rights and privileges this condition conferred on them, to protect their economic position and defend themselves from their male partners' assertions of total dominance. Ultimately, most women in El Teniente married, formed families, and worked as housewives. Within the private space of the nuclear family, they were forced to draw on the dominant cultural codes and social institutions that underpinned the gender regime in the camps in order to resist complete sexual and economic subordination. Marriage represented an extension of the sexual contract that governed the less formal and nonlegal relationships single women established with male workers. On a spectrum that began with outright sex-work and passed through informal sexual relationships based on the exchange of goods and money for sex and company, marriage lay at the other end, in many cases a logical next step. The sexual contract in marriage, however, provided women with rights and guarantees denied to single women who entered into similar contractual arrangements outside the sphere of the nuclear family.

As Carole Pateman has argued in the case of industrializing England, the sexual segregation of the labor force, which entailed the construction of the workplace as a preserve of men and the restriction of women to low-paying occupations (primarily domestic service), meant that marriage became economically beneficial to women.[42] One woman recalls, for example, that "women married someone from El Teniente because of their economic situation." And, as another added, "it's the security, not that the wages are so high, but the security."[43] As these women remembered, the El Teniente workers enjoyed a rare economic security provided by relatively high wages and benefits. Married women had access to their husbands' wages, the family allowance, credit at stores, and the protection of the company welfare department and the local court, which recognized their and their children's rights to economic support from their husbands.

Married women frequently put the gender ideology of domesticity to their own use. Unlike single women, they could often use the company Welfare Department and the camps' court to force their husbands to give them their wages and benefits or to protect them from abuse. The company's attempts to control the behavior of husbands who neglected their wives and contributed little to the household budget provided married women with important support. Women drew on their rights as mothers and wives to win control of at least part of their husbands' incomes. The company's close control of family life in the camps, while certainly repressive, may, at times, have served married women's interests. Its stated policy of warning and then suspending or firing men who "through vice cannot fulfill their family obligations," in order to "obtain decent living conditions for a number of mothers and children who . . . suffer conditions worse than those of the unemployed," provided married women with important economic guarantees.

The economic forces that drove some women to enter into marriages were reinforced by social and cultural pressures. Single women workers were stigmatized as immoral, their behavior was policed and regulated by their employers and the state, and they were placed in a socially and sexually vulnerable and insecure position. Single women enjoyed little protection by the law or the company from sexual abuse and male violence. In addition, they had no legal basis to enforce the informal sexual contracts they established with men. Nor did the social codes of the mining community offer them significant support. In the dominant codes that governed gender and sexuality in the camps, single women workers were perceived to be immoral. Women's work in domestic service was often seen as synonymous with prostitution. Fathers, for example, refused to let their daughters work in the camps' canteens and pensions because of the sexual danger believed to be part of such work.[44]

Male violence against single women workers was often seen as legitimate because of empleadas' supposed immorality. In one case, for example, an empleada accused a large group of men of locking her in a room and raping her. In general, the feeling of many men and women in the canteen was that if she had been raped, it was her own fault. Her attitude toward sex and sexuality legitimized the rape in the eyes of the community. Thus the female owner of the canteen where the woman worked cited her employee's statement that "she was the owner of her actions and that nobody was going to interfere in her business" as well as her flirtatious behavior as signs that she "had it coming."[45] As she put it, "From my point of view this girl's head doesn't work right, and if what she says really happened to her, she alone is to blame since she is very backward and I know that she has had relations with a lot of people."

Although single women frequently went to the police with complaints of abuse and rape, the court in the mining camps offered them little protection. In most cases, charges against men accused of abusive behavior were dismissed, or men were warned and threatened that if they came before the court again they would be punished. In almost all rape cases the male defendants were acquitted for lack of evidence or because women simply dropped their charges. In general, single women confronted a community and a set of social codes of gender and sexuality that legitimized male violence.

Married women, unlike single women, could hope to receive protection from the courts and the company welfare department, which attempted to maintain the order and harmony of nuclear families in the camps. In the case of domestic violence, the significant role played by the otherwise despised company social workers and welfare department was clear to women. According to oral testimony, women complained to the Welfare Department about abusive or negligent husbands and often received aid from social workers. One woman remembers, for example, that "we were always close to a social worker . . . and if the social worker heard that a marriage wasn't functioning well, she went to the house and conversed and tried to solve the problem. . . . the social workers were around, very close, in order to help."[46] Similarly, women appealed to the police, who sometimes helped women, although at other times they only talked to abusive husbands. According to one woman, "one could go to the police without worrying . . . if they could help you, they helped you."[47] Thus, while miners and their wives might reject the intrusions of company social workers and the company's private police force, who frequently entered and searched miners' homes, some women found a source of support in these social controls.

Married women took their husbands to court in order to ensure that a violent episode did not repeat itself. Many women brought charges and then dropped them, explaining that they had done so in order to prevent their husbands from getting into the habit of beating them. As one woman explained, "I was upset so I went to the police to denounce him. . . . I did it so that he wouldn't do it again."[48] Another woman testified that she had charged her husband with abuse "so that he not become accustomed to hitting me for any reason."[49] In this way, the company's efforts to regulate and police miners' and their families' domestic lives through the activities of the company police, social workers, and the local court supported women in dealing with their husbands. Married women, unlike single women, could draw on the dominant ideology of domesticity in the camps to win access to their husbands' wages or the family allowance or to limit their husbands' violence.

The price of married women's loss of independence was made clear in their economically and sexually subordinate position within El Teniente's households. Women's dependence on their husbands' wages provoked constant problems. At times, despite company policy, miners refused to hand over their wages to their wives and used the family allowance as a work bonus for themselves. In 1943, for example, the company Welfare Department complained that,

> there has been deception by workers who registered their wives and children as dependents to obtain the family allowance and then only contribute [some of] this to the family sustenance. . . . the Company doesn't want to have workers who do not fulfill their duties as husbands and fathers and who, while they leave their families with a starvation ration, spend on themselves ten times the sum they concede to their families to maintain themselves.[50]

The company's distress at the complaints they received from women whose husbands neglected to share their wages and bonuses with them reveals two points. First, it demonstrates women's vulnerable position within the nuclear family. Without control of financial resources they were rendered completely dependent on their husbands and the company. Second, it shows that miners often fell short of or rejected the company's ideal of domesticity and the nuclear family. They resisted the company's efforts to mold them into responsible heads of household. In a sense, this constituted an extension of a workplace culture of rebellion against the company's regimes of discipline and efforts to create efficient workers and model male heads of household.

Yet, while miners may have struggled against the pressures to make them reliable husbands and fathers, they did extract advantages from their dominant economic position in relation to their wives. Men spent their wages in activities proscribed to women. They gambled, drank, and frequented brothels. While married women had to stay home, men could spend their days off in bars, often with female lovers or prostitutes. El Teniente's social landscape was dominated by male institutions. Men gathered in mutual aid societies, social clubs, recreational clubs, and union halls, where women had no place. Often the identities of these clubs corresponded to work sections, thus reproducing in the social sphere both the masculine bonds of work-based solidarity and the exclusion of women. While workers could come together outside the mine to play in their own soccer team against other work sections, to frequent their own mutual aid society, or to drink and gamble in social clubs, women had no equivalent public social institutions or spaces.

Men's control of their families' incomes and their monopoly of public space allowed them the freedom to leave both the domestic sphere and the camps. The social and sexual freedom men derived from their economic power was revealed in the cases of adultery and bigamy. Given the nature of the sexual contract in El Teniente, men were able to have more than one wife or to have permanent lovers because of their economic resources. Oral sources describe how many miners had more than one wife or a number of lovers in addition to their wives. These men shared their wages among their wives and lovers. The opposite was rarely true. Married women simply didn't have the income or the kind of social/sexual freedom that would allow them to establish sexual relationships with more than one man.

Women's subordinate position within the family was also revealed by a company social workers' report that "in general the amounts given by the married workmen to their wives for the weekly food bill is far below what they could allow."[51] The company report condemned some workers for forcing their wives to take in laundry, boarders, and sewing, while they spent their wages and bonuses on "wine, women, and song." While the company may have been discussing a small group of workers and an extreme situation, its report reveals the social and sexual privilege that monopoly of the labor market and public space in the camps bestowed on men. Women's lack of control over their husbands' wages could leave them in a precarious position. The company's statement that some miners left their wives and children "underfed and badly clothed" revealed its own, often unsuccessful, efforts to impose an ideal of family life and of the male head of household on El Teniente's working-class community. It also indicated the vulnerabilities experienced by women in miners' families.

Domestic violence was another area in which men expressed their social power over women. As in relationships between miners and single women, marriage in El Teniente was viewed as an exchange of services for goods and money. And, as in the relationships between empleadas and miners, married men perceived this sexual contract as giving them certain rights over women's bodies and behavior, as well as over their labor power. At times, when women rejected their husbands' efforts to control their social lives or were perceived to be neglecting their domestic duties, men resorted to some form of violence.

Domestic violence cannot be separated from the web of social codes and practices that structured gender relations in El Teniente. Men's economic power, the masculinization of public space and work in the camps and the mine, and the accompanying restriction of women to the household contributed to men's capacity to use violence against women. Few of the domestic violence cases heard in the El Teniente court dealt with women's violence against men. The appearance of domestic violence in El Teniente, a reflection of the company's and the state's new interest in administering gender relations, was also defined and structured by the sexual and economic inequalities between men and women created by the formation of nuclear families and a new gender regime in the camps.

Domestic violence became an expression of the imbalances in the sexual contract that governed marital life in El Teniente. A large number of domestic violence cases were caused by men's anger at their wives' failure to perform their expected domestic duties or at their failure to behave obediently and compliantly. Abusive husbands often marshaled arguments about their wives' lack of submissive respect ("she talked back to me") or refusal to follow their orders as a way of defending and justifying their actions.[52] In court, miners frequently justified hitting their wives because they nagged them, scolded them, refused to accept orders, or were generally *porfiadas* (stubborn or hardheaded), a complaint that was echoed many times.

Women's failure to accommodate men's attempts to restrict their social lives and discipline their domestic labor also provoked violence. A wife who went out by herself or with friends risked her husband's ire. In one case, Elsa Saaverda de Beltrán went out one night to buy medicine, leaving her children alone for a short while. Her husband returned from work and, believing that she had been with another man, beat her and had her arrested for abandoning the home.[53] The state's involvement in supporting husbands' efforts to police their wives' social and domestic lives was made clear in the case of one woman, who was often absent from her home because of her involvement in union activities. The court supported the husband, who had beaten his wife, and lectured the woman on her domestic duties: "the court . . . made the wife see that she was neglecting her fundamental duties that are principally to attend to the home."[54] A married woman could only hope for protection from male violence if she fulfilled her prescribed role as housewife.

Miners, the Ideology of Domesticity, and the Masculinization of Work

Domestic violence expressed both a fundamental economic and sexual inequality between men and women in El Teniente's families and male workers' particular sense of masculinity. While the state and the company coincided in their efforts to form nuclear families based on a male wage earner and a female housewife, male workers played an important role in supporting and reaffirming the implementation of the ideology of domesticity. As a number of writers have pointed out, the sexual, as well as economic, basis for women's subordination within the nuclear famly has been revealed historically in male workers' consistent support for the exclusion of women from the labor market and for the prerogatives and privileges this gives to men.[55] In El Teniente, while the miners resisted the company's efforts to force them into marriages and monogamy, they embraced the control over women's labor and sexuality that the new organization of gender relations in the camps gave them.

The process of proletarianization in the El Teniente mining enclave involved the creation of an entirely male labor force drawn to work in the mine by high wages and work incentives and induced to form nuclear families and settle in the camps by company regulations and financial incentives. Miners built a work culture based on an intense sense of masculinity that both supported the company's efforts to transform them into reliable workers and responsible heads of household and provided the basis for opposition to company authority. Like miners around the world, the El Teniente workers constructed an identity based on a masculinized understanding of their work and figured the object of their labor, the mine, as feminine. The masculinized work culture, based on codes of independence, a challenging attitude toward company authority, and solidarity among workmates, shaped miners' class identity and politics and inscribed their militancy. It also, however, implied a fundamental exclusion of and antagonism toward the experiences and worlds of women and reinforced the prevalent ideology of domesticity within the camps.

The fact that the El Teniente workforce was entirely male and that for years men lived together in close quarters in the barracks played a role in the elaboration of an intensely masculinized sense of identity. For years, work and recreation took place in almost entirely male spaces that women almost never entered. As men smuggled alcohol, gambled, drank in groups, played soccer, or frequented social clubs, they reproduced ties and solidarities built at work inside the mine—forms of friendship and community that excluded women. Within the masculine worlds of work and recreation, miners developed their own culture. They spoke a language and shared a vocabulary foreign to anyone outside the mine. They had jokes, code words, and style (*manera de ser*) that marked them as miners.[56] Workers had an arrogance and cockiness, even a way of dressing, that distinguished them immediately as El Teniente miners. Store owners in the camps or in Rancagua could instantly recognize a miner for his bearing and for his *pinta* (look). Miners all wore suits and dressed sharply. They also usually had a lot of available cash and an arrogant and overbearing attitude, according to those bar or store owners who had to serve them. This form of identity, this miners' pride, found its roots in the culture nurtured within the mine, in the common language, references, myths, and work in teams. To be a miner was to be something more than an ordinary worker. In their stride and strut the miners constructed a manera de ser rooted in a sense of masculinity that found expression in physical strength, the capacity for hard and strenuous work, and the sacrifice and costs of labor in the mine.

Within the mine, men competed among themselves to prove their strength and skill as miners. Workers won respect from their fellow workers and from foremen for their capacity to work hard. The company helped both to foster this cult of physical strength and to reinforce it with a system of competitions and contests. The company offered prizes and bonuses to work groups, workers, and foremen with the highest production. For example, company-sponsored contests included drilling competitions, in which workers would compete to see who could drill most skillfully. The miners also participated in a series of other competitions, according to one observer, "of perfectly useful works, competitions stimulated and awarded by the company."[57] In fact, the miners took great pride in their capacity to work hard and in their skills in negotiating and managing the difficult terrain of production in the mine.

To work inside the mine implied a certain stature and status. As Baltazar Castro, a former miner himself, writes, "I never looked down upon my *compañeros* in the mills and the workshop, nor at the others who worked above ground, but I can't deny that my aspiration was always to be transferred to the mine, to feel that I was a miner in every sense of the word."[58] True manhood and respect from one's comrades could only be won by working in the mine and proving one's strength and skill. For Castro, the prospect of working in the mine inspired the desire to dominate the mine itself and thus to prove himself. He writes that "the incentive to penetrate and remove what was there inside grew every day."

Miners' strength became an essential element of their masculinity. Castro's texts, for example, construct an iconography of physical force and of the miner's body, with frequent references to the miners' "wide hands," "wide shoulders," "firm arms like two hammers," and "impressive moustaches."[59] One miner is described as a "mountain of tight muscles . . . massive, robust."[60] The tough jobs in the mine won miners respect, and they derived a sense of dignity from their work. As Castro writes, they "knew that sensation of triumph, that action as victors, when the *minero de avance* thunders the twenty-five explosions and the *enmaderadores* hurry to extend the tunnel."[61] They also found pride in the physical skills required by their jobs in the mine. For example, Castro writes appreciatively of a "skilled *minero de turno* who knows the effects of the explosion in all its details, who had located the perforations in such a way that . . . the explosion blew the rock away in an extensive stretch: each explosion supporting the other successively until all twenty or twenty-five had thundered."[62] Similarly, he describes a miner "who enjoyed fame as a true enmaderador, capable of stepping on the heels of the explosions as he advanced into the mountain."[63] Manhood was expressed and demonstrated in skill and hard work.

All of the El Teniente miners' myths imagined a female presence in the mine or defined the mine as feminine. In figuring the mine as female, miners sexualized their labor. They frequently described their work as the act of making love. One popular song described, for example, how "el pico del minero es el mas duro que hay / parte a pedazos la roca y le saca el mineral" (the miner's pick is the hardest that there is / it breaks the rock to pieces and extracts the [copper] ore).[64] Similarly, a miner in one of Castro's stories declares that "the mine is that way, you enter her and you can't leave no matter how hard you work. She's a very vexing and chastising woman."[65] The penetration of the mine could be dangerous because it involved a kind of sexual conquest, domination, and betrayal. Thus one miners' story describes how "the mountain, alive, wounded, bloody, revenged itself against those miserable men for the desecration of its millenary bowels."[66]

The miners' elaboration of a masculinized work culture reflected anxieties about male control of female sexuality. Eroticized, work became an expression and a fulfillment of manhood. But in its deeply alienating, dangerous, and dehumanizing quality, work inside the mine also rendered masculinity, as a basis for dignity and self-worth, quite precarious. Uneasiness about women permeated the miners' codes and underlined miners' fears about the dangers of work in the mine and their loss of control over their labor. Miners, to this day, maintain the belief that a woman entering the mine provokes accidents. They spoke of the mine as a jealous and punishing woman. The miners invoked the female figure of the Virgin Mary (the *viejita linda*), alternately begging her for aid and cursing her for misfortune. They attributed accidents to female spirits (*animitas*) or to the ghost of a woman, *la llorona* (the crier). Other miners' tales described the activities of the ghost of a woman who was executed for killing her miner husband and chopping him into pieces. Similarly, miners believed in a spirit called *la lola* (the girl), who dwelled in the mine and did away with workers. One miners' story described la lola as "a horrible and disheveled woman whose cries drive the listener insane" or as "a strange monster, mixture of monkey and woman, who guards a secret treasure in the mine."[67]

Miners expressed their sense of loss of control over their labor and lives in the mine in anxieties about their manhood. Fear of adultery permeated the culture of the mine. Many miners attributed the distinctiveness of their *manera de ser* to turbulent marital lives. Miners had their own terms to describe unfaithful wives. They used the phrase *hacer las diez ultima* (to do the last ten) to signify infidelity to a husband.[68] The miners also had a name for a man who slept with miners' wives, *Jorge*. It was a custom to joke or taunt, calling an unfaithful miner Jorge, or telling a miner that his wife had been seen with Jorge.[69] Similarly, miners sang a little refrain about adultery to taunt and torment the many miners who had left their wives behind and gone up to the mine alone: "El minero en las minas 'ta trabajando / y la mujer abajo lo esta gorreando" (the miner in the mines is working / and the woman below is deceiving him).[70]

During the 1960s, social workers employed by El Teniente ascribed the miners' extraordinary combativeness to a general dissatisfaction based mainly on anxieties about adultery and turbulent marital lives.[71] In oral histories, many miners also emphasize adultery as prevalent and as a fundamental way to explain their distinctive manera de ser.[72] For one miner and union leader, the miners' work hours, the dehumanizing and consuming quality of the work, the exhaustion, the sickness, and the little time spent with families led to constant family problems, adultery, and alcoholism. This fact, he believed, helped shape miners' sense of being different, their machismo, and their sense of hardship and sacrifice, and ultimately explained their discontent and combativeness.[73] Miners' fears about their lack of control over their labor was reflected in the sense of sexual uneasiness that informed their work culture and structured their class identity.

The culture of masculinity within the mine served the company's purposes. By masculinizing and sexualizing their labor, the miners naturalized women's exclusion from the world of work and thus reaffirmed the company's gendered social welfare policies, which restricted women to the domestic sphere. Miners' masculine work culture also served the company's interests in increasing production. Competition between and within *caudrillas* led workers to intensify their labor in order to prove their manliness. The miners' pride in their skill and capacity for work contributed to higher productivity. The turbulent work culture of the mine, with its emphasis on combat, conquest, and control, did not necessarily contradict the company's interests. As they strove to exert control over their own work and the mine and to emerge as "victors" through hard work, they filled the company's production quotas. The miners' code that dictated that men prove their manhood through the struggle with the (feminized) mine and the demonstration of skill and capacity for hard labor bolstered the company's efforts to get the miners to work harder and produce more.

While furthering certain company objectives, however, the miners' work culture of masculinity also reinforced combative notions of manhood that could be directed against employers and their representatives. "A manly bearing toward the boss" was crucial inside the mine.[74] Workers frequently fought with, made fun of, and mocked their Chilean foremen and North American supervisors. They applied special insulting names to North American supervisors and ridiculed them behind their backs.[75] Fights between workers armed with knives were common, but so were bloody fights between workers and foremen or supervisors. Company records, the local court, and the union paper record constant fights between workers and their bosses, both inside the mine and outside in the camps.[76] In some cases, workers actually murdered their foremen or supervisors.[77] Workers who ingratiated themselves with foremen and supervisors were figured as *maricones* (fags), and scabs and strikebreakers were perceived as feminine and homosexual. In one case, a scab was tried in a mock union court and then dressed in women's clothes and paraded through the camps.[78] Many fights broke out when workers felt that their honor had been insulted because they had been called *chupas de los jefes* (those who suck up to the boss).[79] In El Teniente, fights, wildcat stoppages, and strikes were figured in the mine's language of masculinity. The deeply male culture of the mine was also a class culture that defined antagonisms between workers and the company.[80]

Miners expressed their antagonisms to the company first in the language of the mine, where strength, independence, and a "manly bearing toward the boss" formed the basis of their manera de ser. But they also drew on the new gendered language of the nuclear family and the male-headed household to articulate both their sense of manhood and their conflicts with the company. The miners' union frequently invoked the company's gender ideology to justify strikes. As respectable and reliable heads of household, miners argued, it was their right and duty to fight for their families' welfare. The miners drew on their newly prescribed responsibilities and rights as husbands and fathers to legitimize labor conflicts. They thus invoked a model of manhood based on notions of respectability and responsibility culled from the company's ideology of domesticity. While these two notions of working-class manhood were in some ways contradictory, they coincided in defining masculinity in terms of men's control of women's sexuality and labor. Like the unruly mine worker, the male head of household signified his dignity in terms of his domination of women. In this sense, both models of manhood available to workers drew on and affirmed the company's gender ideology of domesticity.

Conclusion: Gender and Politics in El Teniente

By the 1940s, the Braden Copper Company had succeeded in establishing a constant and stable labor force of married workers in the El Teniente mine. As the Second World War approached and markets for copper once again expanded, the company could rely on a permanent workforce that lived in family units in the mine's camps. By 1937, for example, almost half of El Teniente's workers were married (3,503), and 3,000 women lived in the camps, a considerable increase from the 1920s.[81]

Contrary to the Braden Copper Company's expectations, the settling of workers and their wives into stable households, rather than bringing accommodation and discipline to the workforce, coincided with an explosion of labor militancy. With the support of the newly elected Popular Front government of Pedro Aguirre Cerda in 1938, the El Teniente workers were able to reorganize their union and engage in the first major strikes in the copper mines since 1919. The miners' union, led by militants of the Communist Party, launched five major strike movements between 1938 and 1948, and during this decade the miners engaged in innumerable wildcat work stoppages to protest working conditions and the inflated cost of living in the camps.[82]

Women played a major role in these conflicts. They organized support committees and *ollas comunes* (communal kitchens), walked the picket line with their husbands and children, and spoke at rallies. The strike, more than a collective conflict between workers and employers, was a battle between El Teniente's working-class community and the company that dominated every aspect of their lives. The miners' union recognized the importance of women's participation when it argued that a 1939 strike could not depend "exclusively on the workers. . . . This mobilization must embrace all the women and families."[83] Women in El Teniente also organized a chapter of the Movement for the Emancipation of Chilean Women (MEMch), which participated actively in miners' strikes and organized political support for the Popular Front governments.

The solidarity between men and women in labor struggles reveals the ways in which the mine and the company penetrated every aspect of workers' lives, from work to housing, the cost of living, recreation, education, and cultural activities. In the mining enclave, workers' petitions included demands for better housing, schools, recreational facilities, parks, stores, and food—all areas dominated by the company. And in the system of gender relations constructed in El Teniente, these areas of struggle all fell within the sphere of activity to which women were consigned. Women's mobilization in collective movements in El Teniente was rooted in their role as housewives. According to the company ideology of domesticity, women had responsibility for the welfare of miners' families. Women's participation in cost-of-living and other committees focused on demands pertaining to the assigned female sphere—consumption, food prices, and education for their children. Thus women's dependence on their husbands for wages and benefits, and on the company for the education of their children and food for their families, frequently placed them at their husbands' sides in opposition to the company. Their desire to ensure the security and the rights promised by the company's social welfare policies and dominant gender ideology often led to their participation in collective movements.[84] In ways different from other industries, because of the structures of both the mining enclave and gender relations, women in El Teniente had fundamental interests in common with men in struggles with a shared enemy, the company. Men understood this and strove to mobilize their wives and family members during labor conflicts.

The company's strategy of creating a community of stable nuclear households backfired. As more women stayed in the camps and took on roles as housewives and mothers, and while more men began to stay on in the camps with their families, a permanent community took shape in El Teniente. The company had been mistaken in its assumption that single workers were the culprits in organizing strike movements. Later, the company reported that married workers had organized a major strike in 1938. Single workers, rather than organizing unions or strikes, had the alternative of leaving in search of new jobs. But married workers and their wives began to plan their lives in the mining camps and thus struggled to make their future there better. While single women might have threatened the domestic order of miners' lives and contributed to the propagation of "vices," married women organized committees, participated in the MEMCh, and walked the picket line. Men who stayed on in El Teniente participated in the elaboration of an intensely masculine and combative work culture that served as the basis for endemic labor conflicts. In addition, in their new roles as heads of household, miners strove to improve their lives and fulfill their family responsibilities by engaging in collective action.

The unity of interest between men and women in labor struggles was predicated on women's economic dependence on their husbands and their subordination within the nuclear family. Miners' masculinized work culture defined militancy as an expression of manhood and produced a class identity shaped by the ideals of the male wage earner and the female housewife. This was reinforced by miners' reaffirmation of their central role as breadwinners and heads of household. This meant that women's role in community movements and strikes was limited by their relegation to the domestic sphere. While the gender division of labor and the organization of sexuality in the El Teniente mine established the basis for a combative and cohesive working-class community, they also severely limited women's autonomy and impeded the development of a politics that might have challenged the intertwined constructions of class and gender that had reshaped working-class men's and women's lives.

Notes

1   For accounts of the strike see *El Mercurio, La Epoca, Análisis,* and *Página Abierta,* January 1990.

2   Examples include Hernán Ramírez Necochea, *Historia del movimiento obrero en Chile: Siglo 19* (Santiago: Austral, 1956); James Petras and Maurice Zeitlin, *El radicalismo político de la clase trabajadora chilena* (Buenos Aires: Centro Editor de América Latina, 1969); Jorge Barría, *El movimiento obrero en Chile* (Santiago: Ediciones de la Universidad Técnica del Estado, 1971); and Charles Bergquist, *Labor in Latin America* (Stanford: Stanford University Press, 1986). For a critique of the traditional labor historiography's emphasis on miners see Peter DeShazo, *Urban Workers and Labor Unions in Chile, 1902–1927* (Madison: University of Wisconsin Press, 1983).

3   In general, women have been absent from the histories of Latin American workers, and Latin American labor historiography has yet to integrate an analysis of gender. See Emília Viotti da Costa, "Experiences versus Structures: New Tendencies in the History of Labor and the Working Class in Latin America— What Do We Gain? What Do We Lose?" *International Labor and Working Class History,* no. 36 (fall 1989): pp. 3–24.

4   This is particularly true for the literature on African miners. See, for example, Jane Parpart, *Labor and Capital on the African Copperbelt* (Philadelphia: Temple University Press, 1983); Charles van Onselen, *Chibaro: African Mine Labour in Southern Rhodesia, 1900–1933* (London: Pluto Press, 1976); Charles Perrings, *Black Mineworkers in Central Africa* (New York: Africana, 1979); and Michael Burawoy, *The Colour of Class in the Copper Mines* (Manchester: Manchester University Press [for] the Institute for African Studies, University of Zambia, 1972). For an excellent study of proletarianization, peasant resistance, and the development of mining in Peru see Florencia Mallon, *In Defense of Community in Peru's Central Highlands: Peasant Struggle and Capitalist Transition, 1860–1940* (Princeton: Princeton University Press, 1983).

5   One notable exception concerning Africa is Jane Parpart, "Class and Gender on the Copperbelt: Women in Northern Rhodesian Copper Mining Areas," working paper no. 53, Boston University African Studies Center, 1982.

6   For a seminal work on gender and working-class history see Joan Wallach Scott, *Gender and the Politics of History* (New York: Columbia University Press, 1988). For a critique of historians' use of gender-blind class analysis see Sally Alexander, "Women, Class, and Sexual Difference in the 1830s and 1840s: Some Reflections on the Writing of a Feminist History," *History Workshop Journal* 17 (autumn 1984).

7   For histories of the Braden Copper Company see Guillermo Drago and Pedro Villagra, *Historia general del mineral El Teniente, 1823–1988* (Rancagua: n.p., 1989); and Luis Hiriart, *Braden: Historia de una mina* (Santiago: n.p., 1962). For data on copper production see Chile, Senado, Oficina de Informaciones, "Antecedentes

económicos y estadísticas relacionadas con la gran minería del cobre," *Boletín de Información Económica,* no. 157, 1969.

8　In 1917, only 22.4 percent of the El Teniente workforce was permanent, and in 1918, only 23.8 percent, according to a study performed by Alejandro Fuenzalida Grandon (*La vida i el trabajo en el mineral "El Teniente"* [Santiago: n.p., 1919]). In 1922, of the two thousand workers hired by the infamous *enganche,* only 9 percent stayed on in El Teniente to work (H. Mackenzie Walker to L. E. Grant, May 2, 1923, Archive of the Braden Copper Company [ABCC]). The transience of the copper labor force was consistent with Chilean workers' long history of migrations. Since the nineteenth century, laborers had traveled the country, from the agricultural regions of the southern and central valleys, to the northern nitrate fields, through ports like Valparaíso and Antofagasta, and to urban centers like Santiago, in search of work opportunities. Most workers spent time at a number of different jobs in different sectors of the economy. For studies of the nineteenth- and early-twentieth-century workforce and migration see Gabriel Salazár, *Labradores, peones, y proletarios: Formación y crisis de la sociedad popular chilena del siglo 19* (Santiago: Ediciones SUR, 1985); and Arnold Bauer, *Chilean Rural Society from the Spanish Conquest to 1930* (Cambridge: Cambridge University Press, 1975).

9　Welfare Department, annual reports, 1922, 1924, 1926, and 1927, ABCC.

10　Mine superintendent to Judge Julio Maldonado, August 22, 1915, ABCC.

11　Welfare Department, annual report, 1922, ABCC.

12　Of the 155 women who listed their origins, only 44 had come to the mine with their families or male partners. Over 100 women, then, had come to El Teniente by themselves. Out of the same 155 women, only 14 married men from their hometowns. It is probable that these women either accompanied their prospective spouses to El Teniente or followed them later on. The rest apparently either met their partners in El Teniente or in other regions of the country before coming to the mine. Only thirteen had parents in the mining camps and had moved with their families to the mine (*Registro de Matrimonios, El Teniente, Registro Civil, Machalí,* 1917).

13　In another case, a woman from the south-central agricultural town of Talca married a man from Valparaíso. The couple legitimized their child born in Santiago, where it is likely that they had met. In another case, a woman from Valparaíso married a man from the central agricultural town of San Felipe. The two had had children in Valparaíso, where it would seem that they had met, and in Santiago. One final case reveals the extraordinary geographic mobility of the men and women who journeyed to El Teniente. A woman from Santiago married a man from the northern port of Iquique. The two had had children in two other port cities, Valparaíso and Talcahuano.

14　Twenty-two women came from Santiago, eight came from Concepción, and ten came from the ports Coquimbo, Valparaíso, Antofagasta, and Talcahuano.

15　See Bauer, *Chilean Rural Society;* and Salazár, *Labradores, peones, y proletarios.*

16   In one typical case, Juana Zamorano García was arrested for selling alcohol
to Angel Sepúlveda and to "the prostitute Carmen Soto Rojas." The pair were
found drinking in one of the bedrooms of the house (*Juzgado de Letras de Menor
Cuantía, Sewell, Causa No. 6036,* December 11, 1940, Conservador de Bienes y
Raíces, Rancagua [CBRR]). In another case, police apprehended three prostitutes
whom they discovered sitting around a table in a "dance room" drinking pisco
and Bilz, a popular soft drink (*Juzgado de Letras de Menor Cuantía, Sewell, Causa
No. 10.093,* June 4, 1945, CBRR). In another, Juana Donoso Saavedra was arrested
for clandestinely selling wine to three miners. Donoso had converted her own
house into her "place of business" (*Juzgado de Letras de Menor Cuantía, Sewell,
Causa No. 4947,* March 10, 1939, CBRR).

17   *Juzgado de Letras de Menor Cuantía, Sewell, Causa No. 2768,* June 24, 1935, CBRR.

18   In 1939, for example, women working in El Teniente's laundries earned between
$5 and $7 pesos a day in contrast with the $30 peso daily minimum wage for a male
worker in the mine (*Despertar Minero,* August 31, 1939). In 1941, domestic workers
in the camps' canteens earned between $60 and $80 pesos monthly, while the
average wage for a male worker was between $30 and $45 pesos a day (*Despertar
Minero,* January 30, 1941).

19   Baltazar Castro, *Un hombre por el camino* (Santiago: Editorial Cultura, 1950), p. 174.

20   *Juzgado de Letras de Menor Cuantía, Sewell, Causa No. 10.945,* August 28, 1946, CBRR.

21   The nature of these semi-stable relationships based on the exchange of sex for
money or goods is revealed in one empleada's testimony to the Sewell court
about a miner who had stabbed her in the chest. According to Cristina Ferrera
López, José Ortíz Monsalves was a pensioner in the canteen where she worked
and had made a number of passes at her which she had rejected. In her statement, she denied that he had given her money or clothes and stated that she had
refused to have relations with him. She was echoed by her attacker who, claiming not to understand why he had attacked Ferrera, also made a point of the fact
that he hadn't had a relationship with her, and stated, "I haven't given her anything, nor has she asked me for money or clothes" (*Juzgado de Letras de Menor
Cuantía, Sewell, Causa No. 10.033,* May 3, 1945, CBRR).

22   Welfare Department, annual report, 1922, ABCC.

23   *Informe,* Welfare Department, Braden Copper Company, n.d., ABCC.

24   June Nash notes a similar attempt to build nuclear families in the Bolivian tin
mines after 1954, when "the beneficial effects of a stable family life in creating a
more dependable work force were recognized by the administration of the mines
after nationalization" (*We Eat the Mines and the Mines Eat Us: Dependency and Exploitation in Bolivian Tin Mines* [New York: Columbia University Press, 1979], p. 59).

25   *El Teniente,* 1922–1942.

26   Oral sources describe many miners' disgruntlement because their wives or
female partners had abandoned them and left the camps. They expressed their
discontent in letters of protest to the company Welfare Department.

27   Fuenzalida, *La vida i el trabajo,* p. 101.

28   Ibid.

29   Oral sources.

30   Braden Copper Company to Hernán Cousiño Tocornal, January 1946, ABCC. In 1919, for example, a study reported that miners frequently rented or purchased forged marriage licenses to avoid the company's regulations for civil marriage, and in 1939 the head of the company Welfare Department wrote that "there exist families without legal status; there have even arisen cases of the complete falsification of the civil marriage license book. . . . We have seen cases where the license of a legitimate marriage is presented to cover up another illegitimate union" (letter to Ana Pino Santibanez, February 3, 1939, ABCC).

31   *Informe.*

32   For descriptions of the schools and classes see *El Teniente,* 1922–1942.

33   Oral sources.

34   *Juzgado de Letras de Menor Cuantía, Sewell, Causa Civil No. 2189,* CBRR. Also see *Juzgado de Letras de Menor Cuantía, Sewell, Causa Civil No. 2200,* CBRR, for a similar case.

35   *Mensaje Obrero,* May 14, 1939.

36   Oral sources.

37   Welfare Department, letter to presidente, Sindicato Industrial Braden Copper Company "Sewell y Mina," July 31, 1943, ABCC.

38   See Thomas Miller Klubock, "Class, Community, and Gender in the Chilean Copper Mines: The El Teniente Miners and Working-Class Politics, 1904–1951" (Ph.D. diss., Yale University, 1993).

39   In one case, for example, an empleada was arrested after she was hospitalized following an illegal abortion. According to her fellow workers, she had had other clandestine abortions before (*Juzgado de Letras de Menor Cuantía, Sewell, Causa No. 9926,* March 23, 1945, CBRR). For other cases of women arrested for illegal abortions see *Juzgado de Letras de Menor Cuantía, Sewell, Causa No. 6049,* July 14, 1940; and *Causa No. 9926,* March 23, 1945, CBRR.

40   For more about women arrested for abandoning their husbands see *Juzgado de Letras de Menor Cuantía, Sewell, Causa No. 5458,* November 5, 1940, CBRR.

41   Welfare Department, "El Departamento de Bienestar," 1921, ABCC.

42   Carole Pateman, *The Sexual Contract* (Stanford: Stanford University Press, 1988), p. 132.

43   Oral sources.

44   Oral sources.

45   *Juzgado de Letras de Menor Cuantía, Sewell, Causa No. 13.599,* July 26, 1951, CBRR.

46   Oral sources.

47   Oral sources.

48   *Juzgado de Letras de Menor Cuantía, Sewell, Causa No. 11.342,* June 12, 1947, CBRR.

49   *Juzgado de Letras de Menor Cuantía, Sewell, Causa No. 11.334,* March 31, 1947, CBRR.

50   Welfare Department, confidential memorandum, July 28, 1943, ABCC.

51 H. Mackenzie Walker to W. J. Turner, September 6, 1939, ABCC.

52 A classic case was that of Ramiro del Carmen Herrera Rodríguez, who beat his wife, María Cruz Castro, because he didn't like the way she was serving him, and because when he scolded her she answered back (*Juzgado de Letras de Menor Cuantía, Sewell, Causa No. 12047,* July 13, 1948, CBRR).

53 *Juzgado de Letras de Menor Cuantía, Sewell, Causa No. 2842,* July 26, 1935, CBRR. In another case, when Olga Moya Hall de Marchant went to the cinema with a cousin and a friend without permission, she received a beating when she arrived home. According to her husband, "I hit her in the head because she doesn't obey me and leaves the children abandoned so that she can go to the theater alone" (*Juzgado de Letras de Menor Cuantía, Sewell, Causa No. 6266,* November 14, 1941, CBRR).

54 *Juzgado de Letras de Menor Cuantía, Sewell, Causa No. 10.955,* September 2, 1946, CBRR.

55 See, for example, Pateman, *The Sexual Contract;* and Scott, *Gender and the Politics of History.*

56 Oral sources. These traditions flourished when miners entered El Teniente in the 1950s and continue to this day.

57 Account published in *La Semana,* November 12, 1921.

58 Baltazar Castro, *Mi camarada padre* (Santiago: Editorial Nascimento, 1963), p. 267.

59 Ibid., pp. 11–18.

60 Castro, *Sewell* (Santiago: Editorial Zig-Zag, 1966), p. 25. Castro's iconography of the male body is startlingly similar to George Orwell's fascination with British coal miners' physical strength. Writing around the same time as Castro, Orwell described coal miners as "hammered iron statues . . . splendid men . . . most of them have the most noble bodies; wide shoulders tapering to slender supple waists, and small pronounced buttocks and sinewy thighs" (*The Road to Wigan Pier* [New York: Harcourt Brace Jovanovich, 1958], p. 23). A study of British coal miners during the 1950s commented on the ways in which "in the pit itself, among his workmates, the miner is proud of doing his job as a good man should. . . . pride in work is a very important part of the miner's life. Old men delight in stories of their strength and skill in youth" (Norman Dennis, Fernando Henriques, and Clifford Slaughter, *Coal Is Our Life: An Analysis of a Yorkshire Mining Community* [London: Tavistock, 1956], p. 73). Similarly, Michelle Perot notes that with industrialization and proletarianization in France, "the symbols of the working class . . . became more and more masculine: it has been represented by the barrel-chested male worker with broad shoulders, swollen biceps, and powerful muscles" ("On the Formation of the French Working Class," in *Working-Class Formation: Nineteenth Century Patterns in Western Europe and the United States,* ed. Ira Katznelson and Aristide R. Zolberg [Princeton: Princeton University Press, 1986], p. 99).

61 Castro, *Sewell,* p. 26.

62 Ibid., p. 39.

63   Ibid., p. 89.

64   See *Página Abierta,* October 12–25, 1992.

65   Castro, *Un hombre por el camino,* p. 202.

66   Gonzalo Drago, *Cobre: Cuentos Mineros* (Santiago: Zig-Zag, 1960), p. 82.

67   Ibid., p. 18.

68   Castro, *Sewell,* p. 126.

69   Oral sources.

70   Drago, *Cuentos mineros,* p. 99.

71   Manuel Barrera, "El conflicto obrero en el enclave cuprífero," *Revista Mexicana de Sociología* 40 (April–June 1978): p. 37.

72   Oral sources.

73   "You see, the worker arrives tired . . . from work and sleeps, gets up, drinks, arrives home drunk . . . he doesn't have a good relationship with his family, he doesn't have a good relationship with his wife. . . . Life in the camps is harder because there you noticed more those women that cheated on their husbands and everyone knew that the woman cheated on her husband . . . and we even had a name for this . . . *la boca del fiero* [the cruel mouth?]" (oral sources [Rancagua, 1991]).

74   See David Montgomery, *Workers' Control in America: Studies in the History of Work, Technology, and Labor Struggles* (Cambridge: Cambridge University Press, 1979), for a discussion of this workplace code of behavior in the industrializing United States.

75   For descriptions of miners' mocking jokes and pranks see Fuenzalida, *La vida i el trabajo,* p. 112.

76   See, for example, *Juzgado de Letras de Menor Cuantía, Sewell, Causa No. 11.142,* January 14, 1947; and *Causa No. 7824,* January 21, 1942, CBRR.

77   See *Despertar Minero,* June 25, 1939; *Despertar Minero, Primera Quincena de Noviembre de 1944;* and "General Manager's Report—1940, Braden Copper Company," ABCC, for accounts of murders.

78   *La Tribuna,* March 5, 1942.

79   For examples of these kinds of fights see *Juzgado de Letras de Menor Cuantía, Sewell, Causa No. 6134,* November 3, 1941; *Causa No. 10.546,* February 6, 1946; and *Causa No. 5430,* January 15, 1940, CBRR.

80   Yonne de Souza Grossi describes a similar masculine work culture in the Brazilian gold mines, where the company also promoted competitions among workers and work groups. The discourse of virility divided the miners and stimulated individualist tendencies. At the same time, however, de Souza Grossi argues that this sense of virility based on hard physical labor created the potential for militant collective action (*Mina de Morro Velho: A extracão do homem* [Rio de Janeiro: Paz e Terra, 1981], p. 267).

81   *Censo de la Braden Copper Company, 1937,* ABCC.

82   Klubock, "Class, Community, and Gender."

83 *Despertar Minero,* April 25, 1939.

84 This appears similar to Temma Kaplan's argument that "accepting and enforcing the division of labor by sex . . . can bring women into conflict with authorities" ("Female Consciousness and Collective Action: The Case of Barcelona, 1910–1918," *Signs* 7, no. 3 [spring 1982]): pp. 545–66.

Household Patrones

Wife-Beating and Sexual Control
in Rural Chile, 1964–1988

HEIDI TINSMAN

In June 1993, in the aftermath of Chile's seventeen-year military dictatorship, three hundred women fruit workers gathered in Santiago at the First National Meeting of Female Temporary Agricultural Workers. Sponsored by Chile's four campesino labor confederations, the conference stressed employer exploitation as the central locus of female oppression and called on the female temporary workers (*temporeras*) to join male agricultural workers in reviving the rural labor movement. The women in attendance did not refute the need for a united labor front, but during the floor discussion a young woman rose to question the presumption of gender solidarity:

> *Compañeras,* it is all fine to talk about solidarity with men, but how many of you have husbands who wash dishes or take care of children? How many of you have husbands who let you go to meetings or like the fact that you work? And—I know none of us wants to talk about this—but how many of you have husbands who are abusive, who beat you for whatever whim?

As other women applauded in agreement, an older woman stood up to contribute:

> My dear, this is nothing new. Women have always suffered men's abuse, but in the old days it was much harsher. My husband beat me, my father beat my mother, my grandfather beat my grandmother. But women didn't complain or run off, they stayed with the family. Not like today. No, back then women had to be strong, because a husband was worse than the *patrón.*[1]

This chapter explores the dynamics of working-class wife-beating in rural Chile between 1964 and 1988. Most Latin American social and labor histories have ignored male aggression toward women as a meaningful subject of study. When mentioned at all, such violence is generally attributed to a vague machismo or to the brutality of class oppression.[2] In this chapter, I argue that men's violence against women is not a simple outcome of male frustration in the wake of poverty, patrón abuse, or alcohol consumption. That a husband systematically hits his wife and not a chair begs explanation of how violence is specific to gender relations within class.

As several pioneering works have demonstrated, violence against women is historically and politically specific.[3] Men do not always beat their wives or conjugal partners; and if they do, they do not always beat them for the same reasons. Definitions of unacceptable and acceptable physical aggression between spouses vary according to changing notions of proper gender roles and organizations of sexuality within the family and broader society. Moreover, conflict between husbands and wives arises from struggles in which conjugal partners contest real resources within specific circumstances. Wife-beating has both material and sexual bases; it is conditioned by the ways in which the experience of class is fractured by gender and gender is constructed by sexuality.

As one of the most overt examples of female subjugation to male authority, wife-beating offers a window into contemporary notions of masculine prerogative and feminine obligation and into how these norms are negotiated and contested. Conjugal violence tells us not only about power relations within the family but also about how the sexual hierarchies enforced within the household are shaped by, and help to shape, broader social relations. The content of what men and women fight about changes over time. While wife-beating may always involve conflict over masculine and feminine roles, the meaning of male and female at a particular moment varies and reflects other ideological and material factors in society as a whole.

This chapter argues that husbands' use of physical force against wives in rural Chile between 1964 and 1988 was rooted in the dependence of rural masculinity on the control of female sexuality; but that definitions of manhood and the parameters of sexual control were conditioned by the changing political and economic context that gendered men and women's lives. Specifically, I examine the shifting boundaries of wife-beating during two historical periods: first, the dismantling of Chile's hacienda economy during the Agrarian Reforms undertaken by the consecutive Christian Democratic and Popular

Unity governments, between 1964 and 1973; and, second, the evolution of a capitalist fruit-export economy under military dictatorship, between 1973 and 1988. I maintain that, although men employed violence against women in both periods, during the 1960s and early 1970s men used violence to bolster an already existing male social and sexual privilege that was in many ways reinforced by the process of Agrarian Reform; while under military rule and export capitalism, men used violence in reaction to a relatively greater social and sexual agency assumed by women.

I do not attempt to measure the rise or fall of domestic violence over time. Given the limited nature of my sources and the concealed character of conjugal abuse, this is necessarily a qualitative rather than a quantitative study. What interests me is how the conflicts underlying conjugal violence changed in form between 1964 and 1988, and what this tells us about the changing nature of women's subordination to men: What were couples fighting about when men used violence, and what does this say about how masculinity and femininity were constituted in a sexualized hierarchy within the household? How and why did women react or not? And, finally, how and why do these dynamics shift over time?

This chapter takes as its case study the Department of San Felipe in the Central Valley province of Aconcagua, today the showcase for Chile's U.S. $450,000,000 fruit-export industry. San Felipe's history is representative of the dramatic changes that have occurred in the Chilean countryside over the last thirty years. In the early 1960s, 90 percent of productive land in the province was owned by less than 8 percent of all property holders.[4] Sprawling haciendas produced grain for domestic consumption and relied on a combined labor force of seasonal wage laborers (who were largely, but not exclusively, male) and resident male peons called *inquilinos* (resident peons) who exchanged their labor in return for access to plots of land within the estates.

During the Agrarian Reforms of Presidents Eduardo Frei (1964–1970) and Salvador Allende Gossens (1970–1973), the state expropriated over 50 percent of productive land in San Felipe and reorganized it into large cooperatives and state-managed farms.[5] The inquilino labor system was abolished, and workers were paid a wage and were involved directly in the administration of Agrarian Reform Production Units. Between 1964 and 1973, rural income tripled, and the rural poor enjoyed unprecedented access to state welfare services in health, education, and nutrition.[6] The Agrarian Reform also generated a massive rural labor movement that gave the rural poor a major voice in national politics for the first time in Chile's history.[7]

Following the violent coup against Allende's leftist Popular Unity government in 1973, the military junta headed by General Augusto Pinochet dismantled the Agrarian Reform and brutally silenced popular mobilization. Land was reconstituted into medium-sized farms, owned and managed by a new entrepreneurial class that took advantage of government credit policies to gear production toward the export of luxury fruits such as grapes and peaches.[8] This conversion to export capitalism ended workers' guarantees of social justice and accelerated the marginalization of the rural poor. Temporary labor contracts replaced permanent ones, and women became workers in fruit-packing plants in numbers approaching those of men. By 1980, less than 20 percent of the agricultural workforce was employed on a permanent basis, and almost 50 percent of it was female.[9]

The history of wife-beating in San Felipe must be understood against this backdrop of political and economic change. The transformation of Chilean agriculture directly shaped the dynamics of men's and women's different and unequal positions within the rural household and thus, I argue, the nature of domestic conflict and violence. I focus on the intersection between structural relations and household dynamics in order to stress the material basis of domestic violence, not to posit a necessary or mechanical relation between the two. Gender relations within the rural household did not change as a direct result of new economic policies and political projects, but rather from men's and women's varied perceptions of, and reactions to, what these broader changes meant for their positions within the family and community. Popular response was mediated by existing ideologies and practices regarding male and female behavior that were generated by multiple interlocutors such as organized religion, the judiciary system, community tradition, local politics, and popular culture. As the term *domestic conflict* suggests, new gender norms did not simply arise to complement a new political-economic order, but were negotiated and contested, frequently by force.

This work relies on women's testimonies in several of the 420 cases of male-on-female assault filed at the San Felipe Juzgado de Crimen between 1964 and 1988. Of the 168 court cases available for this study, roughly three-quarters involved women from poor families engaged in agricultural labor.[10] In addition to judicial records, this work draws on ninety oral histories that I gathered from interviews with rural workers in San Felipe between 1992 and 1993.

The court records provide a view into the content and dynamics of wife-beating rather than statistical evidence of the frequency of such violence. Many case files were incomplete, without an elaboration of why charges were brought. Other files listed in the Criminal Registry were lost or misplaced and not available for examination. Yet even had all cases been available for consideration, they would represent only a tiny fraction of the actual incidence of wife-beating. Because bringing legal charges against husbands involves extraordinary risks for poor women, court cases are necessarily the brave testimony of a minority. This makes them more helpful to examining the qualitative, rather than quantitative, aspect of conjugal conflict.

The reasons for which men appear to have beaten their spouses varied widely, and it is impossible to discuss all the possible causes in this chapter. Nonetheless, in the 168 files examined, I detected certain behavior patterns in men's and women's actions and assertions of why violence had occurred. There were also marked changes over time. The cases referred to in this chapter were chosen because they were representative of certain patterns as well as for their level of detail.

Similarly, the oral histories used in this chapter were chosen for their detail and precision in describing the various reasons for domestic violence given in interviews.[11] When asked, all men and women said that wife-beating was common in rural society both during and after the Agrarian Reform. Women were far more willing than men to discuss their personal experiences in detail, although many men would comment on the behavior they observed in "a neighbor's" relationship. While these informants, like those who testified in judicial cases, comprise a tiny proportion of the San Felipe population, their random selection across lines of gender, age, and occupation helps establish the widespread existence of domestic violence and to interrogate its dynamics.[12]

El Rey del Rancho: Male Authority and Household Violence during the Agrarian Reform, 1964–1973

The Agrarian Reform dramatically reorganized land tenure and labor relations in San Felipe and substantially improved the material well-being of the rural poor. On the roughly one-half of all irrigated agricultural land that was expropriated and incorporated into the government-managed Reformed Sector, campesino workers ceased to labor under the arbitrary and coercive authority of private landowners and became de facto state workers on land that the government promised would one day become their own.[13] Even on haciendas that remained in private hands, powerful rural labor unions that were supported by the state's official sanction and financial backing forced landowners to pay higher wages, honor employment contracts, and fulfill various social-welfare obligations.[14] Simultaneously, the state sponsored an array of programs aimed at ameliorating rural poverty. In less than nine years, illiteracy rates in San Felipe dropped by over 50 percent, infant mortality declined by nearly 25 percent, and thousands of campesino homes were provided with electricity, sanitation facilities, and drinking water.[15]

This project of social uplift, however, was executed in an uneven manner and experienced in unequal ways. The Agrarian Reform targeted only the largest haciendas, those over eighty hectares, and included as future recipients of land only those inquilinos and permanent workers who had formerly been employed on an expropriated estate.[16] This excluded the majority of the rural population: subsistence farmers, seasonal laborers, and permanent workers on smaller, non-Reformed estates.[17] Traditional landowner/worker relationships continued to exist alongside the newer, more privileged arrangements in the Reformed Sector.

If the Agrarian Reform privileged some workers over others, it privileged virtually all men over women. Both the Christian Democratic and Popular Unity governments, as well as the rural labor movement, shared the assumption that the Agrarian Reform's central goal should be to transform impoverished male peasants into able producers and successful providers for their families. Certainly, Centrist and Leftist visions of the Agrarian Reform as a whole differed radically: the Frei administration and the Christian Democratic and Catholic labor unions sought to create a new class of peasant farmers who owned land individually, while the Popular Unity administration and Marxist labor unions attempted to build a more collectively owned socialist economy. All factions, however, shared the belief that it would naturally be rural men who would be the protagonists in the new society. The Agrarian Reform Law required members of Agrarian Reform Production Units to be "household heads" (98 percent of whom were male); the Ministry of Agriculture's technical training programs were open only to former full-time estate employees (98 percent of whom were male); and rural labor unions excluded most women from formal membership because they were not permanent workers.

Women, it was assumed, would benefit through the uplift of their male family members. And indeed, they did, as campesina women enjoyed higher standards of living between 1964 and 1973. Yet the improvement in women's livelihoods evolved as part of a broader project to bolster male-headed families in which men were economic providers and women were dependent wives and mothers. The Agrarian Reform was partly based on and directed at a notion of family that built on sexual divisions of labor already existing in the pre–Agrarian Reform world of the hacienda, but which both the Christian Democratic and Popular Unity governments actively sought to reinforce. Traditional gender arrangements were promoted and bestowed with a new dignity born of a campesino family's material well-being, civic participation, and economic independence.

Domestic violence between 1964 and 1973 developed within the context of rupture and overlap between two different organizations of rural society. The Agrarian Reform did not immediately, or ever entirely, replace latifundia relationships, and new notions about the proper interaction between husbands and wives shared much with those of the recent past. Nonetheless, the Agrarian Reform's promotion of rural men's empowerment and celebration of a particular family ideal touched the lives of all rural people, whether they were incorporated already into the Reformed Sector or waiting expectantly to be let in. Spousal disagreements that ended in men's use of force against women were mediated both by traditions that predated the Reform and by new expectations that the Reform generated.

Between 1964 and 1973, rural women in the Department of San Felipe filed 198 denunciations of their husbands at the Juzgado de Crimen.[18] In a majority of the denunciations, women cited male sexual jealousy as the principal reason for aggression. They stressed the severity of physical injury they had suffered and that such violence had occurred before. Women complained that men used force to police their wives' interactions with other men and to insist that a wife's primary obligation was to serve her husband in the home. Men, in turn, justified violence as an appropriate punishment for their wives' transgressions from the feminine duties of marriage and cohabitation.

Typical of these cases was that of Olivia Acevedo from the *comuna* (county) of Putaendo. In January 1968, Olivia brought charges against her *conviviente* (common-law spouse), Ramón Contreras, for beating her and cutting her with a machete. She complained that since she had become pregnant with his child, he had become "really bad" because she "could no longer have sexual relations with him or fulfill [her] other obligations as a housewife."[19]

Similarly, in October 1970, Sonia Muñoz Guerra, age twenty, reported that her conviviente, José Bruna Covarubias, an agricultural worker in the comuna of San Felipe, had beaten her in the face after she "decided (that she) wanted nothing more to do with him and was seeking other company." José admitted to his actions, but defended them on the grounds of his marital right to castigate his wife for infidelity. He told the judge, "We were making a married life together and I surprised her talking with another man. I asked her for an explanation, and since I had already pardoned her once for a similar situation, I hit her in the face."[20]

In an oral history, Anita Herrera, the child of inquilinos and a lifetime agricultural worker in the comuna of Santa María, remembered coercion and violence as also characterizing her married life with Manuel Rojas. Married in 1951 at age fourteen, Anita bore ten children in her first eleven years as a wife. After the tenth child Anita's doctor insisted she get a hysterectomy, against the protests of her husband. She remembered Manuel's reaction with bitterness:

> After the operation, everything changed between us. That's when he really began to beat me badly. He was furious, said I had gotten sterilized so that I could run around with other men and that now I didn't serve for anything as a wife or as a woman. He refused to have [sexual] relations with me, started seeing other women and staying out for months. When he came back, he'd be drunk and he'd beat me. He split my head open several times.[21]

Cases involving male jealousy highlight the degree to which many rural men understood sexual access to women as both a male right and a central definition of marital relations. That many men interpreted women's flirtation, conversations, and informal meetings with other men as infidelity suggests that men presumed that their access would be total and unrivaled. Such men saw marriage and cohabitation as entitling them to sexual ownership of their wives. Physical force was legitimated as justifiably preventing female deviance from the conjugal contract.

Interestingly, cases involving male jealousy often included accusations of women's inadequacy as housewives. Men cited housekeeping failure as further proof of a woman's sexual transgression. In the cases of Anita Herrera and Olivia Acevedo, men felt that a woman's inability to have sex or to procreate made a woman useless as a housewife, generally. The connection suggests that men saw female sexual and domestic services as inseparable duties of a "proper wife." Sexual performance and, specifically, reproductive capacity were understood as part of a wife's household obligations. In turn, the worth of a wife's housekeeping chores was measured in sexual terms: When Olivia could no longer have sex and Anita could no longer have children, their husbands ceased to value their domestic labors. Such men seem to have reasoned that sexually loyal (or functional) wives kept a good house, and good housekeepers were sexually loyal. Failure in one could imply betrayal in the other.

A second common reason for conjugal violence cited by women involved quarrels over women's opposition to male authority in the household. While childrearing and household management were considered female responsibilities, men frequently insisted on their right to override wives' decisions. Women objected to this infringement on their authority—particularly when it came to the care of children—but were often unable to prevail even in matters that were socially defined as female.

In 1965, María Lopez Trancibia was hospitalized with severe cuts on her abdomen and buttocks inflicted by her conviviente, Hernán Guerra, an agricultural laborer in the comuna of San Felipe. María testified that Hernán had turned on her because she had tried to prevent him from disciplining her sixteen-year-old son with a knife. "I told him to hit him with a clean hand and not the knife, so he stabbed me, saying that even though he is not the boy's father, he is the man in the house." [22]

In her oral history, Sonia Cardanes complained of similar conflicts with her husband, Jorge León, an agricultural laborer in the comuna of Santa María:

> When he was around, it was the worst. I'd have my way of disciplining my girls, but when he got home, everything was his way. He'd hit them and me for not having the house exactly as he wanted, if they had forgotten to sweep the floor, he'd hit them, and if I intervened, he always set on me. [23]

"El hombre manda en la casa" (the man rules at home) is the common way that both men and women summarized the domestic balance of power in the 1960s. Unlike the situation for many urban women, the home did not provide rural women with a special sphere of female jurisdiction. A rural woman was less likely to be *la reina del hogar* (the queen of the home) than her husband was *el rey del rancho* (the king of the shanty). In contrast to the urban separation between the barrio and the factory, both the hacienda sector and the Reformed Sector blurred distinctions between individual household economies and that of the estates generally. Men labored both in the patrón's fields or in the commonly farmed portion of Agrarian Reform Production Units *and* on their subsistence gardens behind the family's home in the estate. This meant that when women worked in their homes or took turns cultivating the family subsistence garden, men were often around. Moreover, on non-Reformed haciendas, the servile nature of men's estate work, under the close surveillance of an overseer or patrón, distinguished the rural household as one of the few places where poor men could exercise the autonomy and authority theoretically guaranteed them as men in a patriarchal culture but largely denied them by class.

Men's efforts to rule at home extended beyond their roles as breadwinners, to monitoring the behavior of wives and children and controlling household consumption. Men decided at what age a child would be withdrawn from school to enter work, as well as whether or not a wife would labor as a domestic servant or laundress. Many rural women reported that in the 1960s they rarely handled money: Men would make the family's few purchases at town stores, would market the produce from the family's garden, and would sell female handicrafts. Allowing a woman to go to town was seen as endangering her virtue and therefore threatening a man's sexual prerogative to limit his wife's contact with other men.[24]

The most immediate factor conditioning men's sense of authority over wives' bodies and labor was women's overt economic dependence on men. According to the Agricultural Census in 1964, barely 5 percent of permanent agricultural workers in San Felipe were female.[25] Although nearly one-fifth of rural women worked occasionally for wages as domestic servants, vendors, laundresses, and seasonal agricultural laborers during harvests, the temporary nature of such positions and the low wages they generated meant that few women could earn enough to support themselves and their children without male assistance.[26] Most adult women who did not enter formal sexual unions with men migrated. Indeed, in 1960 only 2 percent of rural households in San Felipe were headed by women.[27]

The Agrarian Reform did little to alter women's economic dependence on men and, indeed, actively promoted the idea that it was men, not women, who should head rural households. The dramatic shift from private to state ownership of land did not radically change the crops produced on ex-haciendas or the overwhelming disproportion of men employed on them. While the commitment of both the Christian Democratic and the Popular Unity governments to raising rural wages was widely celebrated by rural women and men alike, state policies explicitly focused on strengthening men's positions as breadwinners rather than on creating employment opportunities for women. Under both Frei and Allende, the government sponsored a variety of handicraft and sewing projects for rural housewives, to help women generate additional income for their families.[28] However, such home-based activities were not competitive with the wage work of men on estates, Reformed or un-Reformed, and they allowed women to make only minimal financial contributions to the household. Although experiments with fruit cultivation in the Reformed Sector provided several hundred women with new employment as harvesters and packers, such seasonal work lasted only two or three months a year, in contrast with the expanded permanent employment options for men. By the time of Allende's overthrow, women seem to have comprised a slightly smaller percentage of San Felipe's permanent agricultural workforce than they had when the Reform began — 3 percent as opposed to 5 percent.[29]

Women who lived in the Reformed Sector complained that they lost employment options because the flight of landowners decreased demand for domestic service. They also maintained that their husbands often forbade them to work even occasionally for wages and preferred to hire men and women who lived outside the Reformed Unit for seasonal tasks. As one woman explained, this aversion to a wife's wage work flowed from a man's perception that, "because now he was the owner of the land, he was also now el rey del rancho and could support his family without the wife's [financial] assistance."[30]

This sense of male pride and its investment in female economic dependence was bolstered by Center and Left efforts to politically mobilize the rural poor between 1964 and 1973. Rural unions, the largest and most politically powerful working-class organizations in the countryside, were 95 percent male, and their activities dealt almost exclusively with land and wage issues affecting male inquilinos and permanent workers.[31] Unions became important vehicles for refashioning campesino masculinity. All three of the political tendencies within the rural labor movement—independent Catholic, Christian Democratic, and Marxist—stressed that unions served to transform campesinos from children who were dependent on a patrón into men who controlled their own destiny.[32] Rural men were urged to participate in wage strikes and land occupations to vindicate their rights *as men* to fair treatment by landowners and opportunity for economic self-sufficiency. Technical training programs and labor education seminars run by the state also emphasized the importance of self-mastery and economic independence to rural manhood. As Rafael Moreno, the president of the National Corporation of Agrarian Reform, explained, the purpose of state programs for rural workers during the Frei administration was to "convert the modest campesino into a small-businessman, to eliminate his diminutive status and to elevate him to the active consciousness of knowing his worth as a human being."[33] Although during the Popular Unity years, the goal of building socialism would downplay the need to transform campesinos into small-businessmen, themes of masculine agency and pride remained constant. Allende boasted that his government's "true Agrarian Reform" would "make campesinos real men and real owners" with the capacity "to support their wives and children in dignity."[34]

The state and rural labor movement also encouraged rural women's involvement and transformation in the process of Agrarian Reform. Yet female participation was solicited selectively, in ways that built upon, rather than challenged, women's subordination in the family. Between 1964 and 1973, campesina women provided food and lent organizational support to men in rural wage strikes and land occupations through their membership in government-organized groups called Mothers' Centers. They also lobbied for housing, electricity, and water through community institutions known as Neighbors' Councils. These activities offered women important new roles outside the home, encouraging women to think of themselves as political actors on both a local and a national scale. However, they also evolved within the context of domesticity and women's exclusion from paid employment. Mothers' Centers and Neighbors' Councils focused on teaching women handicraft and homemaking skills, while labor unions barred most women from membership on the grounds that they were not, and should not be, permanent workers.[35]

Both the state and the labor movement celebrated the political significance of women as "community activist housewives." Yet they envisioned female activism as supportive, rather than constitutive, of the struggles of all-male unions. Together with the celebration of men's militancy in the primary battles for land and their future capacity as providers, this did not significantly alter the domestic balance of power and even legitimated many men's sense of authority within the household.

A third reason for wife-beating cited by women in cases of conjugal violence involved women's opposition to a husband's sexual liaisons outside the home. If men demanded sexual faithfulness from wives, they jealously guarded their own sexual freedom outside marriage. Although most women were forced to comply with such arrangements, they frequently contested men's sexual libertinage as unjust and argued that marriage should involve greater mutual fidelity.

In 1969, Orfelina Aguirre, a twenty-nine-year-old housewife, denounced her conviviente Luís Vargas, an agricultural worker in the comuna of San Felipe, for beating her in a fight over his habit of frequenting local brothels. Luís insisted that it was none of Orfelina's business if he went to brothels and that she "had an obligation to stick with [him] through the good and the bad."[36] In an oral history, Elena Vera recalled the violence in her marriage in the 1960s to Carlos García, an agricultural laborer and union leader in the comuna of Putaendo, as related to his affairs with other women:

> When I complained about the other women, he would beat me. I felt such shame to walk in the streets with him, because everyone knew he abused me and saw other women. Once I asked him why he felt he had the right to be a womanizer when I fulfilled my obligation as a wife. He

said, "because I'm a man, and I have nothing to lose. You are a woman and can lose everything."[37]

Men insisted on their right to extraconjugal sexual relations *and* to a wife's sexual fidelity. This reflected less a double standard or male hypocrisy than it did a logical extension of the entitlements of rural manhood, conceived of centrally in terms of male sexual privilege. Being a good macho meant access to multiple women, including exclusive rights over at least one woman who served a man at home. Campesino men referred to themselves as *huasos,* a term that when employed by landowning and urban classes, was a derogatory reference to rural ignorance and backwardness, but that to the rural poor implied male virility and freedom. As many men explained in oral histories, "A huaso [was] so strong, independent, and irreverent, that no man had a hold on him, not even the patrón."[38] Or, as one popular campesino melody humorously boasted of this brand of masculinity, "A huaso works like a bull, drinks like a horse, fights like a rooster, and conquers women like a man."[39] Undoubtedly, many huasos also provided for their families, but first and foremost it seemed that being a huaso meant being one's own boss.

The fact that on the un-Reformed haciendas few campesino men could have overtly challenged patrón authority or exercised freedom over the terms of employment, made drinking, fighting, and sexual prowess all the more central to defining masculinity. Carlos García's response to his wife that he could do what he wanted because he had nothing to lose, whereas she couldn't because she would lose everything, was analytically precise, if cruel. Carlos's status as a man—as a huaso—could be enhanced by extraconjugal affairs, while Elena's status as a woman—defined chiefly by being a sexually loyal wife and a mother—would be jeopardized by affairs that would give Carlos just reason for leaving her. Significantly, during the 1960s rural folklore referred to the huaso's appropriate female companion as the *china,* meaning a supple, coy, and available young woman, rather than a huaso's *señora* (wife).

During the Agrarian Reform, the notions about male sexual prowess so central to the definition of a huaso were celebrated as an integral part of worker militancy. In oral histories, rural men recalled the all-male drinking sessions that followed union meetings as times for sharing lewd jokes and fantastical stories about women as well as for arguing over politics.[40] Such competitive banter served both to confirm men's common membership in a fraternity that excluded women and to emphasize the link between men's sexual access to women and masculine agency generally. When national campesino confederations held weekend training sessions in Santiago for campesino leaders, they often provided entertainment featuring all-female dance troupes and skits that humorously dramatized men's perpetual vulnerability to the charms of women.[41] The rural labor press across the political spectrum devoted special comic pages to working-class humor in which cartoons poked fun either at men's thwarted attempts to seduce voluptuous, often half-naked, women or at men who were henpecked or sexually denied by their wives.[42] Such jokes revealed a certain anxiety about female sexuality and men's ability to control it, while encouraging the idea that male sexual privilege was inherent to union manhood.

The Agrarian Reform also provided men with widened opportunities to interact with and pursue relationships with women other than their wives. When union activities involved acts of solidarity with other workers in different parts of Aconcagua, men traveled to other comunas, where they lodged in another señora's home and enjoyed the host comuna's modest festivities of drinking and dancing, frequently in the presence of other women.[43] For top-ranking leaders of unions and Agrarian Reform Production Units the opportunities for heterosexual socializing were still greater since frequent meetings and conferences regularly took them to other parts of the country. Interactions with women ranged from jocular flirting to full affairs. In exceptional cases, men took more permanent lovers and started second families.[44] Men discovered that they not only had increased opportunities to pursue female company, but that their status as "union men" actually heightened their sexual cachet in women's eyes. As Carlos García, the president of Putaendo's communal union recalled, "A lot of men took advantage of being out of the house to meet women and to be with them. There were so many women! And they liked you a lot for being a leader, for having pride. Men found this very exciting. It made them feel they could go around getting lots of women."[45]

Men's heightened sense of sexual freedom placed considerable strain on rural marriages and frequently provoked fights that ended in blows. Rural wives widely suspected husbands of using "union business" as a pretense for sexual promiscuity, and even the most loyal husbands frequently returned home from a labor conference or prolonged land occupation to accusations of infidelity. Ana Sevedra, the wife of a union leader in the comuna of San Felipe, recalled having violent fights with her husband over his nighttime absences and claimed that he became sexually involved with several women who worked as clerical staff at the union headquarters. At one point she threatened to send their children to a sister in Valparaíso, because "he cared only about politics and other women and nothing about his family."[46] Ana's husband, Juan, maintained that he "had always been loyal," but defended both his interactions with other women and his use of force against Ana as the obligations of a labor leader: "I had to show [Ana] I was honorable in my job. I couldn't put up with her jealousy. She just didn't understand that, as president, I [had] to please many people, including the girls [in the union office]."[47]

Despite many women's protests and threats, the vast majority of wives never left violent husbands or convivientes. The dramatic lack of employment options for women, coupled with women's responsibility for children, militated heavily against leaving a relationship, no matter how materially inadequate or physically abusive. Anita Herrera recalled that on the one occasion she fled to her mother's house to escape Manuel's beatings, her mother sent her back the next morning saying, "Well, he's your husband now, he owns you. There's nothing to be done." Anita spoke to women neighbors, but received only the solace of their similar experiences. One friend encouraged her to abandon Manuel, but Anita dismissed the advice immediately: "What was I to do with seven kids at home? They needed their father and I needed a man." She coped by minimizing contact with her husband, putting herself and the children to bed before he arrived home. After thirty-five years of marriage, Manuel finally left Anita for good. Her sense of betrayal is deep: "I put up with so much, but I never abandoned him, never thought of it. I'm not like the women of today who—one fight, one slap and phuff! they leave. No, I worked hard to keep the family together."[48]

If women felt unable to leave abusive situations, they were not necessarily acquiescent to them. By confronting husbands directly or complaining in quiet solidarity to each other, women contested their husbands' view of marriage and sexual entitlement, even if they were unable to change it substantially. Anita's self-perception as a martyr to the family assumes that "a good marriage" *should* have consisted of *male,* as well as female, fidelity and male reliability in providing for the household. Women like Anita embraced the ideal of a workable male-headed household, because they correctly understood it to be their best survival option: Given women's acute economic vulnerability and sole responsibility for childrearing, the male breadwinner who earned an adequate "family wage" offered women material security and possible alleviation from the double burden of wage work. Thus, women articulated objections to domestic violence more on the grounds that it threatened family well-being than because it violated their integrity as individuals. Yet women's accusations of male *failure* to the family condemned male privilege as it was defined and understood by husbands.

During the Agrarian Reform, rural wife-beating in San Felipe was rooted in a domestic ideal that privileged men's roles as economic providers over women's positions as mothers and housewives. Men's sexual monopoly on wives, authority within the household, and sexual freedom outside marriage centrally defined rural manhood and constituted the matrices within which domestic conflict and violence evolved. Despite Christian Democratic and Popular Unity efforts to incorporate women into the process of social uplift, the mobilization of rural women as (dependent) housewives and the focus on rural men as the primary protagonists of social change hardened existing sexual hierarchies, if at a more elevated standard of living.

The Agrarian Reform's emphasis on transforming rural men into able providers and rural women into activist housewives did not, in itself, provoke men to become more violent toward their wives. Although legal accusations of wife-beating were almost one-third more numerous in the 1960s than in the 1950s, these figures may only demonstrate women's heightened willingness to make formal charges. It is even possible that incidents of wife-beating occurred less during the Agrarian Reform than in latifundia society because of decreased domestic tension over money and the formal celebration of family solidarity. Nonetheless, when violence did occur, men justified their actions by invoking a variety of male rights that the Agrarian Reform actively legitimated and promoted. The Agrarian Reform reinforced the preexisting fact of men's privilege over women in the labor market and the idea that men should naturally be caretakers and providers for dependent wives and children. It also celebrated a specific type of masculinity that stressed male combativeness and sexual virility and created opportunities in which rural men could exercise both.

Poverty, Proletarianization, and Conjugal Conflict: Male and
Female Responses to Export Capitalism and Military
Dictatorship, 1973–1988

Military dictatorship radically transformed agrarian society and with it relationships between men and women. Following the bloody overthrow of Allende in September 1973, the new regime quickly abolished popular political organizations and declared its commitment to creating a new economic order based on market efficiency and entrepreneurial initiative. Land was taken away from male campesinos, and by the late 1970s thousands of former landholding men and their female family members had become proletarianized wage laborers on fruit-producing estates and in fruit-processing plants.[49]

The economic livelihood of the rural poor became more vulnerable, while overt challenges to new forms of poverty and social marginalization were made virtually impossible. Although husbands and wives often agreed on survival strategies and their respective obligations within the family, the new realities provoked considerable conflict and dissent.

Between 1973 and 1988, denunciations of wife-beating at the San Felipe Juzgado de Crimen increased from an annual number of ten filings in the 1960s to an average of fifty in the 1980s.[50] While it is uncertain if this reflects an actual increase in the incidence of domestic violence, it clearly demonstrates women's greater willingness to denounce abuse. The content of denunciations also highlights significant changes in why women felt conjugal violence occurred. While themes of male sexual jealousy continued to feature prominently in women's testimonies, a majority of cases now involved disputes over men's work, men's earning power, and male contributions to the household.

On August 16, 1977, Sonia Ruiz, the twenty-nine-year-old wife of José Muñoz, an agricultural worker in the comuna of San Felipe, denounced her husband for severely beating her in the face because she requested money to buy the family's bread. She testified that such beatings frequently occurred when the couple fought about José's contribution to the household. José admitted to hitting his wife, but justified his actions by insisting that she had hit him first and that she was always asking for money when he didn't have any.[51]

Similarly, on May 6, 1986, Nancy Godoy Rosas, age seventeen, brought charges against her conviviente Luís Efraín Ahumada, an agricultural worker in the comuna of Santa María, for beating her in the eyes and nose and causing her to be hospitalized. She testified that Luís hit her for attempting to leave him and that she had long been trying to do so since he was "lazy, didn't work, and spent all of his money on liquor."[52]

Tension over male employment and the percentage of wages men dedicated to the family certainly characterized rural life throughout the 1960s. Yet after the mid-1970s women seemed more willing to criticize men's roles as breadwinners and to leave materially inadequate situations. In part, these conflicts sprang directly from the weakening of men's economic positions as the emerging fruit-export economy undermined prior forms of worker security.

Before and during the Agrarian Reform, only some men had been fully dependent on wages. Resident inquilinos and members of Agrarian Reform Production Units had access to land for subsistence cultivation and received part of their remuneration in food and lodging. Under military rule, the dismantling of the Reformed Sector and conversion to fruit production forced rural workers out of their dwellings in the estates and into self-built shanties on the outskirts of towns. This expulsion of workers ended the landowner paternalism and state guarantees that formerly had provided the rural poor with housing, education, food rations, and—most importantly—land. By the late 1970s, most rural workers had become fully dependent on wages as their only source of income.[53]

The rapid expansion of San Felipe's fruit industry also made agricultural employment less secure. Wages plummeted and unemployment rose in the late-1970s and the 1980s, as the junta withdrew support for the worker-welfare and full-employment goals of the previous governments. Most importantly, the military regime's overt support for the prerogatives of capital at the expense of labor radically transformed the rural labor contract. Agro-industrial employers began to rely heavily on temporary laborers (workers hired for three to four months at a time) in place of the permanent, even lifetime, workers who had formed the core of the labor force during the 1950s and 1960s. By the early 1980s, four out of every five agricultural laborers in San Felipe were temporary.[54]

These changes had dramatic implications for rural men's ability to function as providers. Men's wages fell, and employment became more unstable at precisely the moment that most rural families became solely dependent on wage labor. Moreover, the crushing of the rural labor movement stripped workers of any means for contesting their new vulnerability. The assault on male breadwinning was felt in particularly acute ways, given the prior success of the Christian Democratic and Popular Unity governments at raising rural welfare by strengthening men's positions as providers within a male-headed domestic ideal.

As male breadwinners became increasingly taxed after 1973, their position as sole providers was undermined by the unprecedented large-scale employment of women. Between 1974 and 1986, over fifty new fruit-packing plants ("packings") were constructed in San Felipe.[55] Depending on size, packings hired between twenty and three hundred women, who cleaned, trimmed, classified, and packaged grapes and peaches for export. By 1979, an estimated four thousand women worked in packing plants during the December–April harvest season. By 1988, this number had climbed to six thousand.[56]

Agro-industrialists employed women out of a need to substantially expand their labor force beyond what the resident male population could provide during the short harvest season. They sought local women rather than male migrants, because they understood fruit packaging as an extension of women's domestic food-preparation responsibilities, and because they believed women to be particularly adept at the detail work involved in severing stems and bruised fruit from grape bunches. Furthermore, employers viewed women as socially docile and, therefore, more willing to put up with the intense supervision required to ensure the quality of export produce. Lastly, the three-month packing season was seen as appropriately long for "part-time work for housewives" who were "helping out" with household expenses, but as too short to offer dignified employment to men.[57]

Like men, female packing-plant workers had temporary contracts with restricted benefits and no job security. Since men were employed primarily in vineyard and orchard work rather than in packing plants, they worked an average of twice as many months as did women.[58] However, since packing-plant work paid piece rate and field work usually paid by the day, women could, and often did, earn more than men on a monthly basis.[59]

The employment of women directly contradicted the military regime's aggressive promotion of a cross-class domestic ideal in which men worked and women stayed at home. Throughout the dictatorship, official discourse designated women as the cornerstone of the Chilean *patria* in their role as self-abnegating, apolitical, spiritual, and moral housewives within the sanctity of the home. The sacrificing mother became the female counterpart to the patriotic male soldier, and both were celebrated as the foundation of national progress and social peace. This domestic feminine ideal diverged significantly from the Christian Democratic and Popular Unity ideal of the community activist housewife/mother. From 1974 through the 1980s, elaborate government programs for women—most notably the reconstituted Mothers' Centers headed by Pinochet's wife—propagated an ideology of female domesticity at the same time that the demands of neoliberal capitalism made it increasingly difficult for rural men to keep their wives at home.[60]

Men's heightened economic vulnerability, coupled with women's entrance into wage work, significantly eroded the basis of male dominance as it had been materially and socially defined prior to the 1970s. Stripped of their capacity to function as the household's sole provider, men found their authority challenged within the household generally. Packing-plant shifts began in the early afternoon with the first delivery of harvested fruit and ended as late as 4:00 A.M. the following morning. This meant that women worked in physically separate spaces from most men and labored at night while their menfolk worked in the day. Husbands no longer exercised direct control over their wives' mobility, while packing-plant schedules forced men to take on at least minimal responsibility for child care and food preparation during women's nighttime absences.

Despite employers' efforts to rationalize women's packing-plant work as "appropriate for women," the fact that such work took place at night violated traditional notions about female respectability. Night work meant that mothers were not watching over sleeping children and that wives were not caring for husbands. It also implied sexual promiscuity and danger, since wives and daughters spent evenings under the "care" of male supervisors and walked home on darkened country roads unchaperoned by male family members.

If women's packing-plant work meant that husbands ceased to determine a wife's comings and goings, men also ceased to unilaterally decide household budgets and expenditures. Most women insisted on retaining control over their own wages and on their right to make basic purchases for themselves and the family. In oral histories, both men and women maintained that there was increased domestic conflict over men's failures to find work or to bring home sufficient earnings; however, they stressed that even more volatile fights occurred over *women's* wages, as men tried to control the destination of female earnings.

María Toledo, a forty-six-year-old separated temporera who had worked in packing plants since the mid-1970s, attributed her husband's violence to his view that female work and wages compromised his position as a man:

> You see, [rural] women [in San Felipe] have always worked, but before [the rise of the fruit industry] women worked side by side with men on the same hacienda, and now they work as a big group of women, apart, in the packings, this is what bothers men. Because now women . . . have the same conditions that men have always had—telling jokes, having a good time, gossiping about problems at home . . . a man feels bad. Also, women begin to like their own money and like the fact they often earn more than men. She likes to buy herself things as was never possible before, and men begin to feel displaced, unnecessary. So they hit a woman to feel more in control, to make her give in.[61]

Elena Muñoz, age thirty-seven and a temporera since 1980, also understood conjugal violence as resulting from the threat that female assertiveness over wages posed to masculinity:

> Women are more independent now as temporeras, they have egos and don't like to be accountable to husbands about how they spend their salary. This causes problems. Women think, this is my salary, I'm in charge of it . . . although women almost always spend their wages on their families, maybe at most she buys herself a new blouse, but never anything like on going out with friends like men do. Just the same it bothers women that men want to administer their money. See, men here

are machista—it costs them a lot to admit that their salaries aren't enough so that you can spend all your time serving them, that they, also, need you to work. So that's when the hitting starts.[62]

The proletarianization of women significantly altered women's positions within both the rural household and the broader community. Although the role of wife and mother still figured centrally in women's lives, women now operated in a wider social space that was often heavily female: the world of the packing plant, with lines of temporeras gossiping, quarreling, and joking, paralleled the male work world of camaraderie and conflict. Women not only made proportionally more money than had women a generation earlier, but they often earned more than their husbands during the peak season. Women also now controlled the destination of earnings in their new role as consumers, deciding what to buy for the family and—the unthinkable possibility twenty years earlier—how many pesos might be saved for a woman's own needs. Women's indignation that men attempted to determine the destination of their wages pointed to a growing sense by some women that they had a direct right to the fruits of their labor and that both men *and* women should independently make contributions to the household. This signaled women's bid for both greater independence from and equality with men.

Both men and women complained repeatedly of the disruptive effects of packing-plant shifts on family life: women's night work meant children went unattended until their fathers returned in the early evening; the fact that husbands and wives rarely saw each other caused communication problems; women suffered from exhaustion in their efforts to keep up with housework in addition to wage work; and most destructively—men and women agreed —packing work fomented marital separation. Yet here, men's and women's stories diverged: while men blamed conjugal breakups on women's increased desire and ability to have sexual affairs (with men they presumably met in the packing plants), women argued that separations were caused by fights over money and male suspicion of female infidelity.

Conflicts over women's extraconjugal affairs (presumed or actual) figured centrally in oral accounts of wife-beating. Claudia León, a thirty-three-year-old temporera from the comuna of Panquehue, blamed her sister's violent married life in the late 1970s on male anxiety about the packing environment:

Celi's husband beat her because he just couldn't take it. Men see that there is so much disorder in the packings—grown women flirting with the supervisors or other men. The women make themselves up, wear shorts and miniskirts, make crude jokes. A woman gets off work at three in the morning and walks home with a man who is not her husband. [Husbands] can't take it. Celi might have done something wrong, I don't know, but Leo beat her terribly just because he knew what packing [plants] were about.[63]

María Toledo stressed that her husband's suspicions about how she spent her hours away from home were made more acute by his frequent unemployment:

When I worked there were times my husband had to stay at home [because he couldn't get work]. He got so nervous, he would come pick me up from work or wait up for me until I got home at three or four in the morning, and then he wouldn't be able to sleep. He didn't trust what I was up to, he felt uncomfortable to not have his woman in the house, so he would hit me.[64]

Elena Muñoz also saw men's sexual suspicions as linked to male hostility toward women's nondomestic activities:

It really bothers a man to arrive home and not have a woman there to serve him his food. If he's in bed and she's not there, because she's working, he gets suspicious, he wonders about who she could be with. In my case, Pedro always, always makes me have [sexual] relations with him when I get home from a shift, no matter how exhausted I am, or if I say no. It's a way of testing where I've been. He hits me if I refuse. Men worry about women having affairs, even though men often take advantage of a woman's absence from the home to cheat on her. There can be a case of a good woman, who works very hard, who maybe is forced to look for affection in the packing because her husband is always cheating on her.[65]

Women's status as workers shaped female identity in ways that broke sharply with the rigid domesticity and sexual subordination of the previous generation. María's and Claudia's reflections recognize male anger at women as rooted in women's widened opportunities, especially sexual ones, but criticize men's retaliations as overreactions stemming from male insecurity. On the other hand, Elena's defense of the hypothetical woman who might have an affair because her husband is having one contemplates the viability of women having sex outside conjugal monogamy. While her qualification that such a woman would be *forced* to resort to such measures because of the *prior* actions of her husband suggests that Elena still sees domestic fidelity as her utopia, she stretches to legitimate separating female sexuality from marriage.

Men did not adapt easily to women's new roles and self-perceptions. Female wage work and the changes it implied directly threatened men's sense of authority by undermining men's status as breadwinners and by weakening men's sexual control of women. Some men saw the first as implicating the second. A woman could be sexually unfaithful if she left home to work, and a woman who was not materially dependent on a man might not be sexually loyal to a man. Male concern was not unfounded. The packing plants provided women with new sexual opportunities, ranging from flirtation to affairs, while women's access to cash income enabled new forms of female autonomy, from household purchases without male permission to conjugal separation. By 1986, over one-third of all households in Aconcagua were headed by women.[66] (In contrast, in 1970 this figure had been 3 percent.) While in the majority of cases it was men who left women, women's access to waged employment made survival without a male partner a more viable, if still extremely economically difficult, option than it had been twenty years earlier. This placed women in a stronger position to make demands on husbands. Men who continued to assume that their control over spouses would be absolute employed violence as a backlash against women's expanding sense of entitlement.

During the late 1970s and the 1980s rural women also seem to have taken stronger positions in confronting abuse than had women a generation earlier. More women simply left their husbands, as in the cases of María Toledo and Claudia León's sister. Significantly higher numbers of women filed formal charges against spouses at the San Felipe court. Other women sought public condemnation of their husbands' behavior in an effort to change it. This assertiveness sprang not only from women's relatively more numerous economic options, but, more specifically, from women's new notions about the types of respect and parity they deserved *because* they were both workers and wives.

These ideas were nurtured both by the fact of women's wage work and by women's participation in resistance efforts against military rule. During the 1980s, women comprised a significant proportion of the membership of popular organizations created by antimilitary forces such as the church, human rights groups, and the clandestine labor movement. *Ollas comunes* (soup kitchens) that pooled neighborhood resources, Catholic Church committees on family and community solidarity, and labor education forums on agricultural work all enlisted women's participation in issues that were central to the agenda of the political opposition.[67] These organizations' focus on democracy —as politically and morally antithetical to dictatorship—encouraged women to consider the equity of dynamics within their own households. They also provided women with an organizational means to challenge physical abuse.

Women who ran ollas comunes in the comuna of Santa María in the 1980s rebuked abusive husbands who came to pick up the family's ration.[68] Elena Vera, whose story of refusing to leave Carlos García in the 1960s was described earlier, reported that her activism in a church community program in the mid-1980s helped her take a more assertive tack toward conjugal violence in her children's relationships. When her oldest son Raúl started beating his wife in 1986, Elena took her son aside and slapped him: "I said he had no right to hit her, that if he had a disagreement he should use his mouth and not his fist. Husbands need to respect their wives because they are so sacrificing both in the packing [plants] and at home." Elena also offered advice to her daughter-in-law: "Hit back, my dear, with whatever is the biggest and hardest object around."[69]

If some women felt more enabled to challenge abuse, many still did not. The material difficulties of single motherhood and the social illegitimacy of female sexuality outside the family pressured against taking action. Wage labor hardly made women independent. In the 1980s, temporeras earned between U.S.$500 and U.S.$1000 annually, far below the annual minimum wage calculated as the cost of survival.[70] Women who separated from their husbands or convivientes would necessarily have to pool their salaries with extended family members or find scarce employment opportunities outside the fruit industry to support themselves and their children. Women's access to work also could weaken the social pressure on men to contribute to a wife or family he had left, or to marry a woman who got pregnant.

Lastly, women lacked men's sexual bargaining power. If some temporeras defended women's right to sex outside marriage, this was not a view widely shared. A woman who left or was left by her husband had difficulty finding a replacement. Men seeking to form unions with women generally sought young, unmarried women, preferably with few children. A married man who became involved with a separated woman would rarely leave a wife to set up house with his lover or make financial contributions to her on more than a sporadic basis. While sexual opportunities for women existed in the packing plants, affairs seldom resulted in permanent unions. Women who became involved with male supervisors were particularly vulnerable, since the end of a relationship or a woman's pregnancy could result in the loss of her job. Sexual opportunity did not guarantee women social empowerment.

Nonetheless, from 1973 to 1988, the proletarianization of women in the fruit-export economy significantly altered the parameters of female subordination and the nature of violence that men employed to ensure it. Female wage work and consumerism offered women new spaces of authority, even if such authority did not free women either from poverty or from male dominance generally. Domestic conflict over women's wages and work schedules, men's inadequacy as providers, and *women's*—as opposed to men's—supposed sexual freedom reflected the social stress implicit in men's changing ability "to be men" in ways enabled in the 1960s. They also indicated women's heightened willingness to use new opportunities as leverage against male authority.

The point is not that military rule "improved women's lives." It did not. The replacement of permanent jobs with temporary ones, the overt dependency of workers on inadequate wages, the termination of social welfare programs, and the military regime's brutal hostility to popular mobilization all made the survival of rural families—and, thus, of women in particular—extremely precarious. If women successfully wrested more bargaining power from husbands within their families, they did so under circumstances that made life increasingly difficult. The relative amelioration of female subordination to men was not a feminist windfall of authoritarianism. Both women's wage work and female community activism developed in contradiction to the dictatorship's efforts to depoliticize all workers and to domesticate women in particular. It was not low-wage jobs, family breakdown, and state repression that were "good" for women, but women's access to work, the undercutting of the validation for male-headed and male-dominated families, and women's resistance to new forms of class exploitation and political oppression.

Conclusion

This chapter has focused on the underlying bases of wife-beating and how they relate to men's and women's changing positions in the workplace and family. I have argued that conjugal violence must be considered historically as a shifting relation of power between husbands and wives, rather than as an ever-present pathology of patriarchal societies. Wife-beating is primarily a political issue that stems not from the depravity of individual men, but from the way in which material and cultural factors position men and women differently and unequally within society.

In stressing a connection between violence/sexual control and women's general subordination to men, I suggest that further research is needed on conflict between men and women in general, and on sexuality in particular, if we are to understand gender relations in historical terms. Sexuality is crucial to understanding gender conflict, because it constitutes one of the main loci of male and female interaction and provides the social justification for other forms of gendered behavior. Masculine and feminine norms are defined in sexual terms and in relation to one another. Women's social subordination is rooted in male sexual dominance and cannot be understood without addressing the sexual practices and ideologies that mediate this relationship.

Exploring the historical relationship between violence and sexuality is complex. It can, and should, take multiple forms. Men's use of violence, or the threat of violence, to control women's sexuality is not limited to conjugal relations. Conflict and issues of sexual domination are also present in nonconjugal family relations (between fathers and daughters, for example), in relationships between male employers and female workers, and in interactions between nonmarried or noncohabiting men and women of the same class. Men do not invent ways to dominate women, but act within the parameters of proper male behavior established by state policy, religious ideology, and community tradition. Nor are women simple victims. As this chapter demonstrates, women exercise considerable agency both in their response to violence and in their innovation on sexual practice.

I emphasize the need to study the adversarial nature of gender relations within family life, not because husbands and wives are always at odds, but because conflict—violent or not—allows us to consider the power dynamics of conjugal relations. Marriage and cohabitation also involve high degrees of cooperation and consent between spouses. Agreement may outweigh disagreement, and not all dissent ends in violence. Yet much of marriage and family life fundamentally involves collaboration between unequal partners, not simply partners with different roles. Historicizing domestic violence allows us to interrogate the bases of this inequality and the way in which it is negotiated, contested, and transformed.

Notes

All translations are the author's.

1 Author's notes from the Primer Encuentro Nacional de la Mujer Temporera, sponsored by the Comisión Nacional Campesina at Canelo de Nos, Santiago, Chile, June 6–8, 1993.

Loosely translated, *patrón* is the Spanish word for *boss*. In rural Chile, however, this word takes its specific meaning from the class relations of the agrarian hacienda society, in which patrón refers to a wealthy landowner who commands authority over a servile labor force. In this context, *patrón* connotes *master* as well as *boss*.

2   In social and labor histories, several authors mention conjugal violence as commonplace in rural and urban society throughout the nineteenth and twentieth centuries. See, for example, Gabriel Salazár, *Labradores, peones, y proletarios: Formación y crisis de la sociedad popular chilena del siglo 19* (Santiago: SUR, 1986); and Peter DeShazo, *Urban Workers and Labor Unions in Chile, 1902–1927* (Madison: University of Wisconsin Press, 1983).

3   Historical studies of violence against women are still quite rare. This chapter is particularly indebted to the pathbreaking works of U.S. historian Linda Gordon on family violence in working-class Boston: *Heroes of Their Own Lives: The Politics and History of Family Violence* (New York: Penguin Press, 1988); and Brazilian historian Rachel Soihet on women and violence in turn-of-the-century Rio de Janeiro, *Condição feminina e formas de violência: Mulheres pobres e ordem social, 1890–1920, Rio de Janeiro* (Rio de Janeiro: Forense Universitária, 1989). Both Gordon and Soihet address multiple forms of family violence, including women's abuse of children and father-daughter incest, as well as wife-beating.

4   *Censos agropecuarios* (Santiago: INE, 1954–1955 and 1964–1965).

5   Author's study of Fichas de Expropriación, San Felipe–Los Andes, Ex-Corporación de la Reforma Agraria, 1966–1978, Sociedad Agropecuaria y Ganadera, Santiago. The Chilean Agrarian Reform technically began during the Conservative and Liberal Party government of Jorge Alessandri, 1958–1964. The first law giving the state extensive rights to expropriate private property was passed in 1962. However, the Alessandri administration was firmly opposed to widespread land reform and expropriated merely 60,000 hectares during its six-year tenure. Significant expropriation and redistribution projects only began under the Christian Democrats after 1964.

6   Comisión Central Mixta de Sueldos, *Estadísticas laborales* (Santiago: INE, 1976), p. 41.

7   For a discussion of the campesino labor movement during the Agrarian Reform see Brian Loveman, *Struggle in the Countryside* (Bloomington: University of Indiana Press, 1976); and Almino Affonso, Sergio Gómez, Emilio Klein, and Pablo Ramírez, *Movimiento campesino chileno* (Santiago: ICIRA, 1970).

8   Since the mid-1970s, fruit exports have constituted Chile's third leading source of foreign currency, ranking behind copper and lumber. The most important fruit export was and is table grapes, nearly 80 percent of which have been sold to the United States. For a description of the emergence of the fruit-export economy in Aconcagua see Daniel Rodríguez and Sílvia Venegas, *De praderas a parronales: Un estudio sobre la estructura agraria y mercado laboral en el valle de Aconcagua* (Santiago: GEA, 1990).

9   Gonzalo Falabella, "Trabajo temporal y desorganización social," *Proposiciones,* no. 21 (1992): pp. 65–78; and Ximena Valdés, "Feminizacíon del mercado de tra-

bajo agrícola: Las temporeras," in *Mundo de mujer: Continuidad y cambio* (Santiago: CEM, 1988).

10 *Registro de Crímenes,* San Felipe Juzgado de Crimen, San Felipe. Chilean court cases involving conjugal violence are placed in the broader category of "woundings" (*lesiones*). By examining individual cases, I found that 127 of the available 168 cases involved poor rural women filing charges against legal husbands or common-law husbands (*convivientes*). The balance of cases not available for study had been lost, misfiled, or partially destroyed.

11 For purposes of privacy, the names of all persons cited in this chapter have been changed.

12 I conducted interviews with a wide range of campesinos: single and married men and women, people who had been working adults during the Agrarian Reform, people who were workers primarily during the 1970s and 1980s, former members of Agrarian Reform Production Units, subsistence farmers, small farmers, fruit workers, and members of all political factions.

13 Between 1964 and September 1973, the state expropriated 157,462 hectares in the Department of San Felipe. This accounted for 50 percent of all irrigated agricultural land and 66 percent of all arid, nonirrigated land in the department (Fichas de Expropriación and Roles de Impuestos Internos, Ex-Corporación de la Reforma Agraria, 1960–1973, Sociedad Agropecuaria y Granadera, Santiago).

During the Agrarian Reform, most expropriated lands were organized into Agrarian Reform Production Units known as *asentamientos* (settlements). An asentamiento consisted of one or more former haciendas. Its land legally belonged to the state and was farmed and coadministrated by former inquilinos and other workers who were selected to be *asentados* (seated members). In 1971 the Popular Unity (UP) government established a new type of Agrarian Reform Production Unit called the Centro de Reforma Agraria (CERA, or Agrarian Reform Center). The CERA was a larger unit intended to take advantage of economies of scale and to be a building block for socialism. Like asentamientos, CERAS were legally defined as transitional units, and their ultimate form of land tenure was left purposely ambiguous. However, there was strong pressure within the UP government to maintain CERAS permanently as collectively farmed entities.

14 Between 1964 and 1973, membership in rural labor unions leapt from a few thousand to roughly 250,000, or approximately 65 percent of the rural labor force (Luís Salinas, *Trayectoria de la organización campesina* [Santiago: AGRA, 1985]). The 1967 passage of the Law of Campesino Unionization (Law 16.250) greatly facilitated the mobilization of the rural poor. Law 16.250 overturned legislation dating from the 1940s that, in practice, had made rural unions illegal. Law 16.250 also created a mechanism for financing unions by requiring both employers and workers to contribute to a national unionization fund.

15 In 1960, the illiteracy rate in rural Aconcagua was 48 percent. In 1970, it was 20 percent (*Censo de población y vivienda: Aconcagua* [Santiago: INE, 1960 and 1970]). In

1965, the infant mortality rate in San Felipe was 89.5 deaths per 1,000 live births. In 1973, this figure had fallen to 67.7 deaths per 1,000 live births (*Defunciones y causes de muerte* [San Felipe: SNS San Felipe–Los Andes, 1988]).

16   Membership in asentamientos was determined by an elaborate point system in which applicants were weighted by such factors as marital status, the number of dependents, occupation (with preference given to inquilinos and permanent workers), and specific skills in mechanics, tractor driving, fruit cultivation, and irrigation. The vast majority of asentamiento members were men who had been permanently employed on expropriated estates.

17   Estimates of the number of rural workers who were formally included in the Reformed Sector as full members of Agrarian Reform Production Units vary widely. In one of the most respected studies of the Chilean Agrarian Reform, Salon Barraclough and J. A. Fernández estimate that less than 20 percent of rural workers in the Central Valley ever belonged to Agrarian Reform Production Units. See the summary of Barraclough and Fernández in Lorenzo Caballero, "The Reformed Units" (Swedish University of Agriculture, Uppsala, 1975, Collection of the University of Wisconsin at Madison Land Tenure Center, photocopy).

18   In the 1960s, the Department of San Felipe was divided into five smaller administrative units called *comunas*. Each comuna consisted of a central urban center or town and the surrounding rural areas, both of which were overseen by a local council and mayor. The comunas comprising the Department of San Felipe were Santa María, Putaendo, Panquehue, Catemu, and San Felipe.

19   Case file S350;26768, San Felipe Juzgado de Crimen, 1968.

20   Case file B27;27615, San Felipe Juzgado de Crimen, 1970.

21   Oral history of Anita Herrera, Santa María, April 12, 1993.

22   Case file S319;25030, San Felipe Juzgado de Crimen, 1965.

23   Oral history of Sonia Cardanes, Santa María, April 12, 1993.

24   Oral sources.

25   *Censo agropecuario: Aconcagua* (Santiago: INE, 1964–1965).

26   In 1960, 18 percent of women over age fifteen were listed as economically active in the Department of San Felipe. In the comunas, excluding the urban center of San Felipe itself, this figure was 12 percent. Of those women employed in the province of Aconcagua, 40 percent were listed as domestic servants, 14 percent as weavers or seamstresses, 7 percent as venders, and 9 percent as agricultural workers (*Censo de población y vivienda: Aconcagua,* 1960). In 1964, rural women in San Felipe comprised 17 percent of the seasonal agricultural workforce (workers hired for between one and six months annually), but fully half of these female workers were hired for less than three months annually (*Censo agropecuario: Aconcagua*).

For discussions of men's and women's different positions within the hacienda economy on the eve of Agrarian Reform see Ximena Valdés, *La posición de la mujer en la hacienda* (Santiago: CEM, 1988); Rafael Baroana and Ximena Aranda, *El valle de Putaendo: Estudio agrícola* (Santiago: Instituto de Geografía de la Universidad de Chile, 1960); and Ximena Aranda, *Mujer, familia, y sociedad rural: El valle de Putaendo* (Santiago: Ford Foundation, 1981).

27   Cuadro 30, *Censo de población y vivienda: Aconcagua,* 1960.

28   Through the Institute for the Development of Agriculture and Livestock, a subdepartment of the Ministry of Agriculture, the state financed various income-generating projects that campesina women could operate out of their homes. These included raising chickens and rabbits, running small restaurants, and commercializing women's weaving and knitting production. In addition, through the Ministry of the Interior, the state facilitated the financing of over one thousand sewing machiens to women in San Felipe and its neighboring Department of Los Andes. The sewing machines were intended both to help women meet their families' clothing needs and to encourage women to make clothing and handicrafts for sale.

29   *Censo agropecuario: Aconcagua,* 1974–1975.

30   Oral history of Isabel Antimán, Santa María, October 15, 1992.

31   On women's exclusion from the campesino labor movement during the Agrarian Reform see Ximena Valdés, "Hacía la generización de las demandas de las trabajadoras del agro," and Pilar Campana, "La problemática de la organización de la mujer rural en Chile," *Agricultura y Sociedad,* Santiago, May 1987; Patricia Garret, "La reforma agraria: Organización y participación de la mujer en Chile, 1964–1973," in *Las trabajadoras del agro,* ed. Magdalena León (Bogotá: ACEP, 1982).

32   Throughout the Agrarian Reform, the campesino labor movement was ideologically diverse and organized along distinct political lines. The heavy patronage by both the Christian Democratic and the Popular Unity governments of unions sharing their respective political visions meant that Chilean rural unions were beholden more to political parties than to the state. However, all political tendencies within the rural labor movement shared the idea that the purpose of Agrarian Reform was to uplift campesino men from a state of oppressive dependence into one of economic independence and political participation. The metaphor of transforming "children into men" was invoked repeatedly by various union newspapers and rural labor leaders.

33   Press statement of Rafael Moreno, CORA President, reprinted in *La Nación,* July 28, 1967, p. 4.

34   Press statement of President Salvador Allende Gossens, reprinted in *La Nación,* March 14, 1972, p. 13.

35   For a discussion of Mothers' Centers see Edda Gaviola, Lorella Lopresti, and Claudia Rojas, "Chile, Centros de Madres: La mujer popular en movimiento?" in *Nuestra memoria, nuestro futuro* (Santiago: ISIS, 1988).

36   Case file S356;27066, San Felipe Juzgado de Crimen, 1969.

37   Oral history of Elena Vera, Putaendo, June 4, 1993.

38   Various oral sources.

39   Untitled cueca rhythm dating from the late 1950s. Performed and explained by Anita Herrera and Ramón Martínez, Santa María, September 18, 1993.

40   Various oral histories, including Emilio Toledo, Santa María, May 25, 1993; Daniel Cordova, Panquehue, April 12, 1993; Raúl Flores, Santa María, February 14, 1993; and Robinson Lira, Santiago, November 2, 1992.

41   Oral histories of Carlos García, Putaendo, June 13, 1993; Emilio Toledo; Raúl Flores; and Pedro Muñoz, Catemu, June 14, 1993.

42   For example, see *Tierra y Libertad,* April (official paper of the independent Catholic-affiliated Union of Christian Campesinos); and *El Siglo,* April 23, 1968, and May 5, 1972 (national daily).

43   Oral histories of Pedro Reyes, San Esteben, March 11, 1993; and Juan Plaza, San Felipe, October 20, 1992.

44   In oral histories, both men and women recalled the Agrarian Reform as a time of increased tension in their marriages. Men complained that their wives became jealous of their heightened political obligations outside the home and, in particular, of their overnight stays at union conferences, etc. While only a few men openly acknowledged that they became sexually involved with other women during these periods, they spoke at length about their friends and union comrades who did succumb to such "temptation and disorder."

   Women, on the other hand, insisted that their husbands' infidelity while engaged in "political work" was extremely widespread, and a majority claimed to have had personal experience with this in their own relationships. Interestingly, in three interviews, women who claimed that their husbands took permanent lovers during the Agrarian Reform were married to men who, in separate interviews, professed their own fidelity and elaborated on the affair of a specific "friend."

45   Oral history of Carlos García, Putaendo, June 14, 1993.

46   Oral history of Ana Savedra, San Felipe, April 15, 1993.

47   Oral history of Juan Plaza, San Felipe, May 20, 1993.

48   Oral history of Anita Herrera.

49   For an overview of the development of the fruit-export industry see María Elena Cruz and Cecilia Leiva, *La fruticultura en Chile despúes de la reforma agraria* (Santiago: GIA, 1982); Jaime Crispi, "Neo-liberalismo y campesinado en Chile," working paper no. 5 (Santiago: GIA, 1981); and Rodríguez and Venegas, *De praderas a parronales.*

50   *Registro de Crimenes,* San Felipe Juzgado de Crimen.

51   Case file I15;30964, San Felipe Juzgado de Crimen, 1977.

52   Case file S545;39166xB, San Felipe Juzgado de Crimen, 1986.

53   For a discussion of this process in San Felipe see María Elena Cruz and Cecilia

Leiva, *La fruticultura en Chile despúes de 1973: Una area privilegiada de expansión del capitalismo* (Santiago: GIA, 1981).

54 Falabella, "Trabajo temporal." The literature on the social and economic impact of the fruit industry in Chile is rich and extensive. Because of the importance of Aconcagua to national production, many studies are specifically about San Felipe. See Rodríguez and Venegas, *De praderas a parronales;* Sílvia Venegas, *Una gota al día . . . un chorro al año: El impacto social de la expansión frutícola* (Santiago: GEA, 1992); and Sergio Gómez and Jorge Echenique, *La agricultura chilena: Las dos caras de la modernización* (Santiago: FLACSO, 1988).

55 *Directorio agro-industrial frutícola de Chile* (Santiago: CIREN, 1988).

56 Estimates were calculated from production levels of individual packings, recorded in *Directorio agro-industrial frutícola de Chile,* 1979, 1983, 1984, 1988, and 1993. To date, there is no published statistical record of the number of packing temporeros by region, province, or comuna in Chile. I calculated these figures by dividing a packing's total annual production by a modest estimate of the average production levels of individual workers. These figures may significantly underestimate the number of women employed.

57 For a discussion of employer attitudes toward female fruit workers see Julia Medel R., Soledad Olivos M., and Veronica Riquelme G., *Las temporeras y su visión del trabajo* (Santiago: Centro de Estudios de la Mujer, 1989).

58 Fruit production involves a strict sexual division of labor. Men largely perform planting, harvesting, and cultivation tasks in orchards and vineyards. Women work primarily in the fruit-processing plants, where they clean, disinfect, weigh, wrap, and box fruits for export. Smaller numbers of women also work in the orchards and vineyards as pruners and harvesters. In such cases, most female field workers labor in separate teams from those of men and are assigned to the "lighter" and more "detail-work-requiring" produce such as almonds, olives, and tomatoes. Small numbers of men are also employed in the fruit-packing plants in the capacity of plant supervisors, mechanics, and machine operators.

59 There is a growing literature on the impact of the fruit industry on sexual divisions of labor and women's position in society. For example, see Ximena Valdés, "Feminizacíon del mercado de trabajo agrícola: Las temporeras," in *Mundo de mujer: Continuidad y cambio* (Santiago: CEM, 1988); Valdés, *Mujer, trabajo, y medio ambiente* (Santiago: CEM, 1991); Gonzalo Falabella, "Organizarse y sobrevivir: Democracia y sindicalización en Santa María" (paper presented at the Forty-seventh Americanist Congress, New Orleans, July 1991); and María Soledad Lago, "The Neo-Liberal Model in Chile," in *Rural Women and State Policy,* ed. Carmen Diana Deere and Magdalena León (Boulder, Colo.: Westview Press, 1987).

60 On Centros de Madres under military rule see Teresa Valdés, Marisa Weinstein, María Isabel Toledo, and Lilian Letelier, "Centros de Madres, 1973–1989: Solo disciplinamiento?" (Santiago: FLACSO, 1989).

61 Oral history of María Toledo, Santa María, October 26, 1992. María's claim that

rural women worked on the haciendas prior to the development of the fruit-export industry is a reference to women's full-time responsibilities for non-remunerated subsistence cultivation on family plots and women's seasonal wage employment during harvests.

62   Oral history of Elena Muñoz, Santa María, May 31, 1993.

63   Oral history of Claudia Muñoz León, San Esteben, June 7, 1993.

64   Oral history of María Toledo.

65   Oral history of Elena Muñoz.

66   Estimates of Servicio Nacional de la Mujer for the 1980s are quoted from Venegas, *Una gota al día.*

67   For a discussion of rural women's participation in forms of popular mobilization during the 1980s see Falabella, "Organizarse y sobrevivir"; Ximena Valdés, "Entre la crisis de la uva y la esperanza en crisis" (work presented at the Forty-seventh Americanist Congress, New Orleans, July 1991); Valdés, "Una experiencia de organización autónoma de mujeres del campo," in *Cuadernos de la mujer del campo* (Santiago: GIA, 1983); María Soledad Lago and Carlota Olavarría, *La participación de la mujer en las economías campesinas: Un estudio de casos en dos comunas frutícolas* (Santiago: GIA, 1981); and Veronica Oxman, "La participación de la mujer campesina en organizaciones," unpublished manuscript, courtesy of ISIS-Santiago, 1983.

68   Oral history of Rosa Tolmo, Santa María, June 4, 1992.

69   Oral history of Elena Vera, Putaendo, June 14, 1993.

70   Calculating exact wage earnings in packings is almost impossible, since employers pay slightly different piece rates and because earnings are determined by harvest production levels and a worker's individual productivity. Although the earning power of temporeras is greatly debated, most investigators and all campesino labor confederations argue that temporeras earn only slightly above official minimum wage rates. Since women work in packings or other agricultural labor for between three and six months annually, I estimated women's yearly earnings between 1974 and 1988 by multiplying the official minimum monthly wage by six. For official minimum wages see Comisión Central Mixta de Sueldos, *Estadísticas laborales.* This may significantly overestimate the annual earnings of most temporeras.

Oral History, Identity Formation, and Working-Class Mobilization

JOHN D. FRENCH AND DANIEL JAMES

The goal of this volume has been to broaden labor history by aiming for a fullness of representation of all spheres and dimensions of the lives of women workers, including women's participation in trade union and political party activity. As Farnsworth-Alvear suggests in a different context, labor historians only achieve greater understanding when they refuse to flatten working people's interactions solely "into meanings derived from their subaltern status." Rather than forcing every investigation into a resistance/accommodation dichotomy, she suggests, they should more fully explore "the contradictions inherent in their being human beings," whether at work or at home.[1]

To incorporate the subjective dimension into historical explanation requires a shift in the nature of the sources used, the tools with which they are approached, and the questions asked of them.[2] French and Cluff's brief discussion of the neglected topic of women's voting, for example, suggests that much can be learned about women's electoral behavior in working-class communities through the creative use of female voter registration statistics.[3] And the Tinsman and Klubock chapters in this volume likewise demonstrate that court records about domestic violence can be used to deepen our understanding of such "traditional" labor history categories as proletarianization, class formation, and working-class mobilization. With his skillful use of oral and folkloric sources, Klubock offers new perspectives on the history of masculinity and male identity among Latin American workers, while Farnsworth-Alvear and Lobato show perspicacity in their combination of oral testimony with factory personnel and disciplinary records.

Oral sources occupy pride of place in this collection, which is not surprising given the crucial role that oral testimony has played in rescuing the hidden voices suppressed in other types of historical sources.[4] In studying women workers, oral sources have been used largely to document the lives of those doubly silenced by virtue of their class and gender. This impulse has uneasily coexisted with an impoverished use of oral testimony primarily as a source of additional "data" to supplement "direct evidence" or to add human flavoring to the standard narrative.

The last ten years have seen important theoretical and methodological breakthroughs in the use of oral history. As can be seen in this volume, few today would subscribe to the naive fiction that oral history allows the analyst to achieve direct or unmediated access to the thoughts, feelings, desires, and aspirations of those they study. This volume does, however, demonstrate the many ways that oral history can be used to deepen our understanding of the complex nature of individual and collective consciousness and identity.

We have shown, for example, how working-class women take elements of a hegemonic discourse that is strongly gendered in male terms, and deploy them creatively to contest the inequalities they face as women. This enables them to better cope with the tensions and anxieties produced by the discrepancy between lived experience and formal rhetoric, between material conditions and aspirations. As Farnsworth-Alvear suggests, "prescriptions are not descriptions," and even description does not tell us how the individuals involved feel about their roles and lives. As she and other contributors show, the process of manipulating dominant cultural values and gender constructs is a profoundly conflicted one whose traces can be found in the contradictions, gaps, and silences present in oral testimony.[5]

The contributions to this volume take different approaches to the generation of oral testimony and its analysis. Lobato and Tinsman, for example, use oral sources to generate observations about specific issues. While they generalize from the universe of oral histories they have collected, Veccia and Farnsworth-Alvear explore the individual life stories of a smaller group of women workers in more detail. Their chapters on São Paulo and Medellín offer an ethnographic richness of detail about women's individual lives and experiences and show the complicated mixture of love and resentment, solidarity and rivalry, that characterizes interpersonal relations in the family and on the shop floor. The net effect is to shatter the implied homogeneity of pre-existing categories such as "workers," "women workers," or "women," with their implied corollary that members of the category feel or respond in uniform ways.

Levenson-Estrada offers a sensitive meditation on the biographical details that emerged from her interviews with labor activist Sonia Oliva. Wrestling with pressing questions facing feminist and union activists, she places Oliva's story within the context of her fellow female textile workers, her male union counterparts, and the urban working-class community from which they come. More strikingly still, she offers a depth of psychological insight that suggests the real possibility of achieving a socially committed existentialist labor history.

Yet Levenson-Estrada does not focus primarily on the autobiographical narrative as text for what it could reveal about other aspects of Oliva's consciousness. It is precisely this approach that distinguishes the chapters by James and Farnsworth-Alvear, who are acutely aware that the women being interviewed bring their own agendas to the interaction; they are not just informants but storytellers. As Farnsworth-Alvear shows for Medellín, the stories told by these women workers navigate "between the conventional signposts of compañerismo, obedience, and rebelliousness." She also shows, however, that the stories are not univocal in their meaning. Even "tales of resistance against ingrained stereotypes of femininity" may be placed alongside "narratives of obedience" and conformity.

The advantages of paying attention to the narrative form of an oral testimony can be shown by examining a wonderful story told to Theresa Veccia by dona Ermínia Albertini. Discussing her first job at age eleven, at a distant cracker factory, Albertini offers a self-dramatization that adheres to the conventions of traditional melodrama. Indeed, her story is Dickensian in its documentation of employer avarice and heartlessness in dealing with the most vulnerable of all workers, children. Her narrative tells of starving thirteen-year-old girls forbidden by a Scrooge-like employer from eating the crackers they make. Moreover, the narrative even highlights the action of a good soul, the factory's baker, who at Christmastime makes them a *panettone* cake from leftovers. These events unfold within a narrative that ends, as she has told us at the outset, with the employer firing Albertini and her sisters because her mother, who has regularly sent them to work at four in the morning, acts one day to protect them by not allowing them to depart during a powerful rainstorm.

The form of an oral narrative, as James suggests, is as significant as the content. It is only at the end of Albertini's narrative that she suddenly undercuts the familiar expectations about child labor that she has created through her use of the melodramatic form. While we expect to discover that this early experience has awakened a deep sense of class antagonism in the young girl, Albertini now reveals that her anger and indignation came from her reinterpretation of the experience years later. "At the time, I didn't see it. I was a young girl. I wasn't aware of what was going on. I wanted to have fun, right? That's what I wanted, to have fun." In a sense, she has now problematized the narrator, herself, by revealing that her own story is an interpretation of her experience rather than a direct expression of it; thus spawning a double hermeneutical process involving both the life story–teller and the historian.

Albertini's confession reminds us of the dangers that we face as historians. The oral historian must bear in mind, as James suggests, that "if oral testimony is indeed a window onto the subjective in history, the cultural, social, and ideological universe of historical actors, then it must be said that the view it affords is not a transparent one that simply reflects thoughts and feelings as they really were/are." The unexpected twist in Albertini's story also reminds historians who lack or eschew oral sources of the ease with which meaning is often inferred in an unself-conscious fashion from known "facts." When a historian refers to child labor, for example, the reference carries with it a set of connotations including culturally enshrined images of suffering children and lost childhoods. Consciously or unconsciously, this established trope informs our own and our readers' understanding of the "meaning" of child labor, even for the children who experience it.

The way that Albertini ends her story reflects her unwillingness to allow her own retrospective anger and indignation at her childhood experience to erase how she experienced it as a young girl. In taking this stance, she illustrates the reality of agency and the limits of determination. In the simplified Sartrean formula, you are not what is done to you but what you do with what is done to you.[6] This is true not only at the moment of the experience itself but over the course of your life, since you may come, at a later point, to alter the meaning you ascribe to what has happened to you.

These insights lead us directly to the question of human agency and the constitution of identity. Oral sources are especially fruitful in this regard, because they reveal, to any critical analyst, that identity is not univocal and that consciousness consists of multiple, parallel, and competing claims to identity. The role of the *ama de casa* (housewife), one of the most common of women's identities, can prove illuminating in this regard. As has been shown, the working-class woman in Latin America confronts a powerful gendered discourse that posits her identity in terms of her domestic function as daughter, wife, and mother.[7] "What women do outside the home remains suspect," Levenson-Estrada reports, and "they earn status and a sense of worth for what they accomplish within it." Veccia echoes this: "An adult woman's sense of identity was, in fact, intimately linked to the way she executed the domestic labor that was culturally defined as women's work."

A working-class woman could not easily escape the daily fight against dirt or the tyranny exerted by the powerful expectations that were associated with it. Whether she resisted housework or embraced it, she would still find herself defined from the outside as either a good or a bad housewife/woman. As an individual, she had to come to terms with this limit on her freedom, and in doing so she might choose, whether occasionally or in a more enduring fashion, to make of her household drudgery a source of pride, even though society devalues the very domestic role that it condemns her to perform. Veccia offers a wonderful quote in this regard from a woman who recalls the domestic apprenticeship she served with her mother: "Every week we scoured the aluminum pots and pans. Because we had a shelf up on the wall where we put them for everyone to see. They looked so pretty, the aluminum shined so bright that the pans looked like they were made of silver."[8]

Identity is above all a relational phenomenon or category, a process bound up with culture and material conditions. Identity can only become real within the context of groups, such as family, factory, community, gender, class, region, or nation. This is true because the individual's freedom to choose is also limited by the social legibility, the social credibility, of the identities that one can claim within the context of both the wider world and the groups to which one belongs. Identity formation, in other words, is never purely arbitrary but is a socially contingent and iterative posture that must be researched with an eye to regularities as well as variation. As Emília Viotti da Costa has said,

> Identities, language, and meanings are products of social interaction, which takes place within a specific system of social relations and power, with its own rituals, protocols, and sanctions. The material conditions of people's lives, the way human and ecological resources are utilized and distributed, the concrete ways power is exerted, are as important in shaping identities, defining language, and creating meanings, as the social codes that mediate experience or the conventions used to define what is real. In fact, material conditions and symbolic systems are intimately connected.[9]

The aim of this endeavor should be to establish a more sophisticated understanding of how consciousness operates and how identity is formed within the context of material conditions and structures of power that limit and, to that extent, determine its outcomes. Moreover, claims to identity are always linked to conflict, "difference," and clashing interests, and they acquire credibility and stability to the extent to which they fit the material and ideational world in which they are enmeshed.[10]

Thus there are systemic and not just random linkages between material reality, human agents, and claimed identities, linkages that are revealed, affirmed, or contested through social interaction (whether in the form of acts or speech acts). Identities crystallize, in other words, through a material historical process in which individuals come to recognize shared interests based on like circumstances in juxtaposition to unlike others. The study of female and male workers is thus incomplete unless one takes political economy and legal and institutional structures fully into account; that is, the material manifestations of a given society's structure of power that delineate the boundaries between superordinate and subordinate roles and identities.[11]

This model of identity formation has emerged precisely from an attempt to gender labor history by highlighting the importance of discursive constructions of meaning without reducing reality to an agentless circular logic of abstract categories.[12] The relevance of this approach can best be demonstrated through a gendered examination of the role of women in the trade union and political struggles of workers. The primary interest of traditional labor history, after all, has always been in workers as a collective subject expressed through and embodied in trade unions and political parties. Thus it was not surprising that women "naturally" disappeared as an important focus of scholarly attention; after all, the majority of women were not activists and thus could be safely ignored (along with the majority of male workers, we might add). Within the same logic, this approach to labor history was impoverished by a narrowness of focus that ignored the personal aspects of workers' lives, both male and female.

Before the feminist second wave of the 1960s, the subject of women workers in the class struggle, although acknowledged, was treated as of secondary importance and dealt with in a sexist fashion: women workers and working-class women in particular were most often viewed as a "problem," as a weak link, as "carriers of conservative ideas and habits" within the working class (in a 1970 quote from a Brazilian communist leader quoted by French and Cluff). In treating "class consciousness" as a known deductive category, as French and Cluff observe, it was hard for scholars not "to adopt a crude typology of 'class-conscious' or 'non-class-conscious' workers, the latter being a residual category to which women and other 'failed' or 'backward' workers are relegated."

Breaking with this paradigm, French and Cluff, James, Levenson-Estrada, and Klubock each investigate the impact of female and, to a lesser extent, male identities on class mobilization and trade union activism. How, in other words, does gender affect workers' struggles, and how do they in turn impact gender relations? Addressing women's sociopolitical participation in the community, the union, and electoral politics, French and Cluff offer the hypothesis that "the greater the extent, depth, and intensity of working-class mobilization, the greater the involvement and visibility of working-class women, housewives as well as women workers." In addition, they suggest that "at the mass level, the broader assertion of a common class identity served to lessen resistance to innovation and changes in consciousness, including ideas about gender."

In their examination of the community dynamics of the strikes of early 1946, French and Cluff show that the postwar upsurge of industrial militancy and political radicalism in São Paulo opened the door for the incorporation of housewives into struggle and change. In supporting their husbands during these strikes, they suggest, even "women who were conservative about matters of gender roles could still feel comfortable with this small expansion of their family role as wives 'loyal' to their husbands." For other working-class women, however, the years 1945–1947 offered a dramatic opportunity to break with "traditional" roles by entering into activism in the male-dominated public sphere at the very moment when women and workers in Brazil first gained the effective right to vote.[13]

The existing literature on women's trade union activism, as summarized by French and Cluff, has found that women's participation is highest during moments of intense class mobilizations such as strikes, while "women have been largely absent from the ongoing organizational activities of the workers' movement." Although active at the peaks of intense working-class mobilization, women were "more likely to quickly abandon systematic trade union work than were men in the aftermath."

The controversy has revolved around how one is to interpret these findings. Is the behavior of women workers fundamentally different from that of male workers? And if so, how and why? In answering these questions, one might be tempted to deny that such observations contain any truth at all. It could be that these claims about lesser female union participation are in fact a sexist libel on women workers by male trade union and scholarly establishments that seek to erase the reality of women's vanguard role within the working class.[14] One might then explain women's diminutive role in union leadership and ongoing labor militancy as the by-product of exclusion by an overwhelmingly male leadership cadre.

The observations of scholars and women working-class activists, however, suggest that such an explanation is too facile, and the examination of the lives of women working-class activists in this volume by James and

Levenson-Estrada suggests the need for a more gender-conscious approach to this subject. Before we turn to their studies of María Roldán and Sonia Oliva, respectively, it is important to emphasize, as do French and Cluff, that we are dealing in part with an illusion of fundamental male/female difference due to a process of gender-biased generalization. For too long analysts have drawn conclusions about the nature of women workers' consciousness without applying the same standard to male workers. Scholars, for example, have routinely offered high turnover rates among women in the factories as part of their explanation for female "passivity." Yet they have not offered similar generalizations about *male* workers who also often came and went without the "labor commitment" idealized by the U.S. industrial sociologists of the 1950s.[15] In addition, most male workers have, like women, been unwilling to enter into conflict with their employers most of the time, and only a small minority of men have ever become active in union affairs on an ongoing basis. When looked at statistically, in other words, the distinctions between male and female workers are a matter of degree. As French and Cluff note, "the widespread pattern of [women's] intense yet intermittent participation is not unique to women but rather mirrors in an exaggerated way the ups and downs of male working-class participation as well."

The essays by French and Cluff, James, and Levenson-Estrada in this volume explore the dynamics of women's role as working-class leaders. Both the cases of the Brazilian Carmen Savietto (French and Cluff) and the Argentine María Roldán (James) stem from the immediate post–World War II years, when workers in both countries were drawn into trade union and political activity on an unprecedented scale. As French and Cluff suggest, the dynamics of women's sociopolitical participation emerge more clearly in such unusual periods of popular ferment. This is equally true for the Guatemalan Sonia Oliva, who became an activist during the popular upsurge that swept Central America in the 1970s, when the prospect of popular revolutionary victory seemed on the horizon.[15]

While French and Cluff were limited to written sources, James and Levenson-Estrada were able to draw on interviews with two women labor activists: a married woman drawn into activity in the 1940s during her thirties (Roldán), and a young single woman who became active in the 1970s during her twenties (Oliva). Both women were mothers and labor militants, but each stood in a very different relationship to established gender norms. In many ways, the older, married mother Roldán better captures the prevalent mix of attitudes about gender identified by Levenson-Estrada in her discussion of Oliva's fellow women union members. Like them, Roldán violates female norms of behavior but does so without articulating it at the level of a formal critique. Sonia Oliva, by contrast, represents a working-class feminism whose lonely path is described with empathy by Levenson-Estrada.

James and Levenson-Estrada seek to answer two central questions: What has it taken for women to become labor activists? And what does being a woman mean for a female labor activist? In both cases, it is clear that male-female inequality and patriarchal gender ideology are fundamental factors in explaining women workers' lesser propensity to become union or political activists than men. These chapters break new ground precisely because they explain how these factors shape the process by which some women *do* become activists as well as how those women *experience* that transgressive activist commitment.

James examines the life of Doña María Roldán, a union shop steward at Swift in the 1940s and 1950s and a Peronist militant until her death. During the dramatic years that marked the rise and consolidation of the meatpacking union and its ally Juan Perón, Roldán lived a life of intense political and union participation on the shop floor, in the union hall, and as a Peronist political campaigner not only in Berisso but elsewhere. In a country where women gained the right to vote only in 1947, her intense engagement in the male public sphere underlined her radical difference from other women of her class. She was, as she liked to say, *una mujer atrevida* (a daring woman).

It is tempting to celebrate the activism, class consciousness, and political awareness of Roldán by allowing her to metonymically stand in for her fellow working women. Roldán's trajectory looks radically different, however, if we understand that she was not only defined by her union or political identity but was also part of a historically specific, gendered working-class culture. She shared a common habitus with the nonactive working-class women in Berisso. Despite her heretical status, she reacts to, and works within, the same gender constructs as other women but handles them differently.

If Roldán is looked at as a woman and not just as a union or Peronist activist, her life can in fact tell us much about the factors shaping nonactivist women as well. The story of Roldán's entry into the packing plants offers a clear example. She had lived for ten years in Berisso without working outside the home, which suggests the strength of either her or her husband's rejection of paid employment for wives. Her years as a *doña de casa* were made possible by her husband's relatively well-paid job deboning meat (*depostador*), which also meant that there was no socially accepted "necessity" for her to go to work. The event that eventually led to and justified her entry into the plant was the need to buy medicine for her son, who had polio, but then she continued to work after his death. And when she decided after a decade to leave the plant, and thus her union role, Roldán spoke of her desire to take better care of her other children.[16]

Doña María's narrative of how she became involved in the union is crafted so as to deny any element of conscious initiative on her part. She was recruited, she says, after being approached by union leader Cipriano Reyes, who said, "I come on behalf of your husband, he is already in agreement, and if you want to be the delegate for this section, because you have the qualities, your husband says it is fine." Although we cannot establish the truth of her account, it nonetheless suggests the social conventions within which she operated: it had to be her husband's request to which she acceded, thus denying that her own desire played any role in the decision. Even if this version is a retrospective projection, the device still reveals her defensiveness about what is viewed by others (and perhaps by herself) as transgressive behavior.

Roldán's mention of her husband's approval also echoes French and Cluff's finding that female activists were often recruited from among the wives and daughters of militant workers. As noted in a study of female activists in the São Paulo metalworking industry in the 1980s, "It is hard to find a married woman who is a union activist whose husband is not" also one (cited by French and Cluff). Yet this observation should not be misread, as Levenson-Estrada reminds us, as a statement that all, or even most, male trade unionists allowed or encouraged their wives to become involved in the unions; their preference in most instances was to maintain their women at home away from the fray.

In trying to square her behavior with the gender ideals to which she adhered, Roldán always talked about her activity as a shop floor delegate in maternalist terms, as a means of helping and orienting others.[17] In this way, she legitimated her union activity as an extension of her proper role as a woman. Moreover, this self-representation of her shop floor leadership was quite different from that offered by men, who tended to tell stories about their aggressive defense of workers in "battles" with the employers. These gender-differentiated representations of leadership are no doubt closely linked to the differing styles of shop floor conflict that characterize men and women, as analyzed with such acuity by John Humphrey in the Brazilian case.[18]

The events that precipitated Sonia Oliva's entrance into the leadership of the textile workers union at the ACRICASA factory also illustrate the powerful obstacles that stand in the way of activism by women. As French and Cluff note, women's participation in trade union and political activities was often discouraged "by disapproving parents, husbands, or boyfriends." Indeed, the male union organizers at ACRICASA first approached not Sonia but a married woman, but she resigned the next morning because her mother, husband, and everyone else at home had yelled at her when she told them what she had done. Such social disapproval could even take the form—in an example mentioned by Klubock—of a man beating his wife because she frequented the union hall.

Oliva was thus the second woman to be approached, and her background was broadly similar to those of the women activists discussed by French and Cluff: "Young working women in their mid-twenties who . . . were single, reflecting the fact that a full political life placed demands on individuals that were hard for married women with children to fulfill." Oliva was not married, and this reality was reflected in her matter-of-fact answer to Levenson-Estrada's question of how she got involved: "There was no one at home to stop me, . . . no husband, mother, father, mother-in-law, father-in-law. I was alone." In telling her own story, as Levenson-Estrada notes, Oliva explained "that she had to be 'alone,' outside of normal gender relations, to be an activist. That was *how* she became an activist."

In their struggles in the ACRICASA factory, women union members often violated the norms of "ideal" or "proper" female behavior. Yet most did not avow this transgression in their public discourse as did Oliva, who was acutely aware "of the oppressive nature of gender roles and ideologies." Instead, they lived with "the tension between accepting and rejecting one's 'proper' role, rights, and obligations as a female . . . and it remained a largely unresolved matter." This lack of resolution, Levenson-Estrada suggests, should not be viewed as surprising or discouraging, since "normative gender identities have had time, habit, culture, and social structure on their side, and most intensely, emotions, since most affective relations and families have been built around gender roles. Feminism [in this context] has felt like a threat to love."

The exploration of the subjectivity of women activists by James and Levenson-Estrada suggests that the exceptional cases of activist women cannot be understood without reference to what they share with the nonactivist majority. After all, if it was hard for women to justify entering a factory to work, as we have shown, then it is easy to imagine how difficult it was for a woman to become a public figure in the trade union. Trade union activism, as Levenson-Estrada demonstrates for Guatemala, has a radically different meaning for men than for women. For an individual man, an activist role coincides with the most valued aspects of a discourse of masculinity. For a woman, by contrast, "the personal nonconformism that trade unionism has demanded threatens an important means whereby women have achieved an identity and have received love and status." The story of Sonia Oliva, Levenson-Estrada argues, is that of a rebel against a gender as well as a class hierarchy. "She had to be outside the relations that imprisoned her as a woman in order to live her life as a woman class activist."

For women to be trade unionists, in other words, they "had to carry on two struggles—one against the company and the state, and another against sanctioned models of gender behavior—while men have had to wage the first and not the second." This observation speaks strongly to another marked characteristic of women workers during periods of intense class mobilization. When women workers did join in struggle, as Leite's informants in São Paulo suggested, they were "extremely combative and enter[ed] into the fight with passion, with an immediate involvement even greater than that of men" (cited by French and Cluff). In other words, participation in the class struggle served to empower women in different ways than men. It was the thrill of transgression, of turning things on their head, of letting loose, of breaking away from rigid gender norms that accounts for the enthusiasm and passion that marked women workers' actions when they did join strikes en masse. In São Paulo, for example, women often participated intensely in the picketing that marked the generalized mass strike movements of the post–World War II era. As one male metalworker recalled about 1953, the mass picketers that descended on his factory, mainly women, were angered when the men failed to join them, and they exploited the gender reversal implied by their own actions. Throwing stones at the factory, they taunted the nonstriking men by asking "if they wanted to wear skirts, why don't they wear skirts."[19] When female ACRICASA workers passed nearby nonunion factories, Levenson-Estrada tells us, they too taunted the men for their failure to organize when women had.

Women workers also inverted the conventions of respectability by exploiting male "embarrassment" to win victories in their less dramatic day-to-day struggles in Medellín and Guatemala City. Interviewed by Farnsworth-Alvear, Cristina Monsalve tells a story about a female *vigilanta* (factory matron) who was spreading rumors that Cristina was pregnant (for which she could be fired). Her response, she says, was to go directly to Don Antonio of higher management. "And I took off my apron, . . . and I told him: 'You are a married man, go right ahead, check me, because it's easily known." At the ACRICASA factory, Levenson-Estrada recounts the story of a woman who had been reported to management for the "excessive" length of her lavatory visit. During the ensuing meeting between herself, management, and union representatives, she rushed out and returned with a soiled sanitary napkin, which she placed on the manager's desk: "'If you want to know why I was in the bathroom so long, here's why!' and with this the clocking of workers . . . stopped." On another occasion, a group of young single mothers confronted management over their union's demand that they too receive the paid holiday accorded married mothers. Infuriated, one woman threatened the manager: "'I will lie on your desk and you bring a doctor in here to decide in front of everyone whether I am a mother,' and management, embarrassed, gave in immediately."

Yet the fact that women's activism was a transgression exacted a high price, especially for those individual women who took a stand or assumed a leadership role. "The courage which young women need to make a labor protest," Fiona Wilson wrote in her study of clandestine manufacturing workshops in Michoacán in the late 1980s, "should not be underestimated. Not only can confrontation in the workshop (and in the town) be hurtful and humiliating, taking a case before the authorities in Morelia demands that a young woman [go] . . . into a world of men where the lawyers and public officials share gender, class, and age characteristics with workshop owners. She therefore becomes the 'outsider' breaking many conventions."[20]

This outsider status is reflected in both the anguish about gender exhibited in María Roldán's oral testimony and in the life and struggles of Sonia Oliva. A nontraditional mother, Oliva took her young son Pavel into her world of activism and, by bringing him to work with her, she got the company to open a day care center during the day; later she forced the company to provide such services at night by leaving Pavel at the factory at the end of the day. Such actions by Oliva, it must be emphasized, did not necessarily meet with the approval of her fellow women workers. Although many women may have admired her commitment and audacity, they parted company with Oliva on the issue of her "mothering, [in terms of] *those* maternal politics." In her detailed analysis of the day care issue, Levenson-Estrada offers a suggestive critique of those who have recently emphasized a Latin American women's politics based on "their gender identity as mothers, wives, and daughters," or on their "femaleness, whether that is understood as a real essence or as a social construction."

Roldán's and Oliva's experiences of activism in the male public sphere cannot be understood without analyzing their relationships with their male union counterparts. The two women were clearly exceptional, and they "won" their right to participate in a male union and political world by being rendered "not women." As Levenson-Estrada shows, this convention neutralizes a potential threat to patriarchal gender norms by masculinizing the female activist. "Because of class realities men could not reject these women; because of gender concepts they could not accept them as women. 'So and so has more pants than most men I know,' ran the typical remark about forceful, outspoken, and effective women trade unionists." And in Berisso, at least one man recalled Roldán as having had more *pelotas* (testicles) than many of the male workers. "In this way," as Levenson-Estrada comments, "men kept trade unionism very masculine—these women were more male than most men!—to maintain unionism as their own, even if it included women."

Yet the masculinization of class activism is, Levenson-Estrada suggests, a potentially damaging and illusory tactic, even for men. After all, brave or courageous behavior is not gender-specific, and even male trade unionists in Guatemala were aware that masculine gender roles often worked at cross-purposes with "the intellectual and worldly clarity" demanded for successful class mobilization: "thinking with one's balls" was also a negative referent among these male labor leaders. Moreover, Levenson-Estrada also points out that the very association of *worker* with masculinity and toughness was itself part of a package that associated manual labor with stupidity and a lack of intellectual capacity.

The story of Oliva and her Guatemalan union brothers and sisters suggests the falsity of pitting the workers' "immediate" struggles with capitalism against their "secondary" struggles over women's rights and liberation. "Oliva's history indicates that this is a false dilemma: she had to challenge sexism to be a class activist. There is no 'more important' or 'prior' issue—class or gender—these are inside one another, and the struggle against gender conventions and sexist ideologies is integral to any project of liberation." In constructing a common class project appropriate to the collective interests of workers, male and female, a labor movement gains strength to the extent to which it addresses all forms of inequality and hierarchy. To do so requires an androgynous vision of the future that is based, above all else, on what it means to be human *tout court*.

Notes

1   The analyst "must respect the complications of [working] people's lives," anthropologist Josiah Heyman suggests, and take care not to override the details of their lives with abstract labels. This is especially important, he goes on, as we move "towards the study of the many working peoples of the world. . . . Our understanding should not become simply a localized, human version of the 'working class' that other social scientists have already produced." Above all, we must avoid slipping "into the assumptions and terminologies inherited with

these topics until they have proved useful" (*Life and Labor on the Border: Working People of Northeastern Sonora, Mexico, 1886–1986* [Tucson: University of Arizona Press, 1991], pp. 2–3).

2   In 1986, Charles Bergquist had been doubtful that a North Atlantic–style "new social history" was in fact practical in Latin America, given the state of the field and the material resources it would require. If this skepticism was justified in the case of (male) labor history, it would apply with even more force to women's labor history in the region. As this volume suggests, Bergquist was in fact excessively pessimistic about the advances that could be made through the discovery of new sources and, more importantly, the use of those sources in innovative ways (Bergquist, *Labor in Latin America: Comparative Essays on Chile, Argentina, Venezuela, and Colombia* [Stanford: Stanford University Press, 1986], pp. 382–83).

3   The utility of voter registration statistics is developed further in John D. French and Mary Lynn Pedersen Cluff, "Once Women Vote: The Politics of Female Enfranchisement in São Paulo, Brazil, 1932–1982" (paper presented to the Berkshire Conference on the History of Women, New Brunswick, N.J., June 7–10, 1990).

4   Sherna Berger Gluck and Daphne Patai, eds., *Women's Words: The Feminist Practice of Oral History* (New York: Routledge, 1991). See also Patai's introduction to her fine book of interviews with women from many walks of life, *Brazilian Women Speak: Contemporary Life Stories* (New Brunswick, N.J.: Rutgers University Press, 1988).

5   See also Lesley Gill, *Precarious Dependencies: Gender, Class, and Domestic Service in Bolivia* (New York: Columbia University Press, 1994), p. 13.

6   Jean Paul Sartre, *Search for a Method* (New York: Vintage, 1968).

7   This female domestic role can, as Temma Kaplan suggested in a pioneering article, lead to women's mobilization: "Female Consciousness and Collective Action: The Case of Barcelona, 1910–1918," *Signs* 7, no. 3 (1982): pp. 545–66.

8   Emília Viotti da Costa, *Crowns of Glory, Tears of Blood: The Demerara Slave Rebellion of 1823* (New York: Oxford University Press, 1994), p. xv.

9   In their discussion of consciousness, Lourdes Benería and Martha Roldán give group interests, whether long- or short-term, a crucial analytical role (*The Crossroads of Class and Gender: Industrial Homework, Subcontracting, and Household Dynamics in Mexico City* [Chicago: University of Chicago Press, 1987], pp. 12, 139–40).

10 "Although class and gender may be analytically distinguishable at a theoretical level," note Benería and Roldán, "in practice they cannot be easily disentangled. The problem before us is to build a unifying theory and analysis in which material and ideological factors are an integral aspect" (*Crossroads,* p. 10).

11 Individual identity is profoundly influenced by the dominant discursive constructions in the wider society, but it is not unilaterally defined by it. Societal discourses are internalized and serve to define a range of alternatives from which one composes an identity, but these external discourses are not equal to one's identity; they do not constitute "you." Rather, these discourses must be inter-

preted and reinterpreted in order to make them fit an individual or a group's understanding of self and society, especially with an eye to the material realities of scarcity or abundance that shape their lives. For more on the Scott debate see Kathleen Canning, "Feminist History after the Linguistic Turn: Historicizing Discourse and Experience," *Signs* 19, no. 2 (1994): pp. 368–404.

12 For a fuller treatment of the postwar conjuncture see John D. French, *The Brazilian Workers' ABC: Class Conflicts and Alliances in Modern São Paulo* (Chapel Hill: University of North Carolina Press, 1992); and *O ABC dos operários: Lutas e alianças de classe em São Paulo, 1900–1950* (São Paulo: Hucitec; São Caetano do Sul: Prefeitura Municipal de São Caetano do Sul, 1995).

13 This is the thrust of Joel Wolfe's argument in *Working Women, Working Men: São Paulo and the Rise of Brazil's Industrial Working Class, 1900–1955* (Durham, N.C.: Duke University Press, 1993), although most reviewers have been skeptical. See also his "Anarchist Ideology, Worker Practice: The 1917 General Strike and the Formation of São Paulo's Working Class," *Hispanic American Historical Review* 71, no. 4 (1991): pp. 809–46; and the response by French, "Practice and Ideology: A Cautionary Note on the Historian's Craft," ibid., pp. 847–55.

14 In demonstrating the existence of a large group of longtime women workers, Veccia's factory data suggest the importance of disaggregating the idea of the "woman worker." It is important to carefully distinguish between the experience, meaning, and justification of women's factory labor when it involves short-term as opposed to long-term employment (see also Virve Piho, "Life and Labor of the Woman Textile Workers in Mexico City," in *Women Cross-Culturally: Change and Challenge,* ed. R. R. Leavitt [The Hague: Mouton, 1976], pp. 35–63). Clearly, women's job stability may vary not only between industries (seasonal in fruit packing versus year-round in textiles) but even for factories within the same industry (Veccia's textile plant, compared with the one studied by Vangelista), not to mention the possible variation by section or skill within a given workplace. We must also pay closer attention to the generational dimension of women's consciousness and behavior. Lobato suggests, for example, that autonomy or self-fulfillment appears more commonly as a motive for paid employment in the testimony of women who went to work in the 1960s than it did earlier. Finally, we may also find interesting dynamics among generations of women in a given factory, between older factory matriarchs and women workers in their late teens or early twenties (Kevin Yelvington, *Producing Power: Ethnicity, Gender, and Class in a Caribbean Workplace* [Philadelphia: Temple University Press, 1995]).

15 For general background on the labor struggles of these years in Argentina, Guatemala, and Brazil, see Daniel James, *Resistance and Integration: Peronism and the Argentine Working Class, 1946–1976* (Cambridge: Cambridge University Press, 1988; paperback, 1993); Deborah Levenson-Estrada, *Trade Unionists against Terror, Guatemala City, 1954–1985* (Chapel Hill: University of North Carolina Press, 1994); and French, *Brazilian Workers' ABC.*

16   In a world of domestic inequality and women's preeminent responsibility for
      children, it is not surprising that a working woman might feel a powerful in-
      ternal conflict over any perceived neglect of her children (see Virginia Guzmán,
      Patricia Portocarrero, et al., *Dos veces mujer* [Lima: Centro de la Mujer Peruana
      Flora Tristan, 1985], p. 119). A story in Veccia illustrates the reality of this emo-
      tional economy within the family. After getting married, Vicente, whose mother
      had worked in the textile industry, told his new wife that he didn't want his kids
      "to grow up on the streets like he had done."

17   For more on the dynamics of female participation see Guzmán et al., *Dos Veces,*
      pp. 107–12; Estela Teresita Soto, "Mujeres delegadas de fábrica en Argentina,"
      Latin American Labor News nos. 10–11 (1994), which is excerpted from *Boletín
      CEIL* 16, no. 21, pp. 39–46.

18   John Humphrey, *Gender and Work in the Third World: Sexual Divisions in Brazilian In-
      dustry* (London: Tavistock, 1987), pp. 137–41.

19   Interviews with Maria Salas and Fortunato S. Silvestre Depinedo, cited in Hélio
      da Costa, *Em busca da memória: Comissão de fábrica, partido e sindicato no pós-guerra*
      (São Paulo: Scritta, 1995). See the discussion of women strikers waving skirts at
      nonstriking men in Ann Farnsworth-Alvear, "The Mysterious Case of the Miss-
      ing Men: Gender and Class in Early Industry Medellín," *International Labor and
      Working Class History* 49 (1996): pp. 73–92; Nancy A. Hewitt, " 'The Voice of Vir-
      ile Labor': Labor Militancy, Community Solidarity, and Gender Identity among
      Tampa's Latin Workers, 1880–1921," in *Work Engendered: Toward a New History of
      American Labor,* ed. Ava Baron (Ithaca: Cornell University Press, 1991), 158–59.

20   Wilson also provides a wonderful example of the ingenious discursive strategy
      adopted by one young woman. Refusing to be fooled by her employer's attempt
      to replicate the "household model" in the workshop, she used patriarchal as-
      sumptions to challenge the legitimacy of his claim: "Why are you shouting at us?
      You have no right to. You are not my father. You should not treat us this way.
      I am a worker and I demand that you treat me with respect as a worker" (Fiona
      Wilson, *Sweaters: Gender, Class and Workshop-Based Industry in Mexico* [New York:
      St. Martin's Press, 1991], p. 155).

Contributors

MARY LYNN PEDERSEN CLUFF received her master's degree in history at the University of Georgia. She currently teaches at Weber State University in Ogden, Utah.

ANN FARNSWORTH-ALVEAR received her Ph.D. from Duke University, where she developed a passion for comparative labor studies and feminist theory. Her area of expertise is twentieth-century Colombia, and her research has focused on urban industrial work and oral history. She is Assistant Professor of History at the University of Pennsylvania.

JOHN D. FRENCH is Associate Professor of History at Duke University. He is currently completing a book titled *The Metalworkers of ABC: Linking Consciousness and Mobilization, 1950–1980*. His other research interests include the history of labor transnationalism, women and voting, and color and class in Brazil.

DANIEL JAMES is Associate Professor of History at Duke University. He is currently finishing a book dealing with oral history titled *Doña Maria's Story: Life History, Memory, and Political Identity*. His larger ongoing project is titled "Berisso Obrero."

THOMAS MILLER KLUBOCK received his Ph.D. in History from Yale University in 1993. He is currently Assistant Professor of History at Ohio State University. His forthcoming book, *Contested Communities: Class, Gender, and Politics in Chile's El Teniente Copper Mine, 1904–1951*, deals with the history of working men and women in the El Teniente copper mining community.

DEBORAH LEVENSON-ESTRADA is Associate Professor of Latin American History at Boston College. She received her Ph.D. from New York University in 1988. She is currently writing a social history of childhood and modernity in Guatemala since the late nineteenth century. She is also researching the ideological uses of the category *youth* in the same time period.

MIRTA ZAIDA LOBATO is Professor of History at the University of Buenos Aires. Her work has focused on the meatpacking industry, with a special emphasis on the labor process and women workers. She is also codirector of the "Berisso Obrero" project.

HEIDI TINSMAN received her Ph.D. from Yale University in 1996 and is currently Assistant Professor of History at the University of California, Irvine. Her work focuses on gender and labor relations in rural Chile.

THERESA R. VECCIA received her Ph.D. in History from the University of Wisconsin–Madison in 1995. Her dissertation was titled "Family and Factory: Textile Work and Women's Lives in São Paulo, Brazil, 1880–1940."

BARBARA WEINSTEIN is Professor of History and former Director of Women's Studies at the State University of New York at Stony Brook. She received her Ph.D. in History from Yale University in 1980. Her most recent book is *For Social Peace in Brazil: Industrialists and the Remaking of the Working Class in São Paulo, 1920–1964*. She is currently working on a study of regional and national identities in Brazil.

Library of Congress Cataloging-in-Publication Data

The gendered worlds of Latin American women workers : from
household and factory to the union hall and ballot box / John D.
French and Daniel James, editors.
p.   cm. — (Comparative and international working-class
history)
Includes index.
ISBN 0-8223-2000-2 (cloth : alk. paper). — ISBN 0-8223-1996-9
(pbk. : alk. paper)
1. Women—Latin America—Economic conditions.
2. Working-class women—Latin America—Economic
conditions.   3. Women—Identity—Latin America.
4. Feminism—Latin America.   I. French, John D.   II. James,
Daniel.   III. Series.
HD6100.5.G46   1998
331.4'098—dc21   97-20053   CIP